Adult Education

John M. Peters
Peter Jarvis
and Associates

Foreword by Cyril O. Houle

Adult Education

Evolution and
Achievements
in a Developing
Field of Study

Jossey-Bass Publishers

San Francisco   •   Oxford   •   1991

ADULT EDUCATION
Evolution and Achievements in a Developing Field of Study
by John M. Peters, Peter Jarvis, and Associates

Copyright © 1991 by: Jossey-Bass Inc., Publishers
350 Sansome Street
San Francisco, California 94104
&
Jossey-Bass Limited
Headington Hill Hall
Oxford OX3 0BW

AAACE
1112 16th Street, N.W.
Washington, D.C. 20036

Library of Congress Cataloging-in-Publication Data

Peters, John M., date.
    Adult education : evolution and achievements in a developing field
of study / John M. Peters, Peter Jarvis, and associates.
        p.   cm.
    Includes bibliographical references and index.
    ISBN 1-55542-381-7
    1. Adult education — Study and teaching.   2. Adult education — Study
and teaching (Graduate).   3. Adult education teachers — Training of.
I. Jarvis, Peter, date.   II. Title.
LC5215.P436   1991
374 — dc20   91-13977
                                                                 CIP

Manufactured in the United States of America

The paper in this book meets the guidelines for
permanence and durability of the Committee on
Production Guidelines for Book Longevity of
the Council on Library Resources.

JACKET DESIGN BY WILLI BAUM

Sponsored by the American Association of Adult
and Continuing Education

FIRST EDITION

Code 9183

The Jossey-Bass
Higher and Adult Education Series

Consulting Editor
Adult and Continuing Education

Alan B. Knox
University of Wisconsin, Madison

Contents

Contents

Foreword

We met on the fertile prairie of central Illinois, enjoying but feeling a little awed by the grandeur of Allerton Park, whose imposing mansion had just become a conference center. For three beautiful days in late May 1955, ten faculty members who taught university courses in adult education (perhaps presumptuously, we called ourselves professors) met together, along with five additional people who were interested in adult education. We had the support of fifteen other faculty members who could not attend but who sent papers to our session or in other ways indicated their interest in it.

Both present and absent members had a clear purpose: to see whether we could express for ourselves and others the nature of adult education as an academic discipline. It had been a field of university research and teaching since its introduction at Columbia in 1930, but its growth had been a slow, though diligent, search for identity. Each leader of the new academic field perceived it in a distinctive way, but, unlike the fabled six blind men of Hindustan, nobody was sure that there actually was an elephant. Moreover, the existing adult education programs had little national impact. The organizers of the Allerton Park conference could find no more than twenty-eight professors of adult education in North America, and only fifteen of them had full-time assignments to the area. Their lone voices in various wildernesses needed to be joined together if they were ever to be heard.

We who met at Allerton Park were aware of the great accomplishments of adult education in the service of social purposes. It had helped in the empowerment of nations and of social groups within them; examples could be cited in Scandinavia, in Antigonish, and, most currently, in Britain, with the rise of the Labour party. Adult education had been a powerful instrument in bringing the United States through and out of the Great Depression. It was the means by which many millions of civilians had been trained to win a worldwide war. Now, in the mid 1950s, we asked ourselves, What was the place in society of adult education, both on the grand scale of national and international needs and in the immediate improvement of the quality of life in the myriad communities and groups that influence every mature person? How could university teaching and research best aid in the achievement of this vast mission?

The search for answers to these questions was accompanied by more pressing concerns. The professors present at Allerton Park wanted first of all to talk about the recruitment and placement of their students, the presumed future leaders of the field. We wondered how able people could be attracted as candidates for master's and doctoral degrees and how they could best be guided into useful careers once they had received their degrees. We might have gone on indefinitely talking about how to greet and how to say farewell to our students, but one participant finally noted that recruitment and placement are merely two slopes of a hill — "The peak is what we do with students while they are with us." The central activity of the conference then became the discussion of that peak. Professional people love to engage in shoptalk, and perhaps we most clearly showed our professionalism by our fascination with the structure and mechanics of our own program designs. Curiously enough, we dealt very little with the nature of what was actually to be taught.

The meeting ended with a sense of achievement, perhaps as the result of a successful experience in male bonding. An external evaluator cautiously noted, "At the end of the conference, this observer sensed none of the feeling of frustration which often comes as the climax of adjournment." Subsequent events amply demonstrated that groundwork for further action had been laid at Allerton Park. We had reinforced our belief in the importance of recruitment and placement; a committee drafted an elaborate plan to set up a national system for what was called a "personnel information exchange." We failed to secure financing for this system, but we did receive funding from the W. K. Kellogg Foundation to develop a graduate curriculum in adult education during additional meetings. In 1957 and for four years thereafter, we met at one or another of a tight little circle of midwestern universities to carry further the deliberations begun at Allerton Park.

During the first such meeting, at the University of Michigan, the discussion turned away from shoptalk to a more fundamental discussion of the actual and potential knowledge base of the field. We concentrated on shaping graduate curricula, but it was always evident that continuing education faced a far larger task, particularly in providing learning opportunities for other leaders. We were called on to develop and conduct many instructional presentations both on and off campus.

From its earliest days, the newly named Commission of Professors of Adult Education intended to shape its work into one or more major publications. Even at our meeting in Ann Arbor, individuals were assigned various topics to explore for a publication. The major immediate outcome of the effort was a book issued under the title *Adult Education: Outlines of an Emerging Field of University Study*. The volume was starkly bound in black; therefore, notwithstanding its resounding title and distinguished editors, both spelled out in gold letters on the cover, it became known among the cognoscenti of adult education as the "black book."

In 1964, when it was published, there were 16 well-established graduate programs in adult education in North America. Twenty-seven years later, there are at least 124 programs. Some earlier programs have now disappeared. All the new programs have probably been created or influenced in some way by the black book, and, I must admit, it may have influenced some campus authorities to decide not to start adult education programs. The book is on many reference and personal library shelves, is often cited in the literature, and is discussed frequently, sometimes by people with differing views about what it actually says.

Those readers who have examined it closely have always been surprised at what they have found. It is not a codification of what is known about adult education. No attempt is made to parallel what Blackstone did for law or Osler did for the practice of medicine. It is a portrait of a field in process and, its authors believe, in progress. Each author looks at the subject assigned him (no women were included) in a distinctive and occasionally perhaps idiosyncratic way. Any informed reader who examines the black book is likely to believe that important topics are omitted, that interpretations are wrong, that trivia are described at too-great length, or that some passages are vague. But such conclusions are always likely to be drawn when a work is produced by strong authors who feel that they are in the forefront of a field and who have chosen not to look backward at what they have already learned but forward to record how knowledge is growing and how it will continue to grow.

Now, in 1991, the black book is joined by this companion volume. The book will be warmly welcomed by all readers (may they be many!) who want to examine adult education as a field of academic study, and that welcome will be enhanced by the fact that the professors have finally managed to attract some women into their company. The new book (what, I wonder, will be the color of its cover?) does not exactly parallel the black book, nor is it a replacement for that earlier work. The central intent is the same as before: to describe the processes of analysis and growth, not to report what has already been learned.

To this first external reader doing his first reading, the new work gives clear evidence of the accomplishments of more than twenty-five years. Graduate study in adult education has been advanced in many ways. Additional experience in both research and practice has provided new and more profound concepts and formulations. Adult education itself is now seen in a broader light. Its potential for social change, so dominant at Allerton Park and so strongly expressed in the black book, is heightened in the sequel by a complementary perspective: learning is seen also as a means by which an individual fulfills desires or meets challenges during the mature years.

The two books should stand side by side on the shelf, the second one worthy of comparison with the first. Adult education has not yet found its Blackstone or its Osler, nor has it in any other way achieved a masterful synthesis of what can confidently be said to be the central principles or the basic knowledge of the field. But if any such summation is ever achieved, it will owe much to the ideas expressed in this volume and in its distinguished predecessor. Speaking for all those present or represented at Allerton Park in 1955, I salute the authors of both books.

September 1991   Cyril O. Houle
                                                              Professor emeritus,
                                                       University of Chicago

                                              Senior program consultant,
                                              W. K. Kellogg Foundation

Preface

Adult education is a time-honored field of practice, but as a field of formal study it emerged within the lifetime of many of the adult education scholars who are active today. Only sixty-one years have passed since the first graduate program in North America was formed at Columbia University — a relatively short history compared to that of other areas of professional study, such as medicine and law, as well as most of the social sciences.

Because the study of adult education is a relative newcomer, it is not yet well understood by observers of the academic landscape. For adult education scholars between 1930 and 1950, though, that handicap was minor compared to the complexities of trying to define and then explain to others what they meant by adult education. Professors as a group had accumulated considerable wisdom and experience in adult education, as well as in related disciplines, and they were at home in the institutions of higher education that administered their programs. However, until the mid 1950s, they had not explained to each other, much less to outsiders, what the practice and the academic study of adult education amounted to.

Cyril Houle's Foreword eloquently explains what happened when a small clutch of professors convened in 1955 and began to sort out what they were involved in and how they could communicate to others the essence of their fledgling area of academic study. The work they began at that meeting culminated nine years later in the publication of the benchmark "black book," formally entitled *Adult Education: Outlines of an Emerging Field of University Study* (Jensen, Liveright, and Hallenbeck, 1964).

The black book contains the results of three tasks undertaken by the Commission of Professors of Adult Education (CPAE): (1) to identify the scope of adult education as a field of graduate study, (2) to capture the current thinking of scholars and a good many practitioners about the conceptual foundations of the field, and (3) to describe as completely as possible the intricacies of adult education practice. The authors were apparently much more successful in completing the first two tasks than in accomplishing the third: about 90 percent of the black book's contents are given over to discussion of graduate programs and the conceptual foundations of adult education. Six chapters are devoted to concepts drawn from six social science disciplines, and a section entitled "Conceptual Structure for Some Aspects of Adult Education" comprises an additional three chapters on conceptual foundations. This section is actually the authors' attempt to outline a tentative theory of adult education practice, but it is essentially a discussion of topics basic to the study of adult education, including educational objectives, program development and operation, and evaluation.

As Houle points out in the Foreword to the present work, the black book has served as a guide for many people developing adult education graduate programs who needed some conceptual basis for identifying a curriculum of graduate study. It has also communicated to the educational community at large the nature of adult education as an area of university study.

The CPAE, whose job it had been to produce the black book, decided in the late 1980s that the time had come to reflect on the accomplishments of the field of study since the publication of the black book, to characterize the current status of the field of study, and to consider its future possibilities. These three aims were to guide the preparation of a new book on the academic study of adult education, one that would focus on the study of adult education by primarily university professors and their students. Thus, *Adult Education* is intended to reflect the nature of that academic study and the resulting production of a formal body of knowledge in adult education. This body of knowledge, with its constituent knowledge domains and methods of producing and disseminating them, represents the essence of the formal knowledge base of the field at the present time.

A committee of the CPAE was put in charge of preparing a broad outline for the project and choosing editors to develop it. We were fortunate to be selected as editors of this new and important book. We in turn chose some of the best and brightest scholars in the field to write chapters on particular topics relating to the aims that the CPAE had identified.

We asked the contributors to address their topics in light of the accomplishments of the field since 1964, its current status, and its possible future directions. Some topics were more easily approached this way than others, however, and the reader will discover that some chapter authors focus more on the past than on the present or future. But some authors took this opportunity to say exactly what they think about the field of study and its future. The chapters also vary in scope and depth of treatment, but the resulting "unevenness" that usually characterizes edited collections is in this case a strength. The variety of approaches, views, and directions taken by the authors mirrors the equally diverse forms of thinking that prevail in academic adult education today, especially when scholars from more than one country are involved. While this book focuses on the study of adult education in North America and has both U.S. and Canadian authors, we deliberately included authors from other countries, namely, the United Kingdom and Australia. We did not seek to represent all countries by any means, but we decided early on that it was essential that the contents of *Adult Education* reflect one of the strongest trends in the field today, the internationalization of adult education. The reader will find that authors from the United Kingdom bring to their subjects a perspective different from that usually adopted by writers from the United States. This difference surely adds to our understanding of adult education.

Overview of the Contents

The book begins with an introductory chapter outlining the nature of adult education as a field of study and some of the challenges that lie before it. The six chapters in Part One address in broad terms who studies the field, how we study it, and some of the outcomes.

In Chapter Two, Ronald Cervero explains three perspectives on the relationship between theory and practice. In Chapter Three, Sharan Merriam discusses three paradigms from which researchers work to develop knowledge of the field. Huey Long discusses in Chapter Four the nature of the formal knowledge that has developed in adult education over the past twenty-seven years. In Chapter Five, William Griffith presents his selection of intellectual leaders who have made significant contributions to the field of study in this century, especially those who have influenced the field during the past three or four decades. Ralph Brockett discusses in Chapter Six several ways in which formal adult education knowledge is disseminated and used. Finally, in Chapter Seven, John Peters and Burton Kreitlow examine the special role that graduate programs play in the field of study, and they review the development of graduate programs since publication of the black book.

Part Two contains six chapters, each of which considers the relation of selected disciplines to the study of adult education. The CPAE committee suggested that discussion of the contributions of the related disciplines to the field and the relationship of these disciplines to adult education would be of interest to readers and we agreed. However, we chose for discussion only those disciplines that in our judgment had recently made significant contributions. Additional disciplines might have been included in a lengthier book, and certainly other editors might have selected different disciplines. But Mark Tennant, Alan Knox, Colin Griffin, Kenneth Lawson, Alan Thomas, and Harold Stubblefield, the authors of the chapters on psychology, administration, sociology, philosophy, political science, and history, respectively, provide readers with a variety of viewpoints on what they consider to be of greatest importance in these disciplines and how the disciplines relate to the study of adult education (Chapters Eight through Thirteen).

Part Three contains three chapters whose contents cut across the contents of all of the other chapters—for distinctly different reasons. Phyllis Cunningham's chapter (Chapter Fourteen) critically examines international influences on the field and opens up an exceedingly important area for further dialogue among academics. In Chapter Fifteen, David Deshler, writing about issues that shape the field of study, looks at social, professional, and academic concerns. In the last chapter, Chapter Sixteen, John Peters identifies several themes found in the writings of the other authors as a group and considers the future development of each theme.

We actually do not end the book with the final chapter but instead give the honor over to one of the best-known and most respected adult educators of all time, Malcolm Knowles. His epilogue is what he elected it should be, and it is vintage Knowles. Thus, our "bookends" are "old-timers" in the field; both Houle and Knowles are charter members of the CPAE and contributors to the black book. Two other authors from the black book contributed to *Adult Education*—Burton Kreitlow and Alan Thomas. We hope that by mixing these scholars with others who are relatively new to the field but strong in their own right we have provided a forum for the expression of some of the most vital and interesting ideas possible. Incidentally, the editors of the black book expressed in their preface the wish that the book would "stimulate a growing and ever widening discourse and dialogue about the essential kinds of knowledge and practice which are essential to a thoughtful and effective adult educator" (Jensen, Liveright, and Hallenbeck, 1964, p. xiv). We invite readers to join us and the authors in granting this wish.

We want to acknowledge the considerable help and support given us by our families, friends, and colleagues.

September 1991   John M. Peters
                                                   Knoxville, Tennessee

                                                   Peter Jarvis
                                                   Guildford, England

Reference

Jensen, G., Liveright, A. A., and Hallenbeck, W. (eds.). *Adult
    Education: Outlines of an Emerging Field of University Study*. Wash-
    ington, D.C.: American Association for Adult and Continu-
    ing Education, 1964.

The Authors

John M. Peters is professor of adult education and coordinator of the graduate program in adult education at the University of Tennessee, Knoxville. He received his B.S. degree (1963) in agriculture from the University of Kentucky and his M.S. degree (1966) and Ed.D. degree (1968) in adult education from North Carolina State University. Before coming to the University of Tennessee, he was assistant professor of adult education at North Carolina State University. He also served as visiting professor at the University of British Columbia, Cornell University, and North Carolina State University.

Peters's main research and writing activities have focused on adult learning, adult development, problem solving, and adult education for social change. He served as an executive committee member for the Commission of Professors of Adult Education, chair of the publications committee of the Adult Education Association (now the American Association for Adult and Continuing Education), secretary and vice-president of the Adult Education Association, and book review editor for the journal *Adult Education*. He is editor of *Building an Effective Adult Education Enterprise* (1980), coeditor of *We Make the Road by Walking: Conversations on Education and Social Change* (1980, with B. Bell and J. Gaventa), and author of *How to Make Successful Use of the Learning Laboratory* (1972).

Peter Jarvis is reader in the Department of Educational Studies at the University of Surrey, U.K. He is adjunct professor of adult education at the University of Georgia and was a visiting scholar at the University of Tennessee. Before assuming his position at the University of Surrey, he was senior lecturer at Dudley College of Education (U.K.). He received his B.D. degree (1965) from the University of London, his B.A. degree (1969) in sociology from the University of Sheffield, his M.Sc. degree (1972) in sociology of education from the University of Birmingham, and his Ph.D. degree (1977) in sociology of the professions from the University of Aston. He is coeditor of the *International Journal of Lifelong Education* and serves on the editorial boards of the *Adult Education Quarterly, International Education, Convergence,* and the *Journal of Educational Gerontology.* He also serves as editor of two international book series in adult education.

Jarvis's main research and writing interests are in the areas of adult learning, professional education, and social aspects of education. He has written and edited a number of books, including *Adult and Continuing Education: Theory and Practice* (1983), *The Sociology of Adult and Continuing Education* (1985), *Sociological Perspectives on Lifelong Education and Lifelong Learning* (1986), *Twentieth Century Thinkers in Adult Education* (1987), and *International Directory of Adult and Continuing Education* (1990). His *Adult Learning in the Social Context* (1987) won the 1988 Cyril O. Houle World Award for Literature in Adult Education.

Ralph G. Brockett is associate professor, Department of Technological and Adult Education, University of Tennessee, Knoxville. He received his B.A. degree and his M.Ed. degree in psychology from the University of Toledo and a Ph.D. degree in adult education from Syracuse University. He served on the board of directors of the American Association for Adult and Continuing Education (AAACE) and on the executive committee of the Commission of Professors of Adult Education. He is co-author of *Self-Direction in Adult Learning: Perspectives on Theory, Research, and Practice* (1991, with R. Hiemstra), editor of *Ethical Issues in Adult Education* (1988) and *Continuing Education in the*

Year 2000 (1987), and editor-in-chief of *New Directions for Adult and Continuing Education.*

Ronald M. Cervero is professor in the Department of Adult Education at the University of Georgia. He received his B.A. degree (1973) in psychology from Saint Michael's College, his A.M. degree (1975) in the social sciences from the University of Chicago, and his Ph.D. degree (1979) in adult education, also from the University of Chicago. He has been a member of the executive committees for the Adult Education Research Conference (1982, 1983) and the Commission of Professors of Adult Education (1986–1988) and is currently coeditor of the *Adult Education Quarterly.* He received both the 1989 Cyril O. Houle World Award for Literature in Adult Education and the 1990 Phillip E. Frandson Award for Literature in Continuing Education for *Effective Continuing Education for Professionals* (1988).

Phyllis M. Cunningham is professor of adult education at Northern Illinois University. She received her A.B. degree (1947) in biology/chemistry from Elmira College, her M.S. degree (1950) in nursing and an M.S. degree (1960) in administration, both from Western Reserve University, and a Ph.D. degree in adult education from the University of Chicago (1973). She is editor of the *Participatory Formation of Adult Educators* and was coeditor of the *Journal of Adult Education* and the *Handbook of Adult and Continuing Education* (1989). Active with the International Council for Adult Education, the North American Education of Adults for Democratic Social Change, the Lindeman Center, and Basic Choices, she identifies her intellectual interests as pedagogical practice and theory.

David Deshler is associate professor of adult education at Cornell University. He received his B.A. degree (1952) in psychology from Whittier College, his Th.M. degree (1957) in psychology of religion and clinical psychology from the Claremont School of Theology, and his Ed.D. degree in adult education from the University of California, Los Angeles. His scholarly interests and publications have focused on program evaluation;

futures research and transformative research methods; public policy education approaches, particularly with environmental issues; community development participation in the United States and less industrialized countries; and critical reflective learning in adulthood.

Colin Griffin is senior lecturer at Hillcroft College (U.K.) and part-time staff tutor in the Department of Educational Studies at the University of Surrey. He received his B.A. degree (1958) in philosophy from the University of Birmingham and both his M.S. degree (1962) and his Ph.D. degree (1972) in social and political theory from the London School of Economics, University of London. His research interests lie in the areas of social policy and curriculum development. Griffin is the author of *Curriculum Theory in Adult Lifelong Education* (1983) and *Adult Education and Social Policy* (1987).

William S. Griffith is professor of adult education at the University of British Columbia. He previously served as professor of adult education at the University of Chicago, from which he also received his Ph.D. degree (1963) in adult education. He received his B.S. degree (1953) in dairy science from Pennsylvania State University and his M.S. degree (1955), also in dairy science, from Louisiana State University. He is president of the American Association of Adult and Continuing Education and has served as chair of the Commission of Professors of Adult Education, the Adult Education Research Conference, and the Research Section of the National University Continuing Education Association. Griffith was coeditor (1980–81, with H. McClusky) of the eight-volume *Adult Education Association/USA Handbook Series on Adult Education*.

Cyril O. Houle is senior program consultant of the W. K. Kellogg Foundation and professor emeritus of the University of Chicago. He received his B.A. and M.A. degrees from the University of Florida, both in 1934, and his Ph.D. degree (1940) from the University of Chicago; all three degrees are in education. He holds honorary doctorates from nine universities and is a member of the National Academy of Education. He was on the faculty of the University of Chicago from 1939 to 1976, serving chiefly as a professor of higher and adult education but also holding various administrative positions, including the deanship of the university's extension division. He has written numerous articles and books, including *The Inquiring Mind* (1961), *The Design of Education* (1972), *Continuing Learning in the Professions* (1980), and *Patterns of Learning* (1984). He is also a specialist in the operation of nonprofit and governmental boards, and his chief book in that field is *Governing Boards* (1989).

Malcolm S. Knowles is professor emeritus of adult and community college education at North Carolina State University and previously was professor of education at Boston University, executive director of the Adult Education Association of the U.S.A., and director of adult education at the YMCAs in Boston, Detroit, and Chicago. He received his B.A. degree (1934) from Harvard College and his M.A. degree (1949) and his Ph.D. degree (1960) from the University of Chicago — all in education. He has honorary degrees from Lowell Technical Institute, the National College of Education, and Regis College.

Knowles's main academic and professional interests have been in the theory and practice of adult education. In addition to administering adult education programs and teaching in graduate schools, he has done consulting and conducted workshops for a wide variety of organizations and corporations in North America, Europe, South America, and Australia. His books include *Informal Adult Education* (1950), *The Adult Education Movement in the United States* (1962; rev. ed., 1977), *The Modern Practice of Adult Education: From Pedagogy to Andragogy* (1970; rev. ed., 1980), *The Adult Learner: A Neglected Species* (1973; rev. ed., 1984), and *Andragogy in Action: Applying Modern Principles of Adult Learning* (with others, 1984).

During his retirement, Knowles is serving as a mentor for the Fielding Institute's external degree program in human and organizational development, as national lecturer for the Nova University Center for Higher Education, as adjunct professor of the Union Graduate School, and as a member of the Task Force on Lifelong Education of the UNESCO Institute for Education.

Alan B. Knox is professor of adult and continuing education at the University of Wisconsin, Madison. He earned his B.A. degree (1952) in arts, master's degrees (1953 and 1955) in arts and adult education, and a Ph.D. degree (1958) in adult education — all from Syracuse University. For three decades he held faculty positions at the University of Nebraska, Lincoln; Teachers College, Columbia University; and the University of Illinois, Urbana-Champaign. He served as program coordinator both during the 1950s at University College, Syracuse University, and during the 1970s at the University of Illinois, where he was associate vice-chancellor of academic affairs and director of continuing education and public service. He has taught adults since 1946, and his *Helping Adults Learn* (1987) reflects that experience. More than thirty years ago he organized the Adult Education Research Conference, which he chaired in the early years. He has received two Imogene Okes Awards (in 1977 and 1980) for outstanding research. He was president of AAACE and chair of the Commission of Professors of Adult Education. Educational leadership has been a major theme in his extensive research and publications, as in his graduate courses on the administration and supervision of adult education. His books on leadership include *Leadership Strategies for Meeting New Challenges* (1983) and *Developing, Administering, and Evaluating Adult Education* (1980).

Burton W. Kreitlow is professor emeritus, University of Wisconsin, Madison. He began teaching in a one-room school in 1935, joined the staff of the Cooperative Extension Service as a county 4-H Club agent in 1938, received his Ph.D. degree (1949) in education and sociology from the University of Minnesota, and spent thirty-two years as professor of continuing and vocational education at the University of Wisconsin, Madison. During his retirement, he has been a visiting professor at four universities and continued his involvement in AAACE and the Commission of Professors of Adult Education.

Kenneth H. Lawson is associate director of the Department of Adult Education, University of Nottingham (U.K.), where he teaches certificate, diploma, and higher degree courses. He has written extensively on the philosophy of adult education. He received his B.A. (1955) and M.A. (1960) degrees in philosophy, politics, and economics from the University of Oxford. His Ph.D. degree (1977) in adult education was awarded by the University of Nottingham.

Huey B. Long is professor of adult education at the University of Oklahoma, where he is also director of the Oklahoma Research Center for Continuing Professional and Higher Education. He received both his B.S. degree (1957) in social science and secondary education and his M.S. degree (1958) in geography from Florida State University, and his Ph.D. degree (1966) in adult higher education from Florida State University. He is former president of the Adult Education Association of the U.S.A. and has published books on a variety of topics. His *Adult Learning Research and Practice* (1983) won the Cyril O. Houle World Award for Literature in Adult Education.

Sharan B. Merriam is professor of adult education at the University of Georgia. She received her B.A. degree (1965) in English from Drew University, her M.Ed. degree (1971) in English education from Ohio University, and her Ed.D. degree (1978) in adult education from Rutgers University. Her writing and research activities have focused on adult development and learning and qualitative research methods. She has written or co-authored many books, including *Adult Education: Foundations of Practice* (1982, with G. Darkenwald—winner of the 1985 Cyril O. Houle World Award for Literature in Adult Education), *Case Study Research in Education* (1988), and *Learning in Adulthood* (1991, with R. S. Caffarella). She is also coeditor of the *Handbook of Adult and Continuing Education* (1989, with P. M. Cunningham) and is currently coeditor of the *Adult Education Quarterly*.

Harold W. Stubblefield is professor of adult education at the Virginia Polytechnic Institute and State University. He received his B.A. degree (1955) in social science from Murray State University, his Th.M. degree (1960) in pastoral counseling from

Southern Baptist Seminary, and his Ed.D. degree (1973) in adult education from Indiana University. His principal research interests are the history of American adult education and the development and structure of adult education as a discipline. His book *Towards a History of Adult Education in America* received the Imogene Okes Award for Outstanding Research in Adult Education. He has served as chair of the Commission of Professors of Adult Education.

Mark Tennant is associate professor of adult education in the Department of Adult Education, University of Technology (Sydney). His Ph.D. degree in psychology was granted by Sydney College. Tennant is the author of *Psychology and Adult Learning* (1988), for which he received the Cyril O. Houle World Award for Literature in Adult Education.

Alan M. Thomas is professor of adult education at the Ontario Institute for Studies in Education (OISE). He received his B.A. degree (1949) in English and philosophy from the University of Toronto and both his M.A. degree (1953) in the history of education and his Ph.D. degree (1964) in social psychology from Teachers College, Columbia University. He taught at the University of British Columbia, where he inaugurated the first full-time master's degree program in adult education in Canada, and returned to the Canadian Association for Adult Education as director (1961–1969). After two years as assistant to a federal minister, he joined OISE as chairman of the development of adult education. His major interests are learning in prison, industry, labor unions, and formal institutions of education and the relations between learning and the law. He is the author of *Beyond Education: A New Perspective on Society's Management of Learning* (1991).

Adult Education

CHAPTER 1

Growth and Challenges in the Study of Adult Education

Peter Jarvis

When the original black book (Jensen, Liveright, and Hallenbeck, 1964) was published, adult education was just beginning to establish itself as a field of university study. The very publication of that book was a sign of the growing confidence emerging in the field. Indeed, Liveright claimed that the book had to be written not because the world needed it but because the professors of adult education needed to write it. Their view reflected confidence but also the frustration engendered by the lack of recognition given to adult education. However, the lack of recognition is hardly surprising since in 1964 only sixteen graduate programs of adult education existed in North American universities (Houle, 1964). Growth in the number of programs prior to that time was slow both in North America and in the United Kingdom, where the first department of adult education had been established in 1920. However, in North America, growth in adult education as an area of academic study grew exponentially in the 1960s and thereafter.

The growth in the field of study during the past twenty-seven years has paralleled the growth in the field of practice.

Both have emerged from very marginal enterprises to ones recognized and accepted not only in institutions of higher education but also in society in general. The many organizations offering education for adults have become more prominent in the general field of education. Indeed, the acknowledgment by some of these organizations that they are involved in adult education demonstrates the fact that adult education has become accepted as a field of practice. Throughout the world, adult education has become more visible, especially through the work of such organizations as the International Council for Adult Education and the European Bureau of Adult Education and through the establishment of national organizations in almost every country. Adult education is now studied in universities worldwide. More journals, books, and conferences about adult education exist today than ever before.

In a sense, this book is a celebration of the growth and development of the study of adult education during the past twenty-seven years, but not from a simple, uncritical perspective. Rather, the concern here is both to reflect and to look forward in anticipation; it is to offer an analysis of what has gone before, to look critically at what exists at present, and to look toward the twenty-first century. Without a doubt, adult education will play an even more significant role at that time than it has done in this century. This opening chapter provides an overview of some features of past and future growth and development in the field and in so doing introduces the following chapters.

Developments in the Field of Study

This book and the black book are different in a number of ways. First, the knowledge base in adult education is more substantive today than at the time the black book was written. This book contains the broad outlines of the more formal aspects of that knowledge. Second, this book places a greater emphasis on research and the different ways of thinking about research than the black book does. Third, although this book includes chapters on most of the related disciplines that were discussed in the black book, the disciplines are approached differently by the authors in this book. Here, the disciplines are examined in terms of adult education, whereas adult education was examined in terms of the disciplines in the black book. Fourth, graduate programs have grown in number and their curricula have changed. We are now able to describe that growth and development, much of which was predicted in 1964. Fifth, the study of adult education has become truly international in scope, and features of the internationalization of adult education are captured in this book. Sixth, the relationships between theory and practice differ in this book from those in the black book. The authors of the black book were interested in the applicability of formal knowledge to practice, but, for the most part, they envisioned theory as being applied *to* practice. They also saw practice as a source of knowledge for building theory, but they did not acknowledge the possibility that practitioners also theorize about practice, and they did not consider the political aspects of theory and practice. The editors of this book consider the relationships between theory and practice to be crucial to the study of adult education, and thus include a chapter (Chapter Two) on the subject in the book. I will discuss each of the six differences between the black book and this book in this chapter.

Domains of Knowledge. Adult education as a field of academic study cannot be separated from adult education as a field of practice. The way in which the practice of adult education is conceptualized has much to do with how adult education is studied.

Hallenbeck (1964), in the first chapter of the black book, made the point that adult education will always be a service-oriented occupation, or a field of practice. However, Hallenbeck was only too well aware that it is difficult to locate adult education in a single place and regard it as a single field of practice. He regarded adult education as ubiquitous, pointing out that it was to be found almost everywhere in leisure and work — in schools, churches, synagogues, community centers, and labor union halls. Indeed, the whole of Knowles's (1964) chapter in the black book was an attempt to classify the fields in which adult education practice was to be found; Knowles demonstrated the relevance of adult education to as wide a variety of institutions as possible. Since then, the handbooks of adult education (for example, Merriam and Cunningham, 1989; Titmus, 1989) and other publications (for example, Darkenwald and Merriam, 1982) have adequately captured the variety of the places that practice adult education. The process does not need to be repeated in this book.

The continued development and increasing complexity of the practice of adult education have given rise to at least three different approaches to the study of adult education. However, although scholars are beginning to specialize, they are not yet working exclusively in one of these areas. A growing number of scholars are beginning to focus on the study of a specific field of practice and are becoming recognized as specialists, even though they do not concentrate exclusively on a specific area, such as continuing professional education (Houle, 1980; Cervero, 1988), literacy (Fingeret, 1983; Valentine, 1986), or human resource development (Nadler and Wiggs, 1986). Second, other scholars study the processes of adult education and continue the more general approach to study that was apparent in the black book. This makes their area of study quite different from that of their colleagues who specialize in specific domains of practice. In one sense, however, although they are generalists, the common processes of adult education constitute their field of specialty. These scholars include those who concentrate on teaching and learning, such as Knowles (1980), while I (Jarvis, 1987) studied learning in the social context, and Marsick (1987) examined learning in the workplace. Third, some scholars analyze the field of practice from the perspective of one of the foundation disciplines, such as history (Kelly, 1970; Stubblefield, 1988), psychology (Tennant, 1988), or sociology (Jones, 1985; Jarvis, 1985).

These three broad approaches to studying the field represent both continuity and change in the practice and study of adult education. Continuity is reflected in the study of educational processes, and change is reflected in the evolution of the field and the movement toward specialization and complexity.

In the black book, Jensen regarded adult education as an individualistic enterprise. Hallenbeck (1964) opened the first chapter of the book by claiming that "adult education's first concern will always be helping individual adults to learn, to increase their capacities, to attain a richer and fuller life in their own terms" (p. 5). This view reflects something of the manner in which North American adult education research and theory have developed throughout the past twenty-seven years. That is, the focus has been on the individual rather than the society and on learning rather than the structures within which learning occurs — a psychological rather than a social orientation (Rubenson, 1982).

This orientation is clear in the discussion by Long in Chapter Four of this book of six domains of knowledge that illustrate the knowledge base of adult education. However, as Cunningham (Chapter Fourteen) argues, we have reason to believe that in the future the theoretical base of adult education will almost certainly develop beyond its present confines. Griffin's argument in favor of a critical sociology (Chapter Ten) illustrates the new thinking in adult education that is gaining ground among scholars.

The body of adult education knowledge is a complex and ever-changing phenomenon, overlapping and subdividing. It contains knowledge from research on the practice of adult education in a variety of different specialties and knowledge from analytical and critical examinations from the perspective of one or more of the disciplines.

Research. It is perhaps significant that no chapter in the black book specifically addresses research in adult education, apart from one about evaluation (Thiede, 1964). Over the past twenty-seven years, research has become a significant feature of university study of adult education, contributing to the growth and complexity of the knowledge about the practice of adult education. Like the other social sciences, adult education has passed through an evolutionary pattern in the development of its research procedures. Seeking "scientific respectability," researchers first adopted an objective, positivistic, and quantitative approach, but they gradually realized that that approach has severe limitations when people and their learning are the subject of investigation. Slowly, the research base has broadened as researchers have recognized the strengths of qualitative methods. Researchers now use a variety of different approaches to add to the body of knowledge of adult education and to understand the challenges practitioners face. Action science, critical theory, ethnography, and naturalistic methods are all beginning to find a place in adult education research. In this book, Merriam (Chapter Three) discusses the developments in these and other approaches to research and speculates about future developments.

Related Disciplines. Jensen (1964) claimed that adult education is a practical discipline rather than a theoretical one and that it borrows knowledge from the other disciplines and translates it into a usable form for adult education. This was also the approach adopted by London, McClusky, Essert, and Whipple in the black book. In other words, these authors differentiated between the pure and the applied forms of knowledge. (This is a rather crude distinction, but it is one used in this way in mathematics.) Thus, knowledge in the field of adult education had to be relevant and applicable, but knowledge in theoretical disciplines could have its own internal logic, without reference to its relevance to the practice of adult education.

The assumptions made by Jensen and his colleagues and others were misleading in at least two ways. First, these researchers referred to the so-called foundation disciplines as theoretical, as though a distinction can be made between educational knowledge that is practical and knowledge about education that is theoretical. Second, they felt that adult education was borrowing from theory and applying it to practice in a rather simple way. Actually, practical knowledge emerges from the field and is often codified as a result of research in the practice of adult education. It is integrated knowledge and only when analyzed can it be seen to be a unique constellation of subsections from the applied social sciences. But practical knowledge emerges most frequently from practice itself rather than from related disciplines, so it is not actually borrowed. Neither, therefore, is it actually applied in the sense of taking theoretical knowledge from another discipline and literally applying it to practice. Such knowledge may only be applied, partially, after it is formulated as an integrated subject. The unique integration of these applied disciplines within a conceptual framework of the practice of adult education forms the basis of the practical knowledge (See Boyd and Apps, 1980). It also constitutes a body of knowledge or a theory of practice.

Similar arguments about the body of theoretical knowledge of practice could be made for other fields, such as medicine, nursing, and social work. It might even be possible to detect cultural differences in the way that adult education is studied in different societies, with American scholars tending to emphasize the pragmatic applied approach and European scholars perhaps tending to study the field from the perspective of the foundation disciplines. Yet neither approach is exclusive, and the two overlap.

Graduate Study. Since the publication of the black book, the number of programs and doctoral graduates in adult education has increased nearly eightfold. Over 120 master's programs and 66 doctoral programs are operating at present (Peters and Kreitlow, Chapter Seven). Membership in the Commission of Professors of Adult Education (CPAE) has grown from approximately 20 professors to about 300.

Although the authors of the black book did not specify a core curriculum for graduate programs, one seems to have developed over the past twenty-seven years. Concomitantly, greater numbers of specialty courses, in such areas as continuing professional education, have been added to the curricula. Graduate programs appear to reflect the interests of faculty members in both general domains of knowledge and in selected specialties. Graduate programs will probably continue to mirror the field of practice, insofar as the field continues to grow more complex and diverse in its many programs, agencies, types of learners, and aims. However, this diversity will present a problem for the developers of graduate programs in the future, who will have to find the proper balance between core areas of study and specialized studies and choose among aims — most programs being unable to be all things to all people. Such problems will be exacerbated by the fact that most programs have fewer than four full-time faculty members, a program feature that is likely to continue into the foreseeable future.

The professoriate itself has changed, not only in terms of a larger total number of faculty members at work today but also in terms of the academic preparation of those faculty members. Most professors of adult education in the era of the black book were trained in disciplines other than adult education. Today, the majority have advanced training in adult education. Standards for adult education graduate programs that were recently adopted by the CPAE specify that at least one full-time faculty member will have an earned doctorate in adult education (or other designations such as continuing education or cooperative extension education). The standards say "other full-time faculty will have an earned doctorate in adult education or relevant fields (for example, philosophy, psychology or sociology), with knowledge of and, preferably, experience in adult education." (See the Resource at the end of the book for the full text of the standards.) Therefore, new professors are increasingly expected to have completed advanced study in adult education, rather than to have entered the field from another occupation. Naturally, there are reasons to try to prevent professors with little or no knowledge of adult education from being transferred to adult education programs from elsewhere in universities. However, the adult education professoriate may also seek to exclude scholars whose original discipline would add greatly to an understanding of the practice of adult education.

As the body of knowledge changes, the selection criteria for new entrants to the professoriate will change, but at the same time the selection of the professoriate will have its own effect on the way that the body of knowledge continues to develop. For instance, if the new professoriate is drawn from graduates of pragmatic and practical knowledge-based programs, these new professors might slant future research in a pragmatic direction. But if the new professoriate is drawn from graduates of related disciplines or from the more generic and theoretical streams, the body of adult education knowledge may develop in those directions. Consequently, one of the challenges facing departments of adult education in the future is to ensure that they have a balanced staff, drawn from as wide an academic background as possible, rather than a staff that is drawn exclusively from the pragmatic and practical knowledge-based programs. A balanced staff is necessary not only for teaching and research but also to ensure that the body of knowledge of and about adult education develops in an even manner across the whole of its complexity.

International Aspects. Shortly after the black book was published, educators of adults, including some of the authors of the book, participated in a historic meeting in Exeter, New Hampshire (Liveright and Haygood, 1968). This meeting was probably the first academic gathering in America at which adult education was examined from an international and comparative perspective. Since that time, international and comparative studies in adult education have gradually increased in number, among the most recent being the work of Lichtner (1989). Scholars are now traveling widely between countries and comparing practices. Although the whole world of adult education cannot be examined in this book, the "internationalization" of the field is reflected here.

In contrast to the black book, this book emphasizes the study of adult education as being worldwide and international (see Titmus, 1989). But it is not just the fact that the field has expanded in this way that is important. How scholars and practitioners of adult education have responded to the pressures of the past is also significant. Indeed, they are confronted with unresolved questions, and these and the issues that stand before them in the future are all central to this book.

Theory-Practice Relationships. The problems involved in relating theory to practice are not restricted to the related disciplines. Practitioners are often skeptical of the value of theory developed by adult education scholars. Moreover, the direction that the relationship of theory and practice should take (theory to practice, practice to theory, practice in theory) is not universally agreed upon. Cervero, in Chapter Two of this book, discusses four ways in which theory and practice may be related and how different viewpoints about these relationships have evolved over the past sixty years of formal study of adult education. The first viewpoint discussed by Cervero is simply that practice is guided by common sense and experience and not by reference to formal theory, a viewpoint that was widely held before university study of adult education began in the 1930s. The second viewpoint, which began to develop in the 1930s and persists until today, is that theory is the foundation of practice and is to be applied to practice and that the best theory is scientifically derived knowledge. The third viewpoint is that theory resides in practice, and thus attention is shifted away from mainly discipline-based, "detached" sources of formal knowledge and priority is given to knowledge developed by practitioners themselves. This viewpoint has received increasing attention in the recent literature of adult education, as has the fourth viewpoint, which, as Cervero says, holds that theory and practice are indivisible because they are part of a single reality. This last viewpoint is the subject of considerable debate among adult education scholars and practitioners because it focuses on the political nature of the development of knowledge and the potential it has for shaping the lives of adult learners.

Conclusion

Jensen (1960) suggests that three aspects of adult education point to its being a discipline: it is factual, normative, and an art or a practice. Liveright (1964) concludes that "In Jensen's terms, adult education should be looked upon as a practical discipline concerned with factual and descriptive elements and with normative elements; it should be looked upon as an art, a practice, and an engineering" (p. 90).

Insofar as the theoretical body of practical knowledge may be regarded as the primary concern of an applied discipline, adult education as an applied discipline has developed in a sophisticated manner in the past twenty-seven years. Clearly, the knowledge base in adult education is evolving and the field of study is international in scope.

Throughout this chapter, I have emphasized the way in which adult education is growing, developing, and becoming more widely accepted as a field of university study. However, the more radical role that education — especially of adults — can play must not be lost on the academic community. Adult education has a long and honorable history as being popular education for the people. Adult education has had radical and political significance, and this aspect of its history must not be lost as it seeks acceptance within the academic world.

Many of the themes that I touched on here will be developed at far greater depth in the subsequent chapters, and they are summarized by Peters in the final chapter. I have attempted no more than to set the scene for the remainder of the book. The study of adult education is entering a significant period in its development, but undoubtedly it has achieved much in twenty-seven years. The next quarter of a century holds promise and challenges and an exciting future for adult education.

References

Boyd, R. D., Apps, J. W., and Associates. *Redefining the Discipline of Adult Education.* San Francisco: Jossey-Bass, 1980.

Cervero, R. M. *Effective Continuing Education for Professionals.* San Francisco: Jossey-Bass, 1988.

Darkenwald, G. G., and Merriam, S. B. *Adult Education: Foundations of Practice.* New York: Harper & Row, 1982.

Fingeret, A. "Social Network: A New Perspective on Independence and Illiterate Adults." *Adult Education Quarterly,* 1983, *33* (3), 133–146.

Hallenbeck, W. "The Role of Adult Education in Society." In G. Jensen, A. A. Liveright, and W. Hallenbeck (eds.), *Adult Education: Outlines of an Emerging Field of University Study.* Washington, D.C.: American Association for Adult and Continuing Education, 1964.

Houle, C. O. "The Emergence of Graduate Study in Adult Education." In G. Jensen, A. A. Liveright, and W. Hallenbeck (eds.), *Adult Education: Outlines of an Emerging Field of University Study.* Washington, D.C.: American Association for Adult and Continuing Education, 1964.

Houle, C. O. *Continuing Learning in the Professions*. San Francisco: Jossey-Bass, 1980.

Jarvis, P. *The Sociology of Adult and Continuing Education*. London: Croom Helm, 1985.

Jarvis, P. *Adult Learning in the Social Context*. London: Croom Helm, 1987.

Jensen, G. "The Nature of Education as a Discipline." In G. Jensen (ed.), *Readings for Educational Research*. Ann Arbor, Mich.: Ann Arbor Publishers, 1960.

Jensen, G. "How Adult Education Borrows and Reformulates Knowledge of Other Disciplines." In G. Jensen, A. A. Liveright, and W. Hallenbeck (eds.), *Adult Education: Outlines of an Emerging Field of University Study*. Washington, D.C.: American Association for Adult and Continuing Education, 1964.

Jensen, G., Liveright, A. A., and Hallenbeck, W. (eds.). *Adult Education: Outlines of an Emerging Field of University Study*. Washington, D.C.: American Association for Adult and Continuing Education, 1964.

Jones, K. *A Sociology of Adult Education*. Aldershot, England: Gower, 1985.

Kelly, T. *A History of Adult Education in Great Britain*. Liverpool, England: Liverpool University Press, 1970.

Knowles, M. S. "The Field of Operations in Adult Education." In G. Jensen, A. A. Liveright, and W. Hallenbeck (eds.), *Adult Education: Outlines of an Emerging Field of University Study*. Washington, D.C.: American Association for Adult and Continuing Education, 1964.

Knowles, M. S. *The Modern Practice of Adult Education: From Pedagogy to Andragogy*. (Rev. ed.) Chicago: Association Press, 1980.

Lichtner, M. *Comparative Research in Adult Education*. Frascati, Italy: Centro Europeo Dell' Educazione (CEDE), 1989.

Liveright, A. A. "The Nature and Aims of Adult Education as a Field of Graduate Education." In G. Jensen, A. A. Liveright, and W. Hallenbeck (eds.), *Adult Education: Outlines of an Emerging Field of University Study*. Washington, D.C.: American Association for Adult and Continuing Education, 1964.

Liveright, A. A., and Haygood, N. (eds.). *The Exeter Papers:*

Report of the First International Conference on the Comparative Study of Adult Education. Boston: Center for the Study of Liberal Education for Adults, Boston University, 1968.

Marsick, V. J. (ed.). *Learning in the Workplace.* London: Croom Helm, 1987.

Merriam, S. B., and Cunningham, P. M. (eds.). *Handbook of Adult and Continuing Education.* San Francisco: Jossey-Bass, 1989.

Nadler, L., and Wiggs, G. D. *Managing Human Resource Development: A Practical Guide.* San Francisco: Jossey-Bass, 1986.

Rubenson, K. "Adult Education Research: In Quest of a Map of the Territory." *Adult Education,* 1982, *32* (2), 57–74.

Stubblefield, H. W. *Towards a History of Adult Education in America.* London: Croom Helm, 1988.

Tennant, M. *Psychology and Adult Learning.* London: Routledge, 1988.

Thiede, W. "Evaluation and Adult Education." In G. Jensen, A. A. Liveright, and W. Hallenbeck (eds.), *Adult Education: Outlines of an Emerging Field of University Study.* Washington, D.C.: American Association for Adult and Continuing Education, 1964.

Titmus, C. J. (ed.). *Lifelong Education for Adults: An International Handbook.* Oxford, England: Pergamon Press, 1989.

Valentine, T., "Adult Functional Literacy as a Goal of Instruction." *Adult Education Quarterly,* 1986, *36* (2), 108–113.

PART ONE

DEVELOPMENT
OF THE FIELD

Adult education is both a field of practice and a field of study, but these two aspects of adult education are not altogether separate. Academics whose professional lives are devoted to studying the field are practitioners in their own right, and the adult educators whose practice is not in graduate programs are sometimes involved in their own studies of adult education. But this book is about the study of adult education in universities. The editors and authors will sometimes necessarily distinguish between the study and practice of adult education as if they are two separate fields of knowledge or endeavor that include exclusive pursuits, activities, and interests. In this sense, we subscribe to convention, for most observers associate study with what academicians do and practice with what people in the "real world" of work do. Unfortunately, this division too often pits the interests of academicians against those of other practitioners, and less is accomplished than might otherwise be the case. Thus, readers should know that the authors of this book, all of whom are academicians, do not see themselves as belonging to an exclusive area of study separate from all other forms of practice, but indeed consider their work a part of the larger territory of adult education practice.

15

Jarvis suggests in Chapter One that formal study of adult education in universities will continue to mirror the field of practice, with a focus on practical knowledge. The term *discipline* evokes controversy and debate when it is used to describe any area of professional study. Our purpose is not to continue this debate here but instead to stress that university professors and their students are engaged in the systematic and rigorous study of practice. They use methods appropriate to that pursuit, although their methods may be different from those employed in other areas of academic study. For these professors and students, adult education is primarily an area of academic study, and their subject matter concerns practice in the broadest sense of the term. They build theories of practice, and they use theory originating in other areas of study and in practice, but their primary concern is not with building theory as an end in itself. In this sense, their work is distinguished from the work of people in disciplines whose primary concern is the generation of knowledge for its own sake. Thus, for adult education scholars, theory and practice must remain tied together. However, the exact nature of this relationship is not always clear in the minds of all academicians or the other practitioners with whom they work. The issue of theory versus practice remains dominant in the field at large.

An academician's view of the correct relationship between theory and practice is certain to influence his or her approach to studying the field. This view helps shape the academician's thinking about the purposes of research, possible sources of knowledge, how to employ methods of research, the proper means and results to be achieved by dissemination and use of the knowledge created by research, and who should control the whole enterprise. To address these issues, we begin Part One of this book with a chapter on the relationships between theory and practice. In this chapter, Cervero discusses the evolution in views about theory and practice that has occurred over the short history of academic study in adult education. He also speculates on what these views mean for our future efforts to understand and improve practice.

The discussion in Chapter Three is very closely related to that in Cervero's chapter. Merriam discusses three paradigms of thought that influence researchers' selection and use of methods of inquiry in adult education. She argues that a researcher's world view dominates his or her decisions about method and, consequently, the kinds of knowledge that research produces. Following these two framing chapters, Long discusses the results of efforts to develop a formal knowledge base in adult education thus far. He discusses six domains of knowledge that illustrate the kinds of formal knowledge developed by academicians and their students in the past quarter century.

The field has been shaped by forces internal and external to it, but the predominant force that shapes the body of knowledge is the people who do the inquiring. Griffith was asked by us to identify the people who in his judgment are leaders in the study of adult education. His selections are presented in Chapter Five. The manner in which the fruits of the labor of these leaders and that of others are disseminated and used is discussed by Brockett in Chapter Six. His chapter highlights the many new vehicles for disseminating knowledge that have been developed in recent years. And he speculates about what needs to be done in the future if we are to improve the dissemination and use of knowledge in the field.

Part One of the book closes with a comprehensive chapter on the development and future of graduate programs in adult education by Peters and Kreitlow. Chapter Seven updates statistics that depict the size and growth of the formal study of adult education in universities, reviews some of the issues that affect graduate study, and speculates on areas that need improvement in the future.

CHAPTER 2

Changing Relationships
Between Theory
and Practice

Ronald M. Cervero

In the great span of human experience, ideas about the relationship between theory and practice in adult education have arisen quite recently. Although these ideas exhibit some variety, the general consensus about the relationship can be summarized quite succinctly: theory and practice should be intimately related. In reality, however, there is a great disparity between theory and practice, which frustrates those who consider themselves practitioners and concerns those who consider themselves theoreticians. There is no shortage of accusations of fault for this disparity; some people blame theory and theoreticians and others locate ⁺he problem in practice and practitioners.

In trying to improve or at least understand this relationship, it is useful for us to consider another relationship that has a much longer tradition in human experience. The Bible expresses an expectation concerning the relationship of women and men in marriage: "And the two will become one. So they are no longer two but one" (Matt. 19:5-6). Many valuable insights can be drawn from considering the analogy between this

relationship and that of theory and practice. The one I wish
to highlight is that both marriage and the relationship between
theory and practice are human inventions whose ideal and actual forms are historically developed, socially organized, and
culturally mediated. Both relationships are social practices that
cannot be worked out "in principle" but must be negotiated by
real people in actual circumstances that involve issues of power
and status.

The central assumption of this chapter is that the relationship between theory and practice is not a naturally occurring one but rather a human invention; therefore, it must have
come into existence at a particular historical moment under certain social conditions to serve certain human purposes. My thesis
is that the existence of this relationship and the language used
to discuss it have their origins in the development of adult education as a field of university study.

Four different viewpoints about the relationship between
theory and practice in adult education are apparent. Each viewpoint has a common core of ideas that differentiates it from the
other three. Even though each of the four has its own history
and future, they exist in relation to each other because to a large
extent they arose in response to each other.

Although people who study adult education believe that
a proper understanding of the relationship between theory and
practice is critical, they do not agree on the meanings of the
terms *theory* and *practice* and their relationship (Bright, 1989).
Thus, this chapter does not offer a single definition of these terms
but rather discusses the concepts in the language used by the
proponents of each viewpoint. Also, most discussions of this issue use the terms *body of knowledge* and *theory* synonymously.
Although the distinction between these two terms may be important to one or more viewpoints, it is of secondary importance to conceptions of the relationship between theory and practice. In this chapter, then, the terms are used interchangeably.

The purpose of this chapter is to show that the meanings
of the relationship between theory and practice have been continually changing since the development of adult education as
a field of university study and that the positions people take on

this relationship have profound implications for the study and practice of adult education. The first sections of the chapter present the four views on the relationship in the order in which they first became identifiable in the field's professional literature. In the first view, adult education is carried out without reference to an organized body of professional knowledge and theory. The second view posits that a body of knowledge developed through the scientific process should be applied to practice so that practice can be improved. In contrast, the third view holds that the best way to improve practice is to uncover and critique the informal theory that practitioners use in their work. The fourth view presents a fundamental unity between theory and practice, highlights the ideological character of all knowledge, and argues that adult education can be improved by fostering emancipation. The final section of the chapter discusses the implications of these viewpoints for the future of adult education as a field of study.

Adult Education Without Theory

The central idea of the first viewpoint is that adult education has been carried out throughout history, including the present, without reference to what is commonly considered a body of knowledge. Many educators of adults are not aware of adult education as a field of study or practice. For these people, there is no body of knowledge. Nor is there for them a practice of adult education because the term *practice* implies being a member of an occupational group that has developed a set of traditions about how to carry out its work. Instead, these educators base their work on a set of ideals and practical knowledge that they have developed through direct experience. They fall into one of three groups: those who educated adults before there was a research-based body of knowledge, those who are unaware of a body of knowledge, and whose who are skeptical of the value of a body of knowledge.

Before adult education became a field of university study, it was an important movement in many societies (Grattan, [1955] 1971). Adult educators went about their work, some better than others no doubt, without reference to a body of knowledge about adult education. In 1970, Laidlaw reflected on the founding members of the Canadian Adult Education Association in 1935 and pointed out that "not one had a course in group dynamics but they sure made things happen" (Welton, 1987, p. 49). Not until after 1935, when the first doctorate in adult education in North America was awarded by Columbia University, could adult educators even possibly be concerned about the existence of a body of knowledge. It was exactly two decades later that university professors met for the first time to consider what that body of knowledge might be.

Before a body of knowledge was developed in universities, adult educators were plying their trade in mainstream institutions such as public schools (Knowles, 1977) and in broader social movements such as Antigonish (Coady, 1939). This tradition continues today because most adult educators work without knowledge of adult education as a field of university study. For example, it is fair to assume that most people involved in the highly significant educational efforts of the civil rights, women's liberation, and environmental movements do not consider their work in terms of being part of a larger field of adult education. Also, Griffith (1985) estimates that 95 percent of the people who carry out continuing education for professional groups in the United States have been trained as members of the groups with which they work rather than in the field of adult education. The relationship between adult education theory and practice is simply not an issue for these people because they are not aware of a body of knowledge in adult education. Many of these people would argue that their "common sense," which was developed through their formal education and practical experience, is the basis of their success as educators.

This common sense was highly valued by some people (but not all, as we shall see in the next section) who sought to develop adult education as a field of study. In fact, some people believe that the field was better off before there was a systematic body of knowledge to which adult educators could look for guidance. Laidlaw said, "Then we were unrespected and disrespectful amateurs. The present-day are respectable and polite professionals. Adult Education has arrived! Now it has been dissected down to the last cell but nobody seems to be working overly hard at it" (Welton, 1987, p. 51). Kidd (1981) also expresses great concern that "bland, homogenized, deodorized, anesthetized" theory was of little use to adult educators (p. 3).

Other people argued that one way theory could be developed was to recover and articulate the concepts implicit in good practice. Knowles (1980) observes that many of the successful teachers who wrote for the *Journal of Adult Education* from 1929 to 1948 "had no theory to support their practices; they were simply being pragmatic and following their intuitions" (p. 41). In preparing practitioners through university study, Houle (1964) asked, "Can the great lore of the creative but untrained pioneers of adult education be studied so that it can be passed on in a more systematic fashion?" (p. 82).

It is important to note that all of these comments were made after adult education had secured a place as a form of university study. For all adult educators up through the 1930s, and for most today, the relationship between theory and practice was simply not a concern. Not until university-based researchers began to produce science-based knowledge did the issue of the relationship between theory and practice arise. It is to this part of the story that we now turn.

Theory as the Foundation for Practice

The fundamental relationship espoused in this viewpoint is that theory should be applied to practice; a body of knowledge generated through the systematic processes of scientific research should be used to provide a solid foundation on which to base the practice of adult education. Thus scientifically derived knowledge is seen from the outset as different from and better than the knowledge that arises through experience and, therefore, should be used to improve practice. The difference between theory and practice is sharply drawn in this viewpoint, yet the ideal relationship between them is symbiotic because "theory without practice leads to empty idealism, and action without philosophical reflection is mindless activism" (Darkenwald and Merriam, 1982,

p. 37). This view also creates a division of labor between those who develop theory (primarily in universities) and those who are practitioners in adult education.

It was not until the 1950s that adult educators began a sustained and self-conscious movement to professionalize the field of adult education. For those people promoting professionalism, common sense was not a sufficient basis for practice. They believed that in order to be a professional field, adult education would need a knowledge base generated through the scientific process. Of course, those people promoting this idea had credible and powerful role models in the university, such as the fields of medicine and engineering. As Schön (1983) argues, the dominant view of professional practice at that time (and today) was "instrumental problem solving made rigorous by the application of scientific theory and technique" (p. 21). Those people trying to professionalize adult education were right in step with the nearly total acceptance in North America of the positivist view of knowledge and functionalist social theory.

In the positivist and functionalist views, education is a kind of applied science, "using empirically tested generalizations as a basis for resolving educational problems and guiding educational practice" (Carr, 1986, p. 181). The positivist view of knowledge claims to be able to describe only what is, not what ought to be. Thus, questions of values cannot be the subject of educational theory. Adult education professors and their students were left with trying to produce a body of theory that interpreted educational practice as a technical activity designed to bring about given ends. The body of knowledge of adult education, therefore, would be similar to that of engineering. Like engineers, who do not decide whether to construct a building but rather how to build it most effectively, the body of knowledge would be a set of value-free principles about how to conduct adult education most effectively.

This viewpoint clearly became dominant in the 1950s, with the formation of the Commission of Professors of Adult Education in the United States, and continues to predominate through the present. This orientation can be seen in the writings of the leadership of the commission in the 1950s, such as Verner (1956), who wrote that the growth of research "holds promise of strengthening the field and laying the foundation for advancement upon a scientifically valid knowledge base" (p. 226). Handbooks of adult education published in 1960, 1970, and 1980 called for more scientifically based theory (Knowles, 1960; Smith, Aker, and Kidd, 1970; Long, Hiemstra, and Associates, 1980).

This science-based body of knowledge was to serve as the basis of the professional preparation of adult educators. Clearly, this idea was the thrust of the first systematic statement of what should form the knowledge base of adult education — the black book (Jensen, Liveright, and Hallenbeck, 1964). Although practitioners have commonsense knowledge, it is deficient because, as London (1964) argues, "Science and scientific method provides a more accurate and ordered body of knowledge than common sense" (p. 114). This same view is represented in what is probably the basic textbook that has been used throughout the 1980s in graduate courses, Darkenwald and Merriam's 1982 work: "Fundamental research must be done, for not to expand the field's knowledge base is to preclude any hope for improving the quality of professional performance" (p. 23).

Some people with this orientation go so far as to claim that the only valid source of knowledge for practice is scientifically produced knowledge. Verner argues that those practitioners who do not have access to this knowledge base may be well intentioned, but "they are incapable of producing truly efficient and effective learning experiences" (1977, p. viii). Noting the absence of a significant research-based body of knowledge for training in business and industry, Spear (1989) finds it remarkable that this training could "be conducted with so little data or knowledge at its foundation" (p. 532).

Many people who subscribe to the viewpoint that theory should be applied to practice are the first to point out that theory usually is not applied to practice, thus creating a "gap" between the two (Elias, 1982). In their recent comprehensive review of program planning theory, Sork and Caffarella (1989) "have the impression that the gap that has always existed to some degree between theory and practice has widened since the publication of the last Handbook of Adult Education in 1980" (p. 243).

Adult educators give varied and sometimes contradictory reasons for the existence of this gap and methods to close it. Kidd (1981) says the problem is that research has been "influenced very little by the needs of learners, or of practice, but by the rituals of our scientific colleagues" (p. 49). Kenny and Harnisch (1982) agree and propose a research model that starts with practice and leads to theory development. Other people believe that the problem lies not in the nature of the body of knowledge but in the process of applying that knowledge (Long, 1983). For example, Boyd and Menlo (1984) propose a prescriptive model for the use of scientific information, in which they describe how to translate scientific knowledge into practical knowledge. Some people want practitioners to have an impact on the research agenda (Ludden and Wood, 1987) and researchers and practitioners to communicate better with each other (Merriam, 1986; Whitney, 1987). In contrast to all of these solutions, Boshier (1980) argues that research-based knowledge has had little impact precisely because it is focused too much on applied problems. In his view, more basic research is needed that is driven by theory, not practice.

Others argue that the problem cannot be solved because of the way it is framed. They see the question, How can we close the gap between theory and practice? as the wrong question. They believe a solution can be found only by changing the question (Carr and Kemmis, 1986). Their effort to do this is examined in the next section.

Theory in Practice

The central characteristic of the third view of the relationship between theory and practice is the belief that theory can be used to help educators interpret their practical situations by uncovering the tacit knowledge and values that guide their work. This orientation is distinguished by a broadening of the sources of knowledge. It holds that practitioners actually do operate on the basis of theories. According to people with this view, in addition to the formal theory generated by researchers, theory can also be found in practice. Theory can be derived from practice by systematically uncovering the structures of subjective meaning that influence the ways that real individuals act in concrete situations. These theories can influence the ways that practitioners understand themselves and help them to change through self-reflection (Carr and Kemmis, 1986).

In this viewpoint, as in the previous one, educational theory is intended to improve practice. However, the sources and functions of theory in relation to practice differ dramatically in this orientation from those in the previous view. In this view, education is a practical activity, meaning "an open, reflective, indeterminate, and complex form of human action" (Carr, 1986, p. 181). Importantly, practice is seen as a social process in which ends and means are continually negotiated in changing contexts marked by conflicting values, not as an instrumental process to achieve fixed ends. Thus, it is misguided to think that practice can be regulated by "applying" scientifically derived theory. As Carr wrote, "Closing the gap between theory and practice is not a case of improving the effectiveness of the products of theoretical activities, but one of improving the practical effectiveness of the theories that teachers employ in conceptualizing their own activities" (1980, p. 67).

This view of the relationship of theory and practice is firmly rooted in "interpretive" approaches to human knowledge and action (Carr and Kemmis, 1986). Interpretive approaches have become quite prominent in philosophy (Bernstein, 1983), the social sciences (Haan, Bellah, Rabinow, and Sullivan, 1983; Bellah and others, 1985), and education (Carr and Kemmis, 1986). One of the most direct applications of the interpretive approach comes from the efforts of Argyris and Schön (1974), who sought to provide a new understanding of professional practice. Their book, appropriately titled *Theory in Practice: Increasing Professional Effectiveness,* argues for professionals to develop their "own continuing theory of practice under real-time conditions . . . microtheories of action that, when organized into a pattern, represent an effective theory of practice" (p. 157). Schön further developed this line of thought in his books (1983, 1987) on the "reflective practitioner," which presented evidence of how professionals use repertoires of practical knowledge to change indeterminate situations into coherent problems that can be solved.

Adult education scholars have reconceptualized the relationship between theory and practice in similar ways. For example, much has been written recently about models of program development being a form of scientifically based principles that do not account for how practitioners actually carry out their work. Collins (1985) argues that these planning models derive from "the ideology of technical competence, but it is not apparent they have much to do with ensuring competent performance of everyday practical and ethical" activities (p. 12). Brookfield (1986) suggests that a solution to building useful theory is to recognize that practitioners have a body of knowledge and theory that guides their work: "If practitioners come to realize that 'playing hunches,' 'using intuition,' . . . are all . . . valued professional behaviors, then the theory-practice disjunction . . . will be significantly reduced" (p. 259). Sork and Caffarella (1989) suggest that researchers in collaboration with practitioners should build on Schön's work by developing a theory of program planning that takes into account the day-to-day responsibilities of practitioners.

In a similar vein, I offer a rationale for understanding practice as a form of deliberation and choice (Cervero, 1988, 1989). I believe that the existing models of program design do not adequately account for the everyday practice of program developers, which is characterized by situations that are unique, uncertain, and marked by conflicting values. These models are incomplete because they do not account for the role of context and values in making planning choices. Orienting principles for effective practice could be developed out of actual practice situations. The starting point would be to identify the choices made by educators in concrete situations and to state clearly the ways they both framed and resolved those choices.

In the most complete statement of this viewpoint of the relationship of theory and practice, Usher and Bryant (1989) have provided a comprehensive framework to connect theory, practice, and research in adult education. By arguing that "adult education as a field of study . . . should be appropriately located in adult education as a field of practice" (p. 1), they reframe the theory-practice question from how to apply theory to how can representation and explanation assist educators' judgment and understanding (Usher and Bryant, 1987). Drawing directly on Schön (1983), they make a case for the centrality of practical knowledge, which they call the mediation of formal or informal theory in the context of specific situations. According to Usher and Bryant, practical knowledge is what educators actually use in their work and has the following characteristics: it is situated knowledge that arises from the adult educator's actions, and it is concerned with the rightness of actions so that ends and means are codetermined within a framework of values.

Because this viewpoint broadens what counts as the body of knowledge, it has implications for the professional development of adult educators. Usher and Bryant (1989) suggest that the starting point for the preparation of adult educators is the description of the problems of practice and knowledge used in practice in order to begin a reflective dialogue about practice. Although this form of knowledge must be the starting point, it cannot be the exclusive content of the body of knowledge in adult education. Educators must critique it with formal theories in order to become free from the constraints of habit, assumption, and unrecognized ideology. Brookfield (1988) offers a similar scheme for the development of "critically reflective practitioners" (p. 317).

Although this orientation includes a recognition of the character of education, its central task is to describe educational practice and help practitioners become more reflective about their own individual actions. It rejects any explicit concern to change the educational realities being analyzed except through the educators' own actions. In contrast, the final viewpoint rests on the assumption that any educational theory "cannot rest content with providing value-neutral accounts, but must confront questions about practical educational values and goals" (Carr and Kemmis, 1986, p. 99).

Theory and Practice for Emancipation

The central idea in this viewpoint is that theory and practice are indivisible because they are part of a single reality. In this perspective, all knowledge is in some sense a social construct and "there is no possibility of an ideologically indifferent theory *or* practice" (Griffin, 1989, p. 122). The most important characteristic of all knowledge, whether it was developed by theoreticians or practitioners, is whose interests are served by that knowledge. By disclosing the relationship that adult education knowledge bears to the "true interests of individuals and groups in society" (Griffin, 1989, p. 137), this viewpoint seeks to emancipate adult educators from "irrational beliefs and misunderstandings that they have inherited from habit, tradition, and ideology" (Carr, 1986, p. 183).

This viewpoint assumes that all knowledge in adult education arises within the social relations of cultural production and reproduction. Therefore, all practice expresses a theory that relates to these processes and all development of theory must be seen as a form of social practice embedded in these processes. In this sense, theory and practice are "mutually constitutive and dialectically related. The transition is not from theory to practice or practice to theory, but from irrationality to rationality, from ignorance and habit to knowledge and reflection" (Carr, 1986, p. 183). This orientation challenges adult educators to understand the ideological bases of their practice by examining the rationality of those practices from historical and cultural perspectives.

Although it has a long tradition in the social sciences, adult education practice has generally not been seen in terms of this perspective. Most proponents of this viewpoint believe that what counts as theory and practice needs to be expanded to include the systems of knowledge and ideologies that have been systematically excluded in the creation of adult education as a field of study. Law and Rubenson (1988) argue that the "official" body of knowledge in adult education has been captive to a particular ideology, namely that of humanist psychology. This ideology, and therefore the knowledge base, has ignored any forms of knowledge and theory that criticize the social order and has left out the interests and knowledge of people not in the mainstream of society. As Cunningham (1988) points out, in the official histories of the field, "Western civilization is celebrated and competing histories are nonexistent. There is no history of black educators of adults, of female educators of adults, of socialist educators of adults" (p. 141). Using Rubenson's (1982) metaphor, the map of the territory of adult education theory and practice is restricted and is not of much help for either practitioners or researchers.

Although this viewpoint of the relationship of theory and practice is of fairly recent origin, its central ideas are being expressed and developed in the professional literature by a number of people (Cunningham, 1988; Griffin, 1983, 1988, 1989; Law and Rubenson, 1988; Rubenson, 1989; Welton, 1987). The most visible work from this viewpoint in adult education is that of Freire (1970, 1985). For Freire, knowledge is found in the connection between human knowledge, human interests, and power relations: "The only authentic points of departure for the scientific knowledge of reality are the dialectical relationships between men and the world, and the critical comprehension of how these relationships are evolved and how they in turn condition men's perception of concrete reality" (Freire, 1985, p. 86).

This orientation holds that the central focus in the relationship of theory and practice is what counts as knowledge and how, where, and by whom this knowledge is produced. The analysis of these issues is undertaken to further the goal of transforming the social relations of the production of knowledge and the type of knowledge produced. For example, participatory research deals directly with these concerns (Hall and Kassam, 1989). Its central objective is the production of knowledge with and in the interests of the poor and oppressed so that they may "regain their capacities to analyze and critically examine their reality, and to reject the continued domination and hegemony of the elite and ruling classes" (Tandon, 1988, p. 11). This is seen as necessary because the dominant classes have controlled the social relations of the production of knowledge and have used this control to further their own interests. Participatory research represents an effort to recover alternative knowledge systems that have been excluded from the "official" body of knowledge in adult education.

This viewpoint is deeply indebted to several intellectual

traditions in Western industrialized societies that originated in, but later became differentiated from, Marxist thought. The most prominent, because of its longevity, is the tradition of critical theory, which originated in the Frankfurt school in the mid 1930s (Held, 1980) and is represented in more recent times by the work of Habermas (1974). Recent traditions out of which this viewpoint grows are critical social science (Fay, 1987) and post-structuralism (Foucault, 1980). The arguments of some feminists illustrate how these traditions underlie this viewpoint: "Theory must be able to address women's experience by showing them where it comes from and how it relates to material social practices and the power relations that structure them. It must be able to recognize the competing subjective realities and demonstrate the social interests on behalf of which they work" (Weedon, 1987, p. 8). The implications of these intellectual traditions for the field of education have been analyzed by Cherryholmes (1988), Giroux (1983), and Carr and Kemmis (1986).

The view of theory and practice for emancipation has also been critiqued by adult educators (Collins and Plumb, 1989; Griffith and Cristarella, 1979) and by those outside the field who are sympathetic to the aims of the viewpoint (Beiner, 1987; Bernstein, 1976). For example, Lather (1986) claims that some neo-Marxists doing research perceive their role as an interpreter of the world. This perception of the researcher's role confounds their intent to demystify the world for the oppressed because the people who are the focus of the research become objects "rather than active subjects empowered to understand and change their situations" (p. 265). In the name of emancipation, these researchers impose meanings on situations rather than construct meaning through negotiation with the people themselves.

Discussion and Future Directions

This overview of the four viewpoints on the relationship of theory and practice is intended to demonstrate that this relationship is not simply a problem to be solved. In fact, the understanding of the relationship as a problem to be solved is a product of a particular set of beliefs that have thus far served as the guiding force in the creation of adult education as a field of study. These beliefs have been promoted so successfully that many have come to see the terms *theory, body of knowledge,* and *practice* as having agreed upon meanings. An acceptance of these meanings implies a particular stand about what is accepted as the body of knowledge and the goals of adult education as a field.

Rather than a problem to be solved, the relationship between theory and practice should be seen as a highly contested issue over which people who subscribe to competing ideologies and epistemologies struggle. We cannot wish away the issue nor can we look for a theory to resolve it because the struggle revolves around fundamentally different claims about knowledge and the purposes of education. Because these claims are supported by belief systems that have given rise to similar unresolved struggles in other fields of study for many years (Bernstein, 1976, 1983), we should not expect a single viewpoint to finally be accepted by everyone.

We must recognize that creating and maintaining adult education as a field of study is not a value-free process but rather is an ongoing social and political process that operates "behind our backs and beneath our feet" (Welton, 1987, p. 50). One of the central issues in the process that shapes the purposes and contours of the field of study is the struggle over the meanings of the terms *theory* and *practice* and their relationship. For many years, the adult education professoriate acted in the belief that a "natural" process of developing a body of knowledge, which could serve as the foundation of practice, was occurring. This idea framed much of the activity of those involved in the creation of the field of study, including what kind of research was done and the content of graduate training programs. I do not wish to imply that those working from this orientation have not done much good or place blame on individuals for not being conscious of the choice they made in subscribing to this view. We must remember Marx's aphorism that "men make history but not in circumstances of their own choosing" (cited in Rubenson, 1989, p. 57).

Perhaps the most important circumstance affecting the choices made in building adult education as a field of study is

that this process grew out of a movement toward professionalization and institutionalization of graduate programs in North
American universities in the 1950s (see Peters and Kreitlow,
Chapter Seven). In order to legitimize adult education as a field
of study at this time and in this context, it was "natural" for the
professoriate to subscribe to the viewpoint that theory should
be the foundation for practice. This orientation defined both
the appropriate problems to study and the best strategy for developing knowledge to address those problems. Because this was
the dominant viewpoint in all academic disciplines and professions that were located in universities at that time, it should not
be surprising that the authors of the black book (Jensen, Liveright, and Hallenbeck, 1964), who were also university faculty
members, took this viewpoint for granted. However, as has been
shown in this chapter, this orientation is but one way to conceive of the relationship of theory and practice. For example,
Cunningham (1989) argues that there is a "nascent, yet ener-
getic, stirring among many professional adult educators" (p. 43)
to define the education of adults broadly as a human activity
rather than as a field seeking scientific verification.

Merriam believes the knowledge base of adult education
as a field of study derives from the research conducted (see Merriam's Chapter Three). She further argues that the knowledge
produced through this research is contingent upon the questions
asked and the methods used, which ultimately are a function
of researchers' worldviews. Given the increasing numbers of
adult educators whose worldviews are consistent with the viewpoint of theory in practice or for emancipation, the body of
knowledge of the field is already becoming more pluralistic.

Professors in the 1950s and 1960s worked in a climate
in which positivism reigned supreme. In the 1990s, the university-based professions and academic disciplines exhibit a greater
epistemological pluralism. Some theory and research is consistent with the views of theory in practice and theory and practice for emancipation in most of the professions (Schön, 1987;
Unger, 1986), in philosophy (MacIntyre, 1984), and in all of
the social sciences (Bernstein, 1976, 1983). It should not be surprising, then, that adult education researchers have gravitated

toward these newer conceptions of the relationships between theory and practice. Professors and graduate students should have some success as they seek to form alliances with people in other academic disciplines who share these worldviews. They will have opportunities to collaborate in research projects as well as to receive training involving the variety of theory-practice viewpoints.

In most universities, professors can do research, publish, and teach courses based on these newer conceptions of the relationship between theory and practice and can receive tenure for doing so. Likewise, these professors can direct students who seek to undertake their dissertation research within these perspectives. Although people attempting to work from some of these perspectives have to struggle with the still-prevalent belief that the "scientific" process is the sine qua non of quality research, the alternative viewpoints are sufficiently well established in the academic disciplines so that they will not be alone. We are likely to see these alternate viewpoints achieving greater prominence in the landscape of adult education as a field of study.

As I stated in the opening section of this chapter, the relationship between theory and practice must be negotiated by real people in real situations. Because this chapter (and the entire book) seeks to have a role in that negotiation, it is necessary to ask where this chapter stands in relation to its own message. In this regard, its perspective is clearly that of theory as the foundation for practice, for it does not seek to develop a theory out of a material practice (except my own) nor does it challenge the power arrangements regarding who gets to write books such as these (the editors and authors are university-based professors). My goal is to challenge those engaged in further developing adult education as a field of study to think about their practices from a variety of theoretical positions.

Our choices about how to understand and act upon the relationship of theory and practice appear more difficult now than they were twenty-seven years ago. Of course, this is an illusion created by hindsight. Clearly, however, the positions we take on this issue and the processes through which we present these positions have important consequences for the field of adult education. Although the relationship between theory and practice is not an issue that will be resolved, we should set our sights on understanding and being critical of the circumstances that shape our actions about the issue. It is crucial that we do this so that our ignorance does not prescribe the history we make in these circumstances.

References

Argyris, C., and Schön, D. A. *Theory in Practice: Increasing Professional Effectiveness.* San Francisco: Jossey-Bass, 1974.

Beiner, R. "On the Disunity of Theory and Practice." *Praxis International,* 1987, *7* (1), 25–34.

Bellah, R. N., and others. *Habits of the Heart.* Berkeley: University of California Press, 1985.

Bernstein, R. J. *The Restructuring of Social and Political Theory.* London: Methuen, 1976.

Bernstein, R. J. *Beyond Objectivism and Relativism: Science, Hermeneutics, and Praxis.* Philadelphia: University of Pennsylvania Press, 1983.

Boshier, R. "A Perspective on Theory and Model Development in Adult Education." In P. M. Cunningham (ed.), *Yearbook of Adult and Continuing Education, 1979–1980.* Chicago: Marquis Academic Media, 1980.

Boyd, R. D., and Menlo, A. "Solving Problems of Practice in Education." *Knowledge: Creation, Diffusion, Utilization,* 1984, *6* (1), 59–74.

Bright, B. P. (ed.). *Theory and Practice in the Study of Adult Education.* London: Croom Helm, 1989.

Brookfield, S. D. *Understanding and Facilitating Adult Learning: A Comprehensive Analysis of Principles and Effective Practices.* San Francisco: Jossey-Bass, 1986.

Brookfield, S. D. "Developing Critically Reflective Practitioners: A Rationale for Training Educators of Adults." In S. D. Brookfield (ed.), *Training Educators of Adults: The Theory and Practice of Graduate Adult Education.* London: Routledge, 1988.

Carr, W. "The Gap Between Theory and Practice." *Journal of Further and Higher Education,* 1980, *4* (1), 60–69.

Carr, W. "Theories of Theory and Practice." *Journal of Philosophy of Education*, 1986, *20* (2), 177–186.

Carr, W., and Kemmis, S. *Becoming Critical: Education, Knowledge and Action Research.* London: Falmer Press, 1986.

Cervero, R. M. *Effective Continuing Education for Professionals.* San Francisco: Jossey-Bass, 1988.

Cervero, R. M. "Becoming More Effective in Everyday Practice." In B. A. Quigley (ed.), *Fulfilling the Promise of Adult and Continuing Education.* New Directions for Continuing Education, no. 44. San Francisco: Jossey-Bass, 1989.

Cherryholmes, C. H. *Power and Criticism: Poststructural Investigations in Education.* New York: Teachers College Press, 1988.

Coady, M. M. *Masters of Their Own Destiny: The Story of the Antigonish Movement of Adult Education Through Economic Cooperation.* New York: Harper & Row, 1939.

Collins, M. "Some Further Thoughts on Principles of Good Practice in Continuing Education." *Lifelong Learning*, 1985, *8* (8), 12–13, 28.

Collins, M., and Plumb, D. "Some Critical Thinking About Critical Theory and Its Relevance for Adult Education Practice." In C. C. Collins (ed.), *Proceedings of the 30th Annual Adult Education Research Conference.* Madison: University of Wisconsin, 1989.

Cunningham, P. M. "The Adult Educator and Social Responsibility." In R. G. Brockett (ed.), *Ethical Issues in Adult Education.* New York: Teachers College Press, 1988.

Cunningham, P. M. "Making a More Significant Impact on Society." In B. A. Quigley (ed.), *Fulfilling the Promise of Adult and Continuing Education.* New Directions for Continuing Education, no. 44. San Francisco: Jossey-Bass, 1989.

Darkenwald, G. G., and Merriam, S. B. *Adult Education: Foundations of Practice.* New York: Harper & Row, 1982.

Elias, J. L. "The Theory-Practice Split." In S. B. Merriam (ed.), *Linking Philosophy and Practice.* New Directions for Continuing Education, no. 15. San Francisco: Jossey-Bass, 1982.

Fay, B. *Critical Social Science: Liberation and Its Limits.* Ithaca, N.Y.: Cornell University Press, 1987.

Foucault, M. *Power/Knowledge: Selected Interviews and Other Writings, 1972-1977.* New York: Pantheon Books, 1980.

Freire, P. *Pedagogy of the Oppressed.* New York: Herder & Herder, 1970.

Freire, P. *The Politics of Education: Culture, Power, and Liberation.* South Hadley, Mass.: Bergin & Garvey, 1985.

Giroux, H. *Theory and Resistance in Education.* South Hadley, Mass.: Bergin & Garvey, 1983.

Grattan, C. H. *In Quest of Knowledge: A Historical Perspective on Adult Education.* New York: Arno Press and the New York Times, 1971. (Originally published 1955.)

Griffin, C. *Curriculum Theory in Adult and Lifelong Education.* London: Croom Helm, 1983.

Griffin, C. "Critical Thinking and Critical Theory in Adult Education." In M. Zukas (ed.), *Papers from the Transatlantic Dialogue.* Leeds, England: School of Continuing Education, University of Leeds, 1988.

Griffin, C. "Cultural Studies, Critical Theory, and Adult Education." In B. P. Bright (ed.), *Theory and Practice in the Study of Adult Education.* London: Croom Helm, 1989.

Griffith, W. S. "Persistent Problems and Promising Prospects in Continuing Professional Education." In R. M. Cervero and C. L. Scanlan (eds.), *Problems and Prospects in Continuing Professional Education.* New Directions for Continuing Education, no. 27. San Francisco: Jossey-Bass, 1985.

Griffith, W. S., and Cristarella, M. C. "Participatory Research: Should It Be a New Methodology for Adult Educators?" In J. A. Niemi (ed.), *Viewpoints on Adult Education Research.* Information Series, no. 171. Columbus: ERIC Clearinghouse on Adult, Career, and Vocational Education, Ohio State University, 1979.

Haan, N., Bellah, R. N., Rabinow, P., and Sullivan, W. M. (eds.). *Social Science as Moral Inquiry.* New York: Columbia University Press, 1983.

Habermas, J. *Theory and Practice.* (J. Viertel, trans.) London: Heinemann, 1974.

Hall, B. L., and Kassam, Y. "Participatory Research." In C. J. Titmus (ed.), *Lifelong Education for Adults: An International Handbook.* Oxford, England: Pergamon Press, 1989.

Held, D. *Introduction to Critical Theory.* Berkeley: University of California Press, 1980.

Houle, C. O. "The Emergence of Graduate Study in Adult Education." In G. Jensen, A. A. Liveright, and W. Hallenbeck, (eds.), *Adult Education: Outlines of an Emerging Field of University Study.* Washington, D.C.: American Association for Adult and Continuing Education, 1964.

Jensen, G., Liveright, A. A., and Hallenbeck, W. (eds.). *Adult Education: Outlines of an Emerging Field of University Study.* Washington, D.C.: American Association for Adult and Continuing Education, 1964.

Kenny, W. R., and Harnisch, D. L. "A Developmental Approach to Research and Practice in Adult and Continuing Education." *Adult Education,* 1982, *33* (1), 29–54.

Kidd, J. R. "Research Needs in Adult Education." *Studies in Adult Education,* 1981, *13* (1), 1–14.

Knowles, M. S. (ed.). *Handbook of Adult Education in the United States.* Washington, D.C.: American Association for Adult and Continuing Education, 1960.

Knowles, M. S. *A History of the Adult Education Movement in the United States.* (Rev. ed.) Melbourne, Fla.: Krieger, 1977.

Knowles, M. S. *The Modern Practice of Adult Education: From Pedagogy to Andragogy.* (Rev. ed.) Chicago: Association Press, 1980.

Kreitlow, B. W. "Research in Adult Education." In M. S. Knowles (ed.), *Handbook of Adult Education in the United States.* Washington, D.C.: American Association for Adult and Continuing Education, 1960.

Kreitlow, B. W. "Research and Theory." In R. M. Smith, G. F. Aker, and J. R. Kidd (eds.), *Handbook of Adult Education.* New York: Macmillan, 1970.

Lather, P. "Research as Praxis." *Harvard Educational Review,* 1986, *56* (3), 257–277.

Law, M., and Rubenson, K. "Andragogy: The Return of the Jedi." In M. Zukas (ed.), *Papers from the Transatlantic Dialogue.* Leeds, England: School of Continuing Education, University of Leeds, 1988.

London, J. "The Relevance of the Study of Sociology to Adult Education Practice." In G. Jensen, A. A. Liveright, and W. Hallenbeck (eds.), *Adult Education: Outlines of an Emerging Field of University Study.* Washington, D.C.: American Association for Adult and Continuing Education, 1964.

Long, H. B. *Adult Learning: Research and Practice.* New York: Cambridge Books, 1983.

Long, H. B., Hiemstra, R., and Associates. *Changing Approaches to Studying Adult Education.* San Francisco: Jossey-Bass, 1980.

Ludden, L. L., and Wood, G. S. "Practice Driven Research: A Model for Bridging the Gap Between Research and Practice." *Lifelong Learning,* 1987, *10* (5), 21–25.

MacIntyre, A. *After Virtue: A Study in Moral Theory.* Notre Dame, Ind.: University of Notre Dame Press, 1984.

Merriam, S. B. "The Research-to-Practice Dilemma." *Lifelong Learning,* 1986, *10* (1), 4–6, 24.

Rubenson, K. "Adult Education Research: In Quest of a Map of the Territory." *Adult Education,* 1982, *32* (2), 57–74.

Rubenson, K. "The Sociology of Adult Education." In S. B. Merriam and P. M. Cunningham (eds.), *Handbook of Adult and Continuing Education.* San Francisco: Jossey-Bass, 1989.

Schön, D. A. *The Reflective Practitioner.* New York: Basic Books, 1983.

Schön, D. A. *Educating the Reflective Practitioner: Toward a New Design for Teaching and Learning in the Professions.* San Francisco: Jossey-Bass, 1987.

Smith, R. M., Aker, G. F., and Kidd, J. R. (eds.). *Handbook of Adult Education.* New York: Macmillan, 1970.

Sork, T. J., and Caffarella, R. S. "Planning Programs for Adults." In S. B. Merriam and P. M. Cunningham (eds.), *Handbook of Adult and Continuing Education.* San Francisco: Jossey-Bass, 1989.

Spear, G. E. "Adult Education for Employment: Research." In C. J. Titmus (ed.), *Lifelong Education for Adults: An International Handbook.* Oxford, England: Pergamon Press, 1989.

Tandon, R. "Social Transformation and Participatory Research." *Convergence,* 1988, *21* (2 & 3), 5–18.

Unger, R. M. *The Critical Legal Studies Movement.* Cambridge, Mass.: Harvard University Press, 1986.

Usher, R. S., and Bryant, I. "Re-examining the Theory-Practice Relationship in Continuing Professional Education." *Studies in Higher Education,* 1987, *12* (2), 201–212.

Usher, R. S., and Bryant, I. *Adult Education as Theory, Practice and Research: The Captive Triangle.* London: Routledge, 1989.

Verner, C. "Research-Based Publications." *Adult Education,* 1956, *6* (4), 226–233.

Verner, C. "Introduction." In D. D. Campbell, *Adult Education as a Field of Study and Practice.* Vancouver, Canada: Centre for Continuing Education, University of British Columbia, 1977.

Weedon, C. *Feminist Practice and Poststructuralist Theory.* New York: Blackwell, 1987.

Welton, M. R. "'Vivisecting the Nightingale': Reflections on Adult Education as an Object of Study." *Studies in the Education of Adults,* 1987, *19* (1), 46–68.

Whitney, D. R. "On Practice and Research: Confessions of an Educational Researcher." *Lifelong Learning,* 1987, *10* (8), 12–15, 30.

CHAPTER 3

How Research
Produces Knowledge

Sharan B. Merriam

To measure the growth of a field such as adult education, one can count participants, trace the development of programs and funding, note the increase in publications, or document the growth of in-service and graduate training opportunities. The development of adult education can also be traced through looking at the growth of the field's knowledge base. This is a somewhat less satisfactory method of measurement than the other methods, however, because there is no clear consensus as to what constitutes the knowledge base of adult education. Is the knowledge base what we find in books and other printed materials? Does it include what people know to be true but have not written down? Is it what is produced through research? Does it include personal and philosophical reflections on practice, a priori theorizing, and material borrowed from other disciplines? As the chapters in this book suggest, the knowledge base or "the field," includes all of these things. Adult educators do agree that this amorphous, boundary-less field of adult education has indeed been developing and expanding and that all of the above have in some way contributed to this growth.

The purpose of this chapter is to explore how one of these factors — research — contributes to building the field's knowledge base. I will not attempt to review the accumulation of research of the last twenty-seven years since the publication of the black book. Long provides such an overview in Chapter Four and other reviews can be found in Long, Hiemstra, and Associates (1980); Long (1983); Deshler and Hagan (1989); and Titmus (1989). The focus here is not what research leads to knowing but *how* research leads to knowing more about a phenomenon.

Research is broadly defined as systematic or disciplined inquiry; that is, it is a purposeful, systematic process by which we know more about something than we did before engaging in the process. Shulman (1988) points out that educational research methods are "disciplined in another sense. They have emerged from underlying social or natural science disciplines which have well-developed canons of discovery and verification" (p. 16). Indeed, we shall see how the paradigms discussed in this chapter draw from different disciplines.

The knowledge that is produced through research is a function of the questions the researcher asks and the methods the researcher uses to answer those questions. Where do the questions come from that structure research studies? In adult education, many questions come from practice — we observe something that puzzles us, we wonder about it, we want to know why it is the way it is, we ask whether something can be done to change it, and so on. Questions or research problems also come from the literature related to a phenomenon, from deductions based upon theory, and from current issues. However, what one person is curious about or mystified by may not be what puzzles others. Nor will everyone agree on the best methods by which to approach the same question.

The questions raised and methods used are functions of the researcher's worldview. This chapter will discuss how different kinds of knowledge are produced depending upon the assumptions we make about the world and about how to study it systematically. Drawing from Carr and Kemmis (1986) and Bredo and Feinberg (1982), I will discuss the relationship of research to the production of knowledge in terms of three paradigms: the positivist, or empirical-analytic; the interpretive; and the critical. This framework is based upon Jurgen Habermas's theory of knowledge (1971). For each paradigm, the following factors will be covered: the particular worldview and the assumptions underlying the paradigm, how the paradigm is influenced by different disciplinary and intellectual traditions, what kinds of questions researchers ask about phenomena as a result of working with the paradigm, and, finally, how research is conducted and what type of knowledge is produced from inquiry grounded in the paradigm.

Positivist Paradigm

Most of the research in adult education has been based on the positivist paradigm, although other paradigms are gaining in favor among researchers. The term *positivist* comes from the French philosopher Comte, who used *positivism* to represent a particular view of knowledge in the natural sciences (Bredo and Feinberg, 1982). In this view, scientific knowledge consists of facts that could be subsumed under general laws. According to this view, we gain scientific knowledge through sensory or observational experience combined with logic. The "self-evidently clear and consequential arguments" of this paradigm resulted in logical positivism becoming "*the* paradigm for true knowledge of the world" (Bredo and Feinberg, 1982, p. 14). The basic assumption underlying research inspired by this worldview is the notion of a single, objective reality — the world out there — that we can observe, know, and measure. Researchers amass facts to describe the world, with the aim of uncovering laws that will explain aspects of this reality.

The "scientific method," which is compatible with this worldview, was developed and used with such success in the natural sciences that it was appropriated by most of the social sciences, including education, as the way to build a knowledge base. Carr and Kemmis describe the tasks of educational research under this paradigm: "The first is to discover the relevant scientific laws operative in educational situations so that knowledge of the limits of what it is possible to achieve will be available. . . . The second task follows from the fact that the extent to which any scientific laws effectively operate in any educational situation will depend on the extent to which certain conditions are satisfied. . . . So, by manipulating the conditions and circumstances in which laws operate, desired effects can be either encouraged or minimized and, to this extent, controlled" (1986, p. 58).

Questions of description, confirmation, causal explanation, prediction, and control are important to this paradigm. People and their behaviors become objects for study, with the researcher maintaining as much distance from the researched as possible so as to remain objective. To help maintain objectivity, researchers use inanimate instruments such as scales, tests, surveys, and computers to collect data. They analyze data by predetermined, usually statistical, procedures. The researchers claim that the type of knowledge they produce is neutral, objective, scientific explanation of educational practice. Such knowledge can "be employed to make objective decisions about possible courses of action" (Carr and Kemmis, 1986, p. 76).

In North America this perspective on research in adult education has been seen as legitimate and as contributing to the knowledge base and has therefore been disseminated, reviewed, and cross-referenced in the literature. In the first substantial review of adult education research, Brunner, Wilder, Kirchner, and Newberry (1959) selected some 600 sources for review based on the criteria that they had "valid generalizations applicable to the broad field of adult education" and that the findings "were sufficiently well-developed methodologically to suggest tenable and researchable hypotheses" (p. vi). They defined research as "the use of scientific, standardized procedures in the search for knowledge" (p. 1). Brunner found adult education research up to that point to be "rather chaotic," mostly descriptive, uneven in its coverage of areas of interest to the field, and conducted largely by researchers from other disciplines (p. 2). Five years later, the role of research in the development of the field was only cursorily mentioned by a few of the authors in the black book (Jenson, Liveright, and Hallenbeck, 1964), whose editors noted that adult education was developing its own research "to test the applicability of existing knowledge to the education of adults, and to discover for itself new knowledge or new relationships within existing knowledge" (p. viii).

One of the eight handbooks of adult education published in 1980–1981 was devoted to research methods in the study of adult education (Long, Hiemstra, and Associates, 1980). While acknowledging "other means" of doing research, the book's authors focused on "the scientific method of determining what is real" (p. 5). According to Long, the scientific method "is more reliable than some other means of answering questions" (p. 6), and, "in spite of its limitations, the scientific method is one of the most promising tools available to humankind to extend the frontiers of knowledge and to increase the accumulation of tested and verified truth" (p. 7).

Indeed, until the late 1970s, most research in North American adult education was based on this worldview. In a recently published review of research issues and directions, Deshler and Hagan (1989) delineate three overlapping phases of research history. They characterize the earliest phase as atheoretical descriptions of programs. The second phase, which continues today, they call a period of "improvement of research methods and designs patterned after the natural sciences" (p. 2). The most recent phase emphasizes the building of theory and the definition of research territory. This phase, of which their chapter in the handbook is a good example, includes discussions of topics, methods, and alternative worldviews out of which inquiry can be structured.

Certainly, research conducted within the positivist paradigm has contributed much to the knowledge base of adult education. Early descriptions of practice have helped to delineate and define the field. Large-scale studies of who participates in what kind of adult education and for what reasons have given us needed baseline data from which to ask more sophisticated questions. And studies on why adults participate in learning and how adults go about learning (beginning with Thorndike's seminal work in 1928) have helped us to accumulate a body of knowledge that has defined adult education as a field separate from other areas of education.

Several factors help to explain the predominance of the

positivist paradigm in adult education research in North America. In adult education, as in other developing fields of social practice, research based on the natural sciences was seen as a means of producing unique and legitimate knowledge necessary for the field to be classified as a discipline. Further, the emphasis on the individual learner, which is common in North America, led much of the research in adult education to have a psychological orientation (Rubenson, 1989). Apps notes two other reasons for the predominance of this paradigm — the training of researchers in only the positivist paradigm and "a society that puts considerable stress on those things that are easily measured and on technical accomplishment" (1979, p. 182).

Interestingly, Apps (1979) also points out that the positivist paradigm is at odds with some of the values of adult education. First, adult education emphasizes consulting with learners about their learning needs, but "an implicit assumption of the common research approaches is that adults cannot know their own needs, their own realities. A researcher examines them and on this basis determines their reality for them" (p. 180). Second, "Continuing education programmers proclaim the importance of treating adults as mature, unique individuals, each different from every other," but "research assumes that adults are more similar to than different from one another" (p. 182). Third, "Continuing education programmers stress the self-directed nature of adult learning. Research assumes that the behavior of adults is largely predetermined and that they have little capacity for initiative" (p. 182). For whatever reasons, it was in the 1970s that alternative approaches to the positivist paradigm began to receive more attention in adult education. Most of these approaches can be grouped under what Carr and Kemmis (1986) and Bredo and Feinberg (1982) call the interpretive paradigm.

Interpretive Paradigm

The interpretive paradigm challenges many of the assumptions of positivist-oriented research. This paradigm draws from many disciplines and traditions, including anthropology, history, phe-

nomenology, symbolic interactionism, hermeneutics, and the
Chicago school of sociology (see Bogdan and Biklen, 1982). Research out of this paradigm has been called qualitative, naturalistic, field study, ethnographic, subjective, and grounded theory.
Essentially, this paradigm seeks "to replace the scientific notions
of explanation, prediction and control, with the interpretive notions of understanding, meaning and action" (Carr and Kemmis,
1986, p. 83).

In contrast to the positivist paradigm's single, objective,
static reality, interpretive research assumes that there are multiple realities. In this paradigm, reality is not an object that can
be discovered and measured but rather a construction of the
human mind. The world is a highly subjective phenomenon that
is interpreted rather than measured. In this view, beliefs rather
than facts form the basis of perception. The context and the
meaning of that context to the people in it are of utmost importance, as noted by Bredo and Feinberg (1982, p. 117): "The
problem is that in counting or measuring behavior, the social
scientist who imposes a conception of what he is studying that
is insensitive to the conceptions of those being studied in effect
rips the behavior from the social context which makes it what
it is. Two apparently similar acts may have different meanings,
depending on their contexts, just as two apparently different acts
may have the same meanings."

Approaching the interpretive paradigm from a somewhat
different angle, Torbert (1981) asks why educational research
is so uneducational. Part of the answer, he feels, lies with the
dominance of the positivist paradigm, in which attention "is focused away from the actor (researcher) towards the outside
world, where it is assumed . . . that there are simple facts to
be observed" (p. 145). He notes, furthermore, that in this model
of research one learns while setting up an experiment or survey
and after the data have been collected, not during the study.
"What is actually going on, i.e. one's own action with others
and the assumptions upon which that action is based" is neglected
(p. 144).

The interpretive paradigm presents a dynamic rather than
a static view of the world: "Knowledge continually changes; new

constructs permit new perspectives and subsequent knowledge claims. . . . Objects, events, and especially people are continually changing. The process of that change is as important to study as continuity" (Deshler and Hagen, 1989, p. 4). It is important to consider many different assumptions, because they lead to different questions being asked and hence different knowledge being added to the field.

The questions in interpretive research focus on "*process* rather than outcomes or products. How do certain things happen? What is the 'natural' history of the activity or event under study? What happens with the passage of time? . . . Qualitative researchers are interested in *meaning*—how people make sense of their lives, what they experience, how they interpret these experiences, how they structure their social worlds" (Merriam, 1988, p. 19). These reseachers assume that meaning is embedded in people's experiences and mediated through the investigator's own perceptions. Unlike the natural scientist's view of research, which stresses objectivity and distance from what is being studied, interpretive research cannot get "outside" the phenomenon. In fact, the researcher is typically closely involved with what or who is being researched. The researcher, as the primary instrument for both data collection and data analysis, shares in the world of the researched and then interprets what he or she experienced there. The major data collection strategies of this type of research—interviewing, observing and analyzing documents—directly involve the researcher with the phenomenon under study.

How has the knowledge base of adult education been developed through this form of inquiry? Of particular note are those studies that have generated theory or theoretical constructs that have helped define the field. The generation of hypotheses and substantive theory is one of the strengths of this form of inquiry (Glaser and Strauss, 1967). Rather than testing hypotheses, researchers using an interpretive approach often build abstractions, concepts, hypotheses, or theories inductively. In contrast to researchers oriented toward deduction, who "hope to find data to match a theory, inductive researchers hope to find a theory that explains their data" (Goetz and LeCompte, 1984, p. 4).

Two major areas of research in adult education in particular — participation in education (including motivation) and self-directed learning — are rooted in an early qualitative study by Houle of twenty-two adult learners (1961). Gathering data through interviews and then searching for "patterns that would throw light on the meaning of continuing education" (p. 14), Houle characterized adult learners as primarily goal oriented, activity oriented, or learning oriented. This tripart typology has led to dozens of studies on participation and motivation of adult learners. Houle's study also inspired Tough's (1971) investigation of independent learning projects, which in turn opened up an entire line of research into self-directed learning.

Other contributions to the knowledge base out of this paradigm include those from studies by Clark, Mezirow, and Fingeret. Clark's (1956) field investigation of public schools for adults in Los Angeles led to the incorporation of such concepts as marginality, the enrollment economy, and the service-oriented characteristic of practice into adult education. Mezirow's notion of perspective transformation evolved from a grounded theory study of women reentering the educational system (Mezirow, 1975). Within the last few years, his theory has stimulated much discussion and writing, most of which is based on the critical theory paradigm, to be explored in the next section of this chapter. A better understanding of illiterate adults has also been gained through interpretive research. Of particular note is Fingeret's (1983) ethnography of forty-three illiterate adults and her discovery that such adults are members of strong social networks in which they exchange goods and services. (For other examples of interpretive research in North America, see Merriam, 1989.)

Interpretive research is also found outside North America, especially in Europe. Brookfield's study of independent adult learners (1981) and Charnley and Jones's work in adult basic education (1979) are two examples of interpretive research. Despite the European orientation in favor of interpretive research, however, Rubenson (1989) points out that positivistic research "dominates on both continents" (p. 510). (For reviews of research, interpretive and otherwise, from Latin America,

Western Europe, Eastern Europe, and the Soviet Union, see Titmus, 1989).

In summary, the interpretive paradigm stands in contrast to the positivist orientation to conducting research, in both its underlying philosophical roots and its assumptions about what constitutes reality and knowledge. Consequently, a researcher using this paradigm asks different questions about the world and investigates them using different methods than does a researcher using the positivist paradigm. Contributions to the knowledge base of adult education from this paradigm tend to be of a more theory-generating than theory-testing nature. For some people, however, understanding practice through interpretive research does not go far enough. Carr and Kemmis (1986) state that "while it may be true that consciousness 'defines reality', it is equally true that reality may systematically distort consciousness. . . . One of the major weaknesses of the interpretive model . . . [is] its failure to realize how the self-understandings of individuals may be shaped by illusory beliefs which sustain irrational and contradictory forms of social life" (p. 129). This critique by Carr and Kemmis is related to another "problem" with the interpretive approach — its inherent relativism. No mechanism exists for assessing the value or worth of one set of subjective interpretations over another. As Bredo and Feinberg (1982) point out, "If any intersubjective standards may be used to establish a domain of rigorous, rational discourse, we could have the absurdity of the inmates of a mental hospital establishing *their* standards of rationality and then proceeding to act in a rigorously rational (by this standard), if wildly maladaptive, fashion" (pp. 127–128). In response to these and other criticisms of interpretive research, yet another approach to carrying out systematic inquiry in adult education can be delineated. This approach is derived from critical social theory.

Critical Paradigm

The critical paradigm is based on German philosophy, especially that of Hegel, Marx, the Frankfurt school, and more recently Jurgen Habermas, who has become the most prominent spokesperson of contemporary critical theory. Critical social science, of which feminist literature, French poststructuralist philosophy, and critical research in general are prominent components, "goes beyond critique to critical praxis; that is, a form of practice in which the 'enlightenment' of actors comes to bear directly on their transformed social action" (Carr and Kemmis, 1986, p. 144).

Praxis, the combination of reflection and action, is central to this paradigm. "It is the 'doing' which will be reflected upon in retrospect and which is prospectively guided by the fruits of previous reflections" (Carr and Kemmis, 1986, p. 147). Thus, according to this viewpoint, it is not enough to amass information about practice or to come to understand what is happening or what meanings people attribute to phenomena. Critical research involves a commitment to organized, deliberate, and prudent action — action that will change for the better the social situation of those involved. Not until the 1980s did this orientation have some proponents in the field of adult education. Conferences, publications, and research based in this paradigm are helping to express and illuminate some of the vexing issues of the practice of adult education.

Although it is difficult to distill this complex paradigm into a few basic assumptions, it is worth reviewing several assumptions that, by extension, characterize the way critical research is conducted. First, positivistic notions of rationality, objectivity, and truth are rejected. The practitioner's interpretations of the world and self-understandings are accepted as the bases for developing knowledge (Carr and Kemmis, 1986). Second, the paradigm recognizes that people's interpretations of the world may be ideologically distorted; that is, there may be a contradiction "between the way people behave in practice and the way they understand themselves to be acting" (Bredo and Feinberg, 1982, p. 9). Third, the existing social structure is seen as partly, if not totally, coercive and oppressive. This paradigm requires researchers to reflect critically upon society and their complicity in reinforcing an oppressive structure so that they and the people they research can overcome domination and repression through praxis. Taking action to change the social structure is seen as both freeing and empowering.

Research based upon the critical paradigm has different aims and methods than that conducted out of either the positivist or the interpretive paradigms. Comstock (1982) writes that critical social science diverges from a positivistic approach to social science in its image of society and human nature, the nature of knowledge, the form of scientific knowledge, and the role of the researcher.

Society and human nature are viewed by researchers working with the positivist paradigm as objective, ahistorical phenomena. But researchers using the critical paradigm assume that society and human nature are human constructions that can be "altered through people's progressive understanding of historically specific processes and structures" (p. 372). Knowledge, in the positivist view, is objective and value-free. In critical research, knowledge is viewed as subjective, emancipatory, and productive of fundamental social change. Scientific knowledge, as a special form of knowledge, consists of laws and causal explanations in the positivist paradigm, not the critical accounts or explanations that lead to social change found in the critical paradigm. And the role of the scientist differs in the two paradigms in that a person subscribing to the positivist view separates himself or herself from the phenomenon of study, but the critical researcher "endeavors to *engage* them [persons on whom research is being done] in self-conscious action" (p. 378).

Comstock succinctly summarizes the nature of critical social research in the following excerpt: "Critical social research begins from the life problems of definite and particular social agents who may be individuals, groups or classes that are oppressed by and alienated from social processes they maintain or create but do not control. Beginning from the practical problems of everyday existence it returns to that life with the aim of enlightening its subjects about unrecognized social constraints and possible courses of action by which they may liberate themselves. Its aim is enlightened self-knowledge and effective political action. Its method is dialogue" (p. 378).

Thus, the aims of critical research are enlightenment and empowerment brought about through an educational process that leads to transformative action. In this form of research, "the politics of the relationship between the knower and the known

assumes center stage; the task becomes developing methodological approaches to involve the researched in the negotiation
of meaning and power and the construction and validation of
knowledge" (Lather, 1989, p. 252). Lather goes on to note that
"based on feminist, neo-marxist and Freirian attempts to create democratic, reciprocally educative, and change-enhancing
approaches to knowledge production and legitimation, the development of critical science stands in stark opposition to or-
thodox conceptions of what research in the human sciences is
and might be" (p. 252).

Less has been written on how actually to go about doing
research in accordance with the critical paradigm than with the
other two paradigms. However, Comstock (1982) has delineated
a seven-step approach to doing critical social science research.
Basically, the researcher begins with groups or movements with
"progressive" interests — that is, groups who express "interests,
purposes, or human needs which cannot be satisfied" within the
context of the present social order (p. 380). The researcher tries
to understand the subjects' life-world through dialogue. Out of
this dialogue, the researcher identifies factors that determine and
constrain the subjects' life-world. Then the researcher constructs
models of relations between social conditions and the subjects'
actions. The last steps involve education, which enables the subjects to see the world in new ways, and action aimed at changing the social conditions that led to the problem in the first place.
Table 1 from Comstock (1982) contrasts the steps in critical social science research with the steps in the scientific method of
the positivist paradigm.

The influence of critical social science in adult education
can be seen in action and participatory research and in efforts
to develop learning theory. The term *action research* has several
connotations, one of which is actually positivistically oriented.
Some people use the term to mean solving situation-specific
problems of practice (Isaac and Michael, 1981). Many other
people, however, see action research as a means to bring about
social change. Comstock (1982, p. 162) defines action research
as "a form of self-reflective enquiry undertaken by participants
in social situations in order to improve the rationality and justice

Table 1. Steps in the Research Methods
of Positive and Critical Social Sciences.

Positive Social Science	Critical Social Science
1. Identify a scientific problem by studying the results of past empirical and theoretical work.	1. Identify social groups or movements whose interests are progressive.
2. Develop empirically testable hypotheses which promise to improve the theory's explanatory and predictive power.	2. Develop an interpretive understanding of the intersubjective meanings, values, and motives held by all groups in the setting.
3. Select a setting (community, group, organization, etc.) which is suitable to the scientific problem.	3. Study the historical development of the social conditions and the current social structures that constrain actions and shape understandings.
4. Develop measures and data-gathering strategies based on: Previous research Observations and interviews in the setting The investigator's own "common-sense" Knowledge of social processes	4. Construct models of the relations between social conditions, intersubjective interpretations of those conditions, and participants' actions.
5. Gather data through: Experiments Existing documents and texts Surveys and interviews Observations	5. Elucidate the fundamental contradictions which are developing as a result of actions based on ideologically frozen understandings: Compare conditions with understandings Critique the ideology Discover immanent possibilities for action
6. Analyze data to test hypotheses.	6. Participate in a program of education with the subjects that gives them new ways of seeing their situation.
7. Alter laws and theory in light of findings and restate scientific problem to be addressed by subsequent research.	7. Participate in a theoretically grounded program of action which will change social conditions and will also engender new, less alienated, understandings and needs.
Return to Step 1.	Return to Step 2.

Source: Comstock, 1982, p. 388. Reprinted with permission.

of their own practices, their understanding of these practices, and the situations in which the practices are carried out. . . . A self-reflective spiral of cycles of planning, acting, observing and reflecting is central to the action research approach."

Participatory research is somewhat more familiar to adult educators than action research. Participatory research is a system for producing knowledge "of ordinary people, those who are deprived, oppressed and under-privileged" (Tandon, 1988, p. 6). This type of research questions the origins of the production of knowledge, who has access to knowledge, and whose interests and ends knowledge serves. It involves faith in people's ability to produce their own knowledge through collective investigation of problems and issues, collective analysis of problems, and collective action to change the conditions that gave rise to the problems in the first place. Participatory research is thus more than a method of creating knowledge. It is also a process of education and consciousness-raising and "of mobilization for action" (Gaventa, 1988, p. 19).

Although participatory research has most often been linked with social movements and popular education in the Third World, its presence is being increasingly felt in North America. Gaventa identifies three strategies of this type of research that have emerged in North America. The first strategy is to reappropriate knowledge: "Those who are directly affected by a problem have the right to acquire information about it for themselves" (1988, p. 20). Examples of this strategy can be found in community groups, corporate research groups, and right-to-know movements. The second strategy is to develop knowledge created by the people—for example, through researching popular wisdom or folk medicine. The third strategy is to involve people in the production of knowledge—for example, through the carrying out of collaborative studies such as tracing land ownership in Appalachia.

Participatory research is not without its detractors. Griffith and Cristarella (1979) for example, see it as a form of community development, not research. Deshler and Hagan (1989, p. 9) note that positivist-oriented researchers consider this approach "fine as a device to encourage reflection, learning and action," but not one that produces valid research, largely because what makes the approach a legitimate method for the production of knowledge differs radically from the canons of the positivist paradigm.

Critical social science has had an impact on the development of adult education theory. Freire's and Mezirow's work, in particular, can be located in this paradigm. Freire's theory of education defines an authentic educational encounter as one in which learners "as knowing subjects, achieve a deepening awareness both of the socio-cultural reality which shapes their lives and of their capacity to transform that reality" (1970, p. 27). For him, radical social change is the goal of education. Freire's ideas have been the basis for educational social action programs, especially in combatting illiteracy in the Third World. Mezirow's theory of perspective transformation as the defining characteristic of adult learning draws from critical theory, especially the work of Habermas. According to Mezirow, perspective transformation is defined as "the process of becoming critically aware of how and why our presuppositions have come to constrain the way we perceive, understand, and feel about our world; of reformulating these assumptions to permit a more inclusive, discriminating, permeable, and integrative perspective; and of making decisions or otherwise acting upon these new understandings" (1990, p. 14).

In lively critiques of Mezirow's theory as expressed in his 1981 work, Griffin (1987) and Collard and Law (1989) feel that it falls short of critical theory's mandate for social change. Mezirow (1989) has responded, saying that change need not be only social; it can also be epistemic or psychic. Recently, Hart (1990) and Clark and Wilson (1991) have criticized Mezirow's theory for its lack of attention to power-related issues and contexts. (See Long's Chapter Four for additional information about Mezirow's work.) Other work that draws on Habermas's critical theory in particular can be found in Law (1989) and Collins and Plumb (1989).

Researchers from other disciplines, especially sociology, are investigating questions in light of the critical paradigm, questions that are relevant to adult education. Examples of such

studies include Cutting's (1987) case study of parent education
as empowerment; Luttrell's (1988) study of the effects of gender,
race, and class on how women define and claim knowledge;
Auerbach's (1989) analysis of family literacy programs; and Ellsworth's (1989) analysis of college teaching based upon an empowerment model.

In summary, the critical paradigm is based on some very
different assumptions than either the positivist or interpretive
paradigms. Reflection, action, and collaboration define the type
of knowledge produced by research conducted within this paradigm. Questions related to social structure, freedom and oppression, power and control, drive critical research. Some people argue that research out of this perspective is more consonant
with adult education philosophy than research from the other
perspectives because through education adults are "capable of
learning, of changing, of acting, and of transforming the world"
(Tandon, 1988, p. 5).

Research Paradigms and Adult Education

Bannister (1981) points out that the literature on adult education provides much more guidance on how to design experiments than on how to think about research: "The central issue
of how questions are formulated, how we choose, fantasize about,
create, uncover, and personally explore the topic of our research
is almost totally neglected" (p. 192). He notes that there is a
cyclical process to this thinking stage of research. We are at first
wildly speculative, "bound by no rules and where our mind may
and should wander happily up and down every avenue and blind
alley" (p. 192). Out of this speculation emerges the phase "in
which we invent/choose/discover our issue of concern. We begin to see the kind of questions we want to ask. Finally, we move
into the control phase of the cycle wherein we give our question an operational form" (p. 193). The point is that the issue
we see, the questions we ask, and the "operational form" we decide upon are given shape by the paradigm out of which we
function.

The existence of at least three different paradigms out of

which we can conduct research in adult education raises some interesting questions related to the future development of the body of knowledge. First of all, will the three approaches continue to coexist, each contributing toward a better understanding of adult education? Should the three approaches coexist? Are all three equally valid means of producing knowledge? What position should the adult education researcher assume? How should future researchers be trained?

In addressing the first of these questions, Gage (1989), in a provocative article titled "The Paradigm Wars and Their Aftermath," presents three scenarios from the perspective of the year 2009. In the first scenario, "the positivistic, establishmentarian, mainstream, standard, objectivity-seeking, and quantitative approach had died of the wounds inflicted by its critics. In the second version, peace had broken out, but it was not the peace of the grave. The three approaches were busily and harmoniously engaged in an earnest dialogue, lifting the discussion to a new level of insight, making progress toward workable solutions of educational problems, and generating theory that fit together, as seen from the perspective of each of the three approaches. In the third version, nothing that was true in 1989 had really changed, and the wars were still going on" (p. 10).

Gage urges educational researchers to find "an honest and productive rapprochement between the paradigms," since "educational research is no mere spectator sport, no mere intellectual game, no mere path to academic tenure and higher pay, not just a way to make a good living and even to become a big shot. It has moral obligations" (p. 10).

Certainly researchers in adult education also feel the moral imperative of their work. It is another matter, though, to find a way to accommodate knowledge produced out of different worldviews and to assess whether knowledge produced from different paradigms is equally valid. It would seem that one way of dealing with these questions is to remind ourselves of some of the principles that underlie our practice. Adult education is indeed a moral activity in which we intervene in the lives of women and men in, we hope, positive ways. What happens to our learners is of primary concern. Research then, should be

conducted with this end in mind. Research itself is an intervention, no matter how objective or distant from the phenomenon the researcher tries to be. Whatever paradigm we choose
to work within, intervention should not become intrusion. We
should care what happens to and with our participants. The
question of whether competing research paradigms will or should
coexist fades in importance when set against this larger moral
imperative of our practice. It is in fact from the practice itself
of doing research that answers to these questions will likely
evolve. (For a discussion of the interaction between theory and
practice, see Cervero's Chapter Two.)

Whether or not someone will eventually be able to integrate these paradigms, for the foreseeable future, the positivist,
interpretive, and critical paradigms are likely to coexist. And,
it should be noted, in the real world, research into the practice
of adult education does not always so neatly conform to a particular paradigm. Some mixed research designs would be difficult
to label as one or the other type of paradigm. For example, an
important study of urban adult basic education began with a
grounded theory methodology followed by field and survey
methods (Mezirow, Darkenwald, and Knox, 1975). Tough's
study of independent learning projects is another example (1971).
He conducted in-depth interviews with a nonrandom sample
of sixty-six adults but analyzed the data quantitatively (mostly
through frequency counts). Interestingly, the debate in the current research literature is not over whether or how to bring about
an integration of paradigms but rather about the extent to which
research methods characteristic of particular paradigms can or
should be mixed and matched (Firestone, 1987; Smith and
Heshusius, 1986).

Those people doing research or training others to do research need to be aware of and understand how a certain perspective on the world will lead to the nature of the research being defined in specific ways. Furthermore, it is impossible to
carry out any kind of research without facing ethical questions.
And each of the three paradigms has its own set of ethical questions that should be examined throughout the course of the research. Programs of graduate study should present research as

a value-laden, moral activity—just as other things we do, such as plan programs, teach, and counsel learners, are moral activities. Research should also be seen as an integral part of our practice as adult educators. Graduates of programs that foster such a view of research are more likely to make ongoing contributions to the knowledge base of the field.

Bredo and Feinberg (1982) make the point that the paradigm out of which one is thinking and working "should apply to the knower as well as to the known" (p. 10). Thus, examining ourselves and our practice as researchers is crucial to understanding how research contributes to the development of the field of adult education. We must ask ourselves: What assumptions do we hold about research, about the nature of reality, about knowledge, about adults as learners? How does our worldview lead to the questions we ask about adult education practice? How do these questions structure our research and ultimately our contributions to the knowledge base of adult education?

References

Apps, J. W. *Problems in Continuing Education*. New York: McGraw-Hill, 1979.

Auerbach, E. R. "Toward a Social-Contextual Approach to Family Literacy." *Harvard Educational Review*, 1989, *59* (2), 165–180.

Bannister, D. "Personal Construct Theory and Research Method." In P. Reason and J. Rowan (eds.), *Human Inquiry: A Sourcebook of New Paradigm Research*. New York: Wiley, 1981.

Bogdan, R. C., and Biklen, S. K. *Qualitative Research for Education: An Introduction to Theory and Methods*. Newton, Mass.: Allyn & Bacon, 1982.

Bredo, E., and Feinberg, W. (eds.). *Knowledge and Values in Social and Educational Research*. Philadelphia: Temple University Press, 1982.

Brookfield, S. "Independent and Adult Learning." *Studies in Adult Education*, 1981, *13* (1), 15–27.

Brunner, E. de S., Wilder, D. S., Kirchner, C., and Newberry, J. S., Jr. *An Overview of Adult Education Research*. Washington,

D.C.: American Association for Adult and Continuing Education, 1959.

Carr, W., and Kemmis, S. *Becoming Critical: Education, Knowledge and Action Research.* London: Falmer Press, 1986.

Charnley, A. H., and Jones, H. A. *The Concept of Success in Adult Literacy.* Cambridge, England: Huntington, 1979.

Clark, B. R. *Adult Education in Transition: A Study of Institutional Insecurity.* Berkeley: University of California Press, 1956.

Clark, M. C., and Wilson, A. L. "Context and Rationality in Mezirow's Theory of Transformational Learning." *Adult Education Quarterly,* 1991, *41* (2), 75–91.

Collard, S., and Law, M. "The Limits of Perspective Transformation: A Critique of Mezirow's Theory." *Adult Education Quarterly,* 1989, *39* (2), 99–107.

Collins, M. "Self-Directed Learning or an Emancipatory Practice of Adult Education: Re-thinking the Role of the Adult Educator." In C. C. Collins (ed.), *Proceedings of the 30th Annual Adult Education Research Conference.* Madison: University of Wisconsin, 1989.

Collins, M., and Plumb, D. "Some Critical Thinking About Critical Theory and Its Relevance for Adult Education Practice." In C. C. Collins (ed.), *Proceedings of the 30th Adult Education Research Conference.* Madison: University of Wisconsin, 1989.

Comstock, D. E. "A Method for Critical Research." In E. Bredo and W. Feinberg (eds.), *Knowledge and Values in Social and Educational Research.* Philadelphia: Temple University Press, 1982.

Cutting, B. "Parent Education as Empowerment: A Case Study." Unpublished master's thesis, University of Minnesota, 1987.

Deshler, D., and Hagan, N. "Adult Education Research: Issues and Directions." In S. B. Merriam and P. M. Cunningham (eds.), *Handbook of Adult and Continuing Education.* San Francisco: Jossey-Bass, 1989.

Ellsworth, E. "Why Doesn't This Feel Empowering: Working Through the Repressive Myths of Critical Pedagogy." *Harvard Educational Review,* 1989, *59* (3), 297–324.

Fingeret, A. "Social Network: A New Perspective on Independence and Illiterate Adults." *Adult Education Quarterly,* 1983, *33* (3), 133–146.

Firestone, W. A. "Meaning in Method: The Rhetoric of Quantitative and Qualitative Research." *Educational Researcher,* 1987, *16* (7), 16-21.

Freire, P. *Pedagogy of the Oppressed.* New York: Herder & Herder, 1970.

Gage, N. L. "The Paradigm Wars and Their Aftermath." *Educational Researcher,* 1989, *18* (7), 4-10.

Gaventa, J. "Participatory Research in North America." *Convergence,* 1988, *21* (2 & 3), 19-28.

Glaser, B. G., and Strauss, A. L. *The Discovery of Grounded Theory.* Hawthorne, N.Y.: Aldine, 1967.

Goetz, J. P., and LeCompte, M. D. *Ethnography and Qualitative Design in Educational Research.* Orlando, Fla.: Academic Press, 1984.

Griffin, C. *Adult Education as Social Policy.* London: Croom Helm, 1987.

Griffith, W. S., and Cristarella, M. C. "Participatory Research: Should It Be a New Methodology for Adult Educators?" In J. A. Niemi (ed.), *Viewpoints on Adult Education Research.* Information Series, no. 171. Columbus: ERIC Clearinghouse on Adult, Career, and Vocational Education, 1979.

Habermas, J. *Knowledge and Human Interests.* (J. Shapiro, trans.) Boston: Beacon Press, 1971.

Hart, M. "Critical Theory and Beyond: Further Perspectives on Emancipatory Education." *Adult Education Quarterly,* 1990, *40* (3), 125-138.

Houle, C. O. *The Inquiring Mind.* Madison: University of Wisconsin Press, 1961.

Isaac, S., and Michael, W. B. *Handbook in Research and Evaluation.* (2nd ed.) San Diego, Calif.: EDITS, 1981.

Jensen, G., Liveright, A. A., and Hallenbeck, W. (eds.). *Adult Education: Outlines of an Emerging Field of University Study.* Washington, D.C.: American Association for Adult and Continuing Education, 1964.

Lather, P. "Commentary." In F. H. Hultgren and D. L. Commer (eds.), *Alternative Modes of Inquiry in Home Economics Research.* Yearbook 9. Peoria, Ill.: Glencoe, 1989.

Law, M. "Adult Education for Social Transformation: The

Making of an Idea." In C. C. Collins (ed.), *Proceedings of the 30th Adult Education Research Conference.* Madison: University of Wisconsin, 1989.

Long, H. B. *Adult Learning: Research and Practice.* New York: Cambridge Books, 1983.

Long, H. B., Hiemstra, R., and Associates. *Changing Approaches to Studying Adult Education.* San Francisco: Jossey-Bass, 1980.

Luttrell, W. "Working-Class Women's Ways of Knowing: Effects of Gender, Race, and Class." *Sociology of Education,* 1989, *62,* 33–46.

Merriam, S. B. *Case Study Research in Education: A Qualitative Approach.* San Francisco: Jossey-Bass, 1988.

Merriam, S. B. "Contributions of Qualitative Research to Adult Education." *Adult Education Quarterly,* 1989, *39* (3), 161–168.

Mezirow, J. *Education for Perspective Transformation: Women's Reentry Programs in Community Colleges.* New York: Center for Adult Education, Teachers College, Columbia University, 1975.

Mezirow, J. "A Critical Theory of Adult Learning and Education." *Adult Education,* 1981, *32* (1), 3–24.

Mezirow, J. "Transformation Theory and Social Action: A Response to Collard and Law." *Adult Education Quarterly,* 1989, *39* (3), 169–175.

Mezirow, J., Darkenwald, G. G., and Knox, A. B. *Last Gamble on Education.* Washington, D.C.: American Association for Adult and Continuing Education, 1975.

Mezirow, J., and Associates. *Fostering Critical Reflection in Adulthood: A Guide to Transformative and Emancipatory Learning.* San Francisco: Jossey-Bass, 1990.

Rubenson, K. "Adult Education Research: General." In C. J. Titmus (ed.), *Lifelong Education for Adults: An International Handbook.* Oxford, England: Pergamon Press, 1989.

Shulman, L. "Disciplines of Inquiry in Education: An Overview." In R. M. Jaeger (ed.), *Complementary Methods for Research in Education.* Washington, D.C.: American Educational Research Association, 1988.

Smith, J. K., and Heshusius, L. "Closing Down the Conversation: The End of the Quantitative-Qualitative Debate." *Educational Researcher,* 1986, *15* (1), 4–13.

Tandon, R. "Social Transformation and Participatory Research." *Convergence,* 1988, *21* (2 & 3), 5–18.

Thorndike, E. L., Bregman, E. O., Tilton, J. W., and Woodyard, E. *Adult Learning.* New York: Macmillan, 1928.

Titmus, C. J. (ed.). *Lifelong Education for Adults: An International Handbook.* Oxford, England: Pergamon Press, 1989.

Torbert, W. R. "Why Educational Research Has Been So Uneducational: The Case for a New Model of Social Science Based on Collaborative Inquiry." In P. Reason and J. Rowan (eds.), *Human Inquiry: A Sourcebook of New Paradigm Research.* New York: Wiley, 1981.

Tough, A. *The Adult's Learning Projects: A Fresh Approach to Theory and Practice in Adult Learning.* Research in Education Series, no. 1. Toronto: Ontario Institute for Studies in Education, 1971.

CHAPTER 4

Evolution of
a Formal Knowledge Base

Huey B. Long

The knowledge base of adult education can be defined narrowly or broadly. The restrictive definition limits the knowledge base to formal knowledge; that is, to the concepts, facts, principles, and so on that are included in university degree programs or lead to standard principles of practice. Formal knowledge may be created through research or experience, observation, and philosophy (Houle, 1972b). The knowledge base, broadly conceived, includes the type of knowledge as well as noncodified, unsystematic, informal, or tacit knowledge that is derived from experience. Few people question the existence of that latter kind of knowledge, sometimes referred to as indigenous knowledge. Yet such knowledge by its nature is difficult to catalogue, disseminate, describe, and analyze. Furthermore, given the phenomenological nature of this knowledge, its impact is difficult to determine.

According to my survey of the literature (Long, 1983b), the adult education knowledge base as transmitted and developed through graduate programs of study usually rests on sociology of adult education, psychology of adult education, history and philosophy of adult education, and specialized areas of practice, such as program planning and administration and methods of instruction. (Specific course domains are discussed by Peters and Kreitlow in Chapter Seven of this book.)

Since the questions about the development and delivery of adult education programs emerged from practice, the relationship between research (as a means for generating knowledge) and practice has received substantial attention in the literature (Deshler and Hagan, 1989; Kreitlow, 1960; Cervero, Chapter Two of this volume). Space does not permit me to illustrate the impact of the domains of knowledge discussed in this chapter upon practice. Yet such connections can be demonstrated.

Advances in related disciplines have also had an impact on the adult education knowledge base, affecting it through research methodology, research questions, and theoretical constructs. Chapter Three of this book illustrates how views on research methodology are influenced by developments in other disciplines. Advances in psychology and gerontology have nearly removed the research question of the ability of adults to learn at various ages from current literature. Metacognition is a construct from the discipline of psychology that adds to our understanding of adult learning. Similarly, psychological research into the human life span has moved adult educators beyond the earlier work of Havighurst (1952). I could offer other illustrations of the impact of related disciplines on the adult education knowledge base, but the purpose of this chapter is not to provide a comparative analysis of the knowledge base vis-à-vis related disciplines. (See Part Two of this book for that analysis.)

This chapter is designed to describe the evolution of the formal knowledge base that appears in the published sources primarily identified with the field of adult education. Therefore, the literature of general psychology, sociology, and other disciplines that may contain implications for adult education knowledge is not included here. Most of the literature reviewed for this work is from the United States; however, occasional reference is made to salient international contributions.

This chapter presents an overview of the evolution of the formal knowledge base through discussion of five topics: a brief comment on historical development and selected views of contributors to the original black book (Jensen, Liveright, and Hallenbeck, 1964), a summary of current criticism of adult education knowledge, comments on selected factors contributing to the current status of adult education knowledge, a profile of six major domains of adult education knowledge, and speculations about trends and new directions in the development of knowledge.

Historical Development

Until about 1930, the knowledge base of adult education was provided by adult education practitioners and scholars from other disciplines. Beginning in the 1930s, adult education knowledge was supplemented by the increasing experience of an expanding corps of practitioners, including increasing numbers of practitioners trained in new graduate programs in adult education. The codification of knowledge in adult education (Dickinson and Rusnell, 1971; Long and Agyekum, 1974), systematic study based on other disciplines (Brunner, Wilder, Kirchner, and Newberry, 1959), and adult education research (Clark, 1956; Long, 1983b) have increased since midcentury.

The aims of the authors of the black book (Jensen, Liveright, and Hallenbeck, 1964) included encouraging "further systematic organization of the field" (p. iii) so that adult education might fulfill its mission as "an imperative of our times" (p. x). Accordingly, the authors called for a knowledge base to fill the "vast gaps . . . in knowledge and theory" (p. viii). The goals of the publication and the field, according to the various authors, were to be achieved through graduate study (Houle), professionalization (Liveright), theory (Hallenbeck), and borrowing from other disciplines (Jensen).

Current Criticism

A number of individuals have expressed views concerning the status of adult education research and, by extension, adult education knowledge since 1964 (Cookson, 1983; Kreitlow, 1975; Jarvis, 1987; Long, 1980, 1987). The range of comments varies from pessimistic gloom (Carlson, 1977; Rockhill, 1976) to constructive criticism (Boshier, 1980; Mezirow, 1981; Plecas and Sork, 1986) to moderate optimism (Legge, 1979; Long, 1983b). The critics describe the field as lacking coherence (Carlson, 1977), regressing (Rockhill, 1976), slow moving, and lacking theory building and accumulative effort (Plecas and Sork, 1986). Others characterize the field as atheoretical (Boshier, 1980; Mezirow, 1981), reflecting an absence of research programs (Easting, 1979; Long, 1983b) and limited commitment by scholars (Long and Agyekum, 1974).

Moderate optimism is expressed by Legge (1979), who indicates that negative comments are defense mechanisms and may be caused by mystical, unrealistic expectations that some people hold for research. In 1983, I commented that "adult education research is slowly coming of age. . . . a body of knowledge informed by research is emerging" (Long, 1983b, p. 35).

Selected Factors

Four factors associated with the evolution of the adult education knowledge base are the role of the professoriate, the noncumulative research, the atheoretical research, and the legitimacy of interdisciplinary versus intradisciplinary knowledge. These factors have interacted in the development of six domains of adult education knowledge, discussed later.

Role of the Professoriate. The role of the professoriate in developing a knowledge base is critical. However, it appears that for a time the role of the adult education professor was not clear. Was the professor to be a practitioner, a scholar, or some combination of the two? Those people searching for a hybrid model turned to the medical or law faculties for examples. Yet the placement of adult education professors in graduate programs in colleges of education put these professors in an environment that evaluates performance on factors other than skill as a practitioner (Boyd, 1969).

The adult education professoriate of today is more numerous and has different responsibilities and behavior than the professoriate before 1964. Membership in the Commission of Professors of Adult Education has increased from about 20 members in 1960 to nearly 300 members today. The professors' responsibilities have changed from modeling and teaching professional practice skills based on experience to an emphasis on producing grants, research, and publications. These changes in responsibilities are associated with larger changes in the American university.

Changes in the professoriate generally have resulted in the generation of more research. Therefore, the formal knowledge base has expanded. Because of the growth of graduate programs, as discussed by Peters and Kreitlow in Chapter Seven, more adult educators are trained in research methods. My work (Long, 1977) and the work of Willie, Copeland, and Williams (1985) confirm the assertion that changes in the number and responsibilities of the professoriate have had positive consequences for the knowledge base. In Willie, Copeland, and Williams's survey of Canadian and American adult education professors, 26 percent of the respondents ranked research and writing as their first, second, or third source of satisfaction, compared with 28.7 percent who ranked teaching in the first three positions. Also, 20.4 percent of the respondents reported that they had written seven or more articles in the five years preceding the survey. Some of the professors also revealed that pressures to do research were a source of dissatisfaction but not as great as some other sources of dissatisfaction.

Willie, Copeland, and Williams (1985) and I (Long, 1977) agree that older professors tend to be less productive than younger ones. These findings, based on cross-sectional surveys, however, should be interpreted carefully. The inverse relationship between age and amount of research produced may be an artifact of prior educational preparation. For example, older professors may have begun their careers in the late 1950s or early 1960s, before the current emphasis on research and writing.

Noncumulative Research. Three reviews of *Adult Education Quarterly* (AEQ) and conference proceedings and agendas of the Adult

Education Research Conference (AERC) covering 1950–1970 and 1972–1990, as well as a review I am currently conducting of fifty-one *AEQ* articles published between 1985 and 1989, all reveal that the six most popular topics of adult education articles and papers (Dickinson and Rusnell, 1971; Long and Agyekum, 1974; Long, 1983b) are adult learning, program planning and administration, program area, adult education as a field of study, institutional sponsor, and materials and methods. (See Long and Agyekum, 1974, for definitions of the topics.) The popularity of these few research topics has been consistent since 1950 (Deshler and Hagan, 1989).

A comparison of general research methodologies also reveals a preference for descriptive methods. The descriptive methods used in adult education research are quite diverse, however. After descriptive methods, theoretical formulations and methodological studies seem to be the most popular research methods. Experimental, historical, and philosophical inquiries are rare in adult education research literature (Long, 1983d). (See Chapter Three for additional comments on research approaches.)

Some differences within the categories of topics studied by adult educators since 1950 are apparent. For example, many of the *AEQ* research articles relating to program planning focused on recruitment questions prior to 1985, whereas most of the *AEQ* articles published in this category since 1985 deal with retention. The study of barriers or obstacles to participation in adult education has also recently become more visible. The focus of research on adult learning has also shifted from questions concerning adults' ability to learn to research about learning styles and self-directed learning.

Despite the microshifts in topics, the development of the knowledge base continues to be challenged by a paradoxical situation. Since 1950, the research generally has been dominated by descriptive research and a majority of the thousands of studies have been conducted in six topical areas. Yet the knowledge base does not appear to have deepened, except in a few areas. In other words, the research has been noncumulative. Two of the topics to be discussed later in this chapter illustrate the point. Perspective transformation is a highly visible topic in research, yet most of the writing on the topic is the work of one person. Hundreds of authors have written about program planning, yet the topic is only beginning to have the promise of coherence. Examining another characteristic of the knowledge base, atheoretical research, can help to explain the paradox.

Atheoretical Research. Atheoretical research, defined here as research that fails to have a theoretical foundation and framework, has been a characteristic of adult education research for years (Boshier, 1980; Mezirow, 1981; Long, 1987). The roots of this research seem to be in the early practice orientation of the field, in which a problem of practice was approached as a unique phenomenon.

Hallenbeck (1964) emphasizes a derivative approach. It appears he favored the following procedure: take practical action, collect data (study a phenomenon), interpret the results, and develop a theory. Such a process can be successful and underlies some of the current interest in ethnography and related research procedures. Yet the approach met with limited success in building an adult education knowledge base for several reasons. First, the approach may be too utilitarian, with extremely limited generalizability. Second, theory may never be developed because the investigator could lose interest and no one else would follow up the sequence. Third, even if the investigator tries to develop theory, testing of the theory is not included in the steps. Examples of model building with insufficient testing as well as a general lack of interest in testing abound in the literature on participation. As a result, each year the field is presented with at least one hundred new doctoral dissertations and hundreds of research articles and papers (excluding the multiple reports) that broaden the knowledge base but fail to deepen it.

The atheoretical characteristic of adult education research contributes directly to the noncumulative development of knowledge. The problem seems to involve the researchers' utilitarian motives and preference for descriptive research and the absence of good metareviews of topical areas and philosophies of research (Deshler and Hagan, 1989), all of which affect researchers' conceptualization of knowledge, issues, and problems.

Interdisciplinary versus Intradisciplinary Knowledge. Knowledge in adult education can be divided into three types. The first type of knowledge is based on borrowed theory and is noncumulative. It addresses a narrow question of interest to a small segment of the field but does not contribute to a cluster of additional concepts central to the larger issues of adult education. The second type of knowledge is based on borrowed theory but is cumulative. It addresses clusters of theoretical and practical issues central to the field of adult education. The third type of knowledge is inductively derived from experience, observation, and reflection that is central to the field. Two books by Houle (1961, 1972a) are examples of this third type of knowledge. Note, however, that Houle (1988) began his research for *The Inquiring Mind* (1961) from a psychological perspective.

Adult educators have continued to debate the relative merits of a uniquely adult education discipline versus the creation of an interdisciplinary field (Hermanowicz, 1976) that derives knowledge and theory from related disciplines. Boyd and Apps (1980), Plecas and Sork (1986), and Kreitlow (1960) have supported the idea that adult education knowledge does not necessarily need to be derived from other disciplines, at least not until the study and practice of adult education are more fully conceptualized. While not calling for a uniquely adult education knowledge base devoid of social science influence, my work encourages a recognition of the distinctiveness of adults as research subjects and the development of research procedures appropriate to adult characteristics (Long, 1980).

Six Major Domains of Knowledge

Examples of theory-based knowledge that is borrowed, cumulative, and central to the core issues of adult education include research on andragogy, learning projects, participation, perspective transformation, program planning, and self-directed learning. Collectively, these domains of knowledge are informed by psychological, sociological, and philosophical concepts. Each domain is briefly discussed in the following paragraphs. Space does not permit me to report and discuss criticisms of the six domains nor to explicate their centrality to adult education knowledge.

Therefore, it is sufficient to say that each of the domains is subject to a variety of critical comments, and that they seem to be
central to the study of adult education.

Andragogy. The following discussion of andragogy develops four
points. First, definitions of the concept are presented. Second,
likely sources of Knowles's (1967, 1968) concepts of andragogy
are given. Third, explanations of the persistence of Knowles's
concept are shared. Fourth, some consequences of the introduction of the concept into adult education knowledge are noted.

The adult education literature contains two separate conceptions of andragogy. One of these is European, and the other
is identified with Malcolm Knowles. The European conception
of andragogy is more comprehensive than the American conception even though, according to Young (1985), Europeans
do not use the terms *andragogy* and *adult education* synonymously.
Van Enckevort (1971) describes the European use of the terms
andragogy, andragogics, and *andragology.* Andragogy is "any intentional and professionally guided activity which aims at a change
in adult persons" (p. 41). "Andragogics is the background of
methodical and ideological systems which govern the actual
process of andragogy. . . . Andragology is the scientific study of
both andragogy and andragogics" (p. 42). Young (1985) adds
another dimension to the concept based on Dutch, Afrikaans,
and German literature. He says that the primary critical element
in andragogy is that an adult accompanies or assists one or more
adults to become a more refined and competent adult and that
there should be differences in the aims of andragogy and pedagogy (accompanying or assisting a child to become an adult)
as well as differences in the relationship between teachers and
adult pupils and the relationship between teachers and children.

Knowles's (1968) ideas about andragogy are different from
the European ones. Andragogy, according to Knowles and as
generally thought of in the United States, is much more limited
to assumptions about adults and teaching adults. Knowles defines andragogy as "the art and science of helping adults learn"
(1980, p. 42). The basic concepts underlying andragogy, according to Knowles, are part of the relationship that exists be-

tween the teacher and the learner. Over the years, Knowles has modified these concepts to include three (Knowles, 1970), four (Knowles, 1980) or five assumptions (Knowles, 1984).

Andragogy is an area that is weak in empirical confirmation. Knowles popularized the term and a set of ideals and assumptions that he believed should characterize the adult teaching-learning transaction, and as a result, andragogy is possibly one of the most commonly used terms in contemporary adult education discourse. Yet it is also subject to criticism (Hartree, 1984; Plecas and Sork, 1986; Tennant, 1986). I will not discuss the merits of andragogy itself or of the criticism of andragogy here. Rather, I will address two questions central to the theme of the chapter. First, how was the concept derived? And, second, why has it survived a flood of strong criticism?

Knowles says he was exposed to the term in 1967 by a Yugoslavian colleague, Dušan Savićević (conversation with the author, Apr. 1990). But learning how he ran across the term does not give much substance to the discussion. A more useful source of information concerning the content and philosophy that Knowles associates with andragogy is a presentation he made at a national meeting in 1971 (Knowles, 1972). In this presentation, he described how he developed his teaching philosophy and the sources he read. He identified his sources as psychotherapy and the work of Otto Rank, Carl Rogers, and Arthur Sedlin. He also cited Abraham Maslow, Erik Erikson, Eduard Lindeman, and others. It is possible that his ideas about teaching and learning, which he later identified as andragogy, were more directly influenced by several disciplines than they were by Savićević's comments about andragogy. Until definitive proof to the contrary is offered, it can be asserted that andragogy, as developed by Knowles, is a concept derived from several social sciences.

The second question, Why has andragogy survived the criticism leveled against it? is less easily answered. Speculation about the answer helps to reveal the knowledge base of adult education. Andragogy has probably survived criticism because, first, the humanistic ideas underlying andragogy appeal to adult educators in general. Second, the limited empirical refutation of andragogy has not been strongly convincing (Long, 1983a). Third, Knowles's reaction to criticism has been flexible and encouraging, which has permitted him to incorporate some of the criticism in his later revisions of the concept. Fourth, Knowles is a leader in the field who is widely respected for other contributions. His established reputation could have been a factor in both the early acceptance of andragogy as well as the early criticism. (See Chapter Five for more on Knowles.)

The inclusion of Knowles's concept of andragogy into the adult education knowledge base has provided a framework for integrating several potentially useful ideas about adult learners. Furthermore, Knowles's assumptions can be restated in the form of hypotheses and could be tested and confirmed or rejected. However, Darkenwald and Beder and their students (Darkenwald, 1982; Rosenblum and Darkenwald, 1983; Beder and Carrea, 1988) seem to be among the few researchers involved in testing Knowles's assumptions. Importantly, andragogy has contributed to the study of self-directed learning, about which more is said later.

Unfortunately, it also appears that the inclusion of andragogy in the knowledge base has some negative consequences. One consequence, identified by Brookfield (1986), is the possibility that andragogy has become a kind of orthodoxy for some adult educators who feel a need for an intellectual or symbolic rallying point for defending the field. A second consequence is that the widespread use of the term as conceived by Knowles almost automatically prevents American adult educators from benefiting from the more scientific and orderly European concepts of andragogy. If Americans had been working with the conceptions of andragogy, andragogics, and andragology set forth by Van Enckevort (1971), it is possible that this chapter would contain a great deal more information about research and theory on the subject. Of course, American adult educators could yet benefit from the concepts as defined by Van Enckevort.

Learning Projects. Learning projects research legitimized adult educators' interest in the nonschool learner. Prior to Tough's (1971) work, Verner's (1964) definition of adult education had excluded independent learners. However, he later modified his definition (Dickinson, 1979), and it is possible that the learning projects research influenced him to do so.

Learning projects research also illustrates some of the dangers associated with borrowing from related disciplines, as noted by Boyd and Apps (1980). Specifically, there is a danger that the influence of one or more disciplines may be overlooked by researchers engaged in learning projects research. While Tough's (1971) research seems to have been derived from Houle's (1961) work, he appears to have turned to a specific discipline for his theoretical ideas. References in his 1971 publication indicate that Tough's ideas of self-teaching were not inspired by the education literature as much as by humanistic psychology. To fully appreciate the concept of learning projects and self-teaching, one needs to return to the roots of self-directed therapy and the concepts underlying and associated with the ideas of learning and personal change in humanistic psychology.

The consequences of learning projects research for the adult education knowledge base seem to be more beneficial than otherwise. This research introduced the adult learner who is outside of formal education settings into the knowledge base and is often identified with the more recent research concerning self-directed learning. Learning projects research is also related to questions central to participation in adult education, examined next.

Participation. Even though the literature on participation cannot be separated completely from the disciplines of psychology (Lorge, 1947), social psychology (Lewin, 1947), and sociology (London, 1963, 1970; Verner and Davis, 1964; Verner and Buttedahl, 1964, 1965; Verner, 1968), it addresses a particular adult education problem. The traditional voluntary nature of adult education placed a premium on understanding why adults choose, from among competing activities and roles, to assume the student or learner role and engage in educational activities.

Participation was studied as early as the 1930s (Hoy, 1933), and adult education dissertations were written on the topic in the 1940s. Brunner, Wilder, Kirchner, and Newberry discussed participation in 1959, although their emphasis is more on so-cial participation than on educational participation. Two streams of participation research developed in the 1960s: a sociological stream identified with London (1963, 1970) and Verner (Ver-ner and Buttedahl, 1964, 1965), and a psychological stream identified with Houle (1961). Boshier (1971, 1972) is recognized for his psychometric factor analyses of motives for participa-tion. At least one anthropological study of participation has been identified (that by Marineau and Klinger, 1977). Al-though Rubenson (1982) characterizes the bulk of the partici-pation literature in the 1970s as psychological, no analytical in-ventory of research has been done to support the assertion (Long, 1987).

Since the 1960s, adult educators have shown strong in-terest in determining the *motives* (a psychological term) for adult *participation* (a sociological term) in adult education *programs* (an adult education term). Consequently, at least ten models of adult participation have been reported (Long, 1983b). It is not sur-prising that these models all share some common features. The most conspicuous attribute is their dependence upon psycho-logical, social-psychological, and sociological theory, beginning with Lorge's (1947) model based on human wants and Lewin's (1951) field theory. Other early models developed by Douglah and Moss (1968) and Douglah (1970) are also based on socio-logical and psychological constructs. It is safe to conclude that the various models of participation reported in adult education literature could not exist without the aid of the social science disciplines.

Building on Houle's (1961) learning orientations concept, Boshier (1973) made consistent contributions to the knowledge of participation through his factor analytic studies and the de-velopment of a participation scale. He subsequently developed a model of participation and retention based on psychological theory, including Lewin's field theory and Maslow's self-actuali-zation theory. McClusky (1970) added a "margin" theory, in-fluenced by his commitment to stimulus-organism-response (S-O-R) psychology. Miller (1967) developed a model of partici-pation based on field theory. These models were followed in the literature by a model developed in Sweden that has been reported in the literature by Bergsten (1980) and Rubenson (1977). It is referred to as the Swedish expectancy-valence model. The latest major model, contributed by Cross (1981), is known as the chain-of-response model. The Swedish model and Cross's model are similar to the previously mentioned models in that they too were derived from sociological and psychological theories. They seem to be amenable to testing, but few efforts to test them have been reported. The model building in the research on participation illustrates the proclivity of adult education researchers to push an activity up to a point and then to stop short of meaningful explication and testing.

Other researchers who did not build models but who contributed to the participation knowledge include London (1963, 1970) and Verner (1964). London was particularly interested in social class as a variable, and Verner's interest was in the association of socioeconomic characteristics of adult learners and their learning activities.

The consequences of participation studies for the adult education knowledge base are difficult to identify and comprehend. It is obvious that who engages in learning and why people engage in learning are critical issues. Yet information that could increase enrollments has not been identified through the research. To identify such information, researchers might develop clinical trials based on the theory as it relates to other basic questions about learning, teaching, and program development.

Perspective Transformation. Perspective transformation theory struck a responsive chord among adult educators. Mezirow defines perspective transformation as "the process of becoming critically aware of how and why the structure of our psychocultural assumptions has come to constrain the way in which we perceive our world, of reconstituting that structure in a way that allows us to be more inclusive and discriminating in our integration of experience and to act on these new understandings" (1985, p. 22).

It is interesting to speculate about perspective transformation's place in the core knowledge of adult education. Per-

spective transformation theory is in some ways reminiscent of
the work of Kilpatrick (1933, 1951), Lindeman ([1926] 1989),
Freire (1970), and others who emphasize either the different
kinds of learning, the social construction of knowledge, or radical approaches to knowledge and worldviews. Since at least the
turn of the century, some educators of adults have identified
social change among the purposes and aims of adult education
(Lindeman, ([1926] 1989). These educators believe that in order
to accomplish social change people must critically reflect on society and create new "realities," or raise their consciousness
(Levitt, 1979). These perceptions of new realities may lead people to act (Mezirow, 1985a). Some provocative relationships exist
between ideas in Mezirow's perspective transformation theory
and andragogics as defined by Van Enckevort and some self-
directed learning concepts as noted by Brookfield. Mezirow and
Van Enckevort deal with the ideational and philosophical purposes of adult education while Brookfield emphasizes the autonomous reflection and praxis of individual learners. According to Brookfield (1986), the idea of learning is embedded within
a philosophical framework that emphasizes the socially constructed value of the *results* of learning rather than a view of learning as a *process*. This distinction is also found in Cotton's (1968)
analysis of adult education literature, in which he compares the
social reformist view with the professional orientation. The former, according to Cotton, justifies adult education from a ra-
tional-normative position, whereas the professional orientation
supports adult education based on empirical documentation.
Mezirow (1989) indicates that perspective transformation theory is associated with a liberal-democratic view of society and
by extension is perceived as a reformist concept.

    Transformation theory as espoused by Mezirow is traced
by Collard and Law (1989) to Mezirow's early involvement in
community development work. A review of Mezirow's writing
since 1969 reveals his continuing interest in a theory of adult
education practice, an interest that gradually shifted to perspective transformation and then to a critical theory of adult learning and education. He became interested in critical theory as
espoused by Jurgen Habermas (1971, 1984) and, according to
Collard and Law, by Becker, Geer, and Hughes (1968).

Despite the visibility of perspective transformation theory and critical theory in informal adult education discussions nearly twenty years after Mezirow first wrote on the topic, perspective transformation theory has received limited formal treatment in American adult education literature and conference presentations by scholars other than Mezirow. Although preconference sessions have been conducted on the topic at several annual meetings of the Adult Education Research Conference only a few papers on the topic are included in the published proceedings. A review of more than 400 papers presented at six sessions of the AERC between 1983 and 1990, two sessions of the Canadian Association for the Study of Adult Education in 1988 and 1989, and the 1988 session of the Midwest Research-to-Practice Conference reveals that only five papers were presented on transformation and critical theory. Two of these were presented by Mezirow (1984, 1988). A similar review of the *Adult Education Quarterly* between 1983 and 1991 reveals two articles on the topic (Hart, 1990; Clark and Wilson, 1991). Two Forum pieces in the journal are also identified, a critique of Mezirow's position by Collard and Law (1989) and Mezirow's reply (1989). Mezirow's first book on the topic presents several practical tools for "helping adults identify the frames of reference and structures of assumptions that influence the way they perceive, think, feel, and act on their experience" (Mezirow, 1990, p. xiv). Mezirow (1991) has recently published his first book on the theory.

Several possible explanations can be given for the lack of research on perspective transformation by scholars other than Mezirow. First, the critical orientation of Habermas (1971, 1984), from whom Mezirow received early inspiration, is sufficiently alien to American political philosophy to inhibit adoption of perspective transformation theory. In contrast, it is possible that the recent liberal-democratic approach espoused by Mezirow (1989) may be too "soft" for those attracted to a more radical approach. Second, the concepts, language, and framework of Mezirow's theory may be overly philosophical and obtuse for some. Third, the possibility that the theory excludes too much of what is commonly identified as adult education may also have a negative impact on its adoption. Fourth, since the proponents of critical theory seem to disagree with each other, adherents are difficult to recruit (Inkster, 1988).

The consequences of the introduction of perspective transformation theory into the adult education knowledge base are elusive. The concept returns a freshness to adult education, which is sometimes overly concerned about highly specific learning objectives. It also provides a rallying point for adult educators who favor social reform and appeals to those who are attracted to Paulo Freire's work. Perspective transformation theory attempts to integrate, or at least to recognize, some elements of other major adult education concepts, such as those found in some interpretations of andragogy and self-directed learning (Mezirow, 1985b). Yet, as noted above, Mezirow remains the principal writer and developer of the idea. Unlike Houle's learning orientations, which were quickly adopted and studied and which stimulated additional work by a number of scholars (Boshier, 1973; Boshier and Collins, 1985; Tough, 1971; and others), perspective transformation theory has yet to stimulate a copious body of research or philosophically based literature.

Program Planning. Program planning, or program development as it is sometimes referred to, is an extensive body of adult education knowledge. It is central to the knowledge base, and an argument could be made that it is the most essential part of adult education.

Unlike andragogy, learning projects research, and perspective transformation, the literature on program planning is not usually identified with one person. My review and discussion of the literature related to program planning published since 1960 covers fifty-six pages (Long, 1983b). Three general topics are identified in this review: aspects of program building; needs assessment; and promoting, marketing, and recruiting. Rusnell (1974) says that the program planning literature can be classified according to one of two approaches used to develop planning models: conceptual or flowchart approaches. The conceptual approach includes conceptual functions, but not as specific activities that occur in a particular sequence. The flowchart approach is more specific in terms of activities to be performed.

Rusnell failed to identify a third type of planning model that combines the first two. Illustrations of the third type are provided by Houle (1972a) and Knowles (1980).

The term *program* is often preferred in adult education over the term *curriculum.* Verner (1964) defines a program as "a series of learning experiences designed to achieve, in a specified period of time, certain specific instructional objectives for an adult or group of adults" (p. 43). Boone (1985) more recently defined a planned program as "the master perspective (plan) for behavioral change toward which adult educators direct their efforts" (p. 16). Boone says that a planned program consists of a statement of broad-based educational needs, objectives keyed to those needs, teaching strategies for achieving the objectives, and macro-outcomes of the planned program. According to Boone (1985) program planning contains three major subprocesses of concern to adult educators: planning, design and implementation, and evaluation and accountability.

Sork and Buskey (1986) performed one of the most comprehensive analytical reviews of the literature on program planning. They reviewed seventy-three books and sources on the topic and evaluated thirty-five of them on nine dimensions of the model (such as assessment of client system needs and design of a plan for ensuring participation), taking note of whether the element was absent or not addressed, or low, medium, or high. They found that most of the program planning models are inadequate; that is, most of the identified elements were not addressed at a high level.

The history of program planning knowledge is much more difficult to trace than the history of some of the other topics in the knowledge base. Brunner, Wilder, Kirchner, and Newberry (1959) cite a dissertation completed at Harvard in 1955 by Darter concerning program planning in the Cooperative Extension Service. They also identify a report by Jaccard (1931) concerning the importance of lay participation in planning Cooperative Extension Service programs. Based on a review of the items cited by Brunner, Wilder, Kirchner, and Newberry (1959), it appears that rural sociology may have contributed to some of the earlier studies of program planning. Interdisciplinary contributions to the literature on program planning have been closely identified with Tylerian curriculum models, Deweyian models of decision making, and naturalistic models (Long, 1983b). Since 1964, program planning increasingly has been an intradisciplinary area, with only smatterings of ideas from other disciplines being integrated into the models (Sork and Buskey, 1986).

The continuing fascination of researchers for the problems of program planning and development is easy to understand. Program planning is a practical and basic concern for most educators of adults. Good program planning is assumed to contribute to high levels of participation, and high levels of participation are a hallmark of success for adult education programs. Yet the literature appears to be equivocal in terms of what constitutes a comprehensive procedure for planning programs. Educators may have difficulty using the research to develop models for different kinds of contexts or for different kinds of audiences. Yet it appears that the most progressive research would lead to the determination of a model that would be effective across planning situations.

The consequences of the literature on program planning for the adult education knowledge base are dramatic. Perhaps the most basic elements to adult education knowledge are teaching and learning and program development. Boone (1985) combines them in his definition of a planned program. Implicit in each topic is the suggestion that teaching adults is somehow different from teaching in general and that planning programs for adult learners is different from planning programs for learners of other ages or for other objectives, such as for entertainment.

The corpus of adult education knowledge would be reduced severely without the literature on program planning. The inventories of research articles and papers (Dickinson and Rusnell, 1971; Long and Agyekum, 1974; Long, 1983c) reveal the importance of the topic. However, the definition used in some of these inventories (Long and Agyekum, 1974; Long, 1983c) includes the popular topic of participation, and as a result the literature on program planning appears to be greater than it actually may be if participation is treated as a separate topic.

Self-Directed Learning. Self-directed learning (SDL) is a relatively recent addition to the adult education knowledge base. It emerged in about 1975 with Knowles's book on the topic and was a natural sequel to his andragogical concepts that feature autonomy and self-direction of adult learners. Also, it is frequently identified with Tough's (1965) learning projects research. Self-directed learning quickly became a prominent concern of many adult educators, and students have completed theses and dissertations on the topic at most American universities offering a doctoral degree. Its centrality to adult education knowledge depends on the degree to which one accepts the idea that the adult learning-teaching transaction is based upon self-direction in learning (Houle, 1962). In other words, using Knowles's andragogical assumptions, the self-directedness of adults is a critical consideration in the relationship among teacher, learner, teaching techniques, and content. Thus, if andragogy as proposed by Knowles is a critical element in adult education knowledge it follows that adult self-directed learning is a critical element.

The recent historical development of SDL, as noted above, is directly connected with Tough (1965) and Knowles (1967) by Caffarella and O'Donnell (1987). Yet it appears that Knowles and Tough were possibly discussing two different phenomena in their writing. Tough for example, does not use the term *self-directed learning* in his work. He uses the term *self-teaching* (1978) and writes about learning without a teacher (1967). In contrast, Knowles (1970, 1973, 1975, 1980) seems to be writing about learning with a teacher. The complete title of his 1975 book is *Self-Directed Learning: A Guide for Learners and Teachers.* Despite the possible distinction between these concepts used by Knowles and Tough, many adult educators fail to distinguish between them.

The persistence of self-directed learning as a topic of adult education knowledge is explained by several factors. First, as with andragogy, the concept is philosophically attractive to adult educators. It focuses on the learner rather than the teacher and ascribes positive (adult) characteristics to the learner. Second, it recognizes an idea that many adult educators have long subscribed to: that their role is to develop self-directing learners whose dependence on or need for a teacher is reduced over time. Third, the concept provides for learning beyond a schooling environment. Fourth, unlike perspective transformation and like participation studies and program planning, many adult educators have done research on self-directed learning.

The numerical significance of the research on SDL is apparent when it is noted that 37 (13 percent) of the 286 adult education dissertations accepted between 1985 and 1988 were on self-directed learning. At least 173 dissertations concerning self-directed learning were completed between 1966 and 1989. (Long and Redding, 1991). Many of the dissertations on this topic reported in *Dissertation Abstracts International* were based in part on a variety of theoretical concepts from psychology. Research on self-directed learning employs psychological concepts such as attitudes, ego development, internality, locus of control, motivation, and self-concept. Sociological constructs such as life satisfaction and organizational climate are also included in this research. Guglielmino's Self-Directed Learning Readiness Scale (1978) has been used in many of the studies.

Had SDL not been introduced into the adult education knowledge base, many of the other topics included in this chapter would have been affected. Self-directed learning is central to the humanistic ideas about adult learners that underlie many of adult education's concerns about the teaching-learning transaction.

The discussion of these domains reveals that some areas of study are indeed peculiar to adult education and suggests some rather surprising interrelationships. The problems of educational participation and program planning seem to be idiosyncratically associated with adult education. Inquiry into those topics may be facilitated by theory from other disciplines such as psychology and sociology but the knowledge generated from such combinations is not defined as psychological or sociological. The problems are not strictly psychological or sociological; they are adult education problems.

Trends and New Directions

It is obvious that the adult education knowledge base has expanded since 1964. An enlarged professoriate with specific research responsibilities and greater opportunities for publication has increased research and dissemination of knowledge. Shifts in subtopics have continued since the 1970s. For example, research on adult learning continues, but the focus has shifted from the question of learning ability to questions related to adult lifespan development, cognitive structure, learning styles, and self-directed learning.

Program planning knowledge seems to be lurching to a new level based on the work of several researchers (Boone, 1985; Long 1983a; Sork and Buskey, 1986) who have approached the topic from slightly different directions but who have attempted to base program planning on some theoretical foundations. The intensive meta-analysis constructed by Sork and Buskey provides a useful basis for a move forward, and my effort to relate program planning to macrovariables moves program planning from the microlevel so often found in the literature. Boone develops a conceptual model that appears amenable to testing. Other shifts in the literature on program planning include an increasing interest in marketing as a comprehensive approach that is more sophisticated than early ideas about needs assessment.

The increasing interest in history is in marked contrast to the practical how-to orientation of much of adult education knowledge prior to 1965. Nevertheless, adult educators' attitudes toward history are yet uncertain because history is perceived to be nonutilitarian (see Chapter Thirteen).

One of the most challenging areas for adult education is the increasing research in adult development that is based on biological and physiological theory. Adult educators have often turned to the social sciences for theory, but they have limited experience in dealing with the natural sciences. In 1983, I looked at pharmacological, nutritional, and other research from the natural sciences that has implications for adult education knowledge (Long, 1983a). Other sources of such information are rare to nonexistent in the current literature. It is possible that future findings in the natural sciences will have significant implications for practice and research in adult education. Given the social context, institutional goals, and other forces that affect adult education knowledge, additional emphases on the creation of knowledge will occur in the following areas: distance education; use of electronic media; adult development; biological, physiological, and pharmacological knowledge; and the sociology of adult education knowledge.

Three related needs continue to challenge the development of adult education knowledge: a need for integrated knowledge or paradigms; a need for progressive, in-depth development; and a need for substantive metareviews and analyses of existing subtopical areas, such as the use and results of andragogical techniques, program planning, and self-direction in learning. At least two identifiable practices should be discontinued. The first is a noncritical research approach that fails to examine the rationale and underlying theory of researchers prior to widespread replication of their research as occurred in the areas of learning projects, participation, and self-directed learning. A second practice that could be corrected is the shotgun approach, by which the creation of knowledge lacks any coordination or central organizing structures. The latter can be corrected at each university by the adoption of research programs. Both changes are important to the development of adult education knowledge. Thus, steps need to be taken to ensure that the field is not inundated by a sea of models, postulates, and hypotheses that are never tested. Boshier's practice of sticking with one topical area might be emulated. Individuals who add a new model or a new set of hypotheses to the knowledge base should be expected to carry their research beyond that point. Despite Deshler and Hagan's (1989) suggestion that the research base has gone through three phases and that the second was based on the natural sciences, many researchers have not followed the natural science model very well.

The roots of the above problems are found in the historical and philosophical nature of adult education as a field. The field continues to be characterized by its undisciplined nomenclature and its phenomenological, subjective orientations and preference. Such a condition hampers adult educators' efforts to agree on terms and content and ultimately defeats the development of knowledge.

References

Becker, H., Geer, B., and Hughes. *Making the Grade: The Academic Side of College Life.* New York: Wiley, 1968.

Beder, H., and Carrea, N. "The Effects of Andragogical Teacher Training on Adult Students' Attendance and Evaluation of Their Teachers." *Adult Education Quarterly,* 1988, *38* (2), 75–87.

Bergsten, U. "Interest in Education Among Adults with Short Previous Formal Schooling." *Adult Education,* 1980, *30* (3), 131–151.

Boone, E. J. *Developing Programs in Adult Education.* Englewood Cliffs, N.J.: Prentice-Hall, 1985.

Boshier, R. "Motivational Orientations of Adult Education Participants: A Factor Analytic Exploration of Houle's Typology." *Adult Education,* 1971, *2,* 3–26.

Boshier, R. "The Development and Use of a Dropout Prediction Scale." *Adult Education,* 1972, *22* (2), 87–99.

Boshier, R. "Educational Participation and Dropout: A Theoretical Model." *Adult Education,* 1973, *23* (4), 255–282.

Boshier, R. "A Perspective on Theory and Model Development in Adult Education." In P. M. Cunningham (ed.), *Yearbook of Adult and Continuing Education 1979–1980.* Chicago: Marquis Academic Media, 1980.

Boshier, R., and Collins, J. B. "The Houle Typology After Twenty-Two Years: A Large-Scale Empirical Test." *Adult Education Quarterly,* 1985, *35* (3), 113–130.

Boyd, R. D. "New Designs for Adult Education Doctoral Programs." *Adult Education,* 1969, *19* (3), 186–196.

Boyd, R. D., and Apps, J. W. "A Conceptual Model for Adult Education." In R. D. Boyd and J. W. Apps (eds.), *Redefining the Discipline of Adult Education.* San Francisco: Jossey-Bass, 1980.

Brookfield, S. D. *Understanding and Facilitating Adult Learning: A Comprehensive Analysis of Principles and Effective Practices.* San Francisco: Jossey-Bass, 1986.

Brunner, E. de S., Wilder, D. S., Kirchner, C., and Newberry, J. S., Jr. *An Overview of Adult Education Research.* Washington, D.C.: American Association for Adult and Continuing Education, 1959.

Caffarella, R., and O'Donnell, J. "Research Trends in Self-Directed Learning: Past, Present and Future Trends." In H. B. Long and Associates, *Self-Directed Learning: Application and Theory.* Athens: Adult Education Department, University of Georgia, 1987.

Carlson, R. A. "Professionalization of Adult Education: An Historical-Philosophical Analysis." *Adult Education,* 1977, *28* (1), 53–63.

Clark, B. R. *Adult Education in Transition: A Study of Institutional Insecurity.* Berkeley: University of California Press, 1956.

Clark, M., and Wilson, A. L. "Context and Rationality in Mezirow's Theory of Transformational Learning." *Adult Education Quarterly,* 1991, *41* (2), 75–91.

Collard, S., and Law, M. "The Limits of Perspective Transformation: A Critique of Mezirow's Theory." *Adult Education Quarterly,* 1989, *39* (2), 99–107.

Cookson, P. S. "The Boyd and Apps Conceptual Model of Adult Education: A Critical Examination." *Adult Education Quarterly,* 1983, *34* (1), 48–53.

Cotton, W. E. *On Behalf of Adult Education: A Historical Examination of the Supporting Literature.* Boston: Center for the Study of Liberal Education for Adults, 1968.

Cross, K. P. *Adults as Learners: Increasing Participation and Facilitating Learning.* San Francisco: Jossey-Bass, 1981.

Darkenwald, G. G. "Factorial Structure of Differences in Teaching Behavior Related to Adult/Preadult/Student Age Status." *Adult Education,* 1982, *32,* 197–204.

Darter, V. W. "County Extension Program Development." Unpublished doctoral dissertation, Cambridge: Harvard University, 1955.

Deshler, D., and Hagan, N. "Adult Education Research: Issues and Directions." In S. B. Merriam and P. M. Cunningham (eds.), *Handbook of Adult and Continuing Education.* San Francisco: Jossey-Bass, 1989.

Dickinson, G. *Contributions to a Discipline of Adult Education: A Review and Analysis of the Publications of Coolie Verner.* Occasional Papers in Continuing Education. Vancouver, Canada: Centre for Continuing Education, University of British Columbia, 1979.

Dickinson, G., and Rusnell, D. "A Content Analysis of *Adult Education.*" *Adult Education,* 1971, *21* (3), 177–185.

Douglah, M. "Some Perspectives on the Phenomenon of Participation." *Adult Education,* 1970, *20* (2), 88–98.

Douglah, M., and Moss, G. "Differential Participation Patterns of Adults of Low and High Educational Attainment." *Adult Education,* 1968, *18* (4), 247–259.

Easting, G. "Programme Research and Its Application to Adult Education." *Studies in Adult Education,* 1979, *11* (1), 62–66.

Freire, P. *Pedagogy of the Oppressed.* New York: Herder & Herder, 1970.

Guglielmino, L. M. "Development of the Self-Directed Learning Readiness Scale." Unpublished doctoral dissertation. Athens: Department of Adult Education, University of Georgia, 1977.

Habermas, J. *Knowledge and Human Interests.* (J. Shapiro, trans.) Boston: Beacon Press, 1971.

Habermas, J. *The Theory of Communicative Action.* (T. McCarthy, trans.) Vol. 1. Boston: Beacon Press, 1984.

Hallenbeck, W. "The Role of Adult Education in Society." In G. Jensen, A. A. Liveright, and W. Hallenbeck (eds.), *Adult Education: Outlines of an Emerging Field of University Study.* Washington, D.C.: American Association for Adult and Continuing Education, 1964.

Hart, M. "Critical Theory and Beyond: Further Perspectives on Emancipatory Education." *Adult Education Quarterly,* 1990, *40* (3), 125–138.

Hartree, A. "Malcolm Knowles' Theory of Andragogy: A Critique." *International Journal of Lifelong Education,* 1984, *3* (3), 203–210.

Havighurst, R. J. *Developmental Tasks and Education.* New York: McKay, 1952.

Hermanowicz, A. "Some Realities of Adult Education: One Rhetoricians View." In J. F. Blake and E. D. Keyes (eds.), *From Rhetoric to Reality.* Harrisburg, Pa.: Division of Continuing Education, Bureau of Vocational Education, Pennsylvania Department of Education, 1976.

Houle, C. O. *The Inquiring Mind.* Madison: University of Wisconsin Press, 1961.

Houle, C. O. "Ends and Means in Adult Education Research." *Adult Education,* 1962, *12* (4), 212–217.

Houle, C. O. *The Design of Education.* San Francisco: Jossey-Bass, 1972a.

Houle, C. O. "Afterword." In C. O. Houle, *The Inquiring Mind.* Norman: Oklahoma Research Center for Continuing Professional and Higher Education, University of Oklahoma, 1988. (Originally published 1961.)

Hoy, J. D. "An Inquiry as to Interests and Motives for Study Among Adult Evening Students." *British Journal of Educational Psychology,* 1933, *3* (1), 13–26.

Inkster, R. P. "Critical Thinking, Critical Teaching, Critical Theory: Doubting and Believing." In C. E. Warren (ed.), *Proceedings of the Twenty-Ninth Annual Adult Education Research Conference.* Calgary, Canada: University of Calgary, 1988.

Jaccard, C. K. *Results of Organization Meetings in Kansas.* Manhattan, Kans.: State College of Agriculture, 1931.

Jarvis, P. "The Development of Adult Education Knowledge." In P. Jarvis (ed.), *Twentieth-Century Thinkers in Adult Education.* London: Croom Helm, 1987.

Jensen, G., Liveright, A. A., and Hallenbeck, W. (Eds.). *Adult Education: Outlines of an Emerging Field of University Study.* Washington, D.C.: American Association for Adult and Continuing Education, 1964.

Kilpatrick, W. (ed.). *The Educational Frontier.* East Norwalk, Conn.: Appleton-Century-Crofts, 1933.

Kilpatrick, W. *Philosophy of Education.* New York: Macmillan, 1951.

Knowles, M. S. "Andragogy Not Pedagogy." Delbert Clark Award Address presented at Annual Conference of Georgia Adult Education Association, West Georgia College, Carrollton, 1967.

Knowles, M. S. "Andragogy Not Pedagogy." *Adult Leadership,* 1968, *16* (10), 350–352, 386.

Knowles, M. S. *The Modern Practice of Adult Education: Andragogy Versus Pedagogy.* Chicago: Association Press, 1970.

Knowles, M. S. "The Relevance of Research for the Adult Education Teacher/Trainer." *Adult Leadership,* 1972, *20* (8), 270–272, 302.

Knowles, M. S. *The Adult Learner: A Neglected Species.* Houston, Tex.: Gulf, 1973.

Knowles, M. S. *Self-Directed Learning: A Guide for Learners and Teachers.* Chicago: Association Press, 1975.

Knowles, M. S. *The Modern Practice of Adult Education: From Pedagogy to Andragogy.* (Rev. ed.) Chicago: Association Press, 1980.

Knowles, M. S. "Introduction: The Art and Science of Helping Adults Learn." In M. S. Knowles, and Associates, *Andragogy in Action: Applying Modern Principles of Adult Learning.* San Francisco: Jossey-Bass, 1984.

Kreitlow, B. W. "Research in Adult Education." In M. S. Knowles (ed.), *Handbook of Adult Education in the United States.* Washington, D.C.: American Association for Adult and Continuing Education, 1960.

Kreitlow, B. W. "Federal Support to Adult Education: Boon or Boondoggle." *Adult Education,* 1975, *25* (4), 213–237.

Lawson, K. H. "The Problem of Defining Adult Education as an Area of Research." *Adult Education,* 1985, *36* (1), 39–43.

Legge, C. D. "Research for Higher Degrees." *Studies in Adult Education,* 1979, *11* (1), 56–62.

Levitt, L. "Review of *Education for Perspective Transformation* by Jack Mezirow." *Adult Education,* 1979, *30,* 58–59.

Lewin, K. "Frontiers in Group Dynamics: Concept, Methods and Reality in Social Science." *Human Relations,* 1947, *1* (1), 5–41.

Lewin, K. *Field Theory in Social Science.* New York: Harper & Row, 1951.

Lindeman, E. C. *The Meaning of Adult Education.* Norman: Oklahoma Research Center for Continuing Professional and Higher Education, University of Oklahoma, 1989. (Originally published 1926.)

London, J. "Attitudes Toward Adult Education by Social Class." *Adult Education,* 1963, *13* (4), 226–233.

London, J. "The Influence of Social Class Behavior upon Adult Education Participation." *Adult Education,* 1970, *20* (3), 140–153.

Long, H. B. "Publication Activity of Selected Professors of Adult Education." *Adult Education,* 1977, *27* (2), 173–186.

Long, H. B. "A Perspective on Adult Education Research." In H. B. Long, R. Hiemstra, and Associates, *Changing Approaches to Studying Adult Education.* San Francisco: Jossey-Bass, 1980.

Long, H. B. *Adult and Continuing Education: Responding to Change.* New York: Teachers College Press, 1983a.

Long, H. B. *Adult Learning: Research and Practice.* New York: Cambridge Books, 1983b.

Long, H. B. "Characteristics of Adult Education Research Reported at the Adult Education Research Conference 1971–1980." *Adult Education,* 1983c, *33* (2), 79–96.

Long, H. B. "Descriptive Research in Adult Education in the United States." *International Journal of Lifelong Education,* 1983d, *1,* 385–395.

Long, H. B. *New Perspectives on the Education of Adults.* London: Croom Helm, 1987.

Long, H. B., and Agyekum, S. K. "*Adult Education* 1964–1973: Reflections of a Changing Discipline." *Adult Education,* 1974, *24* (2), 99–120.

Long, H. B., and Redding, T. R. *Self-Directed Learning Dissertation Abstracts: 1966–1991.* Norman, Oklahoma: Oklahoma Research Center for Continuing Professional and Higher Education, University of Oklahoma, 1991.

Lorge, I. *Effective Methods in Adult Education: Report of the Southern Regional Workshop for Agricultural Extension Specialists.* Raleigh: North Carolina State College, 1947.

McClusky, H. Y. "An Approach to a Differential Psychology of the Adult Potential." In S. M. Grabowski (ed.), *Adult Learning and Instruction.* Syracuse, N.Y.: ERIC Clearinghouse on Adult Education, 1970.

Marineau, C., and Klinger, K. "An Anthropological Approach to the Study of Educational Barriers of Adults at Postsecondary Level." ERIC, 1977. (ED 141 511)

Mezirow, J. "Towards a Theory of Practice." *Adult Education,* 1971, *21* (3) 135–147.

Mezirow, J. "A Critical Theory of Adult Learning and Education." *Adult Education,* 1981, *32* (1), 3–24.

Mezirow, J. "Epistemological Foundations." *Proceedings of the Twenty-Fifth Annual Adult Education Research Conference.* Raleigh: Department of Adult and Community College Education, North Carolina State University, 1984.

Mezirow, J. "Concept and Action in Adult Education." *Adult Education Quarterly,* 1985a, *35* (4), 142–151.

Mezirow, J. "A Critical Theory of Self-Directed Learning." In S. D. Brookfield (ed.), *Self-Directed Learning: From Theory to Practice*. New Directions for Continuing Education, no. 25. San Francisco: Jossey-Bass, 1985b.

Mezirow, J. "Transformation Theory." In C. E. Warren (ed.), *Proceedings of the Twenty-Ninth Annual Adult Education Research Conference*. Calgary, Canada: University of Calgary, 1988.

Mezirow, J. "Transformation Theory and Social Action: A Response to Collard and Law." *Adult Education Quarterly*, 1989, *39* (3), 169–175.

Mezirow, J. Transformative Dimensions of Adult Learning. San Francisco: Jossey-Bass, 1991.

Mezirow, J., and Associates. *Fostering Critical Reflection in Adulthood: A Guide to Transformative and Emancipatory Learning*. San Francisco: Jossey-Bass, 1990.

Miller, H. L. *Participation of Adults in Education: A Force-Field Analysis*. Occasional Paper, no. 14. Boston: Center for the Study of Liberal Education for Adults, 1967.

Plecas, D. B., and Sork, T. J. "Adult Education: Curing the Ills of an Undisciplined Discipline." *Adult Education Quarterly*, 1986, *37* (1), 48–62.

Rockhill, K. "The Past as Prologue: Toward an Expanded View of Adult Education." *Adult Education*, 1976, *26* (4), 196–207.

Rosenblum, S., and Darkenwald, G. G. "Effects of Adult Learner Participation in Course Planning and Achievement and Satisfaction." *Adult Education Quarterly*, 1983, *33* (3), 147–153.

Rubenson, K. "Participation in Recurrent Education: A Research Review." Paper presented at meeting on Developments in Recurrent Education, Center for Educational Research and Innovation, Organization for Economic Development, Paris, 1977.

Rubenson, K. "Adult Education Research: In Quest of a Map of the Territory." *Adult Education*, 1982, *32* (2), 57–74.

Rusnell, A. D. "Development of an Index of Quality for the Planning of Management Training Problems." Unpublished doctoral dissertation, Department of Adult Education, University of British Columbia, 1974.

Sork, T. J., and Buskey, J. H. "A Descriptive and Evaluative Analysis of Program Planning Literature 1950–1983." *Adult Education Quarterly*, 1986, *36* (2), 86–96.

Tennant, M. "An Evaluation of Knowles' Theory of Adult Learning." *International Journal of Lifelong Education,* 1986, *5* (2), 113–122.

Tough, A. "The Teaching Tasks Performed by Adult Self-Teachers." Unpublished doctoral dissertation, Department of Adult Education, University of Chicago, 1965.

Tough, A. *Learning Without a Teacher: A Study of Tasks and Assistance During Adult Self-Teaching Projects.* Educational Research Series, no. 3. Toronto: Ontario Institute for Studies in Education, 1967.

Tough, A. *The Adult's Learning Projects: A Fresh Approach to Theory and Practice in Adult Learning.* Research in Education Series, no. 1. Toronto: Ontario Institute for Studies in Education, 1971.

Tough, A. "Major Learning Efforts: Recent Research and Future Directions." *Adult Education,* 1978, *28* (4), 250–263.

Van Enckevort, G. "Andragology: A New Science." *Aontas Review,* 1971, *1* (1), 37–52.

Verner, C. "Definition of Terms." In G. Jensen, A. A. Liveright, and W. Hallenbeck (eds.), *Adult Education: Outlines of an Emerging Field of University Study.* Washington, D.C.: American Association for Adult and Continuing Education, 1964.

Verner, C. "Cultural Diffusion and Adult Education." *Adult Leadership,* 1968, *17,* 49–51, 91–93.

Verner, C., and Buttedahl, K. "Socio-Economic Characteristics of Participants in Extension Classes." *Continuous Learning,* 1964, *3* (1), 21–27.

Verner, C., and Buttedahl, K. "Characteristics of Participants in Two Methods of Adult Education." *Adult Education,* 1965, *15* (2), 67–73.

Verner, C., and Davis, G. S., Jr. "Completions and Drop-Outs: A Review of Research." *Adult Education,* 1964, *14* (3), 157–176.

Willie, R., Copeland, H., and Williams, H. "The Adult Education Professoriate of the United States and Canada." *International Journal of Lifelong Education,* 1985, *4* (1), 55–67.

Young, G. "Andragogy and Pedagogy: Two Ways of Accompaniment." *Adult Education Quarterly,* 1985, *35* (3), 160–167.

CHAPTER 5

The Impact of
Intellectual Leadership

William S. Griffith

Adult education as a field of study has continued to change since the publication of the black book in 1964. Probably the most important influence on the field has been the diverse impacts of intellectual leaders who have promulgated their points of view through doing research, writing, speaking, and training adult education graduate students.

The process of identifying the major intellectual leaders who have been shaping the study of adult education since 1964 is complex. It would be possible to identify those people who have written the greatest number of books and articles or who have published the largest number of research reports. The sheer quantity of an individual's publications, however, is not by itself sufficient evidence of leadership in the field. The correlation between quantity and quality of publications is far from perfect, and leaders also exert influence in ways other than through scholarly writing. Quantitative measures are inadequate to capture the intangible essence of influence. However, personality and leadership traits are not so easily measured. Since

97

estimated past, present, and future influence is the elusive quality I am considering, it is clear that I must use more than purely quantitative approaches.

Another approach to determining the intellectual leaders in adult education would be to identify a suitable group of knowledgeable adult educators, such as the members of the Commission of Professors of Adult Education, and to ask them to name those individuals whom they believe have exerted the greatest influence on adult education as a field of university study. To follow such an approach would exclude the majority of practicing adult educators from the judging process and thus seriously restrict the perspective of the judges. It might also be possible to canvass all of those people who have earned doctorates in the field since 1935 to obtain their thoughts. I did not use either of these approaches because doing so might be no more than a sort of popularity scaling that could mistake notoriety for constructive influence. Visibility alone is not an appropriate index of intellectual leadership.

Given the difficulty of assessing the relative influence of selected intellectual leaders on the study of adult education, it seems defensible to base the identification on a number of approaches: (1) noting the frequency with which individuals' publications were cited in scholarly literature, (2) scanning previous publications dealing with the leaders in the field, and (3) reflecting on my personal experience based on twenty-seven years as a member of the Commission of the Professors of Adult Education and active involvement with research conferences and professional associations. I acknowledge that the choices I made are subject to my personal limitations and should be viewed in that light.

The focus of this chapter is on those intellectual leaders from English-speaking North America, that is, Anglophone Canada and the United States. Significant international influences are reported in Chapter Fourteen. Accordingly, only those leaders who have spent a considerable amount of time in North America and who have written publications that have received recognition on this continent are included in this chapter. Further, little attention is paid to those leaders who made their contributions prior to 1964 because these individuals and their influence have already been recognized elsewhere.

The intellectual leaders who initially influenced the study of adult education were individuals who brought concepts from social science to the investigation of adult education phenomena. In recent years, individuals have earned their doctorates in adult education and have sought to address problems of practice without first establishing their credentials in an established discipline. This evolution was anticipated by Gale Jensen (1964).

Adult education graduate study initially attracted professors whose academic preparation had been in the social science disciplines of philosophy, psychology, social psychology, and history. This foundation, in the United States and Canada, inadvertently rather than intentionally, omitted anthropology, economics, political science, and other social science disciplines that address adult education phenomena. The unfortunate persistence of this limited perspective on the appropriate characteristics of adult education professors is reflected in the 1986 *Standards for Graduate Programs in Adult Education* adopted by the Commission of Professors of Adult Education. (For the text of the standards, refer to the Resource at the end of this book.) These standards indicate that in addition to the full-time professor with a degree in adult education, each graduate program ought to have additional full-time faculty with doctorates in a "relevant field (e.g. philosophy, psychology, sociology), with knowledge of adult education." Although the editors of this book recognize the fortuitous nature of the evolution of the field (see Chapter Four and Chapter Seven) and include political science as one of the contributing disciplines (see Chapter Twelve), not all people in the field accept the value of breaking away from the myopic views of those whose conceptualization of the field was distorted by the chance collection of disciplines that were represented at the founding meetings of the commission.

For reasons that have not been identified, adult education as a field of study has not attracted research-oriented individuals from established disciplines. Cynics might observe that the relative status of the field among discipline-oriented departments in universities is not high enough to attract these people.

Also, because of our limited perspective on where adult education research is or should be conducted and the domination of the various research conferences in adult education by universities, individuals from complementary areas of study and researchers in private consulting firms have not yet become identified as integral members of the cadre of researchers who are systematically advancing knowledge in adult education.

Intellectual Leaders

In this chapter the intellectual leaders are discussed in terms of the era in which they first made significant contributions to the field of adult education. The reporting is organized as follows: First, those who made their contributions in the era before the publication of the black book (1950–1964) will be mentioned briefly, providing a background for the subsequent discussion. Second, intellectual leaders who made significant contributions during the black book era and beyond will be presented. Third, leaders who began to make their contributions in the post–black book era (1964 and beyond) will be discussed, followed by a fourth group of younger scholars whose influence is being felt now, but who are likely to exhibit even greater impact on the field of study in the decades of professional practice ahead of them.

Before the Black Book. Several names stand out in an examination of adult education as a field of study in the period before 1950. These individuals are primarily identified with one of the social science disciplines, usually psychology. Edward L. Thorndike in his studies of adult learning (Thorndike, Bergman, Tilton, and Woodyard, 1928) and adult interests (Thorndike, 1935) provided the foundation for establishing a psychology of adult learning and systematized the study of adult interests. Lyman Bryson (1936) addressed the concept of educational needs and worked to advance adult education as a field of study distinct from the social science disciplines. Irving Lorge (1936), yet another psychologist, addressed the importance of an individual's power to learn in contrast to the individual's speed of learning, an important contribution to those who are concerned with adults' capacity to learn. The social reformist view was addressed by Richard H. Tawney in England (United Kingdom, 1919), and by his admirers in North America. Eduard Lindeman (1926) promoted the view that adult education was more than simply a technical practice and insisted that the study of adult education ought to address its social purposes, a message that must be retold to each succeeding generation of adult education professionals.

Black Book Era. The intellectual leaders who made significant contributions between 1950 and 1964 (and later) provided a foundation for the expanding study in the field and furnished the leadership for systematic inquiry into various aspects of the field. Several of these individuals are continuing to contribute to the literature, to play leadership roles, and to do research.

Paul E. Bergevin, the key figure in the Bureau of Studies in Adult Education at Indiana University, called attention to philosophical issues and exerted a major influence on adult religious education. He wrote: "The professional field of study of adult education is not unconcerned about economics and vocational competence, but it is deeply concerned with helping the adult discover how to live a fruitful and satisfying life by balancing his vocational concerns with a variety of other activities which might include cultural, spiritual, recreational, and political pursuits as well as community service" (1967, p. 61).

Bergevin emphasized the need to study the processes of adult education and proposed a glossary of terms that has received less attention than it merits. Working at an institution with one of the largest university education faculties, Bergevin sought to stimulate thoughtful inquiry in adult education as a field that is not confined to the development of technical expertise alone.

Edmund de Schweinitz-Brunner is an intellectual leader whose greatest influence was felt near the end of the era before publication of the black book, through his leadership in the development of the landmark publication *An Overview of Adult Education Research* (1959). Brunner reviewed research in nonvocational adult education, furnishing the major categories and identifying lacunae. His analysis has been instrumental in stimulating research and possibly in providing an operational definition that honored the conventional identification of the relevant social science disciplines. In his work he may inadvertently have discouraged efforts to secure the collaboration of other researchers with complementary disciplinary backgrounds. Nevertheless, his compilation of important adult education research remained as the only one of its kind until the early 1980s, when Huey Long (1983) assembled literature on adult learning, a contribution discussed later in this chapter.

Alexander N. Charters served as president of the Adult Education Association of the U.S.A. (now the American Association for Adult and Continuing Education), the National University Extension Association (now the National University Continuing Education Association), and the Association of University Evening Colleges (now the Association for Continuing Higher Education). He also established the adult education graduate program at Syracuse University and provided a model of innovative programming for its University College. His most important contribution to the study of adult education has been his work in comparative international adult education. He has consistently attended international conferences and has written and edited books such as *Comparing Adult Education Worldwide* (Charters and Associates, 1981) that stress the questions to be addressed in comparative international adult education and the potential benefits to be gained through international cooperation in research and the exchange of research findings. No other individual in the United States has so consistently promoted comparative international adult education over the past twenty-seven years. See Chapter Fourteen for additional information on Charters.

Burton Clark became a respected figure in adult education research with the publication of *Adult Education in Transition: A Study of Institutional Insecurity* (1956), in which he addressed the sense of insecurity among adult education practitioners and scholars. Clark's popular concept of marginalization has been overgeneralized and used quite indiscriminately without rigorous research to examine the generalizability of the findings to settings outside of the public schools and community colleges. Perhaps Clark's concept illustrates the danger of a research-generated concept become fashionable without its serving as a springboard for significant follow-up inquiries by other researchers. (An exception is Jack London's analysis, 1973, of the positive aspects of a marginal position for adult educators who wish to go about their business with minimal interference from their parent institutions.) Clark's subsequent work has been identified with higher education, although its relevance to adult education is clear to those who approach it from that perspective.

Cyril O. Houle, professor emeritus of the University of Chicago, will be better appreciated in the future as serious scholars discover his objective and penetrating analyses of selected aspects of adult education. Houle has turned his attention at various times to adult education in the armed services, the library, and the university; residential continuing education; continuing professional education; external degrees; program planning; participation; and graduate study in adult education itself. His aim is to study practice rather than to extend existing disciplinary concepts. He writes not as a social science scholar from one of the established disciplines but as a confirmed adult educator. Houle has a degree in adult education.

He has not restricted his research to a single disciplinary perspective, but rather has succeeded in approaching contemporary issues in the field by disciplined but not discipline-restricted inquiries, illuminating areas of practice in brilliant presentations. His slim volume, *The Inquiring Mind* (1961), has stimulated more research, both quantitative and qualitative, on participation in adult education than any other book in the history of the field. *The Design of Education* (1972), an analysis of the program planning process that does not have the normative overtones of other American program planning literature, is as yet an underrated publication. It may be underrated because the book is not committed to any one way of viewing the purposes of adult education and does not provide a normative set of linear steps for planning programs. With the passage of time, serious scholars in adult education will give this book greater attention than it has received to date.

A rigorous researcher, Houle has served as a model of the incessantly inquiring adult educator. He has been persistently skeptical, although never cynical, as he has carried out his research and provided a role model for contemporaries and generations to follow. It is noteworthy that the American Association for Adult and Continuing Education has established its highest award for literature in adult education in his honor.

J. Roby Kidd, Canadian humanist, teacher, and profession-builder, was the secretary-general of the International Council for Adult Education, which he conceived and nurtured. He also was Canada's leading adult educator from 1951, when he was named director of the Canadian Association for Adult Education (CAAE), until his untimely death in 1982.

In 1935, like many other adult educators, Kidd began his work in the field at the YMCA. He retained his commitment to the education of underprivileged adult learners throughout his life. He was the first Canadian to earn a doctorate in adult education. In 1957, he taught the first university-level graduate course in adult education in Canada at the University of British Columbia, an indication of his commitment to the improvement of the professional practice of adult education. He served as chairman of UNESCO's advisory committee on adult education, and in 1960 he was elected president of UNESCO's Second World Conference on Adult Education, which was held in Montreal. In 1966, he was named the first chairman of the Department of Adult Education at the newly established Ontario Institute for Studies in Education (OISE), which has become one of the most highly regarded adult education graduate programs in North America. He founded the International Council for Adult Education in 1972. The council has consistently addressed the concerns of equity and justice in Third World countries through adult education.

Kidd was a prolific author. His best-known book, *How Adults Learn* (1959), has been reprinted in at least nine languages and continues to inspire students of the field to investigate his ideas. His dedication to the improvement of life for all people, the force of his personality, and his commitment to the importance of the "animateur" in this field have made an impact on both the study and the practice of adult education worldwide. (See Chapter Fourteen for further details on Kidd's international contributions.)

Malcolm S. Knowles is the best known American adult educator. His reputation may be a result of his leadership as executive director of the Adult Education Association of the U.S.A. from 1951 to 1960, but is more likely a result of his writing and his presentations in countless countries, where practitioners have heard his gospel of andragogy. His book *A History of the Adult Education Movement in the United States* (1977) is a standard text in U.S. graduate adult education programs. Even more popular, both in the United States and elsewhere, is his book *The Modern Practice of Adult Education: From Pedagogy to Andragogy* (1980). The first edition of this book popularized the word *andragogy*. Since 1970, adult educators have debated whether andragogy is a theory of adult education, an ideology, or a collection of postulates and assumptions that represents one way of thinking about the practice of adult education. (See Chapter Four for further discussion of this issue.) Although andragogy has been perceived by many readers and by those who have listened to Knowles's persuasive speeches as a polar opposite of pedagogy, that is not the position Knowles holds today.

The commonsense approach used by Knowles in his primarily descriptive rather than analytical writing has a wide appeal. His presentation of andragogy as a fresh way of thinking about adult education has attracted thousands of disciples from the ranks of practicing adult educators. Unfortunately, the persuasiveness of his approach may account for the fact that Knowles's system of education for adults has not generated a significant amount of rigorous research. However, his concept of andragogy has undoubtedly inspired countless practicing adult educators to adopt the term, to embark upon graduate study in the field, and to profess allegiance to their perception of the concept. Knowles has also stimulated a great deal of interest in the self-directed learner and the use of learning contracts. The orientation toward practice of his publications makes them attractive to teachers of adults in diverse settings and very likely has resulted in increasing the effectiveness of these teachers.

Burton W. Kreitlow, professor emeritus of the University of Wisconsin, brought a practical rural orientation to the examination of the literature of adult education. With the sponsorship of the U.S. Department of Agriculture and the U.S. Office of Education, he analyzed the research literature and pointed out areas that he felt were in need of further research. He bridged the gap between adult education scholars and practicing adult educators in the Cooperative Extension Service, commonly regarded as America's largest adult education institution. He was a leading figure in the National Agricultural Extension Center for Advanced Study at the University of Wisconsin, and he exerted a powerful influence on the graduate education of a generation of administrators in the Cooperative Extension Service. In retirement, Kreitlow is continuing his study of the education of older adults, and it is conceivable that his most significant contribution to the study of adult education will be written in the future.

Howard Y. McClusky was the first president of the Adult Education Association of the U.S.A. and was the enduring symbol of adult education at the University of Michigan. He founded the adult education graduate program at Ann Arbor and fostered the idea of community schools and community education, bringing together notions of community organization, community development, and adult education. He assisted in the development of a network of community educators, which grew into the National Community Education Association.

McClusky's widely known theoretical concept was that of *margin,* which he defined as the difference between the level of an adult's power and the level of an adult's load (McClusky, 1970). One of the better known terms in American adult education, *margin* was readily accepted by adult educators because it coincided with what most of them were ready to believe. Its commonsense nature was apparently so self-evident that almost no one was stimulated to attempt to operationalize the concept, and no satisfactory instruments to measure load or power exist.

In fact, McClusky never discussed how to measure power and load. Nevertheless, margin was used to explain participation and nonparticipation for adults in all walks of life and at all ages.

In his later years, following his official retirement from the University of Michigan, McClusky directed his attention to educational gerontology and served as an adviser to the White House conferences on aging. He coedited the 1980 Handbook of Adult Education series, a series that demonstrated the diversity of study in adult education. He and his students addressed the problem of learning and aging and proposed a number of formulations that are likely to be tested in the future as the attention of adult educators turns inevitably to this growing segment of the population.

Alan M. Thomas is a professor of adult education at the Ontario Institute for Studies in Education, where he is noted for his continuing studies in the area of adult education and public policy. Thomas is the only North American adult educator who has both the practical experience gained from working for the Parliament of Canada and from serving as the director of the Canadian Association for Adult Education (1961–1970). Thomas analyzes provincial and federal legislation from perspectives that provide new and useful insights for adult educators who are interested in this as yet underdeveloped area of study. Like some of his European counterparts, Thomas is more concerned with the social significance of governmental influence on the distribution of adult learning opportunities among the various sectors of the public than he is with the technical aspects of adult education practice. Thomas's research on governmental control of adult education is destined to become much more widely known among North American adult educators as their sensitivity to the consequences of public financing and control of adult education emerges.

Coolie Verner was a rural sociologist and professor of adult education who worked in community development at the University of Virginia. He was largely responsible for the awareness by members of the Commission of Professors of Adult Education of the potential importance of sociology to the study of adult education (Verner, with Booth, 1964). He was the found-

ing professor of the adult education graduate program at Florida
State University. Subsequently, he became the first full-time
professor of adult education in Canada in that country's first
adult education graduate program when he accepted appointment as professor and head of the Department of Adult Education at the University of British Columbia.

As he noted in the black book, Verner was troubled by
the inconsistent use of terms by adult educators, a condition
he felt was incompatible with scholarly progress in the field.
Although he was not successful in persuading his colleagues in
the commission to adopt either his or any other glossary of adult
education terms (a frustration he experienced in common with
Paul Bergevin), he continued to impress upon his graduate students the necessity for rigor and consistency in this area. Verner
also believed that both practitioners and those who were writing as scholars in the field were not well acquainted with their
own literature. Under his leadership, graduate students synthesized the findings of research studies on methods, techniques,
and devices, an area of adult education study that continues to
be woefully neglected. The influence of Verner's ideas since his
death in 1979 has not been great; nevertheless, among those
people who are committed to the rigorous study of adult education, his systematic and rigorous approach to synthesizing the
knowledge of the field continues to provide a guide for contemporary efforts. Interestingly, Verner's contributions to the field
of cartography, his avocation, are at least as significant as his
work in adult education.

Post–Black Book Era. Adult educators of the post–black book
era include leaders whose influence is difficult to assess, not only
because they are still engaged in productive scholarship but also
because of their present highly visible positions. At the risk of
overlooking many influential people, I restricted the following
discussion to eleven of the most prominent leaders.

Jerold Apps, professor of continuing and vocational education at the University of Wisconsin, Madison, is a prolific con-
tributor to the literature of adult education and, especially, adult
higher education. He has become the best-known adult educa-

tion consultant in higher education in North America. His interests are broad, and his publications range from philosophical discourses to practical discussions of managing continuing education programs. Apps has attempted to redefine the discipline of adult education, assuming that the field can only be a true scholarly discipline if the researchers in the field have a set of common organizing assumptions (Boyd and Apps, 1980). Although Apps is not closely identified with a particular concept or theory, service in the CPAE and the AAACE, his wide-ranging publications, and his leadership within the Wisconsin graduate program make him one of the most effective representatives of academic adult education both within and outside of universities.

K. Patricia Cross, a respected scholar primarily identified with higher education, has been dealing with aspects of adult higher education as well as with adult education in general for over twenty years. After analyzing the studies of participation and persistence in adult education, she synthesized what she calls a chain-of-response model of participation in adult education. The model includes the variables that had been proposed previously in at least four other researchers' attempts at theorizing and is more than a summation of such explanatory mechanisms (Cross, 1981). The clarity of her writing and the insightfulness of her critiques have earned her the respect of scholars and the appreciation of graduate students who are trying to deal with the phenomena of participation and persistence.

Cross has also directly questioned whether anything could now be called a theory of adult education, saying that andragogy is a collection of postulates or guidelines for practice. As a speaker at events of the American Association for Adult and Continuing Education (AAACE), she has impressed audiences with her incisive observations and has influenced the nature of studies dealing with participation and how approaches may be devised to overcome obstacles to such participation. Her perspective, commendably, is broader than that of most authors who address participation and persistence.

Paulo Freire, although not from North America, has been a pervasive influence in North America, as well as in other parts of the world, on the thinking of adult educators whose primary clientele are illiterate, underprivileged, or otherwise powerless and oppressed. Through his use of the term *conscientization,* he has convinced many teachers that the use of generative words, photographs, and pictures and the identification of "oppressors" is an appropriate way to stimulate some adults to learn to read and write, to develop a feeling of empowerment, and to confront the forces they believe are responsible for their oppression (Freire, 1973). He has been effective in working within the educational and political establishments in the United States, Brazil, and many other countries. He has used his positions to encourage critical political consciousness among literacy teachers and social activists. No other person is better known in the field of literacy education than Freire. Whether or not one agrees with his analysis, his influence on the practice of adult education is undeniable. His influence seems pervasive, but he provides assumptions rather than hypotheses for subsequent research. Unfortunately, many of those who write about his ideas tend to be sycophants, and so the resulting literature rarely questions the basic assumptions on which his system rests.

Peter Jarvis, reader in the Educational Studies Department at the University of Surrey, has enjoyed a productive relationship with a major publisher of adult education books and is the only contemporary British scholar included in this chapter. He is included because he has spent a considerable amount of time in North America, is affiliated with the CPAE, has participated in the annual conferences of the AAACE, and has received the Cyril O. Houle Award for his contribution to the literature of adult education, *Adult Learning in the Social Context* (1987). Jarvis has written on the sociology as well as the theory and practice of adult education. Unlike most of the other leaders in the post–black book group, Jarvis has only begun contributing to the North American study of adult education relatively recently. But his impact to date suggests that even greater contributions are probable in the future.

Alan B. Knox is a professor of continuing and vocational education at the University of Wisconsin, Madison. He first attracted widespread attention in the scholarly community with the publication of *Adult Development and Learning* (1977). The work presents an encyclopedic overview of research from a variety of disciplines concerned with the relationship between age and its attendant physiological changes and adults' propensity and ability to acquire new information and skills. After the publication of that work, Knox examined aspects of the development, administration, and evaluation of adult education in one of the best selling books in the Adult Education Association Handbook series (Knox and Associates, 1980). In addition to pursuing his own continuing research interests dealing with learning through the life span, Knox has served as the key figure in the editing of the New Directions for Adult & Continuing Education series, the best known among the series that are oriented toward the practice of adult education.

Knox has served as president of the American Association for Adult and Continuing Education (1985–1986). He is one of the founders of the National Seminar on Adult Education Research (now known as the Adult Education Research Conference). The range of his interests, the scope of his publications, and his continuing leadership in the building of the AAACE through the building of the Adult Education Foundation make him an exemplar for the field.

Huey B. Long is a professor of adult education at the University of Oklahoma and formerly was a professor of adult education at the University of Georgia and president of the Adult Education Association of the U.S.A. Long has conducted historical studies of the adult education field in colonial times and has written on contemporary adult education in the United States. However, his best-known work is a synthesis of the research on adult learning, *Adult Learning: Research and Practice* (1983), for which he received the Houle award. In this ambitious undertaking, Long sought to bring together the literature on adult learning that had been published since Brunner, Wilder, Kirchner, and Newberry's *Overview of Adult Education Research* (1959). As the senior researcher at the research center at the University of Oklahoma funded by the Kellogg Foundation,

Long is in a position to continue and to broaden his research and writing. His stature as a leading thinker and researcher in the field will probably continue to increase.

Jack Mezirow is identified with Teachers College, Columbia University, where he has persistently enjoyed playing the role of skeptic and challenging the successive waves of fads that have swept over adult education. His own research contributions are diverse, but he is probably best known for his writing on perspective transformation — the potential influence of expertly planned and conducted adult education programs on the development of adults. Perspective transformation has restored some semblance of balance to the field when researchers have exhorted their colleagues to adopt a narrow version of the purpose of adult education. Mezirow's latest work on transformative learning (1990) is consistent with his view of the importance of adult educators' thinking clearly about the ends and not merely the means of adult education. His earlier work on community development and his insightful investigation of adult literacy programs have stimulated critical thought and are likely to generate further research that challenges traditional assumptions. His designing of an innovative doctoral degree at Columbia University that does not require a residency is evidence of his concern for the continuing education of practicing adult educators who want to study at the doctoral level but who feel unable to pursue traditional residency programs.

Leonard Nadler, who joined the faculty of the George Washington University in 1965 and remained at that school until his retirement, has consistently been identified with the field of training and development. As a leader in the growing area of human resource development (HRD) and a member of the American Society for Training and Development since 1954, Nadler has sought to enlarge the concept of training to include not only job training but also the education and further development of employed adults. From his perspective of seeing the human resource developer as a consultant, he has consistently and persistently sought to educate his colleagues within the Commission of Professors of Adult Education to the need for preparing broadly educated professionals who will be equipped to serve as advocates, experts, stimulators, and change agents in business and industrial settings (Nadler, 1970). As a consultant to a major publisher of books in the field of human resource development, he has played the role of a gatekeeper in selecting the ideas and concepts that are to be disseminated in the areas of training and development.

John Ohliger is the only leading influential scholar in this chapter who voluntarily relinquished a tenured professorship at a university to pursue his independent style of scholarly life. He is possibly best known for his leadership in producing the periodical *Basic Choices,* a newsletter dedicated to revealing the contradictions within adult education. As an opponent of mandatory continuing professional education, Ohliger organized the National Alliance for Voluntary Learning. He is a critic of lifelong education, and he questions whether it is really a means of promoting the notion of permanent inadequacy and the development of lifelong schooling as the antidote. With his dedication to adult learning as a vehicle for improving the quality of life, Ohliger has served as the self-appointed conscience of the field, stimulating serious examinations of the commonly accepted popular notions of the appropriate use of adult education (Ohliger, 1989).

Robert M. Smith, professor of adult education at Northern Illinois University, was associated with the graduate program in adult education at Indiana University before he undertook international assignments to broaden his knowledge of adult education in the Third World. At Northern Illinois University, Smith has been studying how to help adults learn how to learn and has written the book *Learning How to Learn* (1982) in which he sets forth the processes of learning and suggests aspects for further study. He received the Houle award for this work. His continuing research focuses on the process of self-directed learning and addresses approaches to increasing its effectiveness as well as its appropriate use. With the increasing interest shown in self-directed learning and ways of developing that process in adults of all kinds, Smith's research will be the starting point for many future researchers in addition to the many who have already been stimulated by his thinking.

Allen Tough, professor of adult education at the Ontario Institute for Studies in Education, began his study of self-directed learning while he was a graduate student studying with Cyril Houle. His research is internationally known and his study *The Adult's Learning Projects* (1971) has provided the data collection instrument used by dozens of other researchers in various settings. His attention has recently been directed to the use of education as a means of facilitating intentional changes. Those who aspire to serious scholarship on self-directed learning must consult the thinking and research of Tough, for without including his work no investigation in this area of inquiry would be complete.

The Emerging Scholars. Any assessment of the leading future intellectual leaders of the field is a hazardous undertaking, for it is never clear whether those who are currently displaying a zeal for writing and the skill to convey their ideas effectively in writing and speaking will continue to display such competence and dedication. Nevertheless, assuming that the best predictor of future performance is past and present performance, the following four thinkers and researchers appear destined to be influential. Others who have not yet demonstrated their abilities in conspicuous ways may yet emerge to eclipse all of those who have been identified in this chapter.

Stephen D. Brookfield, professor of adult education at Teachers College, Columbia University, is currently the most prolific young author in adult education. Brookfield was a protégé of H. Arthur Jones, the University of Leicester's eminent adult educator. Brookfield spent a year at the University of British Columbia before returning to England, where he was research officer for the National Institute for Adult and Continuing Education. That position gave him a unique opportunity to acquire a national perspective on the provision of adult education and the problems of the field. At Columbia University, Brookfield has written or edited books on adult learners, adult education and the community, self-directed learning (based in part on his own dissertation research involving such learners), understanding and facilitating adult learning, training educators of adults, and developing critical thinkers. He has received the Houle award both in 1986 and in 1989 and the 1986 Imogene E. Okes Award for Outstanding Research in Adult Education. Brookfield is in great demand as a speaker, and he effectively carries his ideas to a wider audience than is prepared to read his books. Should he be able to maintain the impressive pace that he has thus far set, he will establish himself as one of the most influential adult educators of this century.

Ronald M. Cervero, associate professor of adult education at the University of Georgia, is studying continuing professional education and publishing the findings of that research (Cervero, 1988). While still a graduate student, he began to write for publication based on his research on approaches to the measurement of adult competence. During his tenure at Northern Illinois University, he turned his attention to continuing professional education, directing student dissertations and pursuing his own inquiries in this area. His book, *Effective Continuing Education for Professionals* (1988), has been lauded by Donald Schön and is destined to become one of the best-known and most highly regarded books in this area of adult education. Its excellence is indicated by Cervero's being given both the Philip E. Frandson Award by the National University Continuing Education Association and the Houle award. If he continues to devote his energies and talents to the advancement of knowledge in his own specialized sector of the field and if he focuses on reporting his own original research, his contributions will provide the foundation on which knowledge of continuing professional education and other sectors of the field yet to be researched can be advanced.

Hanna Arlene Fingeret, associate professor of adult education at North Carolina State University and current chair of the Commission of Professors of Adult Education, is another of the young scholars who publish very selectively, drawing upon their own research and that of their graduate students as the basis for their writing (Fingeret, 1983). Beginning with her doctoral study of the social behavior and functioning of illiterate adults, Fingeret has consistently devoted her research and writing to the larger questions of literacy education and the improvement of means of delivering relevant and useful learning experiences through unconventional programming of basic education (Fingeret, 1984). Although her work may not be widely known outside of the area of literacy, the thoroughness of her inquiries, her involvement in action research projects, her commitment to deepen and enlarge her understanding of literacy education on both a practical and a theoretical level, and her status within the CPAE presage her future stature in academic adult education.

   Sharan B. Merriam is a professor of adult education at the University of Georgia and was a faculty member at Northern Illinois University and Virginia Polytechnic Institute and State University. She has broad interests in the field and writes on a variety of topics. Her primary area of inquiry, as indicated by her books, is philosophy. She has written or been a coauthor of at least three books dealing with research methods in adult education, including the recent *Case Study Research in Education: A Qualitative Approach* (1988). She has provided guidance for neophyte researchers in navigating the tortuous waters of dissertation research. Merriam's publications follow the tradition of the adult education generalists at a time when the pressure for extreme specialization is strong. While she is not linked with a specific theory or concept of adult education or its practice, her scholarly productivity and wide-ranging interests are likely predictors of her increasing influence on adult education in North America.

Conclusion

University study of adult education has been shaped by diverse intellectual leaders who have employed a broad, but nevertheless circumscribed, range of approaches in their attempts to impose order on the phenomena of the field. Although psychological concepts continue to be the favored vehicles for adult education research, researchers have recently used an increasing variety of disciplinary insights in examining the social and political aspects of adult education policy and organization. Because adult education scholars can be free of the self-imposed constraints characteristic of disciplinary researchers whose approach to studying the world is dominated by the concepts of a single discipline, the field is blessed with an abundance of potential resources. Consequently, the rich profusion of approaches may be misinterpreted by some critics as to be no more than a muddle. But, given the diversity of the field of practice, any narrowly conceived approach to inquiry, whether quantitative or qualitative, would be incapable of addressing the multiple manifestations of practice. One of the most significant positive inferences that we can draw from this review of the intellectual leadership of the field is that scholarship based on sociological, political, and anthropological approaches appears to be on the increase.

Although the field's leaders sought to build rigor into the study of adult education, especially individuals such as Paul Bergevin and Coolie Verner, academic adult educators do not seem inclined to accept the eminently sensible notion that unless they adopt a common vocabulary of concepts and terms, communication will continue to be difficult and progress in the cumulative investigation of primary phenomena will be retarded. Knowledge cannot be built progressively by individuals who insist on using their own glossaries whenever they plan, conduct, and report research. It is extremely difficult, if not impossible, to detect movement toward a common vocabulary of technical terms since the Commission of Professors of Adult Education was established in 1955. Further, it seems that many intellectual leaders of the field are reluctant to accept the idea that a standard set of definitions is compatible with their ideals for adult education.

The intellectual leadership of the field is largely dominated by men because few women have pursued doctoral study until recently. With an increasing number of unquestionably competent women pursuing doctoral programs in adult education, writing scholarly publications, and serving in positions of conspicuous leadership in the field, it seems clear that if a next-generation black book is written, its authors and the field's intellectual leadership will reflect the increase in the proportion of women who are leading the field.

In this chapter, I could single out only a few of the re-

searchers and thinkers in adult education, and the basis for their
inclusion is somewhat arbitrary. Countless action-oriented and
insightful practitioners who have made their contributions outside of academia have not been included in this chapter. Nevertheless, all of those who have been included are recognized by
their peers as persons of integrity whose outstanding professional
performance reflects a commitment to the advancement of adult
education, not simply as an intellectual interest in exploring abstractions but as a means of advancing the welfare of all human beings. It is this commitment to the improvement of the
quality of life for all that distinguishes the intellectual leaders
of adult education as a field of study from those whose primary
goal is the advancement of theoretical knowledge.

References

Bergevin, P. *A Philosophy for Adult Education.* New York: Seabury Press, 1967.

Boyd, R. D., and Apps, J. W. *Redefining the Discipline of Adult
Education.* San Francisco: Jossey-Bass, 1980.

Brunner, E. de S., Wilder, D. S., Kirchner, C., and Newberry,
J. S., Jr. *An Overview of Adult Education Research.* Washington,
D.C.: American Association for Adult and Continuing Edu-
cation, 1959.

Bryson, L. *Adult Education.* New York: American Book, 1936.

Campbell, D. D. *Adult Education as a Field of Study and Practice:
Strategies for Development.* Vancouver, Canada: Centre for Con-
tinuing Education and the International Council for Adult
Education, 1977.

Cervero, R. M. *Effective Continuing Education for Professionals.* San
Francisco: Jossey-Bass, 1988.

Charters, A. N., and Associates. *Comparing Adult Education Worldwide.* San Francisco: Jossey-Bass, 1981.

Clark, B. R. *Adult Education in Transition: A Study of Institutional
Insecurity.* Berkeley: University of California Press, 1956.

Commission of Professors of Adult Education. *Standards for
Graduate Programs in Adult Education.* Washington, D.C.: American Association for Adult and Continuing Education, 1990.

Cross, K. P. *Adults as Learners: Increasing Participation and Facilitating Learning.* San Francisco: Jossey-Bass, 1981.

Fingeret, A. "Social Network: A New Perspective on Independence and Illiterate Adults." *Adult Education Quarterly,* 1983, *33* (3), 133–146.

Fingeret, A. *Adult Literacy Education: Current and Future Directions.* Information Series, no. 284. Columbus: ERIC Clearinghouse on Adult, Career, and Vocational Education, Ohio State University, 1984.

Freire, P. *Education for Critical Consciousness.* New York: Seabury Press, 1973.

Houle, C. O. *The Inquiring Mind.* Madison: University of Wisconsin Press, 1961.

Houle, C. O. *The Design of Education.* San Francisco: Jossey-Bass, 1972.

Jarvis, P. *Adult Learning in the Social Context.* London: Croom Helm, 1987.

Jensen, G. "How Adult Education Borrows and Reformulates Knowledge of Other Disciplines." In G. Jensen, A. A. Liveright, and W. Hallenbeck (eds.), *Adult Education: Outlines of an Emerging Field of University Study.* Washington, D.C.: American Association for Adult and Continuing Education, 1964.

Jensen, G., Liveright, A. A., and Hallenbeck, W. (eds.). *Adult Education: Outlines of an Emerging Field of University Study.* Washington, D.C.: American Association for Adult and Continuing Education, 1964.

Kidd, J. R. *How Adults Learn.* (2nd ed.) Chicago: Follett, 1973.

Knowles, M. S. *A History of the Adult Education Movement in the United States.* (Rev. ed.) Melbourne, Fla.: Krieger, 1977.

Knowles, M. S. *The Modern Practice of Adult Education: From Pedagogy to Andragogy.* (Rev. ed.) Chicago: Association Press, 1980.

Knox, A. B. *Adult Development and Learning: A Handbook on Individual Growth and Competence in the Adult Years.* San Francisco: Jossey-Bass, 1977.

Knox, A. B., and Associates. *Developing, Administering, and Evaluating Adult Education.* San Francisco: Jossey-Bass, 1980.

Lindeman, E. C. *The Meaning of Adult Education.* New York: New Republic, 1926.

London, J. "Adult Education for the 1970's: Promise or Illusion?" *Adult Education,* 1973, *24* (1), 60–70.

Long, H. B. *Adult Learning: Research and Practice.* New York: Cambridge Books, 1983.

Lorge, I. "The Influence of Tests upon the Nature of Mental Decline as a Function of Age." *Journal of Educational Psychology,* 1936, *23,* 100–110.

McClusky, H. Y. "An Approach to a Differential Psychology of the Adult Potential." In S. M. Grabowski (ed.), *Adult Learning and Instruction.* Syracuse, N.Y.: ERIC Clearinghouse on Adult Education, 1970.

Merriam, S. B. *Case Study Research in Education: A Qualitative Approach.* San Francisco: Jossey-Bass, 1988.

Mezirow, J., and Associates. *Fostering Critical Reflection in Adulthood: A Guide to Transformative and Emancipatory Learning.* San Francisco: Jossey-Bass, 1990.

Nadler, L. "Business and Industry." In R. M. Smith, G. F. Aker, and J. R. Kidd (eds.), *Handbook of Adult Education.* New York: Macmillan, 1970.

Ohliger, J. "Alternative Images of the Future in Adult Education." In S. B. Merriam and P. M. Cunningham (eds.), *Handbook of Adult and Continuing Education.* San Francisco: Jossey-Bass, 1989.

Smith, R. M. *Learning How to Learn: Applied Learning Theory for Adults.* Chicago: Follett, 1982.

Thorndike, E. L. *Adult Interests.* New York: Macmillan, 1935.

Thorndike, E. L., Bregman, E. O., Tilton, J. W., and Woodyard, E. *Adult Learning.* New York: Macmillan, 1928.

Tough, A. *The Adult's Learning Projects: A Fresh Approach to Theory and Practice in Adult Learning.* Research in Education Series, no. 1. Toronto: Ontario Institute for Studies in Education, 1971.

United Kingdom, Ministry of Reconstruction, Adult Education Committee. *Final Report.* London: HMSO, 1919.

Verner, C., with Booth, A. *Adult Education.* Washington, D.C.: Center for Applied Research in Education, 1964.

CHAPTER 6

Disseminating and Using Adult Education Knowledge

Ralph G. Brockett

There is perhaps no better way to gauge the development of a field than to critically examine its body of knowledge. As Long has noted in Chapter Four, the knowledge base of adult education has continued to grow, particularly since the early 1970s. However, the potential impact of this knowledge is clearly proportional to the ways in which it is disseminated and used within the field.

The purpose of this chapter is twofold. First, the chapter is intended to describe and analyze how adult education knowledge has been disseminated and used. The term *dissemination* as I use it here refers to a process for transmitting the body of knowledge throughout the field. This discussion will emphasize, but not be restricted to, the professional literature of the field. Second, the chapter will present a number of strategies that have proven successful to date or could be effective avenues for dissemination and use of future knowledge.

Resources in the Knowledge Base

To a large extent, the body of knowledge of adult education is reflected in the professional literature of the field. However, it can also include various forms of media, such as audio and video recordings and computer-based information sources, and the insights and wisdom of individuals who study and practice within the field of adult education. It should be noted that I will use the terms *body of knowledge* and *knowledge base* more or less interchangeably in this chapter.

Although writings on the education of adults have appeared throughout history, the year 1926 can be argued to have been central to the establishment of the adult education professional literature in North America. This was the year in which the American Association for Adult Education (AAAE) was founded. The AAAE played a crucial role in the development of professional literature, particularly through its publication of the *Journal of Adult Education* (1929–1941) and the *Adult Education Journal* (1942–1950) and through monographs such as the twenty-seven volumes in the Studies in the Social Significance of Adult Education series. In addition, 1926 marked the publication of two seminal books: Eduard Lindeman's *The Meaning of Adult Education* and Everett Dean Martin's *The Meaning of a Liberal Education.* The evolution of the professional literature since the 1920s has been addressed elsewhere (see Imel, 1989; Knowles, 1977; Cotton, 1968). When considering and assessing the adult education knowledge base, it is important to remember that what exists today is the product of over sixty years of development and evolution.

In this chapter, I will examine the knowledge base, looking at books, periodicals, monograph series, conference proceedings, dissertations, ERIC documents, fugitive materials, and nonprint materials. In addition, I will examine teaching activities and professional networking.

Books. As might be expected, books are probably the most comprehensive source of knowledge in adult education. These include so-called classics in the field, such as the Lindeman and Martin books mentioned earlier, as well as more "contemporary" works, such as *The Modern Practice of Adult Education* (Knowles, 1980), *Adult Education: Foundations of Practice* (Darkenwald and Merriam, 1982), *Understanding and Facilitating Adult Learning*

(Brookfield, 1986), and *Adult Learning in the Social Context* (Jarvis, 1987).

Periodicals. Periodicals include journals, magazines, and newsletters published on a regular basis. Because of their periodic publication, these sources are important for the dissemination of more current information than can be disseminated through books. The *Journal of Adult Education,* published between 1929 and 1941, was one of the earliest and most influential periodicals in the field (Day, 1981). At present, the American Association for Adult and Continuing Education publishes all three types of periodicals: *Adult Education Quarterly* (journal), *Adult Learning* (magazine), and *Online* (newsletter). Other examples of current journals include the *International Journal of Lifelong Education, Educational Gerontology, Mountain Plains Journal of Adult Education, Studies in the Education of Adults, Training and Development Journal,* and the *Journal of Continuing Higher Education. Training/HRD* is another example of a magazine, and *Adult and Continuing Education Today* is a newsletter.

Another approach to periodicals that is just beginning to become a part of adult education is the "electronic journal." In the electronic journal, manuscripts are submitted and distributed to reviewers electronically, and the journal is distributed to subscribers via computer. *New Horizons in Adult Education,* a refereed journal managed by graduate students through the Adult Education Network (AEDNET) of the Syracuse University Kellogg Project, a network that operates via Bitnet, is the first venture of adult education in North America into electronic publishing. Electronic publishing is likely to have important implications for the way in which knowledge is disseminated and used in the future.

Monograph Series. Monograph series are also important sources of adult education literature. In many respects, these series combine the qualities of books and periodicals. The series Studies in the Social Significance of Adult Education, mentioned earlier, is perhaps the earliest example of this type of publication within the adult education literature. Between 1953 and 1976, the

Center for the Study of Liberal Education for Adults (and, later, Syracuse University Publications in Continuing Education) published several series of monographs, totaling over 150 publications. At present, the quarterly sourcebook series New Directions for Adult and Continuing Education, first published in 1979, provides an up-to-date look at current trends and practices in the field by focusing upon a different topic in each issue.

Conference Proceedings. Papers that appear in the proceedings of various conferences are valuable, but often overlooked, resources. The annual Adult Education Research Conference (AERC) has published a complete book of proceedings every year since 1979. Other conferences that publish proceedings include the Canadian Association for the Study of Adult Education (CASAE), the Standing Committee on University Teaching and Research on the Education of Adults (SCUTREA), the Lifelong Learning Research Conference (LLRC), and the Midwest Research-to-Practice Conference. The major advantage of these publications is that they provide perhaps the most current source of state-of-the-art literature in the field. A disadvantage is that their specialized nature and limited distribution often make them difficult to obtain by individuals who have not attended the conferences.

Dissertations. As is the case with nearly all fields of study, dissertations often represent the cutting edge of research in adult education. Yet dissertations are often overlooked as key resources. Dissertations from most universities are abstracted in *Dissertation Abstracts International,* and complete dissertations can be purchased on either microfilm or paper. Lists of adult education dissertations have been given for many years in the *Adult Education Quarterly* and its predecessor *Adult Education* and, more recently, by the Commission of Professors of Adult Education.

ERIC Documents. The Educational Resources Information Center (ERIC), established in 1966 and operated through funding by the U.S. Department of Education, comprises clearinghouses throughout the United States that specialize in the acquisition of materials from specific areas of education. The ERIC Clearinghouse on Adult, Career, and Vocational Education is located at Ohio State University. Because the ERIC clearinghouse has abstracts of articles from key education journals as well as abstracts and microfiche copies of a wide range of hard-to-find publications, it is the most comprehensive source for adult education materials in North America.

Fugitive Literature. Much of the literature in adult education is "fugitive literature," or literature that is not readily accessible. Project reports, brochures, individual papers, journals and newsletters with a statewide or regional circulation, and conference proceedings are a few examples of such literature. Although ERIC has helped to make fugitive materials more accessible, much of what is written about adult education is still relatively difficult to locate or obtain.

Nonprint Materials. Although the term *professional literature* is most often reserved for print materials, in recent years, nonprint materials have increasingly contributed to the body of knowledge in adult education. Audio and video recordings are perhaps the most obvious examples. A collection of interviews conducted by Stephen Brookfield (1987a) is an example of an audio recording that has added to the knowledge base. The Mentors and Mentors II series produced at the University of Georgia that consist of interviews with several pioneer and current leaders in the field are video recordings that have added to the knowledge base. Other examples of video recordings are "The Women of Summer," a documentary of Hilda W. Smith and her involvement in workers' education for women, and "You Got to Move," about the work of the Highlander Research and Education Center.

   To date, adult education has not used nonprint material nearly to the same extent that other fields (gerontology, psychology) have. One problem, particularly with video, is that the purchase price for nonprint material tends to be considerably higher than the price for books or journals, making it more difficult for individual practitioners to add to their own collections. If we truly wish our field to be on the "cutting edge" of the production and dissemination of knowledge as we move toward the next millenium, we must take a more active role in developing nonprint materials and in finding ways to minimize the cost of such materials.

Teaching Activities. Although the most readily identified strategy for dissemination of knowledge is typically through publication, it is important to recognize that dissemination can occur in many other ways. One of the most important ways in which the body of knowledge is disseminated is through teaching. Galbraith and Zelenak (1989) identify on-the-job training, in-service training, and graduate education degree programs as major avenues for professional development of adult and continuing education practitioners. Universities have played an important role in the training of adult educators since the 1920s (Brockett, 1990b). Brookfield (1988) has assembled a collection of readings addressing the training of adult educators. Through a combination of original and previously published pieces, Brookfield's work provides a look at such topics as theory and practice, conceptual issues in training educators of adults, historical ideas, characteristics and proficiencies of adult educators, criteria of "good practice," and graduate curricula and programs. The importance of graduate study is discussed in greater detail in Chapter Seven. However, I mention it here because graduate programs (and, sometimes, preservice undergraduate courses or programs) serve as major vehicles through which the body of knowledge is passed on to successive generations of individuals.

Professional Networking. Teaching provides a formal mechanism for disseminating and promoting the use of adult education knowledge. Professional networks are another, typically less formal, way through which the knowledge base can be disseminated and used. The most obvious professional networks are professional associations and conferences. However, informal networks are at least as important as more formal approaches. Electronic mail, fax machines, advancements in video technology, and optical scanning are only some of the recent developments that in just a few years have transformed the way in which it is possible for individuals to communicate with one another.

Knowledge for Whom?

Who are the audiences for the body of knowledge in adult education? An issue of continuous concern within adult education (though certainly not unique to adult education) is the chasm that separates theory and research on the one side and practice on the other. Cervero alludes to this issue in Chapter Two, relative to alternative ways of looking at the relationship between theory and practice. The scholar-practitioner dichotomy may be too simple and, thus, inadequate for addressing the question of who the audiences for adult education publications are. As Knox (1972) pointed out, "The scholar's role can be performed by anyone associated with adult education: teacher, administrator, researcher, professor" (p. 49). Similarly, all scholars are engaged in some sort of practice (such as the practice of studying and teaching about the adult education field). Thus, a distinction can be made between scholars of practice and scholarly practitioners.

Instead of focusing on target audiences in the dissemination of the knowledge base, adult educators, it can be argued, should look to target purposes in the dissemination efforts. Griffith (1972) proposed a two-dimensional matrix for categorizing types of publications. In this matrix, one axis (cognitive-symbolic) deals with the purpose of publications and "ranges from the simple objective transmission of information at the cognitive extreme to the intention of influencing the reader's attitude or actions at the symbolic extreme" (p. 35). The other axis (practical-theoretical) focuses on the content of the publication and "ranges from the simple presentation of facts or the reporting of news at the practical end of the continuum to the presentation of explanations of the relationships among concepts at the theoretical end" (p. 35).

It is possible to expand upon Griffith's classification scheme to create a typology of the knowledge base in adult education that identifies four major purposes, each of which reflects a different box in Griffith's matrix. Further, these four categories are relevant to scholars and practitioners alike and can be applied to discussions of the knowledge base in general (as opposed to publications alone). The modified version of Griffith's matrix is presented in Figure 1. In this matrix, the four categories are share new information and ideas, foster professional socialization and reaffirmation, promote critical thinking, and stimulate development of new knowledge.

If adapted as a framework for understanding how the adult education body of knowledge can be used and disseminated, the matrix can provide a helpful tool for better understanding potential consumers of the knowledge base. However, an important point needs to be kept in mind. A given publication can often fit in more than one category. For example, an article on formative evaluation of adult basic education programs might serve as core information to one reader, while for another reader, the same article could stimulate critical thinking about the value of different approaches to formative evaluation. Similarly, a single publication can serve multiple uses to the *same* reader at different times. For instance, a publication might offer an individual new ideas and information and serve as a resource for the individual's research agenda. Thus, the matrix should not be used in a prescriptive way to make discrete classifications among specific publications.

Share New Information and Ideas. One purpose of the knowledge base is to make available basic information and ideas about adult education. Typically, publications that provide them have a descriptive "how-to" orientation aimed at helping readers learn through the descriptive accounts and expertise of others. Although what is most likely to come to mind is publications that deal with techniques of practice (such as marketing, staff development, and teaching techniques), resources on how to use particular research techniques would also fall within this category. The emphasis here is on how material is used rather than on who is using the material. The teaching-learning transaction basically involves sharing information through such activities as lectures, media presentations, and demonstrations.

Foster Professional Socialization and Reaffirmation. A second purpose of the knowledge base is to help socialize new people in the field and to strengthen the sense of professional identity

Figure 1. An Elaboration of Griffith's
Publications Dimensions Matrix.

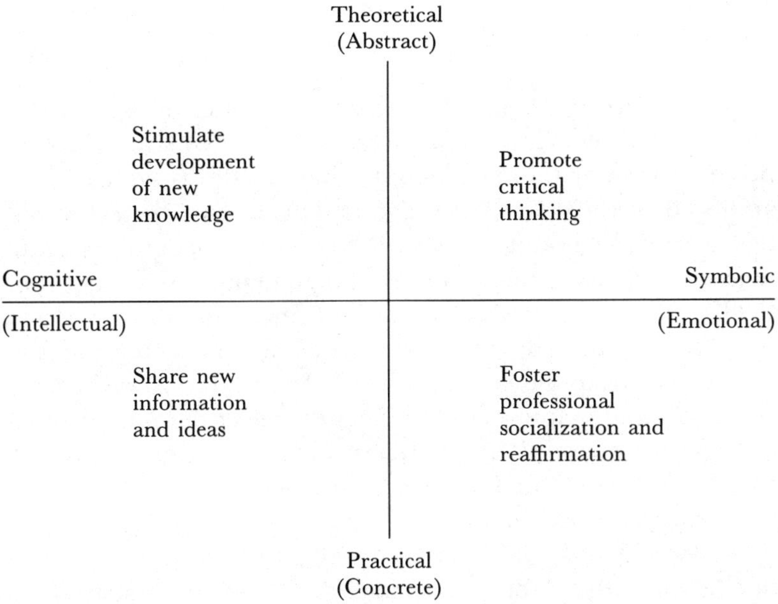

Theoretical
(Abstract)

Stimulate
development   Promote
of new   critical
knowledge   thinking

Cognitive   Symbolic

(Intellectual)   (Emotional)

Share new   Foster
information   professional
and ideas   socialization and
                               reaffirmation

Practical
(Concrete)

Source: Griffith, 1972. Adapted with permission.

among those already in the field. Probably one of the most obvious examples of this use can be found in graduate programs of adult education. As Peters and Kreitlow note in Chapter Seven, one needs to know a lot in order to perform effectively as an educator of adults. The knowledge base becomes an indispensable tool in the process of becoming an adult educator. Thus, dissemination and use of the body of knowledge is an invaluable part of what needs to take place within graduate programs.

This point can be taken a step further, however. The body of knowledge can also help practicing adult educators reaffirm their commitment to the field. Given the diversity (or, as some would say, fragmentation) of the field, the professional literature provides a source whereby it is possible for an individual to gain and maintain a perspective on the field as a whole. Reading professional literature can be an invaluable professional development activity that is both flexible and convenient (Brockett, 1986). As such, it can be a strategy for enhancing one's commitment to the field.

Promote Critical Thinking. A third purpose of the knowledge base in adult education is to serve as a tool to stimulate and promote critical thinking about what we do as educators of adults. Brookfield (1987b) suggests that the two central activities of critical thinking are identifying and challenging assumptions and exploring alternative ways of thinking and acting. Apps (1985) points out that the process of analyzing priorities and practices in adult education offers several benefits to practitioners as well as to the field in general. In general, these benefits center around helping practitioners to reflect upon their practice and to expand their awareness of ways to practice as well as helping the field to develop a "conscience" and a way of critically analyzing its role in society.

How can the body of knowledge be used in this critical thinking process? Publications, in and of themselves, do not lead to critical thought. Rather, they serve as tools for encouraging and supporting critical thinking. The professional literature of adult education is replete with multiple perspectives on institutions, programs, practices, issues, and research within the field. As such, it provides a convenient and often accessible source through which one can engage in the process of critical thinking. However, reading is only one means of stimulating critical thinking; many other ways can be used to encourage individuals to think critically about what they do and why they do it. For instance, Apps (1985) suggests that in addition to reading, participating in the arts, thinking, writing, discussing, and taking action are valuable strategies for analyzing practice. And Brookfield (1987b) stresses the importance of the teaching role in helping adults to be critical thinkers. His emphasis highlights the importance of teaching as a tool for disseminating the knowledge base. Graduate courses, workshops, and informal networks can play an important role in the development of critical thinking.

Stimulate Development of New Knowledge. A fourth purpose of the knowledge base in adult education is to serve as a stimulus for the development of new knowledge. One of the major limitations with the body of knowledge to date has been the lack of sustained research in key areas (Brockett and Darkenwald, 1987). As Long has suggested in Chapter Four, a key to future development of the body of knowledge is the ability of researchers to build new efforts from what already exists. The professional literature is a stimulus for new knowledge as well as new practices or perspectives. For instance, Houle (1988) discussed how his work *The Inquiring Mind,* which was originally published in 1961, served as a point of departure for what can be argued to have been two of the most productive research directions in the past two decades: participation in adult education and self-directed learning. Research, whether conducted by professors, practitioners, or graduate students (as part of the teaching-learning transaction), is an obvious example of how the knowledge base can be expanded.

Describing and Assessing the Literature of Adult Education

What is the nature of the existing body of knowledge of the field of adult education and how valuable is this knowledge? As the field of adult education has evolved, particularly since the publication of the black book (Jensen, Liveright, and Hallenbeck, 1964), researchers have increasingly done studies on the professional literature of adult education. These studies have taken at least three major directions: (1) content analysis investigations of particular publications, designed to offer a basic description of major trends; (2) development studies that focus upon the contributors to the professional literature; and (3) utilization studies that explore how the literature is used and the value ascribed to the literature. Together, these three types of research can provide us with basic data through which we can better understand the body of knowledge and, thus, become more informed about dissemination and use of knowledge in the field.

Content Analyses. Content analysis is a research technique that can be used to systematically discern major themes or trends in a body of literature. Although content analysis is frequently associated with qualitative research methodology, content analyses of the adult education literature to date have been primarily quantitatively oriented.

Perhaps the first effort to look quantitatively at the literature of adult education was a study by Dickinson and Rusnell (1971). In this study, the investigators analyzed the content of *Adult Education* between 1950 and 1970. Based on a quantitative analysis of each article, they concluded that over the twenty-year period, the number of university-based authors, the number of references per article, and the emphasis on the publication of research as opposed to program descriptions or statements of personal belief increased. A subsequent analysis, covering the years 1964–1973 (Long and Agyekum, 1974), suggested that the journal clearly reflected changes taking place in adult education as a discipline. Further, the authors noted that *Adult Education* reflected an "increasing quality and sophistication in research design and importance of research questions in adult education" (p. 113). Still another content analysis of the journal, covering the years 1974–1981 (Peters and Banks, 1982) revealed a continuation of the trends identified by Dickinson and Rusnell.

Other content analyses have included investigations of the *Journal of Adult Education* in the years 1929–1941 (Day, 1981), *Lifelong Learning: The Adult Years* in the years 1977–1981 (Brockett, 1982), *Educational Gerontology: An International Bimonthly Journal* in the years 1976–1986 (Rogers and Brockett, 1988), and several sources of literature on adult basic education (Fisher and Martin, 1987). As with the investigations mentioned earlier, these were studies of major themes and trends in the literature.

Another approach to content analysis is reflected in a study by Pipke (1984). In this investigation, Pipke "examined characteristics of and variables associated with the acceptance of abstracts submitted to the Adult Education Research Conference" selection committee over a three-year period (p. 71). She found that for the most part, the decision to accept or reject was based on characteristics of the abstract (such as "the presence of information concerning theory, instrumentation, data collection, analysis, results, and conclusions"), although reviewers tended to emphasize different variables in different years (Pipke, 1984, p. 82). From this study, Pipke concluded that the "gatekeeping behaviors" of those responsible for editorial decisions are crucial to the dissemination of the adult education knowledge base and, thus, are worthy of further research.

Development Studies. A second line of research consists of investigations of those people who contribute to the body of knowledge. In one such study, Long (1977) examined the vitae and publications lists submitted by eighty-one members of the CPAE. He found that between 1950 and 1973, the members reported a total of 2,098 publications, with an individual range of none to 194. The vast majority of these publications were journal articles or other types of research-related reports; about 10 percent were books. Of the 338 journals in which respondents reported publishing, *Adult Education* (now *Adult Education Quarterly*) and *Adult Leadership* (which was superseded by *Lifelong Learning: The Adult Years* in 1977) were the two most frequently cited.

More recently, I surveyed CPAE members about their professional writing activities (Brockett, 1988). Based on data from 106 respondents, my study made several key findings. First, most professors (82 percent) reported that they think about writing either daily or several times per week; yet only 66 percent of this group reported that they spend two hours or more per week actually writing. Second, nearly 90 percent of the respondents stated that they derive either a great deal or some satisfaction from writing; however, 70 percent reported that they feel either a great deal or some pressure to write for publication. Third, over 80 percent of the respondents stated that writing either greatly or somewhat enhances their effectiveness as teachers. Fourth, I found significant correlations between three attitudinal variables — amount of time spent thinking about writing, degree of satisfaction derived from writing, and the degree to which writing is believed to enhance effectiveness as a teacher. In attempting to expand the role of adult education as a field

of study, it will be essential to develop the literature base continually. Findings of my study suggest that such development
is possible, provided that adult educators increase their present
levels of productivity.

My study looked at scholarly productivity across the adult
education professoriate. Garrison and Baskett (1987) studied
productivity from a slightly different perspective. They inter-
viewed seventeen North American researchers in adult education, selected on the basis of their research productivity. These
individuals reported an average of over fifty-five publications
each during a research career averaging eighteen years. Several
trends emerged relative to research practices, including the use
of various methodologies in research (such as quantitative and
qualitative methodologies) and the identification of an informal
support network of other research-oriented individuals. One of
the more important conclusions drawn by Garrison and Baskett
was that future adult education researchers must be concerned
with the quality of research rather than just the quantity of research. This recommendation is clearly important to the future
development of the knowledge base.

Although most development studies have examined the
publication activity of professors, it is also important to stress
the role that graduate students have played in developing the
body of knowledge. Lee (1979) sent a questionnaire to 162 authors of articles in *Adult Education* between 1968 and 1978. She
found that of these articles slightly over 40 percent were conceptualized by graduate students; 52 percent, by faculty; and
slightly less than 8 percent, by others. When the articles were
actually submitted for publication, however, only 37 percent
of the authors who reported being students when the study was
originally conceptualized were still classified as students. Also,
eight different universities each contributed more than three student research articles to the journal during this period. Lee concluded that graduate student research does, in fact, make an
important contribution to the body of knowledge in adult education. Further, she concluded that because of the blind review
process for selection of articles in *Adult Education,* it is possible
to view student research as equal to all other articles accepted
for publication.

The development studies reported above suggest that adult education does not lack contributors to the knowledge base. At the same time, not unlike most other fields, most of the contributions to knowledge come from a relatively small number of scholars. Nonetheless, the evidence suggests that a potential for further development of a high-quality body of knowledge exists.

Utilization Studies. Content analysis and development studies offer descriptive information about what is contained in the body of knowledge and who has contributed to the development of this knowledge. A third line of research has provided evidence to assess the value ascribed to the body of knowledge and to identify what might be viewed as major sources of knowledge for the adult education field. Essentially, these studies ask respondents to rate the value or usefulness of journals and books in adult education. Indirectly, then, these studies can be used to make inferences about how the literature is used.

Boyd and Rice (1986) surveyed deans and directors of continuing education about the publications that these individuals read. Their findings, based on 131 responses from members of the National University Continuing Education Association (NUCEA) revealed that the most widely read publications were *Continuum* (24 percent of respondents), *Journal of Continuing Higher Education* (10 percent), *Adult Education Quarterly* (7 percent), *Chronicle of Higher Education* (7 percent), *Lifelong Learning* (7 percent), *Journal of Higher Education* (6 percent), and *Change* (3 percent).

In another survey, I questioned adult education professors about their use of professional literature (Brockett, 1990a). Over 77 percent of the respondents reported spending between two and ten hours per week on professional reading. In an open-ended question, respondents were asked to list up to five journals that they believed to be most useful to them in their role as professors of adult education. In contrast with the findings of Boyd and Rice (1986) from practitioners, professors most frequently identified the following journals: *Adult Education Quarterly* (82 percent of respondents), *Lifelong Learning* (64 percent), *Training and Development Journal* (23 percent), *Convergence* (15 percent), *International Journal of Lifelong Education* (12 percent), and

Educational Gerontology (10 percent). *Continuum,* which was by far the most frequently noted periodical in Boyd and Rice's survey of practitioners, was selected by only 5 percent of the professors.

Another study surveyed graduate student members of the AAACE relative to the value they ascribe to the adult education literature (Brockett, Hayes, and Velazquez, 1989). With regard to periodicals, the findings were somewhat similar to the findings for professors in the previous survey. *Adult Education Quarterly, Lifelong Learning, Training/HRD, Training and Development Journal, Educational Gerontology,* and *Convergence* were rated, in descending order, as the six most useful publications.

It should come as no surprise that members of the NUCEA gave the publication sponsored by their association the highest rating while professors and graduate students (all of whom are members of AAACE) rated the publications sponsored by their organization the highest. These publications are a part of the benefit packages of membership in these associations. Perhaps a bit more surprising is that less than 25 percent of the NUCEA respondents stated that they regularly read the publication of their association (Boyd and Rice, 1986). Further, it should be noted that a small but noticeable number of individuals in the latter two studies declined to list any publications as being "most useful" to them. Although these surveys present some indication of basic trends, further research could probe deeper into related questions that go beyond description of trends.

At least three studies have attempted to gauge the value of specific books in the field. Day and McDermott (1979) surveyed graduate students relative to their familiarity with thirty-four historical and contemporary books in adult education. The books that the students most frequently reported to have read, in descending order, were *The Modern Practice of Adult Education* (Knowles, 1980), *The Design of Education* (Houle, 1972), *The Adult Education Movement in the United States* (Knowles, 1977), *Handbook of Adult Education* (Smith, Aker, and Kidd, 1970), and *The Inquiring Mind* (Houle, [1961] 1988). The authors concluded that since the titles that generated most familiarity were more recent publications, graduate students were generally not very familiar with historical writings in the field.

More recently, the survey of graduate students cited

earlier (Brockett, Hayes, and Velazquez, 1989) revealed the five most influential books to be as follows, in descending order: *Understanding and Facilitating Adult Learning* (Brookfield, 1986), *The Modern Practice of Adult Education* (Knowles, 1980), *Adults as Learners* (Cross, 1981), *The Adult Learner: A Neglected Species* (Knowles, 1984), and a tie between *Philosophical Foundations of Adult Education* (Elias and Merriam, 1980), *Adult Education: Foundation of Practice* (Darkenwald and Merriam, 1982), and *Pedagogy of the Oppressed* (Freire, 1970). Interestingly, only three of the books identified in this second study had been published at the time of the Day and McDermott survey.

Perhaps the most comprehensive survey about adult education books is an investigation by Hiemstra, Snow, and Mgulambwa (1989). In this study, 135 individuals (most of whom were adult education professors) reviewed a list of 395 adult education books. Respondents were asked to select the books on the list that they felt were the most important contributions to the field. On the average, respondents selected slightly more than 39 books each. The five most frequently identified books were *Adults as Learners* (Cross, 1981), *The Modern Practice of Adult Education* (Knowles, 1980), *How Adults Learn* (Kidd, 1973), *The Inquiring Mind* (Houle, [1961] 1988), and *The Adult's Learning Projects* (Tough, 1979). Coincidentally, each of these books is identified as an important contribution by Griffith in Chapter Five.

When attempting to use polls such as the ones reported here to assess the quality of the literature, we must bear in mind that these assessments are descriptive opinions of selected individuals recorded at a specific point in time. As such, the findings are clearly limited and cannot be generalized across the field. Thus, while the lists provide us with a baseline from which we might better understand how the literature of adult education is viewed, it is important that these lists not be misunderstood or misused to identify the "best" books in a simplistic, prescriptive way.

Strategies for Enhancing Future Dissemination and Use of Knowledge

Adult education does indeed have a viable body of knowledge. This base has evolved over more than six decades and has provided our field with a rich record of its heritage and evolution. Yet, as Imel (1989) has stated, while most adult educators would agree that the field does, in fact, possess a "distinct knowledge base," they argue over the quality of this base. In the future, several strategies will make it possible to more effectively disseminate and use the body of knowledge of adult education. Some of these strategies emphasize strengthening and expanding existing approaches for disseminating and using the knowledge while others stress new approaches. I close this chapter by identifying several of these strategies.

Expand the Literature Base. It seems a bit trite to say simply that in the future, we will need "more" sources through which the knowledge base of adult education can be disseminated. Yet the fact remains that currently there are relatively few places for adult educators to publish within their own field. For instance, at present *Adult Education Quarterly* is the only periodical in the United States that publishes basic research and theory articles related to the general adult education field (as opposed to specialized areas such as gerontology and literacy). This point is not intended to serve as a call for a proliferation of new publications. Such an approach would probably lead to articles of diminished quality and would ultimately be harmful to efforts to disseminate knowledge. Yet we need to deliberately and thoughtfully create new avenues through which to facilitate further growth of the body of knowledge.

Reinforce the Mainstream Literature Base. If the adult education field is to maximize the use of its literature base in the future, it will be necessary to more clearly define what constitutes that base. The literature of adult education covers the many branches of the field, yet it would probably be accurate to suggest that most educators of adults tend to read primarily from sources within their own particular area of focus. Thus, the findings from the utilization studies, which were cited earlier, are not surprising.

One strategy for further enhancing dissemination and use of the knowledge base would be to encourage people to take a more "inclusive" approach to defining and promoting use of the literature. For example, few people would argue that the *Journal of Continuing Education in Nursing,* the *Journal of Continuing Social Work Education,* or the *Journal of Extension* are not a part of the adult education literature base. At the same time, the readership for these and other adult education publications is typically limited to those people working specifically in that area of practice (that is, nursing, social work, extension). It can be argued that publications such as these have the potential to also be of value to educators of adults who work outside of these areas. An article on program evaluation in nursing continuing education, for example, may suggest techniques or identify problems that are relevant to someone working in an adult literacy program. By stressing the idea of a "mainstream" literature base and by emphasizing a more inclusive view of what is "ours," the body of knowledge in the field is immediately expanded.

Recognize Historical Literature. Many adult educators tend, as reflected in the utilization studies cited earlier, to emphasize only the most recent books and journals. As a result, many of the ideas and individuals who have helped to shape the current field go unrecognized. If we are indeed committed to developing adult education as a field of study, we can ill afford to lose touch with our roots.

As has been pointed out by writers such as Cotton (1968) and Day (1981), the early literature is very rich. Of course, just as is the case with contemporary literature, early publications vary in quality. The challenge to those people who seek ways to disseminate and use the body of knowledge is to carefully and critically search the historical literature in order to uncover the many "buried treasures" that can continue to inform and inspire us today and tomorrow. The Oklahoma Research Center for Continuing Higher and Professional Education has attempted to address this problem by reprinting two long out-of-print works — *The Inquiring Mind* (Houle, [1961] 1988) and *The Meaning of Adult Education* (Lindeman, [1926] 1989). The Kellogg Project at Syracuse University encourages the use of their extensive archival holdings in adult education and the dissemination of historical research through such strategies as conferences, courses, grants to visiting scholars, and innovative approaches to storage and retrieval of documents.

Promote Dissemination and Use of Knowledge in Professional Development. The role of teaching in disseminating the body of knowledge in adult education cannot be stressed enough. A crucial function of graduate programs is to help individuals become informed about the adult education knowledge base and to learn how to effectively use the knowledge base in order to become more informed about the field; develop a professional commitment to the field; become increasingly able to critically analyze programs, practices, and problems in the education of adults; and contribute to the development of new knowledge. In other words, graduate programs can and should essentially strive to help individuals more effectively use the body of knowledge for each of the four purposes listed in Figure 1. This point is discussed more fully in Chapter Seven by Peters and Kreitlow.

The teaching aspect of dissemination is often linked with graduate education, but we must also recognize the importance of conferences, workshops, and informal networks. National, regional, state, provincial, and local conferences provide opportunities for sharing of new ideas and information that frequently do not find their way into the literature. Workshops typically serve as a format for more detailed sharing of knowledge than is found in the shorter duration of conference presentations. Informal networks allow for even more detailed and personalized sharing. Thus, while publishing is typically seen as the primary vehicle for disseminating the body of knowledge, the crucial role of teaching as a form of dissemination must continue to be stressed as well.

Create New Approaches for Dissemination and Use. When looking to the future, we clearly cannot just revise and refine existing approaches to disseminating and using knowledge. Instead, we must create entirely new ways to maximize the impact of adult education's knowledge base. In the 1980s, we witnessed the explosion of such technologies as personal computers and videocassette players throughout society. Computer networks such as Bitnet, as well as fax machines, have greatly expanded and simplified our opportunities to communicate regularly with colleagues throughout the world. As technology continues to develop and improve, the adult education field needs to remain at the forefront, adapting innovations as they become available and creating new ones.

References

Apps, J. W. *Improving Practice in Continuing Education: Modern Approaches for Understanding the Field and Determining Priorities.* San Francisco: Jossey-Bass, 1985.

Boyd, R. H., and Rice, D. "An Overview of Research Activity in Adult and Continuing Education." *Continuum,* 1986, *50* (1), 37–46.

Brockett, R. G. "*Lifelong Learning:* The First Three Years." *Lifelong Learning: The Adult Years,* 1982, *5* (10), 8–9, 27.

Brockett, R. G. "Keeping Up with Professional Reading Is More Than a Luxury." *Community Education Journal,* 1986, *13* (3), 9–11.

Brockett, R. G. "Professional Writing Activity Among Professors of Adult Education." In C. E. Warren (ed.), *Proceedings of the Twenty-Ninth Annual Adult Education Research Conference.* Calgary, Canada: University of Calgary, 1988.

Brockett, R. G. "Development and Utilization of Professional Literature: A Survey of Adult Education Professors." Unpublished manuscript, Center for Adult Learning Research, Montana State University, 1990a.

Brockett, R. G. "Early Ideas on the Training of Leaders for Adult Education." In R. W. Rohfeld (ed.), *Breaking New Ground: The Development of Adult and Workers' Education in North America.* Syracuse, N.Y.: Syracuse University Kellogg Project, 1990b.

Brockett, R. G., and Darkenwald, G. G. "Trends in Research on the Adult Learner." In R. G. Brockett (ed.), *Continuing Education in the Year 2000.* New Directions for Continuing Education, no. 36. San Francisco: Jossey-Bass, 1987.

Brockett, R. G., Hayes, C. W., and Velazquez, L. C. "Graduate Students' Attitudes Toward Professional Development." Paper presented at the annual conference of the American Association for Adult and Continuing Education, Atlantic City, N.J., Oct. 1989.

Brookfield, S. D. *Understanding and Facilitating Adult Learning: A Comprehensive Analysis of Principles and Effective Practices.* San Francisco: Jossey-Bass, 1986.

Brookfield, S. D. *Creating Dynamic Adult Learning Experiences.* San Francisco: Jossey-Bass, 1987a. Audiocassette.

Brookfield, S. D. *Developing Critical Thinkers: Challenging Adults to Explore Alternative Ways of Thinking and Acting.* San Francisco: Jossey-Bass, 1987b.

Brookfield, S. D. (ed.). *Training Educators of Adults: The Theory and Practice of Graduate Adult Education.* London: Routledge, 1988.

Cotton, W. E. *On Behalf of Adult Education: A Historical Examination of the Supporting Literature.* Boston: Center for the Study of Liberal Education for Adults, 1968.

Cross, K. P. *Adults as Learners: Increasing Participation and Facilitating Learning.* San Francisco: Jossey-Bass, 1981.

Darkenwald, G. G., and Merriam, S. B. *Adult Education: Foundations of Practice.* New York: Harper & Row, 1982.

Day, M. J. "Adult Education as a New Educational Frontier: Review of the *Journal of Adult Education* 1929–1941." Unpublished doctoral dissertation, University of Michigan, 1981.

Day, M., and McDermott, W. "Where Has All the History Gone in Graduate Programs of Adult Education?" Paper presented at the National Adult Education Conference, Boston, Nov. 1979.

Dickinson, G., and Rusnell, D. "A Content Analysis of *Adult Education.*" *Adult Education,* 1971, *21* (3), 177–185.

Elias, J. L., and Merriam, S. B. *Philosophical Foundations of Adult Education.* Melbourne, Fla.: Krieger, 1980.

Fisher, J. C., and Martin, L. G. "An Analysis of Research Contributions to the Adult Basic Education Literature 1976–1986." In R. P. Inkster (ed.), *Proceedings of the 28th Annual Adult Education Research Conference.* Laramie: University of Wyoming Press, 1987.

Freire, P. *Pedagogy of the Oppressed.* New York: Herder & Herder, 1970.

Galbraith, M. W., and Zelenak, B. S. "The Education of Adult and Continuing Education Practitioners." In S. B. Merriam and P. M. Cunningham (eds.), *Handbook of Adult and Continuing Education.* San Francisco: Jossey-Bass, 1989.

Garrison, D. R., and Baskett, H. K. "Research and Publishing in Adult Education: A Study of the Approaches and Strategies of the Field's Most Successful Researchers." In R. P. Inkster (ed.), *Proceedings of the 28th Annual Adult Education Research Conference.* Laramie: University of Wyoming, 1987.

Griffith, W. S. "Needs of Associations for Publications in Continuing Education." In A. N. Charters and W. M. Rivera (eds.), *International Seminar on Publications in Continuing Education.* Syracuse, N.Y.: Syracuse University Publications in Continuing Education, 1972.

Hiemstra, R., Snow, B., and Mgulambwa, A. *English Language Adult Education Books: Their Value to Adult Educators* (Technical report no. 4). Syracuse, N.Y.: Kellogg Project, Syracuse University, 1989.

Houle, C. O. *The Design of Education.* San Francisco: Jossey-Bass, 1972.

Houle, C. O. *The Inquiring Mind.* Norman: Oklahoma Research Center for Continuing Professional and Higher Education, University of Oklahoma, 1988. (Originally published 1961.)

Imel, S. "The Field's Literature and Information Sources." In S. B. Merriam and P. M. Cunningham (eds.), *Handbook of Adult and Continuing Education.* San Francisco: Jossey-Bass, 1989.

Jarvis, P. *Adult Learning in the Social Context.* London: Croom Helm, 1987.

Jensen, G., Liveright, A. A., and Hallenbeck, W. (eds.). *Adult Education: Outlines of an Emerging Field of University Study.* Washington, D.C.: American Association for Adult and Continuing Education, 1964.

Kidd, J. R. *How Adults Learn.* (Rev. ed.) Chicago: Follett, 1972.

Knowles, M. S. *The Adult Education Movement in the United States* (Rev. ed.) Melbourne, Fla.: Krieger, 1977.

Knowles, M. S. *The Modern Practice of Adult Education: From Pedagogy to Andragogy.* (Rev. ed.) Chicago: Association Press, 1980.

Knowles, M. S. *The Adult Learner: A Neglected Species.* (3rd ed.) Houston: Gulf Publishers, 1984.

Knox, A. B. "Use of Publications by Adult Education Scholars." In A. N. Charters and W. M. Rivera (eds.), *International Seminar on Publications in Continuing Education.* Syracuse, N.Y.: Syracuse University Publications in Continuing Education, 1972.

Lee, J. "The Contribution of Graduate Research to the Body of Knowledge in Adult Education." Paper presented at the National Adult Education Conference, Boston, Nov. 1979.

Lindeman, E. C. *The Meaning of Adult Education.* Norman: Oklahoma Research Center for Continuing Professional and Higher Education, University of Oklahoma, 1989. (Originally published 1926.)

Long, H. B. "Publication Activity of Selected Professors of Adult Education." *Adult Education,* 1977, *27* (3), 173–186.

Long, H. B., and Agyekum, S. K. "*Adult Education* 1964–1973: Reflections of a Changing Discipline." *Adult Education,* 1974, *24* (2), 99–120.

Martin, E. D. *The Meaning of a Liberal Education.* New York: Norton, 1926.

Peters, J. M., and Banks, B. B. "Adult Education." In H. E. Mitzel (ed.), *Encyclopedia of Education.* (5th ed.) New York: Free Press, 1982.

Pipke, I. "The Gatekeepers: A Multivariate Study of Accepted and Rejected Adult Education Research Conference Abstracts (1978–1980)." *Adult Education Quarterly,* 1984, *34* (2), 71–87.

Rogers, J. M., and Brockett, R. G. "Research and Practice Trends in Education and Aging: A Content Analysis of *Educational Gerontology.*" In C. C. Coggins (ed.), *Proceedings of the 30th Annual Adult Education Research Conference.* Madison: University of Wisconsin, 1989.

Smith, R. M., Aker, G. F., and Kidd, J. R. (eds.). *Handbook of Adult Education.* New York: Macmillan, 1970.

Tough, A. *The Adult's Learning Projects: A Fresh Approach to Theory and Practice in Adult Learning.* (2nd ed.) Austin, Tex.: Learning Concepts, 1979.

CHAPTER 7

Growth and Future
of Graduate Programs

John M. Peters
Burton W. Kreitlow

The authors of the black book outlined for themselves and future professors the conceptual foundations of graduate programs, competencies that graduates should develop, and the role that graduate programs ought to play in the larger field of adult education practice. Their aims were ambitious and their foresight optimistic, for their own ranks were small and their area of study was so new that few other academicians had noticed it or the professors who laid claim to it. Their derring-do was neither wasted nor naive, however, for soon after the book was published, they witnessed a meteoric rise in numbers of graduate programs and graduates from the programs, a plethora of research activities, and the beginnings of a knowledge base to support graduate study in adult education.

The purpose of this chapter is to describe the evolution of graduate programs since the early 1960s, some of the issues and forces that accompanied their development, the current status of graduate programs, and their likely development in the future. We begin by reviewing some statistics that depict program growth over the years, then we describe the features of the curricula offered by universities and colleges, and the programs' organizational structures. We also discuss changes that have occurred in the status of some programs, and we review the standards for graduate programs adopted by the Commission of Professors of Adult Education. We end the chapter with a discussion of possible future directions for the development of graduate programs.

Growth in Numbers

Numbers can be dry and uninteresting, but for professors involved in adult education graduate programs, the numbers that describe the exponential growth of the programs over the past twenty-seven years are important indexes of the health of their enterprise. The first graduate program in adult education began at Columbia University in 1930, but only sixteen programs offered master's and doctoral degrees in North America by 1962 (Houle, 1964). Determining the exact number of programs operating today on the basis of the many surveys and reviews of graduate programs is very difficult (Brookfield, 1988). We read the reports of surveys by Cross (1985), Knott and Ross (1986), Daniel and Kasworm (1985), Kowalski and Weaver (1986), and Brookfield's (1988) own analysis of these works. However, we relied mostly on data from a recently completed survey of programs by Rose and Mason (1990) and the most recent edition of *Peterson's Guide to Graduate Programs in Business, Education, Health, and Law* (1990). Rose and Mason sent us their data, and with their permission we analyzed the data for this chapter. On the basis of these sources, we estimate that currently 66 doctoral programs (Ed.D. and Ph.D.) and 124 master's programs with majors in adult education, continuing education, or extension education operate in North America. Additionally, there are 18 educational specialist degree programs and 9 certificate programs.

A nearly eightfold increase in the number of programs since the early sixties brings with it additional statistics that help depict the evolution of programs since 1964. One set of statistics is the number of people who have graduated from doctoral programs in adult education. Cyril Houle, William Griffith, and their associates have kept a record of these graduates over the years, and their reports show an increase in numbers that parallels the growth in program numbers. By 1965, 556 people had been awarded doctorates in the field (Houle and Buskey, 1966). The number reached approximately 4,000 by the end of 1989 (Griffith, 1988; telephone conversation between William Griffith and Burton Kreitlow, June 1990).

However, the rate of growth in number of graduates has not been steady over the years, and both the number of institutions reporting doctorates and the number of people receiving their doctorates each year have leveled off and declined slightly since the early eighties. The range in the number of graduates between 1975 and 1982 was 157–236; but for the years 1987, 1988, and 1989, the range was 88–163 (Ford and Houle, 1980; Houle and Ford, 1978; Griffith and Parrish, 1986; Griffith, 1988; telephone conversation between William Griffith and Burton Kreitlow, June 1990).

Such fluctuations may in the long run prove to be normal for the graduate programs involved, but for now they seem to be mostly associated with the conspicuous absence in recent censuses of graduates of formerly high-producing programs such as Indiana University, Auburn University, Boston University, and Arizona State University. Although some new programs that were not in existence ten to fifteen years ago are now awarding degrees in the field, they have apparently not yet graduated enough students to equal the decline created by institutions no longer graduating doctoral students. These numbers and their apparent decrease should be interpreted with some degree of caution, however, since reports were not kept on an annual basis in the eighties and there is no assurance that all institutions awarding doctorates in adult education in a given year actually reported them. It should also be pointed out that no such surveys are made of master's degree program graduates or of nonmajors enrolled in graduate courses in adult education.

Not only did the number of doctoral graduates increase over the past twenty-seven years, the occupational backgrounds of the students also became more varied. In the fifties and sixties, most graduate students in adult education were administrators from university-based programs, especially extension programs (Houle and Buskey, 1966). Adult basic education (ABE) teachers, counselors, and administrators began to enter programs in large numbers in the late sixties and the seventies. In the seventies, trainers in private and public agencies, educators from higher education institutions, and health educators also entered the graduate programs in greater numbers. In the eighties, the base of students expanded to include personnel from almost all types of organizations involved in the practice of adult education. One of the significant changes in the student profile has been the enrollment of more foreign students, a trend discussed by Cunningham in Chapter Fourteen. Additional new groups are now enrolling in the graduate programs, such as educators involved in environmental and peace movements (Deshler, Chapter Fifteen).

Another statistic that reveals much about the character of adult education graduate programs is faculty size. According to a survey done by Knox and a committee of the CPAE, faculty size was an issue of great importance to professors who were involved in creating and maintaining graduate programs in the early seventies (Knox, 1973). In the survey, the term *size* referred to the number of full-time and part-time faculty members in a program. The survey found that professors were concerned that the range of content offered by a program can be limited by a small faculty, especially when professors are expected to do research and provide services to the field of practice.

In 1973, Knox reported: "Over the years, most adult education graduate programs have consisted of one or two full-time equivalent (FTE) professors of adult education. Currently most programs consist of two or three FTE professors with very few that have four or more" (p. 33). Today, the "typical" number of full-time faculty members per program is more difficult to estimate. According to the Rose and Mason data (1990), programs vary widely in the number of their full-time and part-time faculty members. Rose and Mason asked respondents to specify the names of full-time and the names of part-time faculty members, but not all of the respondents separated the names into these two categories. We counted the names and put the results in Tables 2 and 3. The first column in Table 2 lists the number of faculty members, or faculty size (for full- and part-time faculty), and the second column lists the number of institutions reporting each faculty size. (It should be noted that seven of sixty-nine respondents did not report the names of faculty members, and thus are not included in Table 2.) Table 2 shows that no particular full- and part-time faculty size characterizes institutions offering graduate programs in adult education. The largest single number of institutions ($n = 9$) report a combined faculty size of three members, but nearly as many ($n = 7$) have a faculty size of eight. Four institutions have between fourteen and eighteen full- and part-time faculty members in adult education.

A more revealing statistic is the number of full-time-only faculty members. Table 3 lists the size of full-time-only faculty in the left column and the number of institutions reporting each faculty size in the right column. (It should be noted that fully a third of the sixty-nine respondents did not list the names of full-time-only faculty members, and they are not included in these numbers.) By far the greatest single number of institutions reported a full-time faculty of two members ($n = 12$), and the next largest number of institutions reported a full-time faculty of one ($n = 8$). While two institutions have between eleven and eighteen faculty members, just over half the institutions ($n = 24$) have faculty sizes of three or fewer. Thus, graduate programs in adult education typically remain small in terms of the number of full-time faculty members, and the majority of programs are no larger than programs in operation at the time of the Knox (1973) survey, at least in the number of full-time faculty members staffing the programs.

What has changed since 1964 (and since the Knox survey) is the number of graduate programs, the number of doctoral graduates, and the total number of adult education professors. But the growth has not been uniform, and some programs have actually ceased to exist. We discuss some of these programs later in the chapter. First, however, we discuss some features

Table 2. Combined Size of Full- and Part-Time Faculty, by Institution.

Faculty Size	Number of Institutions
1	6
2	6
3	9
4	8
5	3
6	5
7	6
8	7
9	3
10	4
11–13	1
14–18	4
	Total 62

Table 3. Size of Full-Time Faculty, by Institution.

Faculty Size	Number of Institutions
1	8
2	12
3	4
4	4
5	4
6	1
7	2
8	2
9	0
10	1
11–13	1
14–18	2
	Total 41

of the existing programs that run beneath the numbers, such as the content of their curricula, the kinds of knowledge being taught and researched, and the way the programs relate to other programs on their university campuses.

Graduate Program Curricula

The authors of the black book did not identify the specific contents and structure that ought to constitute graduate programs.

However, in various chapters, they did make clear that much of the program content should be drawn from the related disciplines. And they proposed a tentative theory of practice that we must assume was meant as a keystone content area for most programs. They also identified some broad knowledge domains that might constitute a curriculum. Liveright (1964) had this to say about possible content domains in adult education: "In addition to courses or seminars (in the disciplines), sound graduate programs of adult education should increasingly include special courses and seminars concerned with the philosophy, values, and ethics of adult education; with its techniques and methods; with its history and social background. The place of adult education in the community, the adult education learning situation, and research methods in adult education, should also be thoroughly understood" (p. 100).

Liveright also stressed that because of the variety of agencies, programs, and methods that characterize the practice of adult education, "a graduate program is likely to emphasize content and subject matter which concerns itself primarily with broad knowledge and understanding . . . rather than with specific skills and a high degree of specialization" (p. 100). It is safe to say that Liveright's expectations were shared by most professors who worked in programs of his day.

About twenty years later, researchers began to examine the nature of graduate programs and to publish or report the results to a wide audience of professors (United Nations Educational, Scientific, and Cultural Organization, 1982; Cross, 1985; Daniel and Kasworm, 1985; Knott and Ross, 1986). These program surveys and others to follow them, however, depicted mainly the courses offered by programs, a common but admittedly somewhat limited representation of program content.

Rose and Mason (1990) asked one professor from each identifiable graduate program to list course requirements in their master's and doctoral programs. All sixty-nine institutions responding to Rose and Mason's survey offered the master's degree. Of the respondents, fifty-seven listed specific course requirements or content area requirements for their master's degree, two replied that no specific courses were required of their students, and ten did not respond to this section of the questionnaire.

Forty-three of the institutions reported that they offered the doctoral degree. Of these, three reported no specific course requirements, and nine did not respond to the survey question. All of the thirty-one remaining institutions listed specific courses or course content areas for the doctoral degree. They indicated that doctoral program requirements included the same courses or course content areas that were required in their master's degree program. Most also listed additional requirements for the doctoral degree; however, only seventeen respondents identified specific courses in adult education at the doctoral level.

We grouped the courses and content areas from the responses to Rose and Mason's survey into course domains, based on course titles or content area descriptions provided by respondents. Table 4 lists the course domain requirements and the number of programs reporting course requirements in each domain for the master's degree.

Table 4 shows that all programs that listed requirements included one or more courses in the introduction/foundations of adult education domain. This domain includes such course titles or content area descriptions as introduction to adult education; foundations of adult education; survey of adult education;

Table 4. Course Domains Required by
Master's Degree Graduate Programs.

Course Domain	Number of Programs (n = 57)
Introduction/Foundations of Adult Education	57
Program Planning	45
Adult Learning and Development	44
Adult Education Methods	30
Administration	14
Seminar in Adult Education	9
Internship/Practicum	6
Research Methods/Statistics	35

adult education in the United States; history, philosophy, and sociology of adult education; principles of adult education; and social foundations of adult education.

The second most frequently cited course domain was program planning, followed closely by adult learning and development. The program planning domain included such course titles or content descriptions as program planning, program development, curriculum development in adult education, and extension program development and evaluation. The adult learning and development domain included titles such as the adult learner, adult learning, adult learning and development, and psychology of adult learners.

The domain of adult education methods was required by slightly more than 50 percent of the programs, and titles and content descriptions in this domain included methods of teaching adults, techniques of teaching adults, teaching adults, and methods of adult education. Administration was the next most frequently listed domain. Included in this domain were such titles as administration of adult education and organization and administration of adult education. Nine programs required seminars in adult education, but the exact focus of these seminars was not specified. Internships and practicums were required by six programs. Research methods and statistics courses were grouped and listed at the end of the table because these courses are not necessarily a content area of adult education but were required by over 60 percent of the master's degree programs.

The statistics on course offerings at the doctoral level are very sketchy. As we mentioned earlier, specific *adult education* courses and content areas for the doctoral degree were listed for only seventeen of the forty-three doctoral programs in the Rose and Mason survey. To repeat, however, all thirty-one institutions for which any doctoral-level courses were listed also indicated that the master's core requirements applied to the doctoral program. Other courses or content areas cited by respondents with doctoral programs were in the areas of research methods and statistics, and all thirty-one programs that specified courses cited one or both of these areas as being required of their doctoral students.

Among the adult education courses at the doctoral level that were specified by respondents, most were in the areas of administration and leadership. The other courses cited most frequently were in the areas of curriculum and instruction, philosophy, history, issues, and advanced learning theories. However, these course areas were scattered throughout the institutional reports, and no more than six programs could be identified as requiring more than one of these course areas. This leaves us with little on which to base any conclusions about the distinction between the master's and doctoral degrees, except that, clearly, doctoral students are expected to develop a more advanced understanding of research and statistics.

We can only generally compare the course domains of the Rose and Mason survey to Liveright's (1964) suggested foci of graduate programs. It seems that programs are offering course work in the areas of philosophy, history, and social background of adult education as suggested by Liveright, but the data summarized here do not reveal to what extent students are studying these areas. For example, we can only assume that these areas are at least touched upon in the obligatory introductory course, but the special courses on history and philosophy that were cited in the Rose and Mason survey (relatively few were cited) probably come closer to what Liveright had in mind. At least 50 percent of the graduate programs in the survey offered courses in techniques and methods, though far more offered courses in program planning and curriculum, a content area not included in Liveright's vision of a graduate program.

It is probably more fruitful to compare our findings from Rose and Mason's survey to contemporary studies of adult education graduate programs. Brookfield (1988) reviewed most of the studies completed by 1987 and concluded: "Notwithstanding ambiguities in definition and classification, and the variations in ranked importance, the core elements of the graduate adult education studies are remarkably consistent" (p. 274). He went on to identify the following as five key areas of adult education curricula: program development, adult learning and development, foundations of adult education, teaching methods and instructional processes, and the management and administration of adult education institutions.

Thus, our findings are consistent with Brookfield's interpretation of other studies, except that he did not mention the areas of research methods and statistics. The findings are also consistent with the results of surveys done by Holmberg (1984) and Touchette (1989), both of whom studied course offerings by institutions around the world but whose statistics on North American programs most closely approximate those in the Rose and Mason survey. It is of particular interest for us to note that adult education course domains have not changed much in the past two decades since Knox (1973) identified essentially the same domains from his survey of graduate programs.

Only one of the studies reviewed by Brookfield (1988) drew a distinction between courses offered at the master's and doctoral levels. It seems useful to review this study in more detail since it relates to our concern about having limited information about doctoral courses. Knott and Ross (1986) reported data on forty-six programs in 1986. Their data base included thirty-three doctoral programs. Knott and Ross were particularly interested in comparing course requirements to the list of courses recommended in the *Standards for Graduate Programs in Adult Education*. (The standards are given in the Resource at the end of the book, and they will be discussed in another section of this chapter). Here is their summary of the findings and their comparisons.

> The recommended [by the standards] course on the study of adult learning was addressed by most programs, with 25 of the 33 responding doctoral programs requiring a course on adult learning or development. The study of methods of inquiry also appears to be well represented, with 21 of the responding programs requiring a course on research in adult education. It is not possible, however, to determine from course titles if these courses are "advanced" beyond the Master's level of study. The recommendation [in the Standards] for an " . . . in depth analysis of social, political and economic forces that have shaped the philosophical foundation of adult education" (p. 4) may be addressed

in the content of the 17 required foundation courses
or the nine history/philosophy courses; it is again
difficult to be certain of the level of depth of these
courses from a title alone. The recommendation for
the study of leadership, including theories of administration and management, appears not to be
met, at least as a required course, with only seven
of the responding institutions reporting a required
course in the administration of adult education. . . .
There is little evidence of specific courses focusing
on the study of issues that impinge on policy formation, with only three required seminar courses
and three problems/controversies courses reported
(p. 29).

The findings by Knott and Ross are practically identical to our
own analysis of the Rose and Mason data. We will have more
to say about the differences in master's and doctoral degrees a
little later in this chapter.

The Rose and Mason (1990) survey also asked respondents to identify specializations offered by their programs. We
found that the term *specialization* was interpreted in different ways
by the respondents, but most of them seemed to relate it to what
they considered to be their program's particular emphasis among
many possibilities in the field of study. Some respondents related
the term to subfields of adult education, such as adult basic education or continuing professional education. Others related it
to knowledge domains, such as adult learning, or thought of
specialties in terms of organizational contexts for adult education, such as the Cooperative Extension Service. A few people
considered the "general field" to be their specialty. Of the sixty-
nine respondents, 70 percent reported one or more program
specializations. Table 5 contains a list of specializations offered
by the programs. Respondents could list more than one specialty
area.

Perhaps the most interesting feature of Table 5 is the large
number of programs that offer a specialty in the areas of human resource development, training, or vocational-technical

Table 5. Specialty Areas Offered by Graduate Programs.

Specialty Area	Number of Programs (n = 49)
Human Resource Development/Training/ Vocational-Technical Education	38
Administration/Leadership	20
Literacy/Adult Basic Education	13
Gerontology	12
Continuing Professional Education	10
General Field of Study	10
Instructional Methods	10
Cooperative Extension	7
Continuing Higher Education	7
Planning and Evaluation	7
International Education	7
Community Education/Development	5
Adult Learning and Development	6

education for adults. These closely related areas were not emphasized by programs in the black book era, and they reflect major new trends in industrial and governmental training that have occurred since then. However, while the area of human resource development is listed by many programs as a specialty, its relationship to the broader field of adult education study and practice is far from clear. Indeed, whether or not it is a specialty area at all is a subject of considerable debate within the professoriate (Griffith, 1986; Watkins, Cameron, and Marsick, 1986). Deshler also discusses human resource development in Chapter Fifteen of this book.

Literacy/adult basic education has become a specialty area within the past twenty years or so, and growth in this area of practice is discussed in a later section of this chapter. Gerontology as a specialty reflects an interest in aging that dates to the graduate programs of the 1950s, but interest in this area seems to be growing. Specializations in continuing professional education

and continuing higher education parallel growth in these sub-
fields of adult education practice, and both are the subjects of
a growing body of literature. International education is gradually attracting the attention of curriculum committees, as the
"internationalization" of adult education increases (Cunningham,
Chapter Fourteen). The remaining areas of specialization on
the list are not unlike what might have been reported by members of the CPAE in the sixties had they been asked the same
survey question. It will be instructive to ask the question again
in ten years; the list will likely grow by then. It is interesting
to note that Jones and Galbraith (1985) identified twenty-eight
different areas of concentration in their survey of graduate programs, and the names of these areas are about the same as the
names of the areas in Table 5.

What appears to be an increase in the number of specializations of programs developed over the past twenty-seven years
since the black book was published relates to faculty size, since
the smaller the faculty the more difficult it is for a program to
offer both core courses and many specialized courses. The top
concern cited by professors of graduate programs in a survey
by Knox (1973) was how to determine the proper balance in
specialty and core courses and which specialty courses to offer
in their programs. Then and now, the usual response to this
problem is for programs to add part-time or adjunct faculty
members to offer courses in their own areas of practice and to
form joint programs with other faculties, such as higher education and vocational-technical education. However, the problem
of balance remains in the face of growing interests in subfields
of adult education and the predominance of relatively small full-
time graduate faculties in the field.

The appropriate mixture of courses in graduate programs
was also reflected in another issue addressed in the Knox survey: how courses in other departments ought to be used in the
adult education curricula. The issue revolves around the desirability for adult education students to take courses in other departments, despite the fact that sometimes such courses are not accessible to nonmajors or simply are not relevant to the interests of
adult education students. This issue also reflects a more historical

and fundamental concern, how adult education programs ought to relate to other disciplines and professional areas of study.

Perhaps the strongest theme expressed in the black book was that the study of adult education should be grounded in related disciplines, such as sociology, psychology, and political science, an assumption that also applies to graduate coursework. The professors who wrote the black book had little choice but to look to related disciplines for inspiration and content, and many of them were guided by their own training in the related disciplines. However, we have little evidence of how strong this reliance on the related disciplines is today. It seems reasonable to assume that as the number and range of specialty course offerings in adult education increase and as more programs stress a core set of required courses in adult education, the number of courses in related disciplines will diminish over time. Another factor that will affect curriculum decisions is the growing body of knowledge in adult education per se.

Jarvis (Chapter One) points out that the discourse in the field of study has shifted away from the related disciplines and that knowledge from the disciplines is increasingly regarded specifically as adult education knowledge. He further points out that this is a sign of growing maturity of the field. Indeed, Boyd and Apps (1980) developed their conceptual model for adult education on the premise that we err in drawing knowledge from the disciplines "until we have clearly understood the structure, function, problems and purposes of adult education itself" (p. 2). One could conclude from these views that adult education as a field of study should be located next to the disciplines, not in them.

Graduate programs may be adopting a less direct and dependent relationship to the disciplines as adult education acquires a knowledge base that is expressed in its own terms for its own aims, applications, and specialties. This would suggest that graduate programs are positioned to further develop needed depth in the theories and concepts of adult education practice and will struggle less in their attempts to translate knowledge found in the disciplines and apply it directly to practice. The development of such depth in theories would be welcomed by scholars who decry the lack of theory in the field and by those who argue that sound theories of adult education are needed and are ultimately practical (Boshier, 1978). It might also appeal to scholars who argue that direct translation of the content of related disciplines into principles of practice is wrongheaded and in any case, technically impossible (Boyd and Apps, 1980; Plecas and Sork, 1986; Usher and Bryant, 1987; Bright, 1988).

However, a move to develop graduate curricula specific to the field at the expense of gaining knowledge from the related disciplines carries with it the very real dangers of programs becoming parochial and isolated within their institutions and the rejection of what many claim should be a necessary interdisciplinary approach to the study of adult education. It is difficult to conceive of a program with no particular relationship to the disciplines, and programs will continue to rely on the disciplines to some extent (Cookson, 1983). How to strike an effective balance between developing adult education knowledge and at the same time drawing needed knowledge resources from the related disciplines is the problem.

Organizational Structure

The issues of graduate programs' faculty size, specialization, and relationship to other disciplines are related to another issue ranked high by professors in the Knox (1973) survey: the advantages and disadvantages of adult education being a part of a joint department. In most universities, a faculty size of two, three, or four full-time members does not justify a freestanding department. This is about the size of most adult education faculties, so there are few such free-standing departments in North America. Indeed, our analysis of the Rose and Mason (1990) survey data reveals that most adult education departments are linked in some form with one or more other programs or are specialty areas within larger departments. We identified thirty-nine different names of departments, divisions, centers, and other organizational units that housed the adult education graduate programs of the respondents to the survey. These names included adult education (only five of these), adult and higher education (five), vocational and adult education (there were several variations of this combined title), leadership and policy studies, human and organizational development, educational studies, adult education and instructional studies, and so on.

These results are reminiscent of the range of program structures reported almost twenty years ago by Griffith and Cloutier (1971), who identified seventeen program designations for doctoral programs. Griffith identified a much greater number of program designations entitled adult education than we did, but we used formal organizational designations, such as departments, within which joint or subprograms in adult education may indeed be titled as adult education. This diversity in what we call ourselves and in the way we are identified within our institutions was seen by Griffith and Cloutier as a major obstacle to professionalization of the field.

There are many pros and cons to this organizational issue. For example, if adult education is a part of a joint department, students have more direct access to a broader range of faculty resources, but the adult education faculty may lose some of its autonomy and flexibility in programming. The additional faculty resources provided by a joint arrangement may help alleviate the problem of a restricted range of course offerings, especially in regard to the balance between core and specialty courses, but the additional resources do not necessarily provide the kinds of curriculum content needed by adult education students. Theoretically, adult education students have access to courses in another program area whether or not the adult education program shares a department with that area. Joint departments are more often justified as an administrative convenience than as a logical structure for curriculum content. But given the realities of university organizational needs and constraints, most small (and sometimes, large) faculties can expect to be located in joint departments or as specialty areas of larger departments.

Another organizational issue involves professorial roles. This issue was uncovered by the Knox (1973) survey and concerns the competencies and appropriate mix of roles that professors play in graduate programs. The issue grew out of a tension between demands of the field and demands of universities and the profession at large. Knox identified at least three broad roles that professors could play in a graduate program. The first role is that of a scholar in a closely related discipline, a role that has little direct connection to practice. For example, a faculty member with training in psychology might be especially concerned with theoretical issues and research relating to adult learning and would contribute this orientation to the curriculum. A second role is that of the clinical professor who focuses on an understanding of adult education practice. The third role is an eclectic one, involving professors who are interested in working "between" the disciplines and practice, helping students relate the formal knowledge base to problems of practice.

Actually, these roles are not so clear-cut, unless faculty members with particular competencies have been carefully selected and hired to fulfill the roles. Most programs have faculty members filling two or more of these roles, and often the same professor will fill all roles. It is usually in those programs that are staffed with one or more professors who have their doctorate in a related discipline that Knox's first role is played out. However, a variation on the discipline-oriented role today is the role of the professor who is concerned with research and theory in adult education but who is not particularly concerned with working directly with practitioner problems as the clinical professor would be. This role may represent a new breed of professor in adult education, made possible by the development and refinement of knowledge about adult learning and adult education processes through research in adult education per se. We may be witnessing the growth of this role today, as an increasing number of professors delve even more deeply into research on, for example, the cognitive aspects of adult learning or readiness for self-directed learning. However, this role may exacerbate a problem long experienced by professors in graduate programs, that of balancing the relationship between theory and practice (Cervero, Chapter Two).

All the above organizational issues in graduate programs have been the subject of constant review and considerable debate within the professoriate. When these issues were discussed at meetings of the CPAE, there were periodic calls for reform, direction, order, and more commonly, standards to guide the inevitable growth of graduate programs. We discuss these standards next.

Standards for Program Development

Beginning with the first signs of explosive growth in the number of graduate programs in adult education, members of the CPAE were concerned that too many programs were being started too quickly with too little information about what constitutes a high-quality graduate program. The Knox (1973) survey was designed to find out from the professors themselves factors that influenced their decisions about content, structure, and other aspects of the development and maintenance of graduate programs. Unfortunately, the survey results were not immediately translated into the desired guidelines for professors to follow as they developed new programs or changed existing ones.

Many of the members of the CPAE remained convinced, however, that something had to be done about the development of graduate programs by overzealous and, in some cases, "unqualified" professors and university administrators who were eager to capitalize on this new and growing area of study and practice. The members decried what they perceived as unwarranted entry into the field by professors from other fields whose programs were dead or dying, by other professors untrained in the field, and by "charlatans" and the shameless exploitation of available funding for the development of new graduate programs. Even if this alarm did not sound loudly enough in the ears of professors who were opposed to credentialing and regulation on any grounds, the time had apparently come to pull in the crazy quilt of diffuse ideas, designs, and false starts and produce for future program planners, deans, and accreditation agencies a coherent set of guidelines for the creation and maintenance of graduate programs in adult education.

In 1986, after years of debate and agonizing over aims and means, the CPAE finally adopted standards for graduate programs in adult education (see the Resource at the back of the book). With the formulation of the standards, the CPAE had achieved a significant milestone in its history of attempting to guide the development and maintenance of graduate programs in adult education.

The standards are the most succinct statement available of the CPAE's view of how a graduate program should be constituted. Unfortunately, the time since their adoption has been too short for anyone to identify their influence on the decisions of professors and administrators responsible for the development and maintenance of graduate programs. And use of the standards by accreditation agencies has not been recorded. However, the standards were debated fairly and are the expression of the vision of three generations of professors who have the benefit of more experience and a greater variety of voices than did their predecessors. The standards communicate to the larger academic community the essence of adult education graduate programs.

Rise and Fall of Programs

The greatest rate of increase in new programs occurred in 1968–1978, and the rate at which programs have been added since then has gradually declined. This pattern of growth roughly parallels the growth curve for higher education institutions in general. It is also closely associated with the infusion of public funds into higher education institutions in the sixties and seventies and with the pattern of growth in college and university student populations, especially the growth in the number of older, part-time adult students.

The black book was written in what Mayhew (1972) called the "euphoric 1960s" for graduate programs. However, by the late sixties, it became apparent that severe inequities existed in terms of access to the riches of higher education by women, minorities, older adults, and the poor. The Carnegie Commission on Higher Education and the Commission on Non-Traditional Study, among other commissions established at the end of the decade, brought these inequities to the attention of academe, government, and the general public. The commissions proposed new forms of higher education to accommodate a wider diversity of educational needs, mainly the needs of the adult population (Gould and Cross, 1972; Houle, 1973; Hall and Associates, 1974). The significance of this increased attention to adult higher education was not lost on professors of adult education, who not only felt vindicated in their ideas about adult learning and participation in education but who also anticipated new sources of students for their programs and new job opportunities for their graduates.

Additionally, major new social legislation, including the Adult Education Act, was passed in the sixties at about the time the black book was published. New educational programs for disadvantaged adults were thrust into place, and thousands of teachers and administrators were hired to staff them, especially in the area of adult basic education. These personnel needed training, and people looked to universities for leadership in providing staff development programs. By the beginning of the seventies, the number of higher education institutions offering some kind of adult education program at the graduate level more than doubled, and most of the growth could be attributed to the response of institutions to the training needs of ABE personnel (Kozoll, 1972).

In the southeastern region of the country, twenty-two institutions developed training programs during 1969–1971 alone. This phenomenal growth occurred under the leadership of the Southern Regional Education Board, which had received funding from the U.S. Office of Education to develop training programs for ABE personnel in the Southeast. By 1972, twelve of the twenty-two institutions had received approval from their respective university councils to offer the master's degree, five were awaiting approval, and two had established new doctoral programs (Kozoll, 1972). Although institutions in the Southeast developed the most new programs, institutions in all regions of the nation experienced an infusion of federal funds that helped spur the growth of graduate programs. No record exists of the exact number of programs that resulted from these funds, however.

Although most of the sixteen graduate programs in place in 1962 also grew during this time (and some of them with the help of federal funding and growth in student populations), by far the bulk of development in programs occurred as the result of new legislation and changes in the climate for adult learning on campuses around the nation. The growth in programs continued during the seventies, and at the same time the public seemed to be paying more attention to the need for adult education of all kinds.

Another consistent source of support for program development has been funding from foundations. Perhaps the most prominent and lasting of these foundations is the Kellogg Foundation, which in 1956 granted $26,500 to the CPAE to aid in its development of graduate programs. In the early eighties, the foundation provided $50,000 to help support the exchange of nine North American and twelve British professors, and later it supported the development of an international research conference (Cunningham, Chapter Fourteen). In the mid eighties, the foundation also funded a two-year program in leadership for young scholars in adult education and provided millions of dollars to create or expand research centers connected to graduate programs at five universities (University of Georgia, University of Oklahoma, Montana State University, Syracuse University, and Michigan State University). All but the Montana State Kellogg-funded center are operating today, although the Montana graduate program remains in operation. This recent infusion of foundation funds clearly has the potential to substantially upgrade the quality of research and teaching available at a few universities. It also adds to the overall capacity of the field of study to develop. The funding is a strong show of faith in graduate programs and their research potential, and thus increases the credibility of the field as a whole.

As impressive as these numbers and descriptions are, however, all developments in graduate adult education have not been positive; some programs have declined even as others have risen. No one has examined in depth the rise and fall of graduate programs. Although some researchers have documented early programs, the best of this research (Brockett, 1990) stops short of the 1960s. We do not have good documentation of how programs are developed from the ground up, and we have little to go on when we try to understand why some programs fail.

Some of the factors that contribute to program decline are obvious, such as the disappearance of external funds, but factors internal to individual institutions are not as obvious. For example, the end of federal funding meant the demise of at least half of the programs in the Southeast that began operations with the stimulus of federal funds twenty years ago. Most institutions simply did not support the programs once the project money was gone. The rise and fall of such programs did not go unnoticed, and the reasons for the changes are generally well understood. However, the inner workings of a program in decline rarely are disseminated to professors in other institutions. When professors whose programs are in decline do share information, they are usually searching for support from colleagues. An example of the problems of an older, well-known graduate program will illustrate what we mean.

The Florida State University program was in decline for at least six years before Kreitlow was asked to intervene as a consultant for one semester. After two weeks on the job "to help solve a problem," Kreitlow knew that he was dealing with a crisis that had but two potential outcomes: "up or down." In the Florida State case, the trigger for the crisis was the death of the most senior faculty member. It took three years, but the program recovered and new development proceeded. When such a recovery occurs, the opportunity for major development is similar to that present at the start of a program.

Many of the details of Florida State's decline were presented in a report to the CPAE (Kreitlow, 1988). The 1988 report identified nine danger signals and discussed steps that should be taken when they first appear. The danger signals are:

1. Isolation from other fields and disciplines
2. Lack of commitment to the department with which the program is affiliated
3. Acceptance of educators not trained in adult education who were unloaded from other departments
4. Homogeneous age range of faculty members
5. Lack of internal communication
6. Decline in funded research, fellowships, and scholarships

7. Limited publication record
8. Decline in image within the school or college
9. Concerns by graduate students as to status of the program relative to programs in other universities

It is easy to see that the reverse of some of these indicators ought to be conducive to the development of new programs and the continuance of long-established programs.

There are other examples of programs in decline. Boston University rebounded from one decline, but after a second decline no further doctoral students were admitted. Arizona State University has also phased out its program and accepts no new doctoral students. The Ontario Institute for Studies in Education can no longer admit students to the Ph.D. program but maintains its doctor of education option. The University of Chicago, unable to replace staff members, eliminated its program in adult education. Another of the early programs in the field, the program at Indiana University, no longer admits doctoral students, and the program is now limited to one faculty member. The same is true of the program at the University of Missouri, Columbia.

Politics, changing social conditions, the loss of strong faculty leaders, changing institutional priorities, hard economic times, lethargy—any of these can account for the decline of graduate programs in any field. However, in a field of study that is new and not entirely understood, such as adult education, time spent in studying what it takes for a program to grow in higher education would be time well spent. Such a study should be done by the CPAE or some enterprising professor and a doctoral student. It could result in lessons from which professors learn to survive! We next examine some other implications for the future development of graduate programs.

Future Program Development

Developers of graduate programs will in the future be faced with some of the same decisions that the founders of today's programs faced, and some new decision factors will undoubtedly arise to challenge their program development skills. We think the old and new challenges will include the need for a coherent framework for determining program content, the need to make sharper distinctions between the various degrees offered by institutions, the problem of program assessment, how to deliver programs to new and old clientele, how to involve students in program decisions and implementation, and finally, what the proper role of the Commission of Professors of Adult Education should be as programs are added, modified, or removed from the field of study. The reader will probably wish to add others, but our list of challenges is discussed in this final section of the chapter.

Framework for Development. A consensus seems to be developing regarding core content in adult education that should be included in all graduate programs. However, the course areas now offered by most graduate programs are not very different from the areas that programs offered twenty or more years ago, despite the proliferation of specialty courses. Moreover, programs do not easily differentiate expectations of students who come from different backgrounds and who perceive different goals for their practices. We need to critically examine what we have developed so far as a basic set of course requirements in the light of the varied aims and processes of the field of practice, in terms of how the core content relates to specialty curriculum content, and in terms of how adult education content ought to be developed with respect to the related disciplines.

A framework for constructing programs is basic to the development of a program with depth, breadth, and relevance. The authors of the black book had their own concepts and ideas in mind when they speculated about the content and structure of graduate programs, but they lacked a coherent framework for constructing programs. Instead, they were guided by their own experiences as professors. Some had training in the social sciences, and they were keen observers of the field. Thus, they were influenced by the possibility of the social science disciplines as sources of content, and they were mindful of the need of practitioners for knowledge about the organization and delivery of educational programs for adults. The professors also believed that certain basic competencies are central to the effective use of this knowledge, so they drew from the few existing studies of adult educator competencies (such as Chamberlain, 1961) for templates of professional adult educators who would carry the banner of a new profession into the strange new world of practice.

As reasonable as this approach was at the time, it was speculative and in some respects before its time, and of course it lacked the luxury of much hindsight. Also, as Cunningham discusses in Chapter Fourteen, their template might have been overly narrow, focused as it was on instrumentalist aims and guided by the scientific method. The list of competencies that helped guide their selection of curriculum content had a strong bias toward administrative competency, further narrowing the scope of the resulting curricula. Finally, the CPAE members could not be fully aware of the tumultuous changes that were about to occur in society in general and higher education in particular, changes that would help shape future decisions about program content and structure.

Since the black book was published, dozens of organizing concepts and frameworks have been developed with the intent to further our understanding of the complexities of the field of practice and study. They have varying levels of implications for the development of graduate programs. These attempts to construct a framework fall into the following five categories:

1.   Conceptualizations of the general field of study and practice (such as Schroeder, 1970, 1980; Boyd and Apps, 1980)
2.   Distinctions in terms of the nature of adult learners and implications for practice and training (such as Knowles, 1980; Fellenz and Conti, 1989)
3.   Identification of competencies needed by adult education practitioners in general (such as Grabowski, 1981) and specializations in adult education (such as James, 1983)
4.   Typologies of adult educator roles (such as Houle, 1970) and the competencies or proficiencies needed by those that play the roles (such as Knox, 1979)
5.   Frameworks developed especially for the design of graduate programs (such as Boyd, 1969; Brookfield, 1988; Usher and Bryant, 1989)

Although these categories and the variety of ideas within them reflect what Brookfield (1988) referred to as the "paradigmatic plurality" that frames adult education study and practice, they do reflect a maturation of the field of study in terms of the determination of its scholars to clarify the basis of study and practice. We need to continue developing frameworks in the future, but with increasing specificity of the factors that enter into decisions about program content and structure.

The level of specificity achieved by Knox (1979) in his identification of proficiencies appropriate to practitioners in general and to three categories of practitioners in particular (administrators, teachers and counselors, and policy makers) is a step in the right direction. However, Boshier (1985) developed a model for the design of training programs that is closer to the ideal of accommodating the multiple factors that enter into programming decisions. Boshier developed his model for an international audience, and his concept of training was broader than graduate education alone. But his model can be applied to the development of graduate programs on a single continent.

The model stipulates that the content and process of graduate education for an adult educator would be shaped by the role occupied by the adult educator, by the educator's primacy or level of professional commitment to that role, and by the outcomes the educator is seeking by performing in that role. Boshier divides the roles of adult educators into those of planners (administrators, programmers, policy makers) and teachers (animateurs, lecturers, and counselors). By the term *primacy*, or *professional commitment*, Boshier essentially means full-time or part-time employment as adult educators. The outcomes in the model are technical competence, social change, social responsibility, and social integration. Boshier's model is broader and more inclusive than competency and proficiency models, as it more nearly accommodates the multiple aims of adult education and the variety of work situations in which adult educators are involved.

This tentative and heuristic device designed by Boshier is the kind of framework professors who are faced with developing graduate programs need. As we mentioned previously, early programs were based on the designer's personal experience and speculation about the general competencies needed by adult educators, regardless of their practice situation and goal. The surveys of graduate programs have shown evidence of a growing number of specialty courses being offered by the programs, in addition to or even at the expense of coursework on such general topics as history and philosophy of adult education, methods, and adult learning. However, adult educators do not agree on a framework for making such curriculum choices, and the choices remain a local one, based on the interests of the professors designing the program.

If we are to have a profession of adult education, we need a coherent and systematic way of preparing professionals at the graduate level, along with a recognizable body of advanced knowledge and a corpus of literature that as Houle says, "lies at the heart of the graduate program and is the central purpose of its existence" (Knowles, Sheats, and Houle, 1972, p. 307). A conceptually critical approach to examining our programs such as the one begun by Boshier would, we hope, help us achieve the necessary balance in our basic knowledge about adult education, our specialized knowledge, and the integration of these with the related disciplines.

Distinction in Degrees. The surveys of graduate programs conducted over the years show few sharp distinctions between coursework required for the master's and doctoral degrees, although the standards of the CPAE clearly delineate such differences (Knott and Ross, 1986). The differences that are reported are primarily in the areas of research emphasis, special seminars, or simply higher expectations for doctoral students. Often, doctoral and master's students participate together in the same courses, further indicating that few distinctions are made in the level of content available to students seeking different degrees.

The lack of clear-cut distinctions in master's and doctoral programs for adult education majors parallels a broader problem in most graduate schools, where little consensus exists regarding the purpose of the master's degree (Mayhew, 1972; Carroll, 1989). In adult education, as in most other fields of education, the master's degree is considered a practitioner's degree, but for many people, so is the doctorate, especially the doctor of education degree. Although it is beyond the scope of this chapter to explore the differences and similarities in the Ph.D. degree and the Ed.D. degree (this issue was explored by Knott and Ross, 1986), suffice it to say that most people who receive either degree end up as practitioners, not as scholars. Thus, the distinction between the master's degree and the doctoral degree about preparing practitioners does not hold up in adult education. Generally, the distinction between the two degrees is assumed to be a function of level of study and level of employment upon graduation. Students pursuing the doctoral degree are expected to study at the most advanced level available at most institutions, and they engage in a more research-oriented program than do students who pursue only the master's degree. Moreover, they usually expect to be employed at higher levels of administration in adult education organizations than do adult educators who hold only the master's degree.

Clearer distinctions between degrees in terms of knowledge domains and levels of study should help improve the credibility of adult education programs in the eyes of our colleagues in higher education institutions and among prospective employers of our graduates. We should be able to clearly communicate to these groups and to our students what they can expect from our programs. Professors should place this issue on their conference agendas and begin to address it in journals and other vehicles they use for dissemination and use of information, with the aim of making necessary curriculum changes to strengthen the relationship among the various degree options.

Program Assessment. The assessment of programs at all levels of higher education, including graduate education, is receiving increasing attention in the 1990s. Several levels of assessment pertain to graduate schools in general, including the strength of the program's knowledge base, the preparation and productivity of the faculty, the quality of the teaching by the faculty, and the impact the programs have on students and their practice. Increasingly, research productivity of faculty members is a gauge of program quality. The research productivity of many adult education faculties is on the increase, and adult education professors may be among the more innovative teachers on campus. Their public service to the field of adult education is among their strengths, although a proper balance between teaching, research, and public service is sometimes difficult to achieve.

However, a much larger problem related to assessment remains unresolved — How effective are adult education graduate programs in terms of their impact on practice? A record number of people with graduate degrees in adult education hold responsible positions in organizations that sponsor adult education programs, but most positions in adult education are filled by people who do not have degrees in adult education (Griffith, 1986; Cervero, 1986). Of what worth, then, is graduate study in adult education?

Houle (1964) asked some very provocative questions about this issue twenty-seven years ago: "Can graduate curricula provide a group of leaders in the field who are so significantly better than those trained by apprenticeship that the cost of such curricula can be justified? Can those who are recruited for graduate training measure up to those who have been chosen by the crude but effective selection which is now the rule? Can the great lore of the creative but untrained pioneers of adult education be studied so that it can be passed on in a more systematic fashion?" (p. 139). Sixteen years later, Griffith (1980) provided his answer to these questions: "The cold hard facts are that we don't have any empirical evidence that people who have been trained academically in the field of adult education do any better in carrying out the roles of adult educators than those who have not been professionally trained" (p. 223).

It is entirely possible that our attempts to sort out the meanings enshrined in the different but somewhat overlapping viewpoints regarding the proper relationship between theory and practice (Cervero, Chapter Two) will result in a clearer understanding of the role that graduate study will play in the larger scheme of adult education practice. But for now, the issue remains unresolved. Knox (1973) summarized this issue succinctly: "It would appear that the professors associated with each adult education graduate program confront a challenge, regarding how well they can achieve sufficient depth and focus to be relevant and to make an impact on the field, while at the same time retain a broad vision of the responsibility of adult education practitioners to the entire society" (p. 56). These challenges confronted professors and administrators in higher education institutions twenty-seven and more years ago, and we still need to search for answers to questions concerning the effect that graduate programs have on the practice of adult education.

Delivery Modes. For the most part, adult education graduate programs in North America have operated in rather traditional ways, being mainly course-bound and each structured along the same lines as most other programs in their university graduate schools. However, some programs have broken out of the mold and offer to their students formats that are more convenient and compatible with the students' personal and professional lives.

The Teachers College at Columbia University offers a doctoral program option in the form of their Adult Education Guided Independent Studies program that essentially follows a monthly weekend schedule coupled with short periods of residency during two summers. Groups of students enter the program and matriculate together, do joint research, and base their learning activities on their professional work. Syracuse University offers its master's degree program in a weekend format option and has experimented with offering courses by electronic mail. The University of Wisconsin, Madison, put some of its courses on a telephone network in the 1960s. The school initiated a weekend format for their master's program in the mid 1970s. Pennsylvania State University employs distance education methods, including teleconferencing, to deliver its program to at least three other centers around the state. The University of Calgary has been a leader in distance education for years.

This is the so-called information age, and our technological capabilities are improving daily. We are fully capable of transmitting programs by satellite and computer-based telecommunications modes to remote locations, and many university programs are delivered in these ways. But too few graduate programs in adult education are taking advantage of this technology. Even though the costs of some of the methods available are prohibitive for institutions facing severe program cutbacks, innovative scholars in adult education can find ways to format their graduate programs so that they are at least consistent with our ideas about distance education, self-directed learning, access to learning, participation in educational programs, and the like. Innovative delivery methods have even increased enrollments at some institutions.

Student Involvement. Another widely held principle of adult education is that learners ought to be involved in the process of planning and conducting their own learning activities. However, there is little evidence of active involvement of student groups in the determination of program content, structure, and method among institutions offering graduate degrees in adult education. The majority of graduate students in adult education are part time, and this militates against their full and consistent participation in program planning and operation. Faculty members may work informally with graduate students and thus involve them in decisions relating to program matters. However, it would seem that more active student organizations would enhance the work of faculty members and possibly result in a greater sense of ownership on the part of students, full or part time.

     One of the best examples of student involvement has been documented by Crew and Lewis (1990). The student organization, named the Adult Education Colloquium, was involved in redesigning the graduate program at Florida State University when the program was in decline and was instrumental in the survival of the program. Other programs that do not have active student organizations might find them useful now and in the future, whether or not they experience any trouble with program retrenchment.

New Roles for the Commission of Professors. The influence of the CPAE on the development of graduate programs has been great indeed. The production of the black book and its use as a benchmark for the further development of graduate programs is perhaps the most visible evidence of this influence, but other less-cited forms of influence have occurred since the sixties. The standards discussed earlier are the most recent formal evidence of the potential influence of the CPAE on programs of the future. Among the less formal influences are the networking that occurs among members of the CPAE, the information exchange that occurs at its annual meetings, and the sense of identity afforded professors by virtue of its very existence. However, as Griffith (1988) pointed out, the professionalization of the field may need to start with the CPAE itself.

The CPAE needs to adopt a more aggressive approach to the development of graduate programs across the field, which means at least the following:

1. The content and structure of programs that now exist or may be developed in the future should be discussed by the CPAE with regard to their adherence to the standards adopted by the CPAE.
2. Members of the CPAE should provide assistance to one another as they deal with problems relating to staffing, curriculum change, restructuring, recruiting, and employment of graduates in the field of practice.
3. The CPAE should adopt a much more visible stance as a body that represents the best professional interests of its members before the academic community and the field of practice in general.
4. The CPAE should become a leader in promoting the positive benefits of professionalism. See Griffith (1988) for more discussion of this topic and Deshler's Chapter Fifteen for discussion of the pros and cons of professionalism.

The CPAE should be a deliberative body, whose interests should be the collective interests of graduate programs in particular and the well-being of the field of practice in general. We can hope that the well-being of all segments of society will be equally served.

It is obvious that graduate programs in adult education have undergone major changes during the past twenty-seven years, and most of them have been very positive changes. There are clear signs of development in the knowledge base on which programs operate, increasing acceptance of programs by university colleagues and administrations, and the development of a stronger professoriate by virtue of its training and experience in the field of study. But these professors must keep a diligent watch over their programs and not sleep on their achievements, for times are still changing in higher education, in the field of practice, and in society at large. Indeed, there are some crucial decisions and moves that ought to be made by professors if their programs are to prosper and not decline. We discuss some of these in this section, but the reader should also consult Deshler's Chapter Fifteen and Peters's Chapter Sixteen for more discussion of issues that will influence the future development of graduate programs.

References

Boshier, R. "A Perspective on Theory and Model Development in Adult Education." Paper presented at the annual conference of the Commission of Professors of Adult Education, Portland, Ore., Oct. 1978.

Boshier, R. "Conceptual Framework for Analyzing the Training of Trainers and Adult Educators." *Convergence,* 1985, *18* (3 & 4).

Boyd, R. D. "New Designs for Adult Education Doctoral Programs." *Adult Education,* 1969, *19* (3), 186–196.

Boyd, R. D., and Apps, J. W. "A Conceptual Model for Adult Education." In R. D. Boyd and J. W. Apps (eds.), *Redefining the Discipline of Adult Education.* San Francisco: Jossey-Bass, 1980.

Bright, B. P. "Epistemological Vandalism: Psychology in the Study of Adult Education." In M. Zukas (ed.), *Proceedings of Transatlantic Dialogue: A Research Exchange.* Leeds, England: University of Leeds Press, 1988.

Brockett, R. G. "Early Ideas on the Training of Leaders for Adult Education." Paper presented at the Kellogg Project, Visiting Scholars Conference in History. Syracuse, N.Y.: Syracuse University Kellogg Project, Nov. 1990.

Brookfield, S. *Training Educators of Adults: The Theory and Practice of Graduate Adult Education.* London: Routledge, 1988.

Carroll, M. A. "Quality Issues in Graduate Education." *Ethical Issues in Graduate Education and Research.* Proceedings of the 18th annual meeting of the Conference of Southern Graduate Schools. Little Rock, Ark., Feb. 1989.

Cervero, R. M. "Professionalization of Selected Adult Education Sub-Fields." In L. H. Lewis and J. A. Niemi (eds.), *Commission of Professors of Adult Education, Proceedings of the 1986 Annual Conference.* Hollywood, Fla.: Commission of Professors of Adult Education, 1986.

Chamberlain, M. N. "The Competencies of Adult Educators." *Adult Education,* 1961, *11* (3), 78–82.

Cookson, P. S. "The Boyd and Apps Conceptual Model of Adult Education: A Critical Examination." *Adult Education Quarterly,* 1983, *34* (1), 48–53.

Crew, E., and Lewis, J. L. "Building a Graduate Professional Culture: A Case for Student Involvement in Developing and Sustaining an Adult Education Graduate Program." Paper presented at the national conference of the American Association for Adult and Continuing Education, Salt Lake City, Utah, Nov. 1990.

Cross, K. P. "Adult/Continuing Education." Unpublished manuscript, Graduate School of Education, Harvard University, 1985.

Daniel, R., and Kasworm, C. "Evaluation of Adult Continuing Education Doctoral Programs Within the Federation of North Texas Area Universities." Report presented at the annual conference of the Commission of Professors of Adult Education, Philadelphia, Nov. 1985.

Fellenz, R. A., and Conti, G. J. *Learning and Reality: Reflections on Trends in Adult Education.* Information series, no. 336. Columbus: ERIC Clearinghouse on Adult, Career, and Vocational Education, Ohio State University, 1989.

Ford, D., and Houle, C. O. "Doctorates in Adult Education, 1978." *Adult Education,* 1980, *30* (2), 123–125.

Gould, S. B., and Cross, K. P. *Explorations in Non-Traditional Study.* San Francisco: Jossey-Bass, 1972.

Grabowski, S. M., and Associates. *Preparing Educators of Adults.*
San Francisco: Jossey-Bass, 1981.

Griffith, W. S. "Personal Preparation." In H. J. Alford (ed.),
Power and Conflict in Continuing Education. Belmont, Calif.:
Wadsworth, 1980.

Griffith, W. S. "Challenging the Future: The Professionalization of the Major Segments of Adult and Continuing Education." In L. H. Lewis and J. A. Niemi (eds.), *Commission of
Professors of Adult Education, Proceedings of the 1986 Annual Conference.* Hollywood, Fla.: Commission of Professors of Adult
Education, 1986.

Griffith, W. S. "1988 Annual Report of Doctorates Conferred
in Adult Education." *Commission of Professors of Adult Education, Proceedings of the 1988 Annual Conference.* Tulsa, Okla.:
Commission of Professors of Adult Education, 1988.

Griffith, W. S., and Cloutier, G. H. *College and University Degree
Programs for the Preparation of Professional Adult Educators, 1970–
1971.* Sponsored Reports Series, Department of Health, Education and Welfare publication no. (OE) 74–11423. Washington, D.C.: U.S. Government Printing Office, 1974.

Griffith, W. S., and Parrish, M. C. "Annual Census of Doctorates Conferred in Adult Education." In L. H. Lewis and
J. A. Niemi (eds.), *Commission of Professors of Adult Education,
Proceedings of the 1986 Annual Conference.* Hollywood, Fla.: Commission of Professors of Adult Education, 1986.

Hall, L., and Associates. *New College for New Students.* San Francisco: Jossey-Bass, 1974.

Holmberg, B. *On the Concept and Academic Discipline of Adult Education.* ZIFF Papiere, no. 52. Hagan, Germany: Zentrales In-
stitut für Fernstudienforschung Arbeitsbereich, Fern Univer-
sität, 1984. (ED 290 010)

Houle, C. O. "The Emergence of Graduate Study in Adult Education." In G. Jensen, A. A. Liveright, and W. Hallenbeck
(eds.), *Adult Education: Outlines of an Emerging Field of University Study.* Washington, D.C.: American Association for Adult
and Continuing Education, 1964.

Houle, C. O. "The Educators of Adults." In R. M. Smith, G.
F. Aker, and J. R. Kidd (eds.), *Handbook of Adult Education.*
New York: Macmillan, 1970.

Houle, C. O. *The External Degree.* San Francisco: Jossey-Bass, 1973.

Houle, C. O., and Buskey, J. H. "The Doctorate in Adult Education 1935–1965." *Adult Education,* 1966, *16* (3), 131–145.

Houle, C. O., and Ford, D. "Doctorates in Adult Education 1976 and 1977." *Adult Education,* 1978, *29* (1) 65–70.

James, W. B. "An Analysis of Perceptions of the Practices of Adult Educators from Five Different Settings." *Proceedings of the Twenty-Fourth Adult Education Research Conference.* Montreal: Concordia University/University of Montreal, 1983.

Jones, G. E., and Galbraith, M. W. "Adult Education: A Study of Graduate Programs in the United States and Canada." Unpublished manuscript, Central Community College, Grand Island, Nebr., 1985.

Knott, E. S., and Ross, J. M. "Survey of Graduate Programs." *Commission of Professors of Adult Education, Proceedings of the 1986 Annual Conference.* Hollywood, Fla.: Commission of Professors of Adult Education, 1986.

Knowles, M. S. *The Modern Practice of Adult Education: From Pedagogy to Andragogy.* (Rev. ed.) Chicago: Association Press, 1980.

Knowles, M. S., Sheats, P. H., and Houle, C. O. "Research in Adult Education: Perspectives and New Directions." *Adult Leadership,* 1972, *20* (8), 270–272, 302–308.

Knox, A. B. *Development of Adult Education Graduate Programs.* Washington, D.C.: American Association for Adult and Continuing Education, 1973.

Knox, A. B. (ed.). *Enhancing Proficiencies of Continuing Educators.* New Directions for Continuing Education, no. 1. San Fransisco: Jossey-Bass, 1979.

Kowalski, T. J., and Weaver, R. A., "Graduate Studies in Adult Education: An Analysis of Doctoral Programmes and Professional Opinions." *Proceedings of the 1986 Midwest Research to Practice Conference in Adult, Community and Continuing Education.* Muncie, Ind.: School of Continuing Education, Ball State University, 1986.

Kozoll, C. E. *Response to Need: A Case Study of Adult Education Graduate Program Development in the Southeast.* Syracuse, N.Y.: Syracuse University Press, 1972.

Kreitlow, B. W. "Danger Signals: Trouble Brewing for Graduate Programs in Adult Education." *Commission of Professors of Adult Education, Proceedings of the 1988 Annual Conference.* Tulsa, Okla.: Commission of Professors of Adult Education, 1988.

Liveright, A. A. "The Nature and Aims of Adult Education as a Field of Graduate Education." In G. Jensen, A. A. Liveright, and W. Hallenbeck (eds.), *Adult Education: Outlines of an Emerging Field of University Study.* Washington, D.C.: American Association for Adult and Continuing Education, 1964.

Mayhew, L. B. *Reform in Graduate Education.* Southern Regional Education Board Research Monograph, no. 18. Atlanta: Southern Regional Education Board, 1972.

Peterson's Guide to Graduate Programs in Business, Education, Health, and Law, 1991. (25th ed.) Princeton, N.J.: Peterson's Guides, 1990.

Plecas, D. B., and Sork, T. J. "Adult Education: Curing the Ills of an Undisciplined Discipline." *Adult Education Quarterly,* 1986, *37* (1), 48–62.

Rose, A., and Mason, R. "Survey of Graduate Programs in Adult Education." Unpublished manuscript, Graduate Studies in Adult/Continuing Education, Northern Illinois University, 1990.

Schroeder, W. L. "Adult Education Defined and Described." In R. M. Smith, G. F. Aker, and J. R. Kidd, (eds.), *Handbook of Adult Education.* New York: Macmillan, 1970.

Schroeder, W. L. "Typology of Adult Learning Systems." In J. M. Peters and Associates (eds.), *Building an Effective Adult Education Enterprise.* San Francisco: Jossey-Bass, 1980.

Touchette, C. "A Comparative Study of Andragogy (Adult Education) as a Field of Academic Study in the World." Paper presented at the 7th World Congress of Comparative Education, Montreal, June 1989.

United Nations Educational, Scientific, and Cultural Organization. *Directory of Adult Education Training and Research Institutions.* Paris: UNESCO, 1982.

Usher, R. S., and Bryant, I. "Re-examining the Theory-Practice Relationship in Continuing Professional Education." *Studies in Higher Education,* 1987, *12* (2), 201–212.

Usher, R. S., and Bryant, I. *Adult Education as Theory, Practice and Research: The Captive Triangle.* London: Routledge, 1989.

Watkins, K., Cameron, C., and Marsick, V. J. "Academic Preparation of Adult Educators and Human Resource Development Professionals: Is There a Nexus?" *Commission of Professors of Adult Education, Proceedings of the 1986 Annual Conference.* Hollywood, Fla.: Commission of Professors of Adult Education, 1986.

PART TWO

MULTIDISCIPLINARY
DIMENSIONS OF
ADULT EDUCATION

The following perspectives about related disciplines were gleaned from the black book (Jensen, Liveright, and Hallenbeck, 1964): "Those who have had the task of building graduate departments of adult education have had to take their content where they could find it" (Houle, p. 78). "Because of the nature of the profession, much of the content of a graduate program must at this time be based upon and borrowed from other disciplines" (Liveright, p. 100). "A future responsibility of the professors of adult education as a group is to arrange for the winnowing of . . . golden grain . . . from other relevant disciplines" (Dickerman, p. 319). The aim of these professors and their colleagues was to extract from the disciplines and from the broader field of educational study the concepts, theories, descriptions, and ideas that could reasonably be translated into principles of adult learning and practice or into hypotheses for research. They also modeled their methods of inquiry on the ones used in related disciplines.

The strategy of borrowing from other disciplines has been criticized in recent years on several grounds (Boyd and Apps, 1980; Plecas and Sork, 1986; Bright, 1988). First, critics say that scholars in adult education run the risk of having the related disciplines define adult education for them, especially if the scholars have not clearly identified their own aims and methods. Second, adult educators may apply concepts and theories to adult education that were not originally developed for adult education situations, thus making their relevance questionable. Third, adult educators who are untrained in the related disciplines run the risk of not fully understanding the complexities of the theories and research they seek to borrow, thus committing an error of interpretation. Fourth, adult educators are in danger of naively mixing basically different philosophical and conceptual constructs as if they had the same origins and thus may transfer to adult education material that is internally inconsistent and perhaps invalid. Scholars in the field have also sounded other warnings. Still, many examples can be found of successful borrowing of concepts from related disciplines, as pointed out by Cookson (1983). Moreover, some adult educators argue that much if not most of the research and theorizing taking place in the social sciences assumes an adult audience, thus making the epistemological distance between the related disciplines and adult education not as great as it first appears to be (Bright, 1988).

This debate sets the stage for this book's consideration of the contributions of relevant disciplines. We thought it worth exploring the particular collection of disciplines that appear here, if only to learn how adult education currently stands in relation to them. Our purpose is not to build a new knowledge base on them but rather to examine how they fit into the total knowledge base now developing in adult education. In this regard, the material in Part Two might be read as an extension of Long's overview (Chapter Four) of the domains of knowledge that have been developed by adult educators in adult education situations. The chapters in this part, combined with Long's chapter, give a good overview of the body of formal knowledge that exists in the field of study today.

One additional introductory remark is in order. We gave the authors a great deal of room to choose their own approach to addressing their particular discipline topics. All authors approached their topic in terms of adult education, not solely in terms of the related disciplines. The reader who has also read the black book will recognize stark differences in the contents of the present chapters and their counterparts in the black book. More formal knowledge about adult education exists today, and the authors of the present chapters build their interpretations of disciplinary content, for the most part, in terms of that formal knowledge. Two of the authors, Griffin and Lawson, challenge the notion that sociology and philosophy, respectively, can simply be "applied" to adult education, and they approach their topics from a much more critical point of view than do the other authors in this part. This difference in approach to relating disciplines to adult education is actually a reflection of some of the differences in disciplinary orientations of British and American academicians in adult education, and its appearance here is thus also illustrative of the value of approaching this book in an international context.

Another explanation needs to be given before the chapters are introduced. All of the related disciplines covered in the black book are also covered in this book, except for social psychology. Philosophy and political science are added in this book. The selection of the six related disciplines discussed in the following chapters is based on our belief that they are the ones that have made the greatest contributions to the body of knowledge in adult education to date. Other disciplines, such as economics and perhaps areas within the biological sciences, might have been selected. However, the literature in such areas is not yet related strongly enough to adult education to merit extensive review. Perhaps the next generation of the black book will include many more disciplines than we have included here.

Tennant's Chapter Eight begins with a brief review of the debate about the applicability of psychological concepts to adult education. He talks about these concepts by interpreting the psychological literature in terms of five themes of adult teaching and learning. Readers should glance back at the discussion of adult learning research in Chapter Four to remind themselves of how vital psychological research is to adult education knowledge.

Educational leadership and program administration are the topics of Chapter Nine, written by Knox. The chapter is

organized around broad and interrelated administrative functions, and it draws from the literature in adult education and
related areas of study such as marketing, curriculum and instruction, and organizational psychology. Knox devotes most
of the chapter to concepts of leadership that undergird and inform his selection of administrative functions.

A contrasting approach to relating knowledge from other
disciplines to adult education is undertaken by Griffin in Chapter
Ten. Griffin begins his chapter with a carefully reasoned argument about what a sociology of adult education could contribute to adult education, a field that he considers overly concerned
with and sociologically naive about the relationship between individual development and social change. The bulk of his chapter deals with explaining the nature of a more reflexive and critical sociology of adult education in place of the mechanical
application of the discipline. Although readers will not find a
list and discussion of such traditional sociological concepts as
social organization and social systems, group behavior, and culture, a close reading of this challenging work will reward readers
with very interesting insights about class, social change, community, and curriculum. Griffin also shares some needed and
useful examples of related literature produced mainly in the
United Kingdom and he challenges readers to rethink some of
the assumptions associated with our use of psychological literature produced mainly in the United States.

Lawson, in Chapter Eleven, argues that there cannot be
a freestanding philosophy of adult education. However, he agrees
with Griffin on the need for more critical analysis of practice
and our theories about practice. He says that philosophical ideas
come mainly from outside adult education but that an interplay between adult education and philosophy can exist on several
levels — not the least of which is when fundamental philosophical ideas and principles inform adult education practice. A central idea of Lawson's chapter is that the best philosophical ideas
to apply to adult education must come from a variety of areas;
not all of these ideas are found in educational philosophy.

In Chapter Twelve, Thomas outlines his view of the relationship between political science and the study of adult educa-

tion. He finds that such subject matter as systems theory, concepts of power, influence, and social action can be applied to adult education. In this sense, Thomas's chapter is a complement to Griffin's chapter. Thomas's seasoned experience and wisdom about relationships between adult education and the government shine through in this chapter, and they alone would make the chapter worth reading.

The final chapter in Part Two discusses the role of history in adult education. In Chapter Thirteen, Stubblefield, an accomplished historian, claims that history provides people in adult education with a unique way of learning. He provides a short but thorough historiography of adult education and discusses some new developments being undertaken by adult education scholars. Stubblefield places all this in the context of educational, intellectual, social, and cultural history, and he ends his chapter with suggestions about teaching and studying in the area of history.

References

Boyd, R. D., and Apps, J. W. *Redefining the Discipline of Adult Education.* San Francisco: Jossey-Bass, 1980.

Bright, B. P. "Epistemological Vandalism: Psychology in the Study of Adult Education." In M. Zukas (ed.), *Proceedings of Transatlantic Dialogue: A Research Exchange.* Leeds, England: University of Leeds Press, 1988.

Cookson, P. S. "The Boyd and Apps Conceptual Model of Adult Education: A Critical Examination." *Adult Education Quarterly,* 1983, *34* (1), 48–53.

Jensen, G., Liveright, A. A., and Hallenbeck, W. (eds.). *Adult Education: Outlines of an Emerging Field of University Study.* Washington, D.C.: American Association for Adult and Continuing Education, 1964.

Plecas, D. B., and Sork, T. J. "Adult Education: Curing the Ills of an Undisciplined Discipline." *Adult Education Quarterly,* 1986, *37* (1), 48–62.

CHAPTER 8

The Psychology of
Adult Teaching
and Learning

Mark Tennant

Many of the questions posed by teachers of adults invite psychological explanation: What motivates students to attend classes? Through what processes do adults learn best? How can I adjust my teaching practices to take into account the learning styles and capacities of my students? How can I encourage the group to become cohesive and supportive? Can I make sense of the anxieties and concerns my students express? What can I do to help those students who experience difficulties in learning? Psychology has something to say in response to each of these questions and others like them. However, the relationship between psychology and adult education should not be cast as a conventional theory-to-practice relationship. It is especially important to be mindful of the differences between psychology as a discipline and adult education as a field of study and practice.

As a science, psychology is very much concerned with prediction and control, and to this end seeks to identify cause-effect relationships. However, a number of considerations limit the direct application to adult education of the knowledge gained from this process. For example, psychological experiments are conducted under controlled conditions. The aim of such experiments is to isolate variables for systematic study, which means that other variables must be controlled either directly (as in laboratory experiments) or indirectly through, for example, sampling techniques that select or randomize those variables that could confound the results. The extent of control in psychological experiments limits how knowledge gained in the experiments can be applied in adult education, because the extent of control in an adult education context is less than in a psychological experiment. Moreover, "control" is not something to which adult educators aspire.

Usher (1986) addresses considerations such as these when he advocates the application of psychological theories derived from therapy to an understanding of adult teaching and learning. He argues that, unlike the approach of "scientific" psychological theories, the approach of these theories is hermeneutic; that is, they seek to interpret behavior and stimulate insight, awareness, and understanding. Freudian psychoanalysis and humanistic clinical psychology are examples of theories derived from therapy.

Usher maintains that the activities of therapists and counselors are more like the activities of teachers than are the experimental manipulations of the scientific psychologists. Both the therapist and the educator are concerned with interpreting ongoing actions and events and adjusting their actions accordingly. Unlike the notions of *prediction* and *control* used in experimental psychology, the terms *interpretation* and *influence* used in therapy imply that the therapist (or teacher) is engaged in a reflexive dialogue with the client (or student). Thus the activity of teaching requires practical judgment in a context in which the operating variables cannot be measured or controlled. This practical judgment, and the action that flows from it, is informed by psychological theory in the sense that the theory provides a framework for interpreting events.

On the whole, Usher's argument is convincing, but it is not necessary to dismiss the results of experimental psychology as irrelevant to the practice of adult education. Such research supplies the practitioner with a corpus of experimental findings that point to the range of likely variables and the subtleties of their interaction.

Also, despite their similarities, the therapeutic context is still fundamentally different from the adult education context, and this difference should be acknowledged. Indeed, adult education practice has its own dynamic, which has been shaped by a range of disciplinary inputs (such as sociology, history, psychology, economics, anthropology) and by practitioners documenting and analyzing their practice. Thus psychology does not have a monopoly in providing insight into questions posed about adult teaching and learning. Indeed, some of the insights of adult educators have been confirmed years later in psychological theory and research. The field of adult education is arguably in a good position to guide the practice of researchers working in some areas of psychology, for example, life-span development or group dynamics.

Historically, however, the flow of information and knowledge has been one way, from psychology to adult education. Adult educators have looked toward psychology to inform, guide, and justify their practices. This is understandable because, if a particular practice can be supported by an independent theory and a body of research data, then the practice is legitimated, and its advocates can proceed with confidence.

The influence of psychology is particularly apparent in the many attempts to distill the principles of adult teaching and learning (for example, Gibb, 1960; Brundage and Mackeracher, 1980; Darkenwald and Merriam, 1982; Mezirow, 1983; James, 1983). These principles, which have not changed significantly since Gibb's (1960) formulation of them, have provided direction for the development of adult education practice and have set the agenda for theory and research. It is with these principles in mind that adult educators have maintained a dialogue with psychology.

This chapter will address the following questions: How has psychology influenced the shaping and articulation of these principles? What areas of psychology can best guide and inform adult education practice? For ease of exposition, the entire gamut

of adult teaching and learning principles are subsumed under
one or more of the following themes: promoting autonomy and
self-direction of learners, acknowledging the experiences of
learners, establishing an "adult" teacher-learner relationship,
meeting the needs of learners, encouraging collaborative group
learning.

Promoting Autonomy and Self-Direction of Learners

The idea of self-directed, autonomous learning is firmly en-
trenched in the adult education literature. It is one of only a
few core concepts that have laid the foundations for the identity of adult education as a distinct field of practice and inquiry.
But like most core concepts, self-directed learning is open to
a range of interpretations. At one end of the spectrum, self-
directed learning is thought to occur when learners determine
goals and objectives, locate appropriate resources, plan their
learning strategies, and evaluate the outcomes (Knowles, 1978;
Tough, 1967, 1968; Moore, 1980). Thus, self-directed learning would be characterized by the mastery of a set of techniques
and procedures for self-learning. At the other end of the spectrum, self-directed learning is thought to incorporate the notion of "critical awareness" (Mezirow, 1983; Brookfield, 1985).
Critically aware learners have the capacity to identify and challenge assumptions governing their lives that they previously took
for granted. They are emancipated from their psychological and
cultural assumptions and more in touch with their authentic
needs. Thus, they are able to make a commitment to learning
on the basis of a knowledge of genuine alternatives.

These approaches to self-directed learning have in common a concern with the psychological growth of the learner.
They both assume that learning and psychological growth are
connected, although the nature of this connection differs in each
case. In the first view, in which self-directed learning is essentially a skill, adults are assumed to have a psychological need
for self-direction. The learning processes based on this view (for
example, the learning contract) are designed to acknowledge
and awaken this need. In the second view, an assumption is

made that constraints on learning originate in the social structure and become internalized by the adult learner. Shedding these constraints or psychocultural assumptions (see Mezirow, 1985) is at once an act of learning and psychological growth in its own right and a precondition for subsequent self-directed learning.

This interest in the connection between adult learning and psychological growth has been informed by an expanding psychological literature on developmental stages, the life cycle, and the phases of adult life. Much of this literature refers to the development of qualities like autonomy, independence, individuality, and the integrated self. For Maslow (1968), an individual's personal growth is geared toward self-actualization, with its increased sense of self and autonomy. For Kohlberg (1969), an individual grows toward autonomous and principled morality. Loevinger (1976) portrays the individual as progressing through a sequence of eight stages, the last three of which she calls autonomous, individualistic, and integrated stages. In these last three stages, an individual makes commitments and choices, while recognizing the relativity of social perspectives and the ambiguities and contradictions in being an individual in a social world (see Brookfield, 1987). Gould (1978) conceives of personal growth in terms of the inner freedom gained through stripping oneself of the false assumptions acquired during childhood. Levinson (1978) refers to the process of individuation as being the hallmark of growth. As individuation proceeds, the person becomes more separate from the world and is more independent and self-generating.

These diverse approaches within developmental psychology employ concepts of growth readily identifiable in the adult education literature on self-direction. All of the approaches include the assumptions that people can change throughout adult life and that this change can be positive in the sense that it promotes more self-awareness, a more accurate perception of reality, or perhaps even more power and responsibility.

An issue that serves to demarcate different positions on personal growth within psychology and adult education is the criteria by which growth is to be judged. This issue is likely to persist because the question of what constitutes growth is not solely a psychological question; it can only be answered with reference to moral, ethical, and political debate.

Quite clearly the different answers to the question serve the interests of different groups. Gilligan (1982), for example, denies that criteria such as separateness, independence, and self-generation indicate personal growth. She argues that the emphasis on the development of individual identity in developmental theories is an aspect of gender bias that pervades the literature. She observes that the identity of women is built upon the perception of sameness, mutuality, attachment, and interdependence, qualities that are undervalued by the developmental literature. A similar criticism can be made of all the research that claims to identify universal phases or stages of life. Invariably, some people, for whatever reason, do not conform to these patterns and are thereby deemed to be psychologically stunted.

Adult educators need above all to be mindful of the diverse ways in which people chart their life course and must avoid subscribing to rigid views about the "proper" course of development. They need to understand the dynamics of change and how people interpret and attribute meaning to their experiences as they progress through life. The literature on lifespan development has made a significant contribution to this understanding, especially in recent years, and it is now an indispensable ingredient in any theory of adult learning.

Acknowledging the Experience of Learners

Researchers ranging from Gibb (1960) and McClusky (1964) to Knowles (1978), Brookfield (1987), and Jarvis (1987) consistently cite experience as a distinguishing characteristic of adult learning. The idea that the experience of adults is an important resource for learning is axiomatic. But what does it mean as an adult educator to acknowledge the experiences of learners?

Clearly the experiences of learners can be acknowledged in different ways. First, at the most basic or superficial level, teachers can link their explanations and illustrations to the prior experiences of learners. By doing so, they build a bridge from the known to the unknown. Second, teachers can attempt to link learning activities to learners' current experiences at work, home, or in the community. Typically, teachers do this by adapting material to the immediate problems and concerns of learners, thereby ensuring that learning is relevant. Third, teachers can create experiences from which learning will flow. In other words, they can design learning experiences that require the active participation of learners, such as simulations, games, and role plays. These learning experiences establish a common base from which each learner constructs meaning through personal reflection and group discussion. Fourth, the meanings that learners attach to their experiences may be subjected to critical scrutiny. The teacher may consciously try to disrupt the learner's worldview and stimulate uncertainty, ambiguity, and doubt in learners about previously taken-for-granted interpretations of experience.

Although adult educators are in consensus about the importance and centrality of experience as a foundation for adult education practice, they disagree about how best to conceive of the relationship between experience and learning. The psychological literature offers different theoretical perspectives on this relationship.

One perspective regards learners as passive receivers of behavior, roles, attitudes, and values that are shaped and maintained by rewards and punishments. The most influential example of this perspective is found in the work of Skinner (1959, 1973). His theory has had an impact on teaching and learning in all sectors of education. In adult education, his theory is most apparent in the importance many adult educators attach to the need for setting behavioral objectives for learners and providing learners with regular feedback and reinforcement. The role of the teacher in this perspective is to engineer the experiences of learners and control behavior through the disbursement of rewards and punishments.

A second, cognitive, perspective on learning attributes a more active role to learners, who are seen as continually trying to understand and make sense of their experiences. In effect, learners reconstruct their experiences to match more closely their existing rules and categories for understanding the world. These rules and categories may also change to accommodate new experiences. Thus the relationship between learning and experience is interactive rather than mechanistic (Piaget, 1978; Bruner, 1966). The role of the teacher in this perspective, then, is to provide quality experiences — that is, experiences that require the active participation of learners and from which learners can extract a better or more complete understanding of the particular concept, issue, or problem being considered.

A third perspective, which can be labeled the psychodynamic perspective or humanistic psychology, draws attention to the emotionally laden nature of the relationship between experience and learning.

Humanistic clinical psychology, particularly the work of Rogers (1951) and Maslow (1968), has had a substantial impact on adult education. Humanistic psychology may be seen as a protest against types of psychology that treat the person as an object for scientific inquiry. It reaffirms the human qualities of the person, such as personal freedom, choice, and the validity of subjective experience. The implication of this perspective is that teachers need to address the feelings learners have about past and present experiences for learning to occur. Learning is literally a matter of *learning to be* (to borrow a phrase from the influential United Nations Educational, Scientific, and Cultural Organization [UNESCO] report, Faure and others, 1972).

The above three perspectives are longstanding, and they have provided educators at all levels with different ways of theorizing about the relationship between learning and experience. But more recent developments within psychology also have direct applicability to the relationship between learning and experience in the adult years. Studies on adult intellectual and cognitive functioning have produced findings that sit very well with the emphasis on experience in adult learning.

Writing twenty-seven years ago in the first black book, McClusky (1964) called for a reworking of the concept of adult intellectual and cognitive ability. He argued that existing intelligence tests were biased in favor of young people and were not fair measures of adult capacity. In the intervening years, a host of research findings have supported this view. Intellectual development during the adult years is now regarded as multidimensional (there are a range of mental abilities) and multidirectional (the abilities develop and change in various ways). Moreover, the component of intelligence that appears to grow during the adult years is said to be based on the experience of dealing with concrete problems and situations at work, in the home, and in community life.

Perhaps the earliest and most widely known application of these concepts to adult development is found in the theory of fluid-crystallized intelligence proposed by Cattell (1971) and Horn (1970, 1982). These researchers separate intellectual abilities into two general clusters labeled *fluid* and *crystallized* intelligence. Fluid intelligence is measured by tests of complex reasoning, memory, and figural relations — tests that measure the basic information-processing capacities of the person. Crystallized intelligence is measured by tests on information storage, verbal comprehension, and numerical reasoning — those sorts of abilities that are normally associated with experience and acculturation (that is, abilities that can be learned). Horn' and Cattell's research reveals that these two dimensions of intelligence change in different directions during the adult years. Specifically, from the teenage years onwards, an individual's fluid intelligence decreases and crystallized intelligence increases. The net result is that intellectual functioning remains relatively stable with age, but crystallized intelligence assumes a more dominant role as a component of intellectual functioning.

A recent expansion of this psychometric view (Baltes, Dittman-Kohli, and Dixon, 1984; Dixon and Baltes, 1986) distinguishes between the mechanics and pragmatics of intelligence. The term *mechanics of intelligence* refers to the "basic architecture of information processing and problem solving. . . . It deals with the basic cognitive operations and cognitive structures associated with such tasks as perceiving relationships, classification, and logical reasoning" (Baltes, Dittman-Kohli, and Dixon, 1984, p. 63). The term *pragmatics of intelligence* refers to the application of the mechanics of intelligence to particular contexts or fields of knowledge. Subsumed under the pragmatics of intelligence are generalized systems of knowledge (compare with crystallized intelligence); specialized knowledge, such as occupational expertise; and knowledge about the intellectual skills relevant to particular contexts (for instance, making judgments about problem-solving strategies). Baltes, Dittman-Kohli, and Dixon, (1984) argue that the growth of the mechanics of intelligence is confined to childhood and adolescence. If anything, adulthood requires the gradual adjustment to losses in this domain. By contrast, during the adult years, growth occurs in the pragmatics of intelligence. This conception opens the way for identifying new forms of intelligence that emerge during adulthood and old age.

This emphasis on the pragmatics of intelligence as an aspect of intellectual growth during the adult years is also found in recent commentary in the cognitive structuralist tradition. The conventional cognitive structuralist view is represented by Piaget (1978). In his description of cognitive development he postulates a number of stages, through which the person progresses in an invariant sequence. These stages represent qualitatively different ways of making sense, understanding, and constructing a knowledge of the world. Thus, children progress through different types of thinking as they develop toward mature adult thought. This process culminates in the attainment of what is termed *formal operations,* which is the capacity to think abstractly and reason logically and scientifically. This capacity develops in early adolescence and is then considered to be applied throughout the adult years. In this account, no further development of any major kind occurs beyond formal operations.

Recent commentary, however, highlights the limitations of formal operations as a description of mature adult thought. Researchers have attempted to extend the cognitive structuralist tradition and identify further postformal stages of cognitive development (for example, Riegel, 1973; Labouvie-Vief, 1980, 1982, 1985; Kramer, 1983; Basseches, 1984; Rybash, Hoyer, and Roodin, 1986). These researchers view mature adult cognition as characterized by the ability to fit abstract thinking into the concrete limitations of everyday life.

Labouvie-Vief captures the spirit of this view: "While the

theme of youth is flexibility, the hallmark of adulthood is commitment and responsibility. Careers must be started, intimacy bonds formed, children raised. In short, in a world of a multitude of logical possibilities, one course of action must be adopted. This conscious commitment to one pathway and the deliberate disregard of other logical choices may mark the onset of adult cognitive maturity. . . . This is our first proposed conclusion: adulthood brings structural change, not just in the perfection of logic, but in its reintegration with pragmatic necessities" (Labouvie-Vief, 1980, p. 153).

Both the psychometric and cognitive structuralist traditions seem to be converging on the view that intellectual and cognitive growth occurs in the adult years and that this growth is located in the experiences of people in everyday life. A number of research programs have emerged from this proposition (see Baltes, 1987; Rybash, Hoyer, and Roodin, 1986). They focus on a variety of areas of growth in the second half of life, such as growth in wisdom (Dittman-Kohli and Baltes, 1986; Smith, 1988), expertise (Chi, Glaser, and Farr, 1988; see also Tennant, 1991), relativistic thinking (Sinnott, 1984; Benack, 1984), problem finding (Arlin, 1975, 1984), and dialectical thinking (Basseches, 1980, 1984). This research is still in its infancy. However, it does focus our attention on the continuing growth of intellectual and cognitive capacity during the adult years, and it is significant that this growth is predicated on experience and measured in contexts that have a high degree of "real life" complexity.

Establishing an "Adult" Teacher-Learner Relationship

A fundamental difference between teaching adults and children is that adults have a general life expertise that children are yet to develop. Thus the expertise of adult teachers vis-à-vis their students, resides solely in their mastery of subject matter and teaching technique, and they cannot be regarded as having a general life expertise beyond that of their students. Teachers and learners are adult peers. Indeed a teacher in one context (or moment) may become a learner in another, and vice versa.

An adult teacher may even be a subordinate of his or her learners in the larger organizational or professional context. (This frequently occurs in organizational training.) Considerations such as these have quite properly led to speculation about the appropriate teacher-learner relationship for an adult teaching environment and how this can be fostered.

A common view of the relationship between teachers and adult learners is that it should be equal, open, and democratic. This view has political, philosophical, and psychological dimensions. The political dimension has to do with how power, in a structural and procedural sense, should be distributed between the teacher and learners and among learners. Who decides when, how, and what will be learned? What are the nature and limits of the teacher's responsibility, and who determines what the teacher's responsibility should be? The philosophical dimension has to do with how the relationship serves the purposes and aims of the educational activity. The psychological dimension has to do with how the relationship is worked out at an interpersonal level. This dimension involves the attitudes and actions of teachers and learners toward each other. Knowles (1984) refers to these attitudes and actions when he writes about setting an appropriate psychological climate for adult learning. He says that this climate should be characterized by mutual respect, collaborativeness, mutual trust, supportiveness, openness, authenticity, and humanness.

The descriptions of the relationship between teachers and adult learners found in the research use the language of humanistic clinical psychology, from which the concept of the learning facilitator was taken. Rogers (1983) describes the qualities of a good facilitator as being realness and genuineness; prizing, acceptance, and trust; and empathic understanding—those qualities that are also a mark of the successful clinical therapist. This emphasis on the personal relationship between the facilitator and the learner is a feature of Knowles's conception of the andragogical teacher, who "accepts each student as a person of worth and respects his feelings and ideas . . . seeks to build relationships of mutual trust [and] exposes his own feelings" (Knowles, 1978, pp. 77–79).

Similar views can be found in much of the literature on adult teaching and learning. Too often, however, the humanistic view is watered down to a set of attitudinal precepts for the teacher to follow. But it is naive to assume that adopting these precepts will guarantee a smooth relationship with learners. For example, a discrepancy will almost certainly exist between the teacher's conception of his or her role and the expectations of learners. This discrepancy needs to be addressed by teachers of adults, but how? No obvious strategies have been devised to address this discrepancy. However, teacher and learner will certainly need to engage in some kind of negotiation. A compromise must be worked out between the fulfillment and violation of learners' expectations.

The adult education literature has paid too little attention to this aspect of adult teaching and learning (a recent exception being Brookfield, 1990) and it may well benefit from a more thorough exploration of various psychodynamic theories. Some researchers have applied basic psychoanalytic concepts to an understanding of the dynamics of teacher-learner interaction (Salzberger-Wittenberg, Henry, and Osborne, 1983). They claim that many of the anxieties expressed by adult learners have their roots in childhood and infancy. Adult expectations of teachers are associated with childhood feelings, especially toward parents and school teachers. In their extreme form these feelings represent hopes or fantasies that can never be fulfilled. The teacher is commonly expected to be a source of knowledge and wisdom, a provider and comforter, an object of admiration and envy, a judge, and an authority figure (Salzberger-Wittenberg, Henry, and Osborne, 1983).

When these expectations are not met, the learner's inevitable disappointment will find expression in some way — usually as a transference of hostility and other feelings toward the teacher. The teacher, too, will bring to the classroom a set of expectations, fears, and aspirations. Teachers may fear criticism, hostility, and losing control. The teacher's response to criticism may be infantile (for instance, refusing to admit an error or being overly apologetic and self-effacing about a small mishandling of an event).

An approach like that of Salzberger-Wittenberg, Henry, and Osborne (1983), then, casts a new light on the teacher-learner relationship. Adult teachers certainly need to make sense of the emotionality of teaching and learning, both from the learners' and teachers' point of view. The dynamics of this process and the way in which teachers and learners negotiate their relationship should feature prominently in the psychology of adult learning.

Meeting Learners' Needs

The concept of meeting needs has a long history in the adult education literature, and many disciplines have contributed to the debate about the nature and purpose of meeting learners' needs. Distinctions are made between different categories, types, and levels of need. Thus one can speak of the need to learn particular things or the need to learn in a particular way or the need to develop certain personal qualities like confidence, assertiveness, and self-esteem. Further distinctions are made between felt needs, expressed needs, normative needs, and comparative needs, and between individual, group, and community needs. (See Wiltshire, 1973; Lawson, 1975; Armstrong, 1982; Griffin, 1983; Long, 1983; Tennant, 1985, for reviews of the concept of needs.) Thus the proposition that programs for adult learners should be based on their needs is open to considerable interpretation and elaboration.

Learners' needs have been addressed from the standpoint of sociological, educational, and philosophical theory. The principal contribution of psychology has been to draw attention to those psychological needs that have a bearing on the adults' motivation and capacity to learn. A number of theories attempt to explain motives for participating in adult education. Some of the better known of these are based on Maslow's (1968) hierarchy of needs, Lewin's (1947) force-field analysis, and McClelland's concept of need for achievement (McClelland, Atkinson, Clark, and Lowell, 1953). For example, Miller (1967) explains social class differences in the benefits sought from education in terms of Maslow's hierarchy. He says that people from lower socioeconomic groups will be attracted by a form of education that satisfies the lower-order needs: survival, safety, and a sense of belonging. People from higher socioeconomic groups will be attracted by a form of education that will enhance self-esteem, achievement, and self-actualization.

Boshier (1973), who also draws heavily on Maslow, refers to the need for congruence between the self, the ideal self, and the learning environment. People with a high discrepancy between the self and the learning environment, for example, are more likely to drop out. Rubenson (1977) has developed an expectancy-valence model of motivation to participate in adult education. He assumes that education is an achievement-oriented activity about which the individual has an expectation for success and the positive consequences that flow from success. Usually, however, people experience a range of both positive and negative consequences of participating in education. The values the individual places on these consequences will determine the valence (net force of attraction and repulsion) for the individual to participate.

These theories, at least in the simple form presented here, appear quite unremarkable. (Indeed, their status as theories, especially those accepting Maslow's hierarchy as given, can be questioned. See Tennant, 1988; Korman, Greenhaus, and Badin, 1977). Nevertheless, when they are applied to the task of encouraging a cross section of adults to participate in education these theories do present some basic concepts from which to work. By using terms like *self-esteem, ideal self, expectation, perceptions of outcomes, consequences,* and *values,* they direct our attention to the psychological aspects of participating successfully in an adult education activity. Unfortunately this work on motivation has been linked almost exclusively to explaining why learners participate or drop out. It could also be profitably applied to explaining the nature of classroom interactions at both the interpersonal and group level. Presumably, for example, the valence of which Rubenson speaks is quite malleable, and it would shift with changes in the learner's perception of the situation. As the valence became negative and expectancy moved toward zero, what kinds of changes would be apparent in the learner and what action could the teacher take to address the situation?

Similarly, in Boshier's model, surely the relationships between self and ideal self, self and the other students, and self and the institutional environment are all fluid relationships that ebb and flow with events in the classroom. And surely when there is a tension arising from a discrepancy, this will manifest itself in some way in the classroom interaction. To reiterate an earlier point, the adult teaching and learning environment is emotionally charged, largely because it is an arena in which people are exploring new definitions of themselves, whether it be in relation to their capacities, values, or achievements. Theories of the self in psychology are important in this respect because they offer insight into the affective needs of adult learners.

In addition to considering the psychological needs discussed above, adult educators should also consider the cognitive needs and capacities of learners. As discussed earlier, the changing nature of cognition and intelligence with age has implications for how teachers structure learning activities for adults. An aspect of cognition that has received a great deal of attention in adult education is the notion of cognitive style, or learning style, which refers to how individuals characteristically organize and process information. A number of attempts have been made to classify the different types of cognitive or learning styles. For example, Messick and Associates, (1978) documents as many as nineteen learning styles referred to in the literature. Smith (1983) tabulates seventeen existing learning style inventories. Squires (1981) notes that learning styles are typically represented as polar opposites on a range of dimensions. Thus learners are described as being field dependent or independent, reflective or impulsive, serialist or holist, a converger or a diverger, and so on.

These different approaches to learning style are not necessarily mutually exclusive; that is, learning style differences between people can be represented in a number of ways. The approach of Kolb and Fry (1975) and Kolb (1981, 1984) is perhaps the best-known representation. These researchers have constructed a model of learning based upon a conceptual distinction between different learning styles. They argue that learning styles can be represented by a preference for one or the other pole of two dimensions: concrete experience versus abstract conceptualization and active experimentation versus reflective observation. The ideal learner has the capacity to operate at either pole of both dimensions. In reality, however, very few people are ideal learners, and most people develop a preference or strength in one of the poles of each dimension (for example, a preference for concrete experience and reflective observation).

The idea that people have different learning styles is an attractive one for adult educators. Perhaps this is because it offers an alternative to the concept of general intelligence, which tends to categorize learners from inferior to superior on a single dimension. Learning styles represent qualitative differences among learners, whose learning potential is governed not by some general intellectual ability but by the way in which the teaching and learning process is conducted. However, some significant conceptual and methodological difficulties in the literature on learning style are yet to be resolved. These difficulties relate to questions concerning the origin, stability, persistence, and modifiability of learning styles and to their empirical base (see Tennant, 1988). In addition, a number of issues relate to the implications of learning style differences for teaching practice. For example, using Kolb's categories, one option is for the teacher to adapt to the learning style needs of the learner. For example, concrete thinkers would be given ample opportunities for concrete experiences in the learning environment, and conceptualizers would be provided with theoretical input. Another option is to arrange activities so that nonpreferred learning styles are required. A third option is to use a variety of techniques so that learners can use their preferred style on some occasions but are required to experience different ways of learning at other times.

Clearly it is not possible, or desirable, to always adapt to the immediate felt needs of learners. Some kind of disorienting or unsettling experience is necessary for learning to occur (see Brookfield, 1986; Jarvis, 1987). Some exposure to a nonpreferred style is desirable. It is at this point that the cognitive and psychological aspects of learning converge; a mismatch of learning styles will almost invariably lead the learner to reappraise at an affective level the relation between self and the learning environment.

Psychological theory and research has clearly alerted adult educators to the complexity of meeting learners' needs. It has done so primarily by providing different frameworks for understanding the origin and nature of needs. Now, research is needed that looks more closely at the adult teaching and learning process, in particular, how needs are defined and pursued by learners, and the role of the teacher in influencing this process.

Encouraging Collaborative Group Learning

Much of adult teaching and learning takes place within groups. In addition, small-group teaching techniques are widely used by adult educators. One reason educators use these techniques is that small-group work acknowledges the experiences of adult learners. Learners are encouraged to pool their resources, express their views, clarify their thinking, and explore new ideas. Small groups are said to promote self-understanding through shared support and mutual feedback. They provide a base of common experience upon which new learning is built, and they enhance the identity and cohesiveness of the larger group.

The interest of adult educators in group dynamics, then, is understandable. As a field of inquiry within social psychology, group dynamics is based on the proposition that the group has its own identity that is more than the sum of the individuals comprising it. That is, groups are more than mere collections of individuals. A related proposition is that individuals behave differently in groups than when alone.

Many of the central questions and issues in group dynamics have a long history. The classic experiments of Sherif (1935), Asch (1956), and Milgram (1965) demonstrate the powerful influence of the group on individual actions, perceptions, judgments, and beliefs. The early work of Lewin (1958) drew attention to the capacity of group decisions to effect behavioral change. Mulder (1960) explored the effect of different communication and decision-making structures on group performance, and Bales (1958) developed a framework for analyzing interactions within groups. Other group phenomena that have received attention are the patterns of leadership within groups, the different roles adopted by group members, conflict and cohesion in groups, individual versus group problem solving, and the nature of group development. A number of standard texts offer a coherent account of the field (see Cartwright and Zander, 1968; Hare, 1976; Shaw, 1981), and a number of attempts have been made to relate group dynamics to adult learning (see McLeish, Matheson, and Park, 1973; Cooper, 1975; Jaques, 1984). Much of the current research activity in group dynamics is derived from the earlier work described in these texts.

When adult learning texts refer to the literature of group dynamics, it is usually with a view to helping the teacher of adults to observe and interpret group phenomena and intervene in the group process. Such an approach assumes that group processes are generic and apply equally to different types of groups. This may well be so, but it is equally plausible that the processes take on a different hue in different group contexts. It may be that learning groups have characteristics that distort, magnify, or diminish the processes shared in experimental groups.

For example, it could be argued that learning groups are essentially artificial in the sense that it is individuals who come to learn and not the group as such. An important role for the adult educator is to help transform a collection of individuals into a cohesive group. This is nearly always an overt demand placed upon adult learners. The way the group functions is subject to scrutiny and reflection by the group itself. Thus the group is conscious of its own processes, and the adult educator actively promotes this awareness. This is very different indeed from the experimental group of the social psychologist, where deceit and subterfuge are standard procedure. Unlike adult educators, experimental social psychologists have a vested interest in keeping the subject ignorant. Are the phenomena observed under these conditions transferable to the adult learning environment? It seems unlikely, but in any event it is certainly worth exploring the dynamics of the adult learning group as a distinct type of group with unique characteristics.

Conclusion

I have attempted to outline some of the ways in which psychology has influenced adult education theory and practice. In so doing, I have focused on some dominant themes in the adult education literature. This should be read as a conscious attempt to allow adult education to set the agenda. Psychology certainly deserves a prominent place in adult education, but it should not be preeminent. Moreover, psychological theory and research should not be accepted by adult educators in an uncritical way. Too often practitioners seize upon an easily assimilated psychological theory and use it as a basis and justification for their practice. Any application of psychological theory should be imbued with a critical spirit. That is, practitioners should be aware of the source, nature, and adequacy of the evidence supporting the theory and should be capable of identifying those aspects of their practice to which it applies. Finally, the relevance of the theory needs to be assessed in the context of considerations beyond the psychological, such as the moral, ethical, and political. Approached in this manner, psychology will continue to contribute toward a better understanding of adult education practice.

References

Arlin, P. K. "Cognitive Development in Adulthood: A Fifth Stage?" *Developmental Psychology*, 1975, *11*, 602–606.

Arlin, P. K. "Adolescent and Adult Thought: A Structural Interpretation." In M. L. Commons, F. A. Richards, and C. Armon (eds.), *Beyond Formal Operations: Late Adolescent and Adult Cognitive Development.* New York: Praeger, 1984.

Armstrong, P. F. "The Needs Meeting Ideology in Liberal Adult Education." *International Journal of Lifelong Education,* 1982, *1* (4), 293–321.

Asch, S. "Studies of Independence and Conformity: A Minority of One Against a Unanimous Majority." *Psychological Monographs,* 1956, *9* (complete volume).

Bales, R. "Task Roles and Social Roles in Problem-Solving Groups." In E. Maccoby, M. Newcomb, and E. Hartley (eds.), *Readings in Social Psychology.* New York: Holt, Rinehart & Winston, 1958.

Baltes, P. B. "Theoretical Propositions of Lifespan Developmental Psychology: On the Dynamics Between Growth and Decline." *Developmental Psychology,* 1987, *23* (5), 611–626.

Baltes, P. B., Dittman-Kohli, F., and Dixon, R. A. "New Perspectives on the Development of Intelligence in Adulthood: Toward a Dual-Process Conception and a Model of Selective Optimization with Compensation." In P. B. Baltes and O. G. Brim, Jr. (eds.), *Lifespan Development and Behavior.* Vol. 6. Orlando, Fla.: Academic Press, 1984.

Basseches, M. "Dialectical Schemata: A Framework for the Empirical Study of Dialectical Thinking." *Human Development,* 1980, *23,* 400–421.

Basseches, M. *Dialectical Thinking and Adult Development.* Norwood, N.J.: Ablex, 1984.

Benack, S. "Postformal Epistemologies and the Growth of Empathy." In M. L. Commons, F. A. Richards, and C. Armon (eds.), *Beyond Formal Operations: Late Adolescent and Adult Development.* New York: Praeger, 1984.

Boshier, R. "Educational Participation and Dropout: A Theoretical Model." *Adult Education,* 1973, *23* (4), 255–282.

Brookfield, S. D. "Self-Directed Learning: A Critical Review of Research." In S. D. Brookfield (ed.), *Self-Directed Learning: From Theory to Practice.* New Directions for Continuing Education, no. 25. San Francisco: Jossey-Bass, 1985.

Brookfield, S. D. *Understanding and Facilitating Adult Learning: A Comprehensive Analysis of Principles and Effective Practices.* San Francisco: Jossey-Bass, 1986.

Brookfield, S. D. *Developing Critical Thinkers: Challenging Adults to Explore Alternative Ways of Thinking and Acting.* San Francisco: Jossey-Bass, 1987.

Brookfield, S. D. *The Skillful Teacher: On Technique, Trust, and Responsiveness in the Classroom.* San Francisco: Jossey-Bass, 1990.

Brundage, D., and Mackeracher, D. *Adult Learning Principles and Their Application to Program Planning.* Toronto: Toronto Ministry of Education, 1980.

Bruner, J. *The Process of Education.* Cambridge, Mass.: Harvard University Press, 1966.

Cartwright, D., and Zander, A. *Group Dynamics.* New York: Harper & Row, 1968.

Cattell, R. B. *Abilities: Their Structure, Growth, and Action.* Boston: Houghton Mifflin, 1971.

Chi, M., Glaser, R., and Farr, M. *The Nature of Expertise*. Hillsdale, N.J.: Erlbaum, 1988.

Cooper, C. (ed.). *Theories of Group Processes*. London: Wiley, 1975.

Darkenwald, G. G., and Merriam, S. B. *Adult Education: Foundations of Practice*. New York: Harper & Row, 1982.

Dittman-Kohli, F., and Baltes, P. B. "Toward a Neofunctionalist Conception of Adult Intellectual Development: Wisdom as a Proto-Typical Case of Intellectual Growth." In C. Alexander and E. Langer (eds.), *Beyond Formal Operations: Alternative Endpoints to Human Development*. New York: Oxford University Press, 1986.

Dixon, R., and Baltes, P. B. "Toward Lifespan Research on the Functions and Pragmatics of Intelligence." In R. Sternberg and R. Wagner (eds.), *Practical Intelligence*. Cambridge, England: Cambridge University Press, 1986.

Faure, E., and others. *Learning to Be: The World of Education Today and Tomorrow*. Paris: UNESCO, 1972.

Gibb, J. R. "Learning Theory in Adult Education." In M. S. Knowles (ed.), *Handbook of Adult Education in the United States*. Washington, D.C.: American Association for Adult and Continuing Education, 1960.

Gilligan, C. *In a Different Voice. Psychological Theory and Women's Development*. Cambridge, Mass.: Harvard University Press, 1982.

Gould, R. *Transformations: Growth and Change in Adult Life*. New York: Simon & Schuster, 1978.

Griffin, C. *Curriculum Theory in Adult and Lifelong Education*. London: Croom Helm, 1983.

Hare, P. *Handbook of Small Group Research*. New York: Free Press, 1976.

Horn, J. L. "Organization of Data on Lifespan Development of Human Abilities." In L. R. Goulet and P. B. Baltes (eds.), *Lifespan Developmental Psychology: Research and Theory*. Orlando, Fla.: Academic Press, 1970.

Horn, J. L. "The Aging of Human Abilities." In B. B. Wolman (ed.), *Handbook of Developmental Psychology*. Englewood Cliffs, N.J.: Prentice-Hall, 1982.

James, W. B. "An Analysis of Perceptions of the Practices of Adult Educators from Five Different Settings." *Proceedings of* the *Twenty-Fourth Adult Education Research Conference.* Montreal: Concordia University/University of Montreal, 1983.

Jaques, D. *Learning in Groups.* London: Croom Helm, 1984.

Jarvis, P. *Adult Learning in the Social Context.* London: Croom Helm, 1987.

Knowles, M. S. *The Adult Learner: A Neglected Species.* (2nd ed.) Houston, Tex.: Gulf, 1978.

Kohlberg, L. "Stage and Sequence: The Cognitive-Developmental Approach to Socialization." In D. Goslin (ed.), *Handbook of Socialization Theory and Research.* Skokie, Ill.: Rand McNally, 1969.

Kolb, D. "Learning Styles and Disciplinary Differences." In A. W. Chickering and Associates, *The Modern American College: Responding to the New Realities of Diverse Students and a Changing Society.* San Francisco: Jossey-Bass, 1981.

Kolb, D. *Experiential Learning.* Englewood Cliffs, N.J.: Prentice-Hall, 1984.

Kolb, D., and Fry, R. "Towards an Applied Theory of Experiential Learning." In C. Cooper (ed.), *Theories of Group Processes.* London: Wiley, 1975.

Korman, A., Greenhaus, J. H., and Badin, I. J. "Personal Attitudes and Motivation." *Annual Review of Psychology,* 1977, *28,* 175–196.

Kramer, D. A. "Post-Formal Operations: A Need for Further Conceptualization." *Human Development,* 1983, *26,* 91–105.

Labouvie-Vief, G. "Beyond Formal Operations: Uses and Limits of Pure Logic in Lifespan Development." *Human Development,* 1980, *23,* 141–161.

Labouvie-Vief, G. "Dynamic Development and Mature Autonomy: A Theoretical Prologue." *Human Development,* 1982, *25,* 161–191.

Labouvie-Vief, G. "Intelligence and Cognition." In J. E. Birren and K. W. Schaie (eds.), *Handbook of the Psychology of Aging.* (2nd ed.) New York: Van Nostrand Reinhold, 1985.

Lawson, K. H. *Philosophical Concepts and Values in Adult Education.* Nottingham, England: Department of Adult Education, University of Nottingham, 1975.

Levinson, D. *The Seasons of a Man's Life.* New York: Knopf, 1978.

Lewin, K. "Group Decision and Social Change." In E. Maccoby, M. Newcomb, and E. Hartley (eds.), *Readings in Social Psychology.* New York: Holt, Rinehart & Winston, 1958.

Loevinger, J. *Ego Development: Conceptions and Theories.* San Francisco: Jossey-Bass, 1976.

Long, H. *Adult Learning: Research and Practice.* New York: Cambridge Books, 1983.

McClelland, D. C., Atkinson, J. W., Clark, R. A., and Lowell, E. L. *The Achievement Motive.* East Norwalk, Conn.: Appleton-Century-Crofts, 1953.

McClusky, H. "The Relevance of Psychology for Adult Education." In G. Jensen, A. A. Liveright, and W. Hallenbeck (eds.), *Adult Education: Outlines of an Emerging Field of University Study.* Washington, D.C.: American Association for Adult and Continuing Education, 1964.

McLeish, J., Matheson, W., and Park, J. *The Psychology of the Learning Group.* London: Hutchinson, 1973.

Maslow, A. *Toward a Psychology of Being.* New York: D. Van Nostrand, 1968.

Messick, S., and Associates. *Individuality in Learning.* San Francisco: Jossey-Bass, 1978.

Mezirow, J. "A Critical Theory of Adult Learning and Education." In M. Tight (ed.), *Adult Learning and Education.* London: Croom Helm, 1983.

Mezirow, J. "A Critical Theory of Self-Directed Learning." In S. D. Brookfield (ed.), *Self-Directed Learning: From Theory to Practice.* New Directions in Continuing Education, no. 25. San Francisco: Jossey-Bass, 1985.

Milgram, S. "Some Conditions of Obedience and Disobedience to Authority." *Human Relations,* 1965, *18* (1), 57–76.

Miller, H. L. *Participation of Adults in Education: A Force-Field Analysis.* Occasional Paper, no. 14. Boston: Center for the Study of Liberal Education for Adults, 1967.

Moore, M. G. "Independent Study." In R. D. Boyd, J. W. Apps, and Associates (eds.), *Redefining the Discipline of Adult Education.* San Francisco: Jossey-Bass, 1980.

Mulder, M. "Communication Structure, Decision Structure and Group Performance." *Sociometry,* 1960, *23,* 1–14.

Piaget, J. *The Development of Thought: Equilibrium of Cognitive Structures.* Oxford, England: Blackwell, 1978.

Riegel, K. F. "Dialectical Operations: The Final Period of Cognitive Development." *Human Development,* 1973, *16,* 346–370.

Rogers, C. *Client-Centered Therapy.* Boston: Houghton Mifflin, 1951.

Rogers, C. *Freedom to Learn for the 80s.* Westerville, Ohio: Merrill, 1983.

Rubenson, K. "Participation in Recurrent Education: A Research Review." Paper presented at a meeting of national delegates on Developments in Recurrent Education, Paris, Mar. 1977.

Rybash, J., Hoyer, W., and Roodin, P. *Adult Cognition and Aging.* Elmsford, N.Y.: Pergamon Press, 1986.

Salzberger-Wittenberg, I., and Henry, G. *The Emotional Experience of Learning and Teaching.* New York: Routledge, Chapman & Hall, 1983.

Shaw, M. *Group Dynamics.* New York: McGraw-Hill, 1981.

Sherif, M. *The Psychology of Social Norms.* New York: Harper & Row, 1935.

Sinnott, J. D. "Postformal Reasoning: The Relativistic Stage." In M. L. Commons, F. A. Richards, and C. Armon (eds.), *Beyond Formal Operations: Late Adolescent and Adult Cognitive Development.* New York: Praeger, 1984.

Skinner, B. F. *Science and Human Behaviour.* New York: Macmillan, 1959.

Skinner, B. F. *Beyond Freedom and Dignity.* New York: Viking Penguin, 1973.

Smith, J. "Explorations of Wisdom and Positive Changes with Age." Paper presented at the 5th Australian Developmental Conference, Sydney, Aug. 1988.

Smith, R. M. *Learning How to Learn.* Milton Keynes, England: Open University Press, 1983.

Squires, G. *Cognitive Styles and Adult Learning.* Nottingham, England: University of Nottingham Press, 1981.

Tennant, M. "The Concept of 'Need' in Adult Education." *Australian Journal of Adult Education,* 1985, *25* (2), 8–12.

Tennant, M. *Psychology and Adult Learning.* London: Routledge, 1988.

Tennant, M. "Expertise as a Dimension of Adult Development." *New Education,* in press.

Tough, A. *Learning Without a Teacher: A Study of Tasks and Assistance During Adult Self-Teaching Projects.* Educational Research Series, no. 3. Toronto: Ontario Institute for Studies in Education, 1967.

Tough, A. *Why Adults Learn: A Study of the Major Reasons for Beginning and Continuing a Learning Project.* Toronto: Ontario Institute for Studies in Education, 1968.

Usher, R. "The Theory-Practice Problem and Psychology as a Foundation Discipline in Adult Education." In M. Zukas (ed.), *Standing Conference on University Teaching and Research in the Education of Adults (SCUTREA): Papers from the [16th] Annual Conference.* Hull, England: University of Hull, 1986.

Wiltshire, H. "The Concepts of Learning and Need in Adult Education." *Studies in Adult Education,* 1973, *5* (1), 26–30.

CHAPTER 9

Educational Leadership
and Program Administration

Alan B. Knox

Adult education scholars give lip service to the importance of educational leadership, but practitioners complain that program administration receives inadequate attention in graduate study and scholarly writing. During the past twenty-seven years, the amount of scholarly and professional literature about program administration has increased. As a result, useful concepts are available to practitioners who provide educational leadership from adult education and related fields of study, on such topics as leadership, planning, attraction of participants, staff selection and development, resource acquisition and allocation, program coordination, and external relations. Concepts related to these topics can be used to strengthen educational leadership and guide future research. It is paradoxical that practitioners seek more attention for the administrative role than scholars are providing.

In the black book (Jensen, Liveright, and Hallenbeck, 1964), Paul Essert provided an overview of basic concepts on organization and administration of adult education. His chapter

217

began with a historical review of concepts from social sciences, general administration, and adult education. He addressed the relationship between individual satisfaction and organizational productivity through the concept of the managerial grid. Applications of the grid have continued to evolve, including application to academic administrators (Blake, Mouton, and Williams, 1981). Another theme addressed by Essert that has continued to receive attention was the conflict between the subsystem of the adult education agency and the total system of the parent organization of the agency (Apps, 1988; Katz and Kahn, 1978; Votruba, 1981). A related theme he addressed was the importance of involving internal and external stakeholders in planning and decision making, a theme that has become more prominent in recent decades with the popularity of strategic planning (Simerly and Associates, 1987). The latter part of Essert's chapter listed propositions based on his literature review regarding major administrative functions that Essert felt should be tested by research on adult education administration. Some of these propositions have been studied. A central concept throughout Essert's chapter was decision making.

During the almost three decades since Essert wrote his chapter, the knowledge base from which adult education administrators can draw has expanded (Courtenay, 1990). That knowledge base includes at least three sources: indigenous knowledge, general knowledge from related fields, and specialized knowledge.

Indigenous knowledge related to the specific local context and history is often neglected. As with administrators and professionals in all fields, adult education practitioners acquire such indigenous knowledge of specific local contingencies anecdotally. One contribution of the professional literature is to help them distill and use indigenous knowledge (Houle, 1980). The second source of knowledge is general knowledge of leadership, planning, administration, curriculum, and organizational dynamics from related fields that can be applied to adult education. The third source is specialized knowledge that deals directly with leadership of adult education in agencies and programs. In North America adult education agencies occur as units of all types of parent organizations and occasionally as freestanding provider agencies. This distinctive third source of knowledge provides a bridge that practitioners in each type of provider can use to select general knowledge from related fields and apply it to their specific local contingencies. The case has been well made that effective administrators use concepts generic to organizational leadership in any context and also concepts that are distinctive to their own type of organization (Bennis and Nanus, 1985; Corson, 1979; Courtenay, 1990; McLagan, 1989; Peters and Waterman, 1982).

During the past three decades, adult educators have shifted from a heavy reliance on writings from related fields toward a combined use of such general writings with specialized writings that cover distinctive features of adult education administration. During this period, articles and books on leadership, planning, organization, and administration in adult education have increased dramatically.

A small but growing number of books deal broadly with administration of educational programs for adults. Scholarly articles and book chapters on this topic have followed a similar trend (Courtenay, 1990). Although a few publications have covered a wide range of providers (Knox, 1982a; Knox and Associates, 1980), most have focused on a segment of the field, such as continuing higher education (Freedman, 1987; Gessner, 1987; Simerly and Associates, 1987, Strother and Klus, 1982), training and development provided by public and private enterprises for their employees (Craig, 1987; McLagan, 1989; Nadler and Nadler, 1989), and public school adult education (Langerman and Smith, 1979; Shaw, 1969).

The increased attention to administrative leadership during the past decade by adult education scholars contrasts with the neglect of the topic during the previous half century in the handbooks of adult education in the United States. The handbooks did describe program offerings of provider agencies and overviews of preparation of adult educators, but they contained no chapters on administrative leadership. The 1970 handbook had no chapter or even index listing on administration (Smith, Aker, and Kidd, 1970). By contrast, one of the set of 1980 handbooks was on developing, administering, and evaluating adult education (Knox and Associates, 1980). The 1989 *Handbook of Adult and Continuing Education,* edited by Merriam and Cunningham, contains a practice-oriented overview of administration (Smith and Offerman, 1989). However, practitioners have repeatedly complained that graduate study and scholarly writing give inadequate attention to administration of adult education (Connellan, 1973; Daniel and Rose, 1982). This neglect is surprising because most people who complete graduate study in adult education work in administrative roles.

This chapter is for people with scholarly interests in leadership of adult education, and draws from related fields of study such as administration, program development, strategic planning, organizational dynamics, and leadership. Intended readers include scholarly practitioners as well as scholars of practice from adult education and related fields. The chapter reviews the evolving scholarly and professional literature on educational leadership for adult education during the past quarter century, mainly in North America. It synthesizes major contributions about program administration from related fields as well as an increasing number of contributions specifically focused on adult education. The chapter also explores connections between scholarship and practice and concludes with suggested research directions.

The term *leadership* as used in this chapter refers to gaining agreement on desirable goals and encouraging contributions to the achievement of goals. The term overlaps partially with the term *administrator.* Not all administrators or managers are leaders and not all leaders are administrators. The focus of this chapter is on educational leadership and attention to external relations as a desirable and distinctive feature of adult education administration, in part because most instructors work for provider agencies on a part-time or short-term basis, which increases the importance of educational leadership by administrators.

In this chapter, an overview of the pertinent professional literature is organized by broad interrelated administrative functions. These functions are administrative leadership, program development, attracting participants, staffing, resources, coordination, and external relations. The professional literature reviewed includes theoretical formulations and research reports from both adult education and related fields that are relevant to adult education practice. It also includes scholarly writings about adult education and even some anecdotal reports to reflect indigenous knowledge that tends to be crystallized and shared orally. Segments of the adult education field are referred to by terms such as *continuing education, training and development, extension, community education, organization development, community development, in-service education, continuing professional education, adult religious education, and staff development.*

Although the administrative functions are reviewed in separate sections of the chapter, in practice they are very interrelated as parts of the open social systems in which administrators function in their provider agency and service area. One unifying feature of the sections is attention to decision making by agency directors and program coordinators, who have both shared and distinctive proficiencies and roles (Knox, 1982a; McLagan, 1989).

Administrative Leadership

Educational programs and services for adults are provided by agencies, most of which are dependent units of parent organizations such as educational institutions, professional associations, and public and private enterprises (business, industry, military, government, hospitals) that provide training and education opportunities for their staff. The term *provider agency* as used in this chapter refers to the organizational unit that is mainly engaged in adult education, and the term *parent organization* refers to the total organization. In provider agencies, the administrative functions of agency directors and program coordinators are especially central because administrators constitute a large proportion of people who work full time in the field. Another widespread characteristic of adult education provider agencies is that most of them are dependent units of parent organizations whose main mission is not adult education. Because most provider agencies have few policies or resources that flow automatically, successful administrators acquire resources, maintain cooperation, and provide coordination to achieve stability and compensate for the lack of institutionalization that characterizes more established and bureaucratic organizations (Votruba, 1981).

Although provider agencies vary in size, location, and relation to their parent organization, many of the distinctive characteristics that confront administrators of these agencies relate to their type of parent organization, such as school, university, enterprise, union, museum, association, or religious institution. This diversity makes comparative analysis of organization and administration of adult education across types of providers difficult but especially valuable (Houle, 1980; Peters and Associates, 1980). Thus a broad perspective on various segments of the field can enrich the leadership strategies of administrators. This broad perspective is one of the advantages of graduate study of adult education. Most of the graduates of university programs with a major in adult education work in administrative and leadership roles. Administrators have access to organized knowledge about educational leadership through publications, professional meetings, and staff development (Knox, 1982a; Votruba, 1981).

Effective administrators are leaders who achieve results with and through other people. They do so by encouraging agreement on desirable goals and contributions to the achievement of goals. Because administrators' behavior is affected by interpersonal, organizational, community, and societal influences, administrators can use an open systems view of organizational dynamics and leadership to deal with these interrelated influences (Blaney, 1987; Havelock, 1969; Katz and Kahn, 1978; Peters and Associates, 1980; Votruba, 1981). A systems view can enable administrators to understand and coordinate internal agency functions and external relations.

The importance of leadership is widely recognized. Improving an agency that provides adult education revolves around effective leadership to strengthen agency impact, image, support, enrollment, and staffing. This leadership includes program development and other agency functions such as finance and staffing. Effective administrators can clearly contribute to agency vitality (Knox, 1982b; Mezirow, Darkenwald, and Knox, 1975).

Leadership has long been crucial for initiating and sustaining adult education programs in the field. The field has relied on the personal vision and dedication of its leaders in part because of the lack of routine institutional procedures in agencies that provide adult education. This situation stands in contrast to the situation at many preparatory education institutions, in which full-time faculty members are responsible for the curriculum and routine procedures for finance and facilities are in place. In adult education, the predominant reliance on part-time and short-term staff members and volunteers to plan and conduct programs makes educational leadership by full-time administrators essential for the success of an agency (Knox, 1982b).

Roles and Decisions. Current generalizations about effective administration emphasize relations among leaders and followers in contrast with earlier attention to characteristics of administrators. Based on his ongoing study of planned change and why leaders fail, Bennis identified four strategies for effective leadership from interviews with outstanding leaders in various settings (Bennis and Nanus, 1985). They are transactions between leaders and followers that focus attention on desirable results; communication of meaning and enthusiasm that creates learning; creation of trust and organizational integrity through positioning and commitment to desirable directions; and recognition and improvement of strengths while compensating for weaknesses to achieve positive self-esteem and improve the fit between abilities and role.

Broad leadership strategies such as Bennis's are reflected in the administrator's quality of performance of various administrative roles. Mintzberg (1973), who studied actual administrative performance through qualitative research methods, concluded that most administration in various organizations is characterized by interpersonal relations, oral communication, and short amounts of time devoted to many activities. He also specified widespread administrative roles, many of which are performed by an administrator. These roles include figurehead, monitor, disseminator, spokesperson, entrepreneur (strategist), disturbance handler, resource allocator, and negotiator. Two additional roles, supervisor and liaison (intermediary), are especially important for program coordinators (Knox, 1982a). Eleven roles and thirty-five proficiencies were identified in training and development. Similar proficiencies were shared by people in each of the administrator, manager, marketer, materials developer, program designer, and change agent roles. Widespread ethical issues were also identified (McLagan, 1989).

While specification of multiple administrative roles reflects the diversity of tasks administrators perform, a focus on leadership of the program development function provides coherence (Freedman, 1987; Knox, 1982a, 1982b; Knox and Associates, 1980; Simerly and Associates, 1987; Smith and Offerman, 1989). Many writers on administration and leadership stress the importance of a distinctive mission (such as Bennis and Nanus, 1985; Peters and Waterman, 1982; Simerly and Associates, 1987). Although adult education has become increasingly central in parent organizations and in society, it remains somewhat marginal in many organizational settings. In the context of educational institutions that emphasize young full-time students, the adult education agency is different because of the focus on adult part-time and short-term students. In the context of noneducational parent organizations, the education and training provider agency is different because it deals with education (Craig, 1987; McLagan, 1989). In each instance, the success of the agency partly depends on the effectiveness of the educational programs for adults and the internal and external cooperation that occurs.

Decision making is central to program development and other aspects of agency administration. Reading pertinent professional literature can help administrators share and make explicit their rationale regarding the chain of decisions they make to maintain the stability of their agency while achieving desired improvements in the functioning of the agency. Reflection on goals as well as procedures is especially important for adult education administrators because many of them are in positions of little power. Thus, they must rely inordinately on winning and maintaining cooperation from many people who can readily withhold cooperation (Forester, 1989).

To make and implement sound decisions, effective administrators involve other people in the decision-making process. Including others in decision making involves deciding who to include in the process, clarifying the problem, agreeing on a goal, exploring options, considering criteria and values, and developing implementation strategies. Writings on administration during the past twenty-seven years have analyzed the political and bureaucratic as well as rational aspects of policy and decision making. The people who contribute to decision making bring general concepts (such as formal and informal organizations and delegation of responsibility and authority) and technical expertise (such as needs assessment or budgeting procedures) to it. They also have communication ability, interpersonal effectiveness, values, beliefs, and aspirations that influence their performance (Knox, 1982a; McLagan, 1989), as illustrated by administrative attention to a combination of prudence and risk taking to do the right thing—in contrast with only doing things right, managing risk, and avoiding difficult but important decisions.

During the past thirty years, there has been fairly stable and widespread agreement about the important functions that adult education administrators actually perform. These functions are similar to the main sections of this chapter; and related concepts can be used for their professional development. Administrators can use findings from studies of adult education administration to connect generalizations from the broad professional literature on administration with their own indigenous knowledge and familiarity with the contingencies in their specific context (Griggs and Morgan, 1988; McLagan, 1989). In agencies that value innovation, full-time administrators with preparation in adult education who are active in an association in the field are more likely than other administrators to encourage staff members to advance professionally (Blackburn, 1989; Darkenwald, 1977; Roloff, 1980). With the diversity of administrative tasks and lack of structure at provider agencies, administrators are understandably concerned about time management.

Priority Setting. Leadership by agency directors and their boards or policy committees entails attention to decision making about the decision-making process (Houle, 1989). The resulting policies reflect the priorities important to achieving agency goals. Such policies and priorities involve current choices made about desired future outcomes. Futures forecasting and invention procedures provide tools for exploring desirable and undesirable trends to consider so that an agency can increase the likelihood that it will survive, prosper, and produce beneficial results (Brockett, 1987; Freedman, 1987; Knox, 1982a; Simerly and Associates, 1987). Administrators can work with their staff to prepare scenarios for alternative futures, analyze the likely costs and benefits of each, and then make decisions likely to lead toward the most desirable and feasible goals.

External influences tend to be especially powerful for adult education provider agencies, which in many instances have more permeable boundaries than their parent organization and depend more on voluntary and unpredictable contributions of support (Corson, 1979; Knox, 1982a; Votruba, 1981). More on external influences is presented later in the chapter. However, contextual analysis is essential to effective policy making, program development, and decision-making generally, so it is briefly noted here. The broad field of adult education is pluralistic and fragmented, with many providers interested in serving adult learners. A perspective on the field can help agency administrators fashion a distinctive mission and niche in a turbulent environment. Contextual analysis procedures such as environmental scanning and use of advisory committees or focus groups can enable administrators to make timely responses to emerging threats and opportunities in their service area. The sources of these societal influences are increasingly global (Knox, 1979b; Simerly and Associates, 1987; Votruba, 1981).

Strategic Planning. One of the most useful and unifying concepts and procedures for adult education administration to emerge in recent decades is strategic planning. The essence of strategic planning is to involve internal and external stakeholders in a combination of long-range planning to achieve consensus on desirable goals and procedures to strengthen implementation (Simerly and Associates, 1987). Internal stakeholders include current participants, instructors, and administrators in the agency along with policy makers in the parent organization. External stakeholders include potential participants, public and private funding agencies, government policy makers, and the mass media. A major weakness of some long-range planning procedures has been insufficient attention to implementation. Involving representatives of such stakeholders in the planning process can improve the plans and increase implementation because of the stakeholders' greater understanding and commitment to the plans (Mitroff, 1983). Broad involvement of stakeholders in strategic planning requires that they have confidence in the person leading the planning effort and that the administrator have a participative leadership style.

Recent writings about reflective practitioners, organizational development, and action science have included specific concepts and procedures that adult education administrators can use to specify positive and negative influences on organizational change. These concepts include attention both to the effectiveness of educational activities to achieve objectives and to the desirability of the objectives themselves (Argyris, Putnam, and Smith, 1985; Mezirow and Associates, 1990). An agency has an organizational culture that also influences change efforts. The culture includes informal norms that can either help or hinder administrative leadership. Administrators can use an understanding of positive and negative influences and organizational culture to harness positive influences and deflect negative influences. Nonadministrators associated with the provider agency can also exert leadership (Schein, 1985).

Effective administrators monitor agency functioning. One source of information for monitoring and leadership is evaluation, which can be used for planning, improvement, and accountability (Deshler, 1984; Knox, 1979a; Knox and Associates, 1980, especially Chapter Four). Full-time administrators are the most likely sources of information on research, evaluation, and general professional literature that could be used to enrich agency decision making, functioning, and evaluation.

In summary, educational leadership by administrators can contribute to agency culture and vitality. Administrative effectiveness and strategic planning also reflect relationships between the agency and stakeholders in its parent organization and service area, along with the administrator's perspective on the adult education field.

Program Development

The most distinguishing feature of adult education administration, in contrast with administration in other fields, is the desirability of leadership for program development. At least in higher education, adult education administrators tend to develop programs quite intuitively, with little reference to pertinent writings (Pennington and Green, 1976). However, about one-third of adult education research is on aspects of program development. It makes up the single largest part of scholarly and professional writing in the field, which is understandable because program development is applicable across all types of provider agencies. At least in university continuing professional education, the quality of educational leadership in and attention to program development were the characteristics most associated with agency vitality (Knox, 1982b). The focus of this section is on educational leadership by program administrators regarding broad course offerings and formats (discussion groups, workshops, organizational development, distance education) and not on decisions by individual instructors regarding coverage of content and teaching methods. Of course, program development by program coordinators involves people in various roles. Program coordinators orient and assist instructors, work with planning committees, and obtain support from policy makers and agency directors. Involving adult learners in the planning and implementation process can be beneficial.

Much has been written about the development of programs in adult education that applies to program administrators in all provider agencies who use any type of program format (Havelock, 1969; Houle, 1972; Knowles, 1980; Knox and Associates, 1980; Sork and Buskey, 1986). Some program development writings, however, are on specific formats and parts of the field, such as community development (Biddle, 1965), organizational development (Argyris, Putnam, and Smith, 1985), conferences and workshops (Ilsley, 1985; Sork, 1984), distance education (Wedemeyer, 1981), and self-directed learning (Smith, 1982). Some writings are focused on specific types of provider agency, such as extension (Boyle, 1981), schools (Langerman and Smith, 1979), museums (Collins, 1981), and hospitals (Cooper and Hornback, 1973; Green, Grosswald, Suter, and Walthall, 1984). The past decade has brought a marked increase in writings on program development for people engaged in the training and development that enterprises of all kinds (business, industry, military, government, schools, hospitals) provide for their employees and volunteers (Craig, 1987; Lindquist, 1978; McLagan, 1989; Marsick, 1988; Nadler, 1982; Schein, 1978).

The specific organization of the program development function and the roles of the people involved in program development vary greatly within type of provider agency as well as across the field. Such variation is associated with agency characteristics of size, clientele, goals, relation to parent organization, availability of experts on the subject area, and so on. Specific organizational contingencies such as agreement on clear tasks and relations between administrators and staff members affect educational leadership (Fiedler and Chemers, 1974; Votruba, 1981). The structure and function of program development is also affected by situational influences other than educational technology and relations with the parent organization, such as the nature of the service area and availability of programs from other adult education providers.

Needs Assessment. A central task of program administrators in adult education is ensuring that new programs and existing programs are responsive to client needs and reflect the provider's purposes and resources. Effective administrators explore multiple sources to identify new program directions that fit both agency mission and unmet educational needs (Knox and Associates, 1980).

Needs assessment by program administrators focuses on types of clients to serve, programs to offer, and delivery formats to use. This type of assessment contrasts with needs assessment by instructors, which focuses on analysis of current proficiencies of participants and selection of content and methods for a specific program and group of learners (Knox, 1979a). Program administrators can enhance decision making regarding needs assessment by paying attention to value judgments (Monette, 1977) and general clientele characteristics (Aslanian and Brickell, 1980; Darkenwald and Knox, 1984; Knox, 1979c; Peterson, 1983), as well as information from and about potential participants in the specific service area. Use of multiple methods of assessment and sources of assessment information, at least one of which is potential participants, increases program success (Knox, 1979b). The influence of program administrators on decisions about goals, staffing, marketing, and external support is increased if they use data-based generalizations about high-priority educational needs (Knox, 1982b).

Contextual Analysis. Another major aspect of program development is contextual analysis, which was neglected in past research reports and professional literature but has received increased attention recently. Contextual analysis can include assessment of the provider's purposes and resources, other agency programs in the service area, and the socioeconomic conditions that affect the service area. Such societal influences are more likely to be considered by program administrators as they prepare proposals, defend budgets, market programs, and seek cooperation than by instructors who focus more on teaching and learning in a specific program.

Environmental scanning is one method of contextual analysis. In this method, agency staff members review and share summaries of publications on topics of interest, which are then analyzed to identify promising new program directions (Naisbitt and Aburdene, 1990; Simerly and Associates, 1989).

Objective Setting. Program administrators use information about needs and context to make decisions about courses to be offered, instructors to teach the courses, and resources to support the courses as well as to orient and assist instructors. The essence of educational leadership is attention to emerging directions and priority setting, in contrast to routine maintenance of existing programs by "making arrangements." When seeking agreement on high-priority goals, program administrators can use several sources of information in addition to conclusions from needs assessment and contextual analysis. One source of information is projection of emerging directions (Brockett, 1987). Another is attention to the value judgments implicit in goal setting, such as the ethical dilemma when seeking to accommodate both individual needs and organizational expectations (Brockett, 1988; McLagan, 1989).

Value judgments and assumptions tend to be implicit and unexamined unless one deliberately and critically reflects on the desirability of goals. Comparative perspectives, such as familiarity with popular education in Latin America (Freire, 1970; LaBelle, 1986) and emancipatory education (Mezirow and Associates, 1990), are especially valuable in analyzing cultural and organizational values in various provider agency settings in the United States (Argyris, Putnam, and Smith, 1985; Mezirow and Associates, 1990). Program administrators can promote explicit priorities through the use of advisory and planning committees that are representative of clients, resource persons, policy makers, and administrators (Knox, 1979b). As in leadership generally, the intended result is agreement on desired goals.

Learning Activities. One use of educational goals and priorities is to guide the selection and organization of content and instructional activities. Although detailed planning and implementation of a sequence of teaching-learning activities is associated with the instructor's role, program administrators make important and distinctive contributions to the process (Knox, 1979b, 1986). Administrators familiar with various instructional methods can use generalizations about the effectiveness of the methods for selecting resource persons to help plan and conduct the program and guide the overall process, especially for conferences, workshops, and other adult education programs with multiple instructors (Ilsley, 1985; Sork, 1984). For any format, administrators familiar with program development can help select and organize learning activities likely to be responsive and effective in a specific program (Houle, 1972; Knowles, 1980; Lewis, 1986). The administrator's contribution to such decision making is especially valuable when the program entails use of educational technology (such as educational telephone networks, television broadcasts, or computer-based education) for which an educational utility or infrastructure at the level of the agency or service area undergirds individual courses or workshops (Niemi and Gooler, 1987; Wedemeyer, 1981).

Program Evaluation. Evaluation of an individual course or workshop tends to focus on instructor evaluation of learner achievement and assessment of participant satisfaction with the course and instructor. By contrast, the scope of program evaluation by agency administrators is much broader. It includes all aspects of program planning, implementation, and impact along with all other aspects of the functioning and improvement of the agency. These other aspects, such as staffing, marketing, finance, policy making, and external relations, are interrelated with each other and with program development. Therefore, evaluation of their relationships is as important as evaluation of the separate aspects and components of program development.

The field of program evaluation has evolved greatly during the past twenty-five years. It has moved from a focus on quantitative tests and measurements used to assess learner achievement of behavioral objectives to a combination of quantitative and qualitative data used to assess the value and effectiveness of the program for purposes of program planning, improvement, and accountability in ways that encourage use of conclusions (McLagan, 1989; Knox and Associates, 1980; Patton, 1978). Impact evaluation studies in various segments of the field demonstrate that well-designed adult education programs can produce substantial improvements in learner performance beyond the program and benefits to people in related roles (Knox, 1979b). Evaluation of an adult education program to improve it is even more extensive than impact evaluation, and a recent review identified many useful concepts and procedures that practitioners can use to strengthen their program evaluation (Deshler, 1984), such as program monitoring, value audits, and metaevaluation. Effective program evaluation uses a combination of internal evaluation for improvement and external evaluation of impact and addresses issues of importance to various stakeholders to whom conclusions are reported (Knox and Associates, 1980; Patton, 1978). Because so many practitioners are unfamiliar with and intimidated by evaluation, a crucial administrative role is to encourage and support evaluation activities likely to be worth the time and effort devoted to them.

Attracting Participants

Most adult education administrators play the numbers game. Ongoing attraction of adult learners as participants is essential for achievement of educational objectives. Also, participants provide agencies with income, directly through registration fees or indirectly through enrollment figures used to justify financial subsidy. Without participants, instructors and administrators would be unnecessary. It is therefore understandable that most adult education administrators emphasize attracting and retaining participants.

Marketing. During the past fifteen years, adult education programs have increasingly adapted and used concepts and procedures from marketing theory, especially those related to nonprofit organizations, to attract participants (Knox and Associates, 1980; Simerly and Associates, 1989). Many authors recommend that agencies use a comprehensive deliberate marketing strategy that has a client orientation as a strong part of program development, agency policies, and daily routines. Research and evaluation enable administrators to audit the current marketing effort; assess client needs by market segments; analyze the service area, including other providers; track marketing results; and evaluate the ongoing marketing program (Simerly and Associates, 1989).

To be effective, each provider should specify its clientele and service area, including the numbers and characteristics of adult learners it seeks to serve. This helps provider agencies to identify the other providers that seek to serve similar learners with similar programs. A basic issue in the field as well as in an agency is what to do to attract and serve the types of adults who are prominent in the mission statement as an intended clientele but are underrepresented in the current participants. Many guidelines for attracting such underserved adults emphasize increasing program responsiveness and decreasing barriers to participation as well as providing persuasive information about the program (Darkenwald and Larson, 1980).

The recent *Handbook of Marketing for Continuing Education* provides the most comprehensive and detailed source on marketing for the field (Simerly and Associates, 1989). Although the chapter authors and examples are oriented toward continuing higher education, the concepts and procedures are readily applicable to most segments of the field of adult education.

Many personal and situational variables affect an adult's decision whether or not to participate in a program. The variables include agency image and price, place, and time of program. Another variable is perceived program quality and benefits. Administrators can use publicity and public relations to increase awareness of a program among potential participants. However, a powerful influence on a participant's decision to participate is word of mouth comments by satisfied participants. Thus, attention to high-quality, varied, and interesting educational opportunities that result in mutually beneficial exchanges is the fundamental way to both retain current participants and attract new ones. Marketing procedures such as direct mail, human interest stories in the media, advertisements, and telemarketing should emphasize client benefits. A person's decision to participate reflects the cumulative effect of such messages communicated by the agency, along with conversations with people familiar with the agency and program, such as past participants and people from community agencies who make referrals.

Reducing Barriers. The potential clients who might benefit from the program but do not participate may not know about the program, may face barriers to participation, or may participate in programs by other providers. Counseling services at agencies or community centers have proven to be effective ways to help adults with educational and career planning and overcoming apprehension and other barriers. Counseling contributes to participation and persistence (DiSilvestro, 1981; Heffernan, 1981; McLagan, 1989). Features of an educational program that especially encourage persistence and application are clear and relevant objectives, individualization, active learning methods that promote deep processing and practice, and evaluative feedback (Hiemstra and Sisco, 1990; Knox, 1986; Merriam and Caffarella, 1991).

Responsiveness. An understanding of adult development and learning helps administrators develop and market responsive programs (Knox, 1977a; Merriam and Caffarella, 1991). The range of individual differences widens during the life cycle, and because of this increasing diversity it is especially important to individualize program options and segment markets to attract and serve distinct categories of adult learners (Boshier and Collins, 1985; Hiemstra and Sisco, 1990; Simerly and Associates, 1989). Adult motivation to engage in educational activity reflects discrepancies between an individual's current and desired proficiencies that are neither trivial nor overwhelming (Knox, 1985). Major role changes trigger a person to participate by creating a heightened readiness to learn, in part due to greater awareness of discrepancies or needs that may have been longstanding (Aslanian and Brickell, 1980; Knox, 1977a). In occupational as in other roles, congruence of individual needs and organizational expectations can encourage both educational activity and application of newly acquired knowledge (Schein, 1978).

Agency administrators can use such concepts to work with other staff members, specialists, and advisory groups to develop and implement a strategy to attract and retain participants, which is an integral part of program development and agency functioning. A comprehensive approach, in contrast with the widespread practice of trying to encourage participation by relying mainly on promotional activities, is most likely to be successful. In most agencies, a comprehensive strategy requires that the director or another staff member understands and uses a rationale for encouraging participation that draws from the type of knowledge base reviewed in this section.

Staffing

Because administrators achieve goals with and through other people, staffing decisions are crucial to agency success. Many of the marketing concepts related to mutually beneficial exchanges that can be used to encourage participation apply as well to attracting and retaining able staff and volunteers to help teach, counsel, coordinate, plan, and conduct educational programs for adults. For example, analysis of exchanges can identify multiple incentives that can motivate staff members to stay.

Personnel Policies and Selection. Underlying specific staffing decisions are policy decisions regarding staff compensation, qualifications, assistance, numbers, and roles. Such personnel policies reflect major decisions and trends regarding program development, finance, and relations with the parent organization. A surprisingly neglected consideration is the amount and type of attention that is given to staff development.

Such specific decisions about staffing are best made as part of broad personnel and staffing policies closely associated with major aspects of planning, program development, finance, and external relations (Brown and Copeland, 1979; Knox, 1982a; Simerly and Associates, 1987). This broad range of decisions is affected by societal conditions, policies of the parent organization, the pool of qualified and interested potential staff members, and opportunities and incentives for staff members to work with other providers and organizations. At the core of these dynamics is a basic supply and demand mechanism.

The lack of institutionalization and routine functioning of most adult education agencies also affects staffing. These conditions are reflected in the small proportion of full-time positions with fringe benefits and long-term commitments at most agencies. Typically, an agency's staff positions will include a mix of full-time, part-time, and volunteer positions for instructors, administrators, and other staff roles. Staff members also include people in key roles in the parent organization who make important contributions that affect agency functioning. These people may be deans and department chairs in higher education, line supervisors and middle managers in enterprises, and business managers in many agencies. If an agency were independent, many of the decisions that people from the parent organization make regarding the adult education function would be made by agency staff, so it is useful to include staff members of the parent organization in personnel and staffing plans and implementation (Ilsley and Niemi, 1981; Knox, 1982a). Sometimes these stakeholders and some potential participants are represented on a planning committee that contributes to staffing decisions.

An important aspect of staffing is attracting and selecting new staff members. This process is typically formal and detailed for the few full-time positions. By contrast, staff selection is usually informal for the myriad part-time and short-term paid and volunteer staff members, whose contributions may be as short as a one-hour presentation and discussion at a conference. New part-time staff members are recruited and selected to replace those who do not continue and to augment the pool of successful staff members whose continuation is important to the stable functioning of the agency. This replacement of people who leave is parallel to participant recruitment and retention. Attraction and retention of able staff members reflects a matching process in which agency roles and multiple incentives are compared by potential staff members and volunteers with their own background, expectations, and alternatives. Financial incentives are typically minor for part-time staff and volunteers, so administrators should give special attention to the range of other incentives and benefits to part-time staff. Some staff members continue because they value helping the clientele, disseminating content, increasing personal visibility, and gaining expertise (Brown and Copeland, 1979; Ilsley and Niemi, 1981; Knox, 1982a; Knox and Associates, 1980).

Staff Development. Most people who help adults learn and contribute to program development have little formal preparation when they start, so they learn on the job. Thus staff orientation and development are especially important for staff improvement, and for part-time staff, development tends to be informal. Administrators working with staff development of instructors should personally use the concepts and procedures for helping adults learn that the instructors should use because such modeling may be more influential than the subject matter content (Knox, 1986).

Agency characteristics that interfere with staff development include funding fluctuations, staff turnover, varied staff backgrounds and schedules, and staff unfamiliarity with important generalizations about helping adults learn. Staff development can be more effective when staff members are expert, committed to lifelong learning for themselves and the learners, interested in improving the program and learner benefits, and willing to use new ideas about helping adults learn. Increasingly, agencies include at least one person familiar with new ideas about learning. That familiarity is a basis for educational leadership and quality improvement.

Many writings about continuing professional education and organizational development are applicable to orientation and development of agency staff (Cervero, 1988; Houle, 1980; Lindquist, 1978). Program administrators must be familiar with such material and committed to using it for staff development. Staff development also depends on materials and assistance, encouragement and benefits to staff members, and interpersonal dynamics in the agency. In North America, universities and associations strengthen staff development through publications, workshops, and consultation. This contrasts with the lack of such assistance in many developing countries. For example, popular education in most Latin American countries is quite separate from government and university assistance. In many developing countries in Asia and elsewhere, in-service programs for adult education instructors include teaching them about subject matter content as well as about the teaching process because of the lack of qualified instructors (Boshier, 1985).

Interpersonal Relations. The supervisory role of agency administrators includes staff selection, development, performance review, and termination. Because many staff members and volunteers work under short-term arrangements, the main influence on program quality is the program administrators' rehiring of only those instructors who perform satisfactorily. This places a major responsibility on the program administrators to understand and use concepts related to helping adults learn as they make decisions about position descriptions, along with decisions about staff selection, development, and termination (Knox, 1979a, 1985, 1986). Administrators can use such concepts to help inexperienced instructors to increase their effectiveness.

With the general lack of personnel policies in most agencies, conflict management is an important consideration for administrators who confront differing expectations (Simerly and Associates, 1987). Handling conflict includes negotiation and win-win strategies. Contingency management concepts are useful for adjusting leadership style or staffing decisions in relation to agency dynamics such as agreement on task structure, satisfactory leader-member relations, and the power positions of the administrator (Fiedler and Chemers, 1974).

Resources

A central administrative concern is acquisition of funds, facilities, and other resources to allow teaching and learning to occur and agency goals to be achieved. To stretch very limited resources to pursue seemingly unlimited program goals calls for substantial expertise in resource acquisition and allocation. Most provider agencies conform to the budgetary and financial policies and procedures of the parent organization. Generally, financial decisions reflect both technical policies and procedures and value judgments regarding the relative desirability of the uses to which resources are devoted. An underlying issue is, Who helps make such judgments and on what basis?

Flow of Resources. Financial decisions should be compatible with program decisions so that financial choices serve program purposes. This goal suggests some decentralization of financial decisions to the program unit in large agencies. Money flows through an agency in a "financial transformation cycle." Typically, funds are acquired from various sources such as participation fees, employer reimbursement, subsidy by foundation grants or tax funds, and assistance by the parent organization. The funds are expended for staff salaries, facilities, materials, and marketing to attract participants. The funds to acquire these ingredients are used to produce outcomes through the teaching/learning transaction and related staff support. The financial transformation cycle begins again when the agency receives fees and subsidies in exchange for services rendered (Knox, 1982a). Agency functioning depends on both an effective financial transformation and on the justification of this transformation to various stakeholders. Effective administrators give adequate attention to technical procedures and value judgments related to resource acquisition and allocations.

Aside from human resources, agency administrators are usually most concerned about money, but money is not the only other resource they seek. Many agencies depend on in-kind contributions that otherwise would require financial expenditures. In-kind contributions include volunteer assistance. Parent organizations may also provide in-kind assistance without charge, such as use of facilities and overhead administrative support. Even though such resources may not be budgeted, they should be planned, coordinated, and accounted for (Matkin, 1985).

Budgeting. Program budgeting is a standard way to coordinate program and financial decisions (Matkin, 1985). The ongoing process of budget preparation, revision, approval, administration, and reporting allows articulation of both types of decisions at various levels in the agency. Matkin's (1985) decision process model helps program coordinators to make accurate budgetary projections of income and expenditures when planning a program and then to use the summary financial report afterwards for planning the next program. Matkin's approach also provides a comprehensive and flexible framework of budgeting and finance concepts and procedures for the total agency. These concepts and procedures could readily be adapted by administrators in any size and type of agency, although Matkin's orientation is toward continuing higher education. His suggestions include achieving consensus on the budget process, setting realistic guidelines and targets in a budgetary system that takes both the internal and external environment into account, doing break-even analysis, and monitoring and reporting on financial performance.

Cost Accounting. Although general financial concepts and practices are widespread, specific procedures vary among agencies, mainly based on the practices in the parent organization. Some practices that vary are the level of fee paid by each participant and the extent of cost recovery from fees that is expected for the agency. This decision about fees is influenced by the client's ability to pay, available subsidy funds, and the fee charged for similar programs of other provider agencies. Average costs per participant learning hour (PLH) also varies greatly by type of agency. The average costs per PLH in 1980 were $2 for adult education in public schools, $3 for proprietary schools, $5 for higher education, $8 for community organizations, $15 for professional associations, and $26 for enterprises (Anderson and Kasl, 1982). These average costs per PLH reflect instructor salary and amount paid for facilities, marketing, and travel expense, in addition to course enrollments. Administrators who understand the typical pattern of expenditures that contribute to such divergent average costs in other types of provider agencies can strengthen financial planning in their own agency.

Acquisition and Allocation. Most provider agencies acquire resources from multiple sources. When they request special funds for an unusual program or pilot project, they sometimes submit a proposal to the parent organization or to external organizations such as philanthropic foundations, government agencies that provide grant funds, and enterprises. Buskey (1981) provides an excellent overview of procedures for preparing successful proposals. Some providers depend heavily on grant funds, and substantial staff time is devoted to preparing proposals and (if the proposal is successful) preparing progress reports.

Resource allocation is another aspect of administration.

It includes allocation of budget, space, and various forms of assistance and supplies. When agencies have prepared program goals, plans, projections, and budgets, resource allocation can be based on plans of work in relation to available resources. Agencies must negotiate with funders when resources are inadequate, and additional plans can be made for acquisitions of additional resources, perhaps from unusual sources. A benefit of strategic planning is that it can strengthen the program rationale and commitment of multiple stakeholders to contributing support. This enables administrators to take the initiative and not just react to budget problems.

Program Coordination

The core of the adult education agency is the educational program that combines participants, instructors, and resources to achieve learner and agency goals. Educational leadership entails coordination largely within the agency and in relation to the parent organization.

Decentralization. In larger agencies, some degree of decentralization and delegation to program units is desirable. The agency director or associate director, along with the heads of the program units in larger agencies, has responsibility for program coordination and supervision. Sometimes educational technology or special facilities, such as learning centers, educational telephone networks, television stations, or conference centers, provide the basis for coordination. The administration of such facilities constitutes a distinctive contribution. Coordination is facilitated by setting forth a few clear and important guidelines in policies and decisions about budgeting and resource allocations. Examples of such guidelines include authorization to make decisions about content coverage and cost recovery.

Most agencies must continually initiate new programs to remain viable because some of the old programs accomplish their purposes and must be replaced. There are many sources of ideas for new programs, including agency mission and resources, professional literature, contextual analysis, needs assessment, environmental scanning, and futures forecasting (Knox and Associates, 1980). The launching of a new program can be more successful if potential new ideas are screened to select the most promising in terms of client appeal, feasibility of program development, provision for trial use, and, if successful, plans for expansion (Knox, 1982a). Planning committees are often used to start a new program.

Organizational Culture. As administrators provide program coordination and seek organizational cooperation and change, they confront a phenomenon called organizational culture. This term refers to the norms and informal as well as formal practices that characterize the people associated with the agency, including pertinent people in the parent organization. The organizational culture can help or hinder achievement of administrative initiatives that depend on congruence of views. Administrators can increase such congruence through staffing and consensus building. Because most adult education agencies function in turbulent and ambiguous environments, the vision, values, and priorities that administrators are able to convey are a major means by which they can gain consensus on goals, efforts to achieve goals, and staff productivity (McLagan, 1989; Peters and Waterman, 1982; Schein, 1985). The leadership style that is likely to be effective depends in part on specific contingencies in the organization, such as staff commitment to goals and acceptance of administrative influence (Fiedler and Chemers, 1974). Organizational development is a major means of organizational change, especially in the workplace (McLagan, 1989).

Parent Organization. Relations with the parent organization can be a crucial part of organizational functioning for some agencies. A mutually beneficial exchange between agency and parent organization is vital for a productive relationship (Votruba, 1981). For example, administrative leadership oriented toward both clientele and the parent organization is a source of vitality in agencies (Knox, 1982b). In public school or community college adult basic education, agency effectiveness also depends on administrative leadership, but this leadership is oriented more toward the agency and the clientele and less toward the parent organization than is the case for university-based providers (Mezirow, Darkenwald, and Knox, 1975). Green, Grosswald, Suter, and Walthall (1984) analyzed "quality elements" for comprehensive planning, implementation, and monitoring of continuing education for health professionals, especially those associated with hospitals and clinics. The quality elements were presented as standards to be used for in-service education of adult education staff and for agency evaluation. The study analyzes generic aspects of organizational dynamics and distinctive features of staff development by health care providers. It has many practical implications for agency administration. The study provides one of the few comprehensive analyses of the many aspects of functioning of a specific type of adult education agency. McLagan (1989) provides a similar analysis fur enterprise training departments. Another example of relations with the parent organization is provided by correctional education, in which parent organization concern about security tends to be a major negative influence on the educational program (MacNeil, 1980).

External Relations

As administrators seek to exert their authority on agency policies and priorities, they confront both internal and external influences. Strategic planning should review internal influences, but should also give special attention to external influences, often grouped as threats or opportunities. Major influences on organizational functioning and change tend to be external, yet these influences are least susceptible to administrative control. External influences include the agency's service area, especially in relation to potential participants, staff, resources, and other adult education providers. External influences also include broader national and international social, political, and economic trends and issues (McLagan, 1989; Knox, 1982a).

Environmental Influences. Realistically, how is a local agency administrator supposed to be familiar with all external influences?

When local strategic planning includes environmental scanning, the resulting overview of pertinent external influences is likely to be very useful (Simerly and Associates, 1989). Otherwise, published overviews of external influences can provide administrators with an efficient orientation and promising ideas. For example, Naisbitt and Aburdene (1990) recently identified ten megatrends for the 1990s that have implications for adult education. They are global economy, the arts, free market socialism, life-styles, privatizations of welfare states, rise of the Pacific Rim, women in leadership, biological metaphors, religious revival, and individualism. Other recent writings provide more depth on topics such as individualism and community (Bellah and Associates, 1985), excellence and productivity (Peters and Waterman, 1982), and relations between higher education and society (Apps, 1988). Such trends enable administrators to explore promising directions for their agency by considering important planning and policy questions they might otherwise ignore.

Legislation such as the initiation of federal support in the United States for the Cooperative Extension Service about seventy-five years ago or for adult basic education about twenty-five years ago has an impact on agency functioning that changes over the years. Other societal trends, such as new technology and competition from other providers, contribute to the evolution that provider agencies experience over the years (Moore, 1982). Administrators who want to strengthen the position and image of their agency in its parent organization and service area can emphasize to external stakeholders the contributions and benefits of the agency that the stakeholders value. It is especially important to emphasize these contributions and benefits on an ongoing basis and not wait until budget cuts or other major problems arise.

Environmental influences and the orientation of the provider agency can interact. Belsheim (1988) found that continuing professional education centers that were oriented toward providing sequential educational opportunities for groups had environments characterized by informal relations with the parent organization, a relationship with an influential professional association, and competition from other providers. By contrast, the centers that were oriented toward informational services to individual professionals had environments characterized by more reliance on external grants and support services from the parent organization and more contact with professionals. Centers with varied missions were characterized by less competition, less dependence on grants, and less difficulty obtaining resource persons than was the case for predominantly education or service-oriented centers. These findings suggest the types of external influences that administrators should consider when analyzing their own service area.

Aside from global influences on the content of adult education, a comparative understanding of educational programs for adults in other national settings helps administrators clarify organizational dynamics in their own situation, especially societal influences. In recent years, a number of publications have presented such a worldwide perspective on adult education (Bhola, 1988; Charters and Hilton, 1989; Knox, 1987; Titmus, 1989).

A benefit for administrators who are active in a comprehensive professional association such as the American Association for Adult and Continuing Education is that its publications and meetings increase their familiarity with educational programs for adults in other types of agencies. This comparative perspective can promote both mutually beneficial collaboration and attention to the external aspects of strategic planning.

Collaboration. Because adult education is pluralistic, adults in rural areas and small towns may be able to choose between a small number of programs, adults in small cities may have hundreds of programs to choose between, and adults in large metropolitan areas may have thousands to choose between. In addition, some community organizations refer potential participants to an agency, and other organizations are recipients of people who complete programs.

Agency administrators can relate to such providers in quite different ways, including collaborating, competing, or remaining uninvolved (Baden, 1987; Beder, 1984; Knox, 1982a). Guidelines are available to help administrators decide the types of interorganizational relations that are desirable and to achieve such relationships, including use of mixed strategies. Partnerships characterized by common goals, complementary contributions, and shared benefits are more likely to be successful than collaborative efforts that lack these features.

It is especially important for adult education administrators to take the initiative regarding collaboration. If an agency has established a distinctive niche, other providers may readily cooperate with the agency. Many providers seek to serve a similar clientele, but their specific program offerings may not be duplicated. This is especially so when an educational institution with faculty members and library materials enters into complementary cooperation with a noneducational organization (such as an enterprise or an association) with members who want to learn (Darkenwald, 1983). Providers may cooperate to pay for an expensive utility such as a telephone or television network. Local or regional adult education councils can promote such cooperation. State agencies provide coordination in some parts of the field, such as adult basic education, retraining, community colleges, and the Cooperative Extension Service. Universities tend not to be included in part because they resist such coordination. State coordinating systems have affected local agency administration through cooperative arrangements for data collection, reporting, accountability, and preparation of handbooks for administrators in the state.

Future Directions for Research

The foregoing sections provided highlights from the knowledge base of pertinent scholarly and professional literature that can be used by adult education administrators to strengthen decision making in their major functions. However, a two-way street runs between research and practice, as indicated in Chapter Two by Cervero on theory and practice and in Chapter Three by Merriam on research. Practice-related concerns of administrators can be combined with reviews of scholarly literature to identify promising research questions.

This concluding section identifies emerging directions for

research regarding the development and administration of educational programs for adults. It follows the pattern of earlier reviews of desirable research directions by building on the overview of emerging issues and directions in the foregoing sections of this chapter and listing some illustrative questions for future research (Knox, 1977b). The questions are grouped by the chapter sections on administrative functions.

Administrative Leadership

1. What is the relative effectiveness of various relationships between agency administrators and major stakeholders?
2. What are the relative influences of rational, political, and bureaucratic models of decision making on agency stability and change?
3. What types of encouragement of staff members by administrators are associated with innovation by staff members?
4. What accounts for unusually strong educational leadership by some agency directors?
5. What influences help account for trends during the past three decades in scholarly attention to the organization and administration of adult education?

Program Development

1. What are the strengths and weaknesses of various ways in which the program development function is organized across various types of providers?
2. What is the relative effectiveness of various combinations of needs assessment procedures across various types of providers and clienteles?
3. What is the cost effectiveness of courses that use educational technology compared with similar courses that do not?
4. What valid and efficient evaluation instruments can be developed to assess outcomes of major types of adult education activities?

Attracting Participants

1. What is the relative contribution of personal and situational influences on learner participation across client and provider characteristics?

2. What is the relative effectiveness of various marketing strategies on attracting various categories of hard-to-reach adults?
3. What are major marketing features of program development and when may a marketing emphasis be inappropriate?
4. What roles do and can administrators play in individualization of instruction?

Staffing

1. What combinations of incentives and rewards best attract and retain able staff?
2. Given the widespread complaint about inadequate staff development for adult education instructors, what are some examples of effective and efficient staff development and why?
3. What are major situational contingencies that relate to effectiveness of agency administrative style?

Resources

1. How can widespread budgeting and finance procedures be adapted for use in small provider agencies?
2. What is the impact on agency vitality of voluntary or imposed policies and practices that result in either financial surpluses or deficits that require subsidy?
3. What is the result of the various strategies recommended for obtaining external funding of grant proposals?

Coordination

1. What administrative roles and organizational dynamics are associated with agency vitality?
2. What is the extent of cooperation that occurs within and among various types of providers?
3. What has been the trend in recent years regarding the marginality or centrality of adult education agencies, and what helps to account for this trend?

External Relations

1. What are the costs and benefits to an agency of environmental scanning?

2. In what ways do agencies change over the years, what internal and external influences contribute to this evolution, and what are the implications of such changes for administrators?
3. What do crossnational comparative analyses of adult education agencies suggest as major societal influences on agency functioning that have implications for local strategic planning?
4. What are the advantages and disadvantages of collaborative, competitive, and mixed strategies for interorganizational relations?
5. How effective are community-based educational and career counseling services for adults, in relation to independent efforts by individual providers?

Adult education scholars can use the foregoing research questions to stimulate attention to educational leadership and program administration. In recent decades there has been a steady increase in the scholarly and professional literature on such leadership, produced by scholars in adult education and related fields of study. Administrators who want to strengthen the functioning of adult education agencies can combine generic ideas from related fields with pertinent ideas from adult education research that address the distinctive realities of practice at the operational level. Combined use of generic and distinctive knowledge can draw attention to many aspects of program administration, including specific incentives and deterrents that influence participation by adult learners, effective incentives and assistance to attract and retain able part-time staff and volunteers, and societal influences on relations with the parent organization and other providers. Especially important is educational leadership to include various stakeholders — learners, instructors, coordinators, and policy makers — in widely applicable program development procedures. Ideas from adult education taken in conjunction with ideas from fields related to educational leadership and administration could help focus scholars' attention on the administrative role and encourage them to provide the information practitioners are seeking.

References

Anderson, R. E., and Kasl, E. S. *The Costs and Financing of Adult Education and Training.* Lexington, Mass.: Lexington Books, 1982.

Apps, J. W. *Higher Education in a Learning Society: Meeting New Demands for Education and Training.* San Francisco: Jossey-Bass, 1988.

Argyris, C., Putnam, R., and Smith, D. M. *Action Science: Concepts, Methods, and Skills for Research and Intervention.* San Francisco: Jossey-Bass, 1985.

Aslanian, C. B., and Brickell, H. M. *Americans in Transition: Life Changes as Reasons for Learning.* New York: College Entrance Examination Board, 1980.

Baden, C. (ed.). *Competitive Strategies for Continuing Education.* New Directions for Continuing Education, no. 35. San Francisco: Jossey-Bass, 1987.

Beder, H. (ed.). *Realizing the Potential of Interorganizational Cooperation.* New Directions for Continuing Education, no. 23. San Francisco: Jossey-Bass, 1984.

Bellah, R. N., and Associates. *Habits of the Heart: Individualism and Commitment in American Life.* New York: Harper & Row, 1985.

Belsheim, D. J. "Environmental Determinants for Organizing Continuing Professional Education." *Adult Education Quarterly,* 1988, *38* (2), 63–74.

Bennis, W. G., and Nanus, B. *Leaders.* New York: Harper & Row, 1985.

Bhola, H. S. *World Trends and Issues in Adult Education.* London: UNESCO/Kingsley, 1988.

Biddle, W. *The Community Development Process.* New York: Holt, Rinehart & Winston, 1965.

Blackburn, D. J. (ed.). *Foundations and Changing Practice in Extension.* Guelph, Canada: University of Guelph Press, 1989.

Blake, R. R., Mouton, J. S., and Williams, M. S. *The Academic Administrator Grid: A Guide to Developing Effective Management Teams.* San Francisco: Jossey-Bass, 1981.

Blaney, J. "Leaders in University Continuing Education: Challenges, Opportunities and Tasks." *Canadian Journal of University Continuing Education,* 1987, *13* (1), 56–74.

Boshier, R. (ed.). "Training of Trainers and Adult Educators." *Convergence,* 1985, *18* (entire special issue 3 & 4).

Boshier, R., and Collins, J. B. "The Houle Typology After Twenty-Two Years: A Large-Scale Empirical Test." *Adult Education Quarterly,* 1985, *35* (3), 113–130.

Boyle, P. G. *Planning Better Programs.* New York: McGraw-Hill, 1981.

Brockett, R. G. (ed.). *Continuing Education in the Year 2000.* New Directions for Continuing Education, no. 36. San Francisco: Jossey-Bass, 1987.

Brockett, R. G. (ed.). *Ethical Issues in Adult Education.* New York: Teachers College Press, 1988.

Brown, M. A., and Copeland, H. G. (eds.). *Attracting Able Instructors of Adults.* New Directions for Continuing Education, no. 4. San Francisco: Jossey-Bass, 1979.

Buskey, J. H. (ed.). *Attracting External Funds for Continuing Education.* New Directions for Continuing Education, no. 12. San Francisco: Jossey-Bass, 1981.

Cervero, R. M. *Effective Continuing Education for Professionals.* San Francisco: Jossey-Bass, 1988.

Charters, A. N., and Hilton, R. J. (eds.). *Landmarks in International Adult Education: A Comparative Analysis.* London: Routledge, 1989.

Collins, Z. W. (ed.). *Museums, Adults and the Humanities.* Washington, D.C.: American Association of Museums, 1981.

Connellan, T. K., Jr. "The Administration of Continuing Education in Public Community Colleges: A Study of Competencies Perceived Critical to Job Success." Unpublished doctoral dissertation, Adult Education, University of Michigan, 1973. University Microfilms no. ADG 73-24545.

Cooper, S. S., and Hornback, M. S. *Continuing Nursing Education.* New York: McGraw-Hill, 1973.

Corson, J. J. *Management of the College or University: It's Different.* Topical Paper, no. 16. Tucson: Center for the Study of Higher Education, University of Arizona, 1979.

Courtenay, B. C. "An Analysis of Adult Education Administration Literature, 1936–1989." *Adult Education Quarterly,* 1990, *40* (2), 63–77.

Craig, R. L. (ed.). *Training and Development Handbook: A Guide* to *Human Resource Development.* (3rd ed.) New York: McGraw-Hill, 1987.

Daniel, R., and Rose, H. "Comparative Study of Adult Education Practitioners and Professors on Future Knowledge and Skills Needed by Adult Educators." *Adult Education,* 1982, *32* (2), 75–87.

Darkenwald, G. G. "Innovation in Adult Education: An Organizational Analysis." *Adult Education,* 1977, *27* (3), 156–172.

Darkenwald, G. G. "Perspective of Business and Industry on Cooperative Programming with Educational Institutions." *Adult Education Quarterly,* 1983, *33* (4), 230–243.

Darkenwald, G. G., and Knox, A. B. (eds.). *Meeting Educational Needs of Young Adults.* New Directions for Continuing Education, no. 21. San Francisco: Jossey-Bass, 1984.

Darkenwald, G. G., and Larson, G. A. (eds.). *Reaching Hard-to-Reach Adults.* New Directions for Continuing Education, no. 8. San Francisco: Jossey-Bass, 1980.

Deshler, D. (ed.). *Evaluation for Program Improvement.* New Directions for Continuing Education, no. 24. San Francisco: Jossey-Bass, 1984.

DiSilvestro, F. R. (ed.). *Advising and Counseling Adult Learners.* New Directions for Continuing Education, no. 10. San Francisco: Jossey-Bass, 1981.

Fiedler, F. E., and Chemers, M. *Leadership and Effective Management.* Glenview, Ill.: Scott, Foresman, 1974.

Forester, J. *Planning in the Face of Power.* Berkeley: University of California Press, 1989.

Freedman, L. *Quality in Continuing Education: Principles, Practices, and Standards for Colleges and Universities.* San Francisco: Jossey-Bass, 1987.

Freire, P. *Pedagogy of the Oppressed.* New York: Herder & Herder, 1970.

Gessner, Q. H. (ed.). *Handbook on Continuing Higher Education.* New York: Macmillan, 1987.

Green, J. S., Grosswald, S. J., Suter, E., and Walthall, D. B., III (eds.). *Continuing Education for the Health Professions: Developing, Managing, and Evaluating Programs for Maximum Impact on Patient Care.* San Francisco: Jossey-Bass, 1984.

Griggs, K., and Morgan, S. D. "What Are the Administrative Tasks and Priorities for Continuing Education Administrators?" *Continuing Higher Education,* 1988, *36* (2), 6–10.

Havelock, R. G. *Planning for Innovation.* Ann Arbor: Center for Research on Scientific Utilization of Knowledge (CRUSK)/ Institute for Social Research (ISR), University of Michigan, 1969.

Heffernan, J. M. *Educational and Career Services for Adults.* Lexington, Mass.: Lexington Books, 1981.

Hiemstra, R., and Sisco, B. *Individualizing Instruction: Making Learning Personal, Empowering, and Successful.* San Francisco: Jossey-Bass, 1990.

Houle, C. O. *The Design of Education.* San Francisco: Jossey-Bass, 1972.

Houle, C. O. *Continuing Learning in the Professions.* San Francisco: Jossey-Bass, 1980.

Houle, C. O. *Governing Boards: Their Nature and Nurture.* San Francisco: Jossey-Bass, 1989.

Ilsley, P. J. (ed.). *Improving Conference Design and Outcomes.* New Directions for Continuing Education, no. 28. San Francisco: Jossey-Bass, 1985.

Ilsley, P. J., and Niemi, J. A. *Recruiting and Training Volunteers.* New York: McGraw-Hill, 1981.

Jensen, G., Liveright, A. A., and Hallenbeck, W. (eds.). *Adult Education: Outlines of an Emerging Field of University Study.* Washington, D.C.: American Association for Adult and Continuing Education, 1964.

Katz, D., and Kahn, R. L. *The Social Psychology of Organizations.* (2nd ed.) New York: Wiley, 1978.

Knowles, M. S. *The Modern Practice of Adult Education: From Pedagogy to Andragogy.* (Rev. ed.) Chicago: Association Press, 1980.

Knox, A. B. *Adult Development and Learning: A Handbook on Individual Growth and Competence in the Adult Years.* San Francisco: Jossey-Bass, 1977a.

Knox, A. B. *Current Research Needs Related to Systematic Learning by Adults.* Occasional Paper, no. 4. Urbana, Ill.: Office for the Study of Continuing Professional Education, University of Illinois, 1977b.

Knox, A. B. (ed.). *Assessing the Impact of Continuing Education.* New Directions for Continuing Education, no. 3. San Francisco: Jossey-Bass, 1979a.

Knox, A. B. (ed.). *Enhancing Proficiencies of Continuing Educators.* New Directions for Continuing Education, no. 1. San Francisco: Jossey-Bass, 1979b.

Knox, A. B. (ed.). *Programming for Adults Facing Mid-Life Change.* New Directions for Continuing Education, no. 2. San Francisco: Jossey-Bass, 1979c.

Knox, A. B. (eds). *Leadership Strategies for Meeting New Challenges.* New Directions for Continuing Education, no. 13. San Francisco: Jossey-Bass, 1982a.

Knox, A. B. "Organizational Dynamics in University Continuing Professional Education." *Adult Education,* 1982b, *32* (3), 117–129.

Knox, A. B. "Adult Learning and Proficiency." In D. Kleiber and M. Maehr (eds.), *Advances in Motivation and Achievement.* Vol. 4: *Motivation in Adulthood.* Greenwood, Conn.: JAI Press, 1985.

Knox, A. B. *Helping Adults Learn. A Guide to Planning, Implementing, and Conducting Programs.* San Francisco: Jossey-Bass, 1986.

Knox, A. B. *International Perspectives on Adult Education.* Columbus: ERIC Clearinghouse on Adult, Career, and Vocational Education, Ohio State University, 1987.

Knox, A. B., and Associates. *Developing, Administering, and Evaluating Adult Education.* San Francisco: Jossey-Bass, 1980.

LaBelle, T. J. *Nonformal Education in Latin America and the Caribbean: Stability, Reform or Revolution?* New York: Praeger, 1986.

Langerman, P. D., and Smith, D. H. (eds.). *Managing Adult and Continuing Education Programs and Staff.* Washington, D.C.: American Association for Adult and Continuing Education, 1979.

Lewis, L. H. (ed.). *Experiential and Simulation Techniques for Teaching Adults.* New Directions for Continuing Education, no. 30. San Francisco: Jossey-Bass, 1986.

Lindquist, J. *Strategies for Change.* Berkeley, Calif.: Pacific Soundings Press, 1978.

McLagan, P. A. *Models for HRD Practice.* Washington, D.C.: American Society for Training and Development, 1989.

MacNeil, F. "Organizational Barriers to the Administration of Correctional Education: An Analysis of a Correctional School District." *Adult Education,* 1980, *30* (4), 208–221.

Marsick, V. J. (ed.). *Enhancing Staff Development in Diverse Settings.* New Directions for Continuing Education, no. 38. San Francisco: Jossey-Bass, 1988.

Matkin, G. W. *Effective Budgeting in Continuing Education. A Comprehensive Guide to Improving Program Planning and Organizational Performance.* San Francisco: Jossey-Bass, 1985.

Merriam, S. B., and Caffarella, R. S. *Learning in Adulthood: A Comprehensive Guide.* San Francisco: Jossey-Bass, 1991.

Merriam, S. B., and Cunningham, P. M. (eds.). *Handbook of Adult and Continuing Education.* San Francisco: Jossey-Bass, 1989.

Mezirow, J., and Associates. *Fostering Critical Reflection in Adulthood: A Guide to Transformative and Emancipatory Learning.* San Francisco: Jossey-Bass, 1990.

Mezirow, J., Darkenwald, G. G., and Knox, A. B. *Last Gamble on Education.* Washington, D.C.: American Association for Adult and Continuing Education, 1975.

Mintzberg, H. *The Nature of Managerial Work.* New York: Harper & Row, 1973.

Mitroff, I. I. *Stakeholders of the Organizational Mind: Toward a New View of Organizational Policy Making.* San Francisco: Jossey-Bass, 1983.

Monette, M. L. "The Concept of Educational Need." *Adult Education,* 1977, *27* (2), 116–127.

Moore, D. E., Jr. "The Organization and Administration of Continuing Education in Academic Medical Centers." Unpublished doctoral dissertation, Department of Administration/Higher and Continuing Education, University of Illinois, 1982. University Microfilms no. ADG 82–09610.

Nadler, L. *Designing Training Programs.* Reading, Mass.: Addison-Wesley, 1982.

Nadler, L., and Nadler, Z. *Developing Human Resources: Concepts and a Model.* (3rd ed.) San Francisco: Jossey-Bass, 1989.

Naisbitt, J., and Aburdene, P. *Megatrends 2000: Ten New Directions for the 1990's.* New York: Morrow, 1990.

Niemi, J. A., and Gooler, D. D. (eds.). *Technologies for Learning Outside the Classroom.* New Directions for Continuing Education, no. 34. San Francisco: Jossey-Bass, 1987.

Patton, M. Q. *Utilization — Focused Evaluation.* Beverly Hills, Calif.: Sage, 1978.

Pennington, F., and Green, J. "Comparative Analysis of Program Development Processes in Six Professions." *Adult Education,* 1976, *27* (1), 13–23.

Peters, J. M., and Associates. *Building an Effective Adult Education Enterprise.* San Francisco: Jossey-Bass, 1980.

Peters, T. J., and Waterman, R. H., Jr. *In Search of Excellence.* New York: Warner Books, 1982.

Peterson, D. A. *Facilitating Education for Older Learners.* San Francisco: Jossey-Bass, 1983.

Roloff, P. W. "The Relationship Between Selected Program and Director Characteristics and Responses in the Innovation-Decision Process to Selected Administrative Practices by Adult Education Directors in Illinois Public Schools." Unpublished doctoral dissertation, Department of Adult and Continuing Education, Northern Illinois University, 1980.

Schein, E. H. *Career Dynamics: Matching Individual and Organizational Needs.* Reading, Mass.: Addison-Wesley, 1978.

Schein, E. H. *Organizational Culture and Leadership: A Dynamic View.* San Francisco: Jossey-Bass, 1985.

Shaw, N. C. (ed.). *Administration of Continuing Education.* Washington, D.C.: American Association for Adult and Continuing Education, 1969.

Simerly, R. G., and Associates. *Strategic Planning and Leadership in Continuing Education: Enhancing Organizational Vitality, Responsiveness, and Identity.* San Francisco: Jossey-Bass, 1987.

Simerly, R. G., and Associates. *Handbook of Marketing for Continuing Education.* San Francisco: Jossey-Bass, 1989.

Smith, D. H., and Offerman, M. J. "The Management of Adult and Continuing Education." In S. B. Merriam and P. M. Cunningham (eds.), *Handbook of Adult and Continuing Education.* San Francisco: Jossey-Bass, 1989.

Smith, R. M. *Learning How to Learn: Applied Learning Theory for Adults.* Chicago: Follett, 1982.

Smith, R. M., Aker, G. F., and Kidd, J. R. (eds.). *Handbook of Adult Education.* New York: Macmillan, 1970.

Sork, T. J. (ed.). *Designing and Implementing Effective Workshops.* New Directions for Continuing Education, no. 22. San Francisco: Jossey-Bass, 1984.

Sork, T. J., and Buskey, J. H. "A Descriptive and Evaluative Analysis of Program Planning Literature, 1950–1983." *Adult Education Quarterly, 1986, 36* (2), 86–96.

Strother, G. B., and Klus, J. P. *Administration of Continuing Education.* Belmont, Calif.: Wadsworth, 1982.

Titmus, C. (ed.). *Lifelong Education for Adults: An International Handbook.* Oxford, England: Pergamon Press, 1989.

Votruba, J. C. (ed.). *Strengthening Internal Support for Continuing Education.* New Directions for Continuing Education, no. 9. San Francisco: Jossey-Bass, 1981.

Wedemeyer, C. A. *Learning at the Back Door.* Madison: University of Wisconsin Press, 1981.

CHAPTER 10

A Critical Perspective on Sociology and Adult Education

Colin Griffin

Considerable debate takes place nowadays over the nature of adult education theory in relation to the so-called foundation disciplines (Bright, 1989; Jarvis, 1987b; Usher and Bryant, 1989). Sociology, as one such discipline, has not played as large a part in the construction of adult education knowledge as have philosophy and psychology. This may be, in part, because a sharp contrast exists between adult education and schooling, and the sociological literature both in Britain and the United States deals with schooling to a considerable extent. As with other social sciences, sociology may be represented by a variety of perspectives, and these have sometimes been set out in relation to adult education (Jarvis, 1985; Elsey, 1986). On the whole, however, sociological approaches have had a relatively low profile in adult education.

Current trends in adult education, both national and international, make the sociological perspective more relevant today, however. Rapid economic and social changes present adult educators with constantly developing areas in which adult learning

259

is needed, and social policy creates new groups of adult learners. The technology of learning also continually moves on, as our knowledge of the scope and diversity of adult education grows. Consequently, the nature of professional practice is under permanent review. Adult educators must have some sociological grasp of social change, social structures, and social relations in order to understand the significance of adult education in people's lives.

Adult education has the capacity to transform individual lives, as writers such as Knowles (1978), Mezirow (1981), and Brookfield (1987) have all argued. Other writers, however, argue that adult education "provides a means for working towards a new paradigm of social thought and organization and a more effective counter to social crises for the 1990s" (Leirman and Kulich, 1987). People who argue along these lines are making massive claims for the capacity of adult education to, in effect, change the world. In testing such claims, the proponents make definite sociological assumptions about the nature of social change, social structures, and social relations. But from any sociological perspective, these claims present many paradoxes. For example, the literature of adult education often refers to the need for people to adapt to changing circumstances, particularly those of economic and technological change in the workplace. At the same time, adult learning practices are determined by a conception of individual autonomy and self-direction. Therefore, although social and economic change are presented as inevitable and subject to some kind of momentum of their own, individual learners are presented as striving for freedom and self-determination. In other words, adult education theory has neglected the relationship between the personal and the political. Too often the assumption is made that social change can be reduced to the sum of individual transformations, or that society itself consists of the sum of the individuals who compose it — the sum of all the pressures upon us to conform to its rules and values, diminishing our individuality.

The Scope of Sociology

Since the time of Comte and Durkheim, sociology has presented a much more complex picture than this of social change, social structure, and social relations, even though sociologists have not necessarily agreed among themselves about how we should understand the picture. The relationship between adult education and social change is problematic, and adult educators would be in a better position to advance and defend their claims if they were better informed by sociological perspective than they have been in the past.

What sociology has contributed so far to adult education has been limited in its scope. As Jarvis says, "Despite its long history, no sociology of the education of adults exists in the same manner as there are sociological studies of initial education" (Jarvis, 1985, p. 3). This is true, but as I suggested, adult education theory nevertheless often contains unwarranted and problematic sociological assumptions when it addresses social change or issues concerning the relationship between the individual and society. Consequently, much of this theory is sociologically naive.

But clearly, many aspects of adult education lend themselves to sociological study, and it is appropriate to review some examples. Perhaps the most fundamental aspect of sociology that applies to adult education is that concerned with structural inequalities in society, such as class, race, and gender, together with other divisions, such as age. From the practitioner's point of view, these categories tend to converge in the issue of participation. Participation in adult education is, in fact, most readily grasped in terms of sociological rather than psychological categories. In Britain, a recent survey of nonparticipant groups identified typical characteristics of the group members that reflect structural inequalities in society throughout the industrialized world. The groups were made up of people with the least previous education or with basic educational needs, the unemployed and those with low incomes, poorly skilled workers, ethnic minorities, women with young children, people with disabilities, and people who lived in the country (National Institute for Adult Continuing Education, 1990).

The theory that educational systems reproduce social inequality, associated with the writings of Bourdieu (1973) and others, is actually substantiated by such studies of participation in adult education. The access of adults to education is currently of some priority in some societies but the reasons for this are

largely instrumental: an aging population, the needs of the economy for a more skilled work force, and so on. From the perspective of some people working in higher education, widening
access to it may be merely an opportunistic device to ensure
full enrollment at a time when the population of young adults
is in decline. Whatever the case, adult education is increasingly
being incorporated into the recruitment of students and workers, with the result that progressive adult learning practices are
being identified in both the workplace (Marsick, 1987) and
higher education (Schlossberg, Lynch, and Chickering, 1989).

Barriers to educational access continue to be an important theme of adult education research, but the sociological processes, about which relatively little theorizing has been done
(Jarvis, 1985), have been overtaken by social and economic
change. What appears to remain constant is the function of the
adult curriculum to reproduce society (Griffin, 1983) and the
patterns of inequality in society. Models of adult learning are
increasingly postulated upon social and political developments,
and adult educators need to be aware of the social forces that
bring into existence those groups of people least likely to participate in adult education.

Adult education as a response to structural inequalities
has often been thought of as the basis of radical movements concerning social class (Taylor and Ward, 1986). This view may
be based upon a classical Marxist approach (Youngman, 1986)
or a community approach (Cowburn, 1986; Lovett, 1988) or
an internationalist approach (Gelpi, 1985). These approaches
are fairly well known to practitioners around the world. Practitioners are less likely to be aware of the sociological analyses
of the failure of radical adult education movements to bring
about structural changes in society.

Rare studies from a political science perspective of the
"policy community" of adult education (for example, Evans,
1987) clearly demonstrate the highly problematic nature of the
attempt to bring about redistributive social change by influencing
governments. Adult education as a profession is not a political
force, and the relation between social movements and public
forms of provision are not generally well thought out. Sociology

has an important contribution to make to our understanding of the social processes that have been termed *marginalization* (exclusion from the central processes of society) or *incorporation* (inclusion in the mainstream), or *reproduction* (transmission of cultural deprivation to the succeeding generation). The acknowledged failure of progressive education in these regards is evident in both theory (Rogers, 1983) and practice.

Progressive adult education methods are perfectly well adapted to maintaining and perpetuating the status quo and prove highly effective in corporate management contexts (Knowles and Associates, 1984). The underlying reasons for this elude the greater part of adult education theory, which has failed to adequately conceptualize the real relationship between individual and social transformations. The current preoccupation with the obscurities of Habermas and critical theory represent a somewhat belated attempt to retrieve the situation, but will probably serve only to widen the gap between theorists and practitioners in adult education. To assume that "the personal is the political" is to mistake metaphor for social reality.

The study of adult education as a bureaucratized profession is also relatively undeveloped. In Britain, for example, attempts have been made to apply organizational theory to adult education (Mee, 1980), but they remain quite scarce. Many existing models of bureaucratic organization might be developed in an adult education context. Developing these models seems particularly important in the light of current trends that may be summarized as the relocation of the site of adult learning. Adults learn at home, in the community, and in the workplace much more often than they do in formal instructional settings. The social context of learning is increasingly recognized as an important element in determining the context of adult education.

Indeed, the distinction between adult learning, about which so much research literature exists, and adult education is of fundamental sociological importance. Relatively little study has been done of learning as a social process (Jarvis, 1987a), except in reductionist terms of group dynamics. Similarly, the social construction of knowledge, of the curriculum, of the personality, of age categories, or indeed of adulthood itself are insufficiently familiar to many adult education practitioners—less familiar, perhaps, than to school and college teachers.

For a long time, it was assumed that the content of formally provided adult education was a direct function of the needs of adult learners. However, these needs were rarely if ever located in a social context of the construction of knowledge or in a political context of class, race, or gender. And knowledge itself was not considered in relation to the hierarchical ordering of society. In Britain, the work of Young (1971) and others, although subsequently subjected to justified criticism, raises vital sociological issues around ideology and the curriculum that have been reflected in other radical critiques in the United States by Apple (1980) and Giroux (1981). Knowledge has been aligned with power in this radical tradition, but this view has had little impact upon the tradition of philosophical analysis or upon the psychologists who have influenced adult education theory and practice.

The social factors that impinge on the formation of personality are not conceptualized in most prevailing schools of adult learning theory. This may be because the concept of *adult* itself tends to be abstracted in a universalistic way and attributed to individual personalities without regard to important, albeit not determining, social factors, an oversight that is clearly evident in the challenge to dominant theory and practice developed by feminist critics (Thompson, 1983). The domestication of women's learning by means of differential access to opportunity is a social and political process that cannot be reduced to one of perspective transformation on the part of individual learners.

In the absence of a sociological perspective of some kind, it is easy for educators to perceive personality, or adulthood, as abstractions rather than as living and dynamic products of individual and social forces. More specifically, the concept of personality reflects a cultural dimension, as evidenced by the neglect of social categories of class, race, or gender in personality theory generally. The familiar argument that adult education is essentially a middle-class activity, especially in its liberal forms (Westwood, 1980), reflects a politicized view of knowledge, curriculum, and personality and does not merely reflect the patterns of participation in adult education by different social groups.

What sociological studies offer to adult educators is an irreducible conceptual framework of class, culture, and curriculum in which to locate their ideas and practices. There can be little doubt that the life-chances of individual learners, men and women, are very often transformed by their experiences of adult education. And these transformations may well have collective outcomes in the form of social and political movements directed toward social change. But it does not follow that society changes as a result of these individual changes nor that the causal effects of adult education upon societal change could be isolated and measured. What is more likely to happen is that society "acts back" upon progressive and other social movements and that processes that sociologists variously describe as incorporation or control or hegemony (exercise of covert power or influence) may occur. This view does not necessarily entail a deterministic position, which denies any connection whatever between adult education and social change, but recognizes that other forces for change that are historically more powerful than education are likely to be operating.

Adult Education and Social Change

In Britain, adult education has been largely transformed into a kind of welfare and employment policy (Griffin, 1987). A series of reports (Russell, 1973; Venables, 1976; Advisory Council for Adult Continuing Education, 1982) have traced the process whereby liberal adult education and continuing education have come to take the forms they have at the beginning of the 1990s in Britain. The social and political processes that have accompanied this transformation must be understood in their own right. They include increased government control over public spending, an ideological trend in favor of an unrestricted market economy, and powerful government intervention in favor of an educational system designed first and foremost to serve the needs of the economy. As a result of such processes, liberal adult education has been consigned to the marketplace; social

welfare education, to the local education authorities; and continuing vocational and professional education, to government
and industry itself. The point of this doubtless overgeneralized
account is to illustrate the capacity of adult learning theory and
practice to serve a wide, if not limitless, range of social and political ends. In other words, the level of abstraction of adult learning theory concepts is such that adult education outcomes may
bear little or no relation to practitioners' intentions. This situation provides for both opportunity and retrenchment and is one
of the most important sociological characteristics of adult education in Britain at this time.

The discourse of professional practice is generally one of
interpersonal relations and the facilitation of learning. These
concepts are at the heart of what all adult educators believe to
be their vocation. An awareness of the social and political context of their practice can only serve to further educators' professional confidence. Many adult educators have always thought of
their vocation as, in some way, related to the conception of a
liberal democratic society. However, the onset of a more "futur-
ological" style has led some of them to adopt a much more pro-
active approach.

We are witnessing in recent trends the extension of the
idea of criticism as a desirable attribute of democratic citizenship, including a view of the adult educator as critic of society.
This is quite different from the view of the adult educator as
critical social theorist. It is by no means a straightforward case
of applying sociological perspectives to adult education practice but rather a conceptualization of the adult educator's role
in society. This role is sometimes projected in extreme terms.
For example, in Britain, the Association for the Development
of Adult Political Education believes that the extent of political
ignorance and alienation in the adult community is such that
the health of democracy is seriously threatened. The literature
of political theory does not generally postulate a correlation between democracy and adult education, despite the conceptual
association between liberal democracy and active or participatory citizenship. So this is not a case of the application of any
particular discipline to adult education but rather of the adult
educator assuming the role of critic of society.

From an adult education point of view, these formulations of practitioners' roles provide us with an example of analysis from a critical sociology perspective. They depend upon attributing widespread ignorance, apathy, and conformity to the mass of the population, although little evidence can be found in support of such propositions. The tendency is not a new one, and it has been criticized as the deprivation and disadvantage thesis (Thompson, 1980) or in terms of needs analysis and social class (Armstrong, 1988). In either case, the focus of sociological interest is not upon unsupported attributions of popular ignorance, apathy, or need but upon the processes of reformulation of the role of adult education and adult educators in society.

The concepts of social change and transformation also illustrate problems both in the adult educator's role. Social change and transformation are processes that illustrate some of the difficulties in discovering this role in society, and they also highlight the way that the disciplines are used in adult education. Critical theory, critical awareness, conscientization, and so on may just as well be analyzed from a psychological or a sociological standpoint, and sometimes they are (Tennant, 1988). The prevailing cultural priorities at the point of origin of the analysis affect the analysis greatly. In a society that stresses personal growth, social transformation may be seen as the sum of individual transformation, either through adult learning as Knowles (1978) has argued or perspective transformation as formulated by Mezirow (1981), among others. Despite the respective influences of Dewey (1916) and Habermas (1971), however, Knowles's and Mezirow's accounts project little sense of the dynamic relationship of society and the social, especially of the ways in which radical or progressive ideas are captured, transformed, or incorporated by precisely those social forces against which they are deployed.

With little access to concepts of social change per se, theorists of personal growth, liberation, and transformation tend to project a static and ahistorical view of society on a system of oppression, patriarchy, or mass culture, against which individuals struggle more or less effectively. Although it was in fact developed in specific historical and political conditions that permitted a collectivist analysis, Freire's concept (1979a) of oppression can be expressed in terms of such generality that it can be applied in a whole range of diverse political and cultural conditions (Kirkwood and Kirkwood, 1989).

An understanding of the processes by which individuals and society both act and react to produce the dynamic relationship of culture and power is extremely important for any understanding of how progressivism may be defeated or incorporated. Oppression and patriarchy are both universal and historically specific and this creates problems in terms both of the international tendencies in adult education and the tendency of adult educators to think in terms of applying universal perspectives and concepts from sociological theory. Few writers have systematically pursued the dialectical processes of progress and reaction, but it seems significant that when this has been done it has been in a context of international relations (Gelpi, 1985). It is certainly not a theme addressed by existing studies in comparative adult education.

From a critical sociology perspective, then, it would seem that we are witnessing in adult education a reformulation of what may loosely be called its liberal tradition, focusing upon individual learning in conditions of social change. It is the argument of this chapter that the relationship of individual learning and social change has not been satisfactorily addressed, in so far as social change is a much more complex affair of action and reaction. Individual perspective transformation and collective learning for social change have been associated with concepts derived from critical social theory, but these concepts do not in themselves constitute a sociology of adult learning, which still proves elusive (Jarvis, 1987a). The main obstacle to the formation of such a sociology appears to be a lack of any sense of the irreducibly "social" in human life—a sense of historical, economic, and cultural forces that shape the possibilities for and the meaning of individual growth and transformation.

Unlike the critical social theorists, adult educators who embrace the objectives of social change do so from a definite professional stance relating to their clients, the adult learners. This not only inevitably involves them in a construction of "good practice" but also leads them to attribute ignorance, powerlessness, passivity, and so on to their clients. Nevertheless, from a sociological point of view, individual transformation and social change may be expected to continue to represent the two polarities of professional adult educators' concerns.

One of the most sociologically significant features of adult education of the last few years has been the adoption of progressive adult learning theories and concepts by social, political, and economic forces — the media, the state, and the business world. These political, economic, and social forces may, in fact, be precisely the kind of forces that shape the possibilities for transformation of individuals and society in democratic as well as in undemocratic countries. Although the defenders of the liberal tradition (for example, McIlroy and Spencer, 1988) have shown some resistance to those processes of incorporation, radical adult educators have never considered liberal adult education to be an effective source of opposition to oppression of any kind (for example, Taylor and Ward, 1986; Youngman, 1986). They believe that it only conferred the illusion of an open and democratic society or else that it actually served to reinforce structural inequalities in society. If anything, individual learning for personal growth has been given a new context in the workplace (Marsick, 1987) and thus, radicals consider, supports the status quo ante.

Sociology and Adult Learning Theory

These tendencies, the dying of the old, politically ambiguous liberal tradition, its criticism from a politically radical standpoint, and its current depoliticization and relocation in the workplace, are among the most significant tendencies in adult education from a sociological point of view. They are, of course, massive generalizations. Radical criticism took its cue from Freire rather than Marx, and, in any case, state and other covert bureaucratic direction could hardly be discounted in any analysis of such tendencies. Nevertheless, these tendencies have been among the primary concerns of adult educators and have brought about a heightened awareness of the conflicts surrounding the individual and social purposes of adult education.

Adult educators have brought to bear on their concerns theoretical approaches from various directions, such as those alluded to under the heading of critical social theory. They have treated theoretical issues with increasing sophistication, as in the case of the theory-practice relationship (Usher and Bryant, 1989). In the course of all this, the contribution of sociology as a discipline has been transformed into one of greater reflexivity. It could be argued from the functionalist perspective that adult education has simply changed in response to wider changes in society and in the world. It is more likely, however, that during the last few years professional adult educators have been struggling with reconceptualizing the traditional individual and social purposes of adult education in the light of provision of learning experiences, good practice, and so on.

In the course of this process, the debate about adult learning theory as the basis of good practice has been overtaken by events elsewhere. Adult learning theory provides us with an example of the need to move beyond an applied disciplines approach to a critical sociological one. The debate about andragogy can be seen in this light as a stage in the identification and construction of good practice in adult education. This debate did not advance our ideas about the sociology of adult knowledge or learning. But it has provided an example of the way in which such learning could be relocated outside the traditional structures of adult education.

The problem of locating adult education itself as a profession has been that of identifying the field of practice that is claimed as its own. The problem has been compounded in recent years by the sheer scale of world problems that adult education is claimed to address as well as by the difficulties of the needs analysis approach already alluded to. Caught between the grandiose claims for the world-historical nature of their field on the one hand and the task of distinguishing between andragogy and pedagogy on the other hand, adult educators have needed a critical sociology of adult learning for their professional sense of identity—in the same way that doctors have access to social conceptions of physical illness and health and lawyers have access to the social processes of law.

In education, the social analysis of schooling is much more established than is social analysis in adult education. Andragogy and many other concepts of good practice have been appropriated uncritically in many areas of adult learning other than those of formal adult education. This leaves us with a sense that familiar distinctions between formal, nonformal, and informal adult learning are only a descriptive gloss rather than a real attempt to grasp the nature of adult learning from a critical sociological perspective.

From the critical sociological perspective, the rapid expansion and development of adult education programs in business and industry is only a reflection of the principle that effective adult learning takes place at the point where knowledge itself is generated. This is not only true of adult learning, of course, but has affected the education of adults much more powerfully than the education of children and young people. As a result, while the institutions of school, college, and university remained more or less in place, those of adult education were dispersed and now present a rather amorphous impression.

The formal systems of education for young people are more or less adjusting to an influx of adults seeking for the most part professional accreditation at initial or continuing levels (Schlossberg, Lynch, and Chickering, 1989). While it must be said, as was said at the outset with regard to critical sociology, that it is possible to overgeneralize concepts of adult learning and provision, nevertheless, demographic and economic trends have helped to relocate adult learning back in the formal educational system. This movement has taken place because professional knowledge has traditionally been credentialed in the formal system. But because concepts of professional knowledge have been changing in the direction of a more reflective or experiential mode (Schön, 1987) the actual sites or locations of continuing education have broadened considerably. We may expect a continuing tension between elements of formal educational systems, organized professional interests, and business and industry around the location and accreditation of continuing education.

As has been suggested, a more reflexive view of professional practice among adult educators has also begun to emerge. Once the task of understanding adult education was associated with "grasping the diversity of provision." But the idea of provision itself needs to be more critically examined. No doubt, heightened concern for professional identity reflects major sociological trends in the location of adult learning, especially insofar as these might seem to suggest a dilution of the professional role itself. The notion that adult education could constitute an all-purpose system to serve all adult learning needs was never really tenable, even though exaggerated claims for it continue to be made.

In recent years, the trends of deinstitutionalization and reinstitutionalization of accreditation have contributed to the new adult education discourse, as it moved away from ideologies of meeting needs, conscientization, andragogy, and so on. The liberal tradition of learning for its own sake was not and never could have been separated from some idea of social and political meaning, however individual learners experienced it. The great tradition of "learning for life," or other forms of lifelong learning ideals that we associate with Lindeman (Stewart, 1987) and other writers, could only have gone hand in hand with some process of induction into a specific cultural tradition. One cannot simply learn for life as distinct from learning for life in America or another society. For one thing, the differential social and cultural significance of adult learning in different societies would inevitably affect the meaning of lifelong education. In Britain, for example, the liberal tradition posed a contradiction between individual social mobility and collective purpose as adult education ceased to be a social movement and took on the characteristics of a system of provision.

The current deinstitutionalization of adult learning, however, does not constitute a return of any kind of characteristics of social movement, despite the continued efforts of some adult educators to revive the social purpose of adult education. Instead, the relocation of credentialed adult learning in the professional workplace and the community is associated with major developments in independent, open, and distance learning (Brookfield, 1986; Paine, 1988; Hodgson, Mann, and Snell, 1987). These developments have also been criticized (Harris, 1987; Robbins, 1988).

They have reflected a variety of changes in technologies of teaching and learning, demographic trends, and demands of work and employment. From a critical sociological point of view, while they have been consistent with a procrustean vision of the functions of adult education and a liberal individualistic ideology, they have occurred simultaneously with shifts in the ultimate control of adult learning: progressive, learner-centered approaches have coincided with trends toward traditional assessment and credentialing features.

In general, while the ideology of adult learning continues to reflect control by individual learners, in fact the state and business and industry play the major role in determining the ultimate shape of much adult learning. This is not, however, inconsistent with the tradition of self-directed learning we have come to associate with Tough and that continues to develop (Brockett, 1988). The fact that adult education can function as a form of social policy (Griffin, 1987) does not in any way contradict our view of adult learning as essentially a self-directed and independent process. Adult education and adult learning are, in some respects, moving apart, and a sociology of adult education now needs to be systematically distinguished from a sociology of adult learning. We seem to have arrived at the point where the issues around adult learning and those around adult education are conceptually different. Sociological interest will perhaps focus upon the social processes whereby adult learning is transformed into adult education. Already the adult educator's role is likely to be reformulated as mentor, facilitator, enabler, and so on, alongside other developing functions in the general area of counseling, guidance, and advice.

From Adult Learning to Adult Education

The transformation of learning into education may be seen in the assessment and accreditation of experiential learning. The typical processes of innovative work are involved as experiential learning is transformed, progressing from adult learning theory (Kolb, 1984) through good practice models (Boud and Griffin, 1987) to its incorporation into formal educational systems

(Evans, 1985). In theory, the deinstitutionalization of some areas of adult learning should be reflected in greater responsiveness and a loosening of control on the part of colleges and universities over the style and content of the learning. In practice, a simultaneous process of reinstitutionalization occurs as alternative systems of assessment and accreditation take their place. Indeed, it could be argued that the bureaucratic centralization required by open and distance learning systems in fact produces only the illusion of independent and self-directed learning, and that to maintain equity and credibility accredited education must have a degree of closure. From a sociological point of view, it is more productive to consider the social processes whereby adult learning processes are transformed into, for example, validated professional knowledge than to apply one perspective or another. And it could only be arbitrary to distinguish experience from education in a mechanical way.

The transformation of adult learning into adult education also involves the state, business and industry, and professionals in the process of direction and legitimation. In industrialized countries, characteristics of a social welfare model of adult education are easy to find: literacy and basic education, workers' education (Hopkins, 1985), paid educational leave (Mace and Yarnit, 1987), treatment of the unemployed (McGivney and Sims, 1986; Senior and Naylor, 1987), education of the elderly (Glendenning, 1985), and women's education in both general and specific educational terms (Thompson, 1983; Faith, 1988). The list of target groups in the population for adult education initiatives can be expected to grow as adult education seeks out and finds these groups. The contribution of sociology is to analyze the place of adult education in the social process, with adult education and adult educators increasingly implicated in demographic, social, and economic change as well as in the worldwide social policies of states.

To accommodate changes in the place of adult education in society, a new discourse of adult education has been formulated and has already been extensively discussed by adult educators in relation to a radical tradition (Lovett, 1988) or by way of a political science analysis and critique (Evans, 1987). The older concerns for good professional practice and for the liberal associations of adult learning have been translated into a newer conceptual scheme as a result of social changes, even though these older concerns may remain the concerns at the heart of individual practitioners' philosophies.

The kind of literature being cited bears witness to the possibilities for critical and reflexive social analysis of many changes that have occurred during the last two decades. Issues once regarded as the proper province of philosophy or psychology are being addressed as exemplifying social processes, especially with regard to the part played by professionals in the formulation of such issues. The literature, in so far as it is a literature of critical sociology, tends to challenge universalistic concepts of learners or of oppression and abstract concepts of the aims of adult education. It is a more skeptical literature, which reflects the tendency of progressive practice and practitioners to become incorporated into existing structures of economic and political power. For example, concepts of andragogy, transformation, personal growth, or experiential learning, which are undifferentiated with regard to class or gender, are, increasingly, seen to be worldwide distributions of peoples' life-chances. Perhaps the critical view of adult learning as a social process has sometimes resulted in a euphoric belief in its capacity to bring about social change, but the rapidity of the reconceptualizations described here have no doubt forced the pace at which sociological perspectives have been brought to bear.

Conclusion

Until fairly recently, the significance of a sociological analysis was diminished by adult education's somewhat unreflective conceptualization of practice. It was conceptualization primarily in terms of teaching and learning methods, and psychological theories of adult learning had much to offer in the formulation of good teaching practices. But this emphasis has had the effect of reducing the content of adult learning to a conception of learning needs, and even now the curriculum content of adult education tends to be treated descriptively and comparatively rather than in analytical terms (Langenbach, 1988).

The dominance of a liberal discourse has been challenged

by recent developments, but Keddie's pioneering analysis of adult education as an ideology of individualism (Thompson, 1980) serves as a reminder that not all practitioners were happy about a discourse that apparently lacked any social structural reference whatsoever and that has resulted in some sociologically naive views of the relationship between individual transformation and social change. A more structural and historical analysis was needed for adult educators to avoid vague conceptualizations of oppression or of society itself. Oppression takes various but specific structural forms, and society exists in other ways than merely as a form of cultural overdetermination.

A critical sociological literature has emerged during the last few years to help adult educators achieve a better understanding of the complexities of the social process. Social change and transformation are social processes that cannot be reduced to the collective sum of individual changes without a significant loss of meaning. The state or the culture or forms of oppression are not static but rather are structures of power capable of reaching back in ways that may incorporate the opposition itself. Those writers who have considered the relevance of Gramsci (Ireland, 1987) have added just as much to our understanding of adult education as those who have looked to Habermas for our understanding of adult learning.

The profile of sociology with regard to adult education is determined by the fact that it cannot be "applied" to adult education in quite the same way that psychology can. Our research knowledge of how adults learn can be applied in the teaching of adults and can help us to formulate clear guidelines for practice (Rogers, 1983), but our research knowledge of social processes is of a different logical order. Unless this is recognized, the attempt to apply sociological perspectives to adult education practice may result in some form of reductionism as has been mentioned: recreating the classical liberal view of the individual versus society, deducing social change from individual transformations, reducing the issues of content to those of methods of learning, assuming that "social purpose" education is more likely to achieve political ends than any other kind of education, and so on.

Many such reductionist tendencies now stand challenged by a critical sociology of adult education. A critical sociology is one that focuses upon the meaning, structure, and action dimensions of adult education as a social process. Sociology, after all, remains essentially a theoretical project and not merely an assemblage of social facts. Durkheim (1933) never believed that sociology was a form of social statistics, and the functionalist tradition itself is based upon a highly contested theory of society. Nevertheless, as a theoretical approach to social structures and processes in specific historical conditions, sociology has much to contribute to adult education.

In contrast to the traditional focus upon structural inequalities of race, gender, and class in relation to the provision of adult education, some other areas of sociologial concern may prove more likely to generate new insights. The internationalizing of adult education in relation to changes in the international division of labor, not to be confused with comparative adult education, would be a sociology on the broadest scale. Other likely focuses of this kind of approach might be the social and economic significance of learning in the workplace and the shifting locations of adult learning in general; the social roles of practitioners, especially in terms of their roles as professionals and, sometimes, critics of society; the social processes of bureaucratization, incorporation, marginalization, and so on, that accompany the transitional stages between social movement and professional provision; the sociology of knowledge and the curriculum and issues around the sites where knowledge is generated. Above all perhaps, we may anticipate a more reflexive and critical sociology of adult education in place of the mechanical application of a discipline.

References

Advisory Council for Adult Continuing Education. *Continuing Education: From Policies to Practice.* Leicester, England: Advisory Council for Adult Continuing Education, 1982.

Apple, M. W. *Ideology and Curriculum.* London: Routledge & Kegan Paul, 1980.

Armstrong, P. *Adult Education and Socialism.* London: Croom Helm, 1988.

Boud, D., and Griffin, V. (eds.). *Appreciating Adults Learning.* London: Kogan Page, 1987.

Bourdieu, P. "Cultural Reproduction and Social Reproduction." In R. Brown (ed.), *Knowledge, Education and Social Change.* London: Tavistock, 1983.

Bright, B. P. (ed.). *Theory and Practice in the Study of Adult Education.* London: Routledge, 1989.

Brockett, R. G. *Self-Directed Adult Learning.* London: Croom Helm, 1988.

Brookfield, S. D. *Understanding and Facilitating Adult Learning: A Comprehensive Analysis of Principles and Effective Practices.* Milton Keynes, England: Open University Press, 1986.

Brookfield, S. D. *Developing Critical Thinkers: Challenging Adults to Explore Alternative Ways of Thinking and Acting.* Milton Keynes, England: Open University Press, 1987.

Cowburn, W. *Class, Ideology and Community Education.* London: Croom Helm, 1986.

Dewey, J. *Democracy and Education.* New York: Free Press, 1916.

Durkheim, E. *The Division of Labor in Society.* (E. Simpson, trans.) New York: Free Press, 1933.

Elsey, B. *Social Theory Perspectives on Adult Education.* Nottingham, England: Department of Adult Eucation, University of Nottingham, 1986.

Evans, B. *Radical Adult Education: A Political Critique.* London: Croom Helm, 1987.

Evans, N. *Post-Education Society: Recognising Adults as Learners.* London: Croom Helm, 1985.

Faith, K. (ed.). *Toward New Horizons for Women in Distance Education.* London: Routledge, 1988.

Freire, P. *Pedagogy of the Oppressed.* New York: Herder & Herder, 1970.

Gelpi, E. *Lifelong Education and International Relations.* London: Croom Helm, 1985.

Giroux, H. A. *Ideology, Culture and the Process of Schooling.* Philadelphia: Temple University Press, 1981.

Glendenning, F. (ed.). *Educational Gerontology: International Perspectives.* London: Croom Helm, 1985.

Griffin, C. *Curriculum Theory in Adult and Lifelong Education.* London: Croom Helm, 1983.

Griffin, C. *Adult Education as Social Policy.* London: Croom Helm, 1987.

Habermas, J. *Knowledge and Human Interests.* (J. Shapiro, trans.) Boston: Beacon Press, 1971.

Harris, D. *Openness and Closure in Distance Education.* Brighton, England: Falmer Press, 1987.

Hodgson, V. E., Mann, S. J., and Snell, R. (eds.). *Beyond Distance Teaching.* Milton Keynes, England: Open University Press, 1987.

Hopkins, P.G.H. *Workers' Education.* Milton Keynes, England: Open University Press, 1985.

Ireland, T. D. *Antonio Gramsci and Adult Education.* Manchester, England: Centre for Adult and Higher Education, University of Manchester, 1987.

Jarvis, P. *The Sociology of Adult and Continuing Education.* London: Croom Helm, 1985.

Jarvis, P. *Adult Learning in the Social Context.* London: Croom Helm, 1987a.

Jarvis, P. (ed.). *Twentieth Century Thinkers in Adult Education.* London: Croom Helm, 1987b.

Kirkwood, G., and Kirkwood, C. *Living Adult Education: Freire in Scotland.* Milton Keynes, England: Open University Press, 1989.

Knowles, M. S. *The Adult Learner: A Neglected Species.* (2nd ed.) Houston, Tex.: Gulf, 1978.

Knowles, M. S., and Associates. *Andragogy in Action: Applying Modern Principles of Adult Learning.* San Francisco: Jossey-Bass, 1984.

Kolb, D. *Experiential Learning.* Englewood Cliffs, N.J.: Prentice-Hall, 1984.

Langenbach, M. *Curriculum Models in Adult Education.* Melbourne, Fla.: Krieger, 1988.

Leirman, W., and Kulich, J. (eds.). *Adult Education and the Challenges of the 1990s.* London: Croom Helm, 1987.

Lovett, T. (ed.). *Radical Approaches to Adult Education: A Reader.* London: Routledge, 1988.

Mace, J., and Yarnit, M. (eds.). *Time Off to Learn: Paid Educational Leave and Low-Paid Workers.* London: Methuen, 1987.

McGivney, V., and Sims, D. *Adult Education and the Challenge of Unemployment.* Milton Keynes, England: Open University Press, 1986.

McIlroy, J., and Spencer, B. *University Adult Education in Crisis.* University of Leeds Department of Adult and Continuing Education, 1988.

Marsick, V. J. (ed.). *Learning in the Workplace.* London: Croom Helm, 1987.

Mee, G. *Organization of Adult Education.* New York: Longman, 1980.

Mezirow, J. "A Critical Theory of Adult Learning and Education." *Adult Education,* 1981, *32* (1), 3–24.

National Institute for Adult Continuing Education. *Education's for Other People: Access to Education for Non-Participant Adults.* Leicester, England: National Institute for Adult Continuing Education, 1990.

Paine, N. (ed.). *Open Learning in Transition.* Cambridge, England: National Extension College Press, 1988.

Robbins, D. *The Rise of Independent Study.* Milton Keynes, England: Society for Research into Higher Education and Open University Press, 1988.

Rogers, C. *Freedom to Learn for the 80s.* Westerville, Ohio: Merrill, 1983.

Russell, L. (chair). *Adult Education: A Plan for Development.* (Department of Education and Science report.) London: HMSO, 1973.

Schlossberg, N. K., Lynch, A. Q., and Chickering, A. W. *Improving Higher Education Environments for Adults: Responsive Programs and Services from Entry to Departure.* San Francisco: Jossey-Bass, 1989.

Schön, D. A. *Educating the Reflective Practitioner: Toward a New Design for Teaching and Learning in the Professions.* San Francisco: Jossey-Bass, 1987.

Senior, B., and Naylor, J. *Educational Responses to Adult Unemployment.* London: Croom Helm, 1987.

Stewart, D. W. *Adult Learning in America: Eduard Lindeman and His Agenda for Lifelong Education.* Melbourne, Fla.: Krieger, 1987.

Taylor, R., and Ward, K. (eds.). *Adult Education and the Working Class*. London: Croom Helm, 1986.

Tennant, M. *Psychology and Adult Learning*. London: Routledge, 1988.

Thompson, J. L. (ed.). *Adult Education for a Change*. London: Hutchinson, 1980.

Thompson, J. L. *Learning Liberation: Women's Response to Men's Education*. London: Croom Helm, 1983.

Usher, R. S., and Bryant, I. *Adult Education as Theory, Practice and Research: The Captive Triangle*. London: Routledge, 1989.

Venables, S. (chair). *Report of the Committee on Continuing Education*. Milton Keynes, England: Open University Press, 1976.

Westwood, S. "Adult Education and the Sociology of Education: An Exploration." In Thompson, J. (eds.), *Adult Education for a Change*. London: Hutchinson, 1980.

Young, M.F.D. (ed.). *Knowledge and Control*. London: Collier-Macmillan, 1971.

Youngman, F. *Adult Education and Socialist Pedagogy*. London: Croom Helm, 1986.

CHAPTER 11

Philosophical Foundations

Kenneth H. Lawson

The purpose of this chapter is to demonstrate the interplay between philosophical thinking and adult education and to discuss ways in which adult educators make use of philosophical ideas. I will argue that philosophy can be regarded as foundational to adult education at different levels or in different senses. At an explicit level, adult educators make use of particular philosophical perspectives or positions such as humanism, existentialism, or pragmatism in order to support and provide a rationale for educational practice. Such philosophical perspectives may also be implicit in educational thought and practice but are not recognized as such by adult educators.

Beneath these philosophical positions, we can discern more general ideas and principles shared by a number of philosophical schools, positions, or perspectives that together make up a broad intellectual tradition. That tradition underpins a total culture of which various forms of education, including adult education, are a part. We might, therefore, think of philosophy as foundational to adult education in "weak" and "strong" senses—

with *strong* representing the universality of the ideas involved and the extent to which they cannot be reduced to yet more fundamental ideas. It is not always clear however, what the term *can* — or *cannot* — means in such contexts. A given idea might be fundamental in the sense that is logically impossible to go beyond it and make a further reduction. For example, we cannot logically go beyond the idea of a "first cause." We might however be contingently mistaken about a particular event that we regard as the first cause and our inability to be otherwise resides in ourselves, because of a lack of information and understanding. There are then both logical and contingent senses in which something can or cannot be done. Clearly, what is logically impossible cannot be contingently possible, but we cannot be sure that what for the time being is contingently impossible is thereby also logically impossible. This makes talk about foundations particularly difficult.

As a preliminary to the discussion and in order to make it manageable within a single chapter, some limitations are necessary. The chapter will concentrate on philosophy and upon adult educational thought and practice, as understood in the English-speaking world and as representing a recognizable cultural tradition. I do not apply these limitations with any sense of cultural arrogance or superiority, but merely to produce a case study of more manageable proportions.

Definition of Terms

The range and complexity of adult education, even within the English-speaking world, is well known. The field is not well defined, and the contributors to the original black book attempted to produce a more unified overview (Jensen, Liveright, and Hallenbeck, 1964). Twenty-seven years later, we still disagree on definitions of what constitutes the field of adult education. Plecas and Sork (1986) could still discuss what they saw as an "ill-disciplined discipline." On the other hand, adult education is a reality for many students and practitioners. Some defining criteria do exist, and clues to them can be found in the black book. Verner (1964) concludes that not all adult learning constitutes adult education. Paterson (1979) has pointed to the significance of adult education being defined in relation to its clients rather than its content. Wiltshire (1964) claims that the methods, purposes, and organization of adult education were derived from the characteristics of adulthood. Knowles (1970) argues in a similar way. A normative concept of adult education may therefore be said to exist.

The idea of adulthood is itself normative rather than descriptive, and it is these normative concepts of adulthood and adult education that are implicitly grounded in what might loosely be called philosophical thinking. They are concepts that share a common philosophy that I propose to call liberal, and it is therefore liberal adult education rather than continuing or technical adult education on which I shall concentrate, although allowance has to be made for differences in transatlantic use of the term *liberal adult education.*

What Do We Mean By *Philosophy?*

Philosophy is an ambiguous term that has both popular and technical meanings. It denotes systems of thought, the academic study of such thought, and also particular techniques of study and analysis. It also suggests a concern for questions and problems that are "behind" the empirical or experienced world.

In some sense, most people philosophize at some point or other. We do so if we ponder on the meaning of life or on the nature of freedom and justice. We philosophize when we consider ethical principles in relation to issues such as abortion.

Most of us have a philosophy in the sense that we have a set of beliefs and values that influence our actions and our judgments. We talk of our philosophy of life or of the philosophy of an institution, and either might be simple or complex and sophisticated. An adult education institution might say that its philosophy is to meet the needs of the community or to encourage personal development, and such claims indicate the beginnings of an educational philosophy. From this may be deduced aims, methods, and curriculum or programs for which the philosophy is a foundation.

Philosophy as Prescription

It is not always clear whether language is being used descriptively to state what is the case or whether it is being used prescriptively to make recommendations about what should be the case in the view of a particular writer or school of thought. Descriptive writing makes use of language in more or less standard ways and general terms follow accepted and recognizable definitions. Even at the everyday level of communication, however, language may be used creatively in novel ways. The poet, for example, stretches language to and beyond its current limits. Sometimes poetry is difficult to understand because words are being given new values and meanings beyond the common currency. In effect, therefore, the poet is saying, "look at things my way" or "try to attach my meaning to otherwise ordinary or common words." In a sense, poetry is an exercise in persuasion.

Philosophical discourse may be seen in a similar light because the abstract nature of many concepts makes it difficult to establish what they really mean. There may be no standard meanings for the concepts because we have no criteria by which to judge them. Terms such as *cause, effect, democracy, society,* and *education* all have ranges of meaning, and individual writers may try to put their own meaning into such terms. They make linguistic recommendations about the use of terms and offer prescriptions embodying their own values that are intended to influence the understanding and behavior of the audience.

It might be argued that all or at least most philosophical discourse is of this nature because, like poetry, it is stretching the limits of our understanding and our response. This argument seems to be particularly true of both political and educational philosophy, which are often closely related. It is this view of philosophy that I call philosophy as prescription.

Dewey and Freire are philosophers who have made recommendations for how they think that education should be conceived of and practiced. In a sense, their philosophy is expressed in the models that each prescribes. For Freire, for example, adult education is a process of conscientization. Knowles's influential concept of andragogy may also be seen as a prescription as to how adults should be educated (as indeed are the philosophical ideas of Plato). For such writers, *education* and *adult education* become normative terms. These writers define education as (in their view) it ought to be. It is not easy to spot when normative prescriptions are being put forward. The reference points, if any, that indicate a positive concept of education as it actually is, as distinct from what it might or should become, are not at all clear. It can be argued that all philosophically based claims are normative, and that they are all based on stipulative definitions.

Philosophy as Justification

An article by Burstow (1984), for whom adult education has a built-in philosophy of its own, illustrates the use of philosophy as justification. She writes, "When I hear terms that have become our hallmark, terms like 'self directed learning' and 'ongoing learning' — I am aware that these imply some sort of image of the learner that is libertarian and emergent. This image appeals to me because it is sensitive to what we really are as human beings." But, Burstow says, "It is a vague free floating image at best. It is not rooted in ontology. That is, it is not rooted in an understanding of what is fundamental to existence generally and human existence in particular" (1984, p. 193).

Burstow is starting from an intuitive commitment to a model or concept of adult education, but her commitment needs intellectual or philosophical validation and support. For answers to "the big questions" Burstow turns, as many have done, "to existentialism for a grounding." In particular she turns to Sartre for "his *understanding* of existence" (my emphasis) (1984, p. 193).

It is interesting to note that in the same journal in which Burstow's article appears, Hartree (1984) makes a related point about Knowles's andragogy. Knowles's theory is popular in part because it, too, gives intellectual support to what adult educators support emotionally. Knowles, claims Hartree, "says what his audience wants to hear" (1984, p. 203). Knowles (wittingly) and Sartre (unwittingly) give different rationales rooted in different intellectual subtraditions for the same or similar characteristics exhibited in a particular model of adult education. That model or concept already contains its philosophy (in one sense) within itself. What is being provided is a philosophical rationale in one case and a scientific rationale in the other (Knowles) but in a different sense of the term *philosophical*.

How, if at all, are we to test philosophical justifications themselves? Philosophy does not prove philosophy; neither does science validate science. Each is, as it were, a logical stopping point beyond which our thought cannot go. What these disciplines can do is provide criteria in their own terms for judging internally valid arguments. A metaphilosophy would be needed in order to judge philosophy. And although some philosophers claim to be in a position to validate or criticize the principles on which science rests, this is a contentious issue to which we shall return. It is, therefore, in this restricted or weak sense that we can have justifications.

By tradition, or at least from Plato, Western philosophy is concerned with providing answers to very general questions about how we know things, what it means to be human, truth, mind, being, society, and so on. Philosophy also asks, How is it possible for us to think at all? This may be seen as the most fundamental issue, and it is asked as a question in the search for ultimate foundations.

A number of approaches to these issues are possible. Some philosophers have provided speculative theories grounded in intuition. Others have confined themselves to analysis of how we actually talk about such issues. For the analytical philosopher, language, the means by which we talk about our world, is the place from which to start. These philosophers start with language rather than the world or reality on the grounds that we cannot give content to the concept of reality without considering the language and the form of discourse in which reality and all other concepts play a part and from which they derive meaning. Thus they distinguish philosophy from science, which attempts to take the phenomena of experience as its starting point. In practice, philosophy and science are closely intertwined.

Some philosophers, of whom Kant is an example, saw their task as providing explanations that in some sense were ultimate and foundational. Philosophy in this model is concerned not so much with particular areas of knowledge and ideas as with general questions about the nature of knowledge and thought. One of Kant's questions was, How is thought possible? He concluded, roughly, that we can think and make sense of our experience only by using categories to organize and interrelate our experience. These categories are deemed to precede experience. They are transcendentally presupposed, predetermined, by the concept of experience. In this sense, Kant's arguments are foundational to all philosophical thought, and most philosophers since Kant have seen themselves as validating or establishing the credentials for the claims of knowledge in the sciences and all the other areas of human thought. This view of philosophy tries to establish philosophy as the "Queen" of the sciences and the arbiter of what constitutes knowledge. If we accept this view, this role of philosophy would apply to the field of education, where philosophy would provide foundational principles for educational thinking. It should be noted, however, that this kind of philosophy assumes a very strong sense of what is meant by foundational, and it is based upon the doubtful assumption that thought can establish the nature of thinking in a circular way.

The view that philosophy is foundational in this sense is not currently fashionable. It has been challenged by thinkers from Nietzsche through Habermas and Gadamer, and the challenge has more recently been popularized by Rorty (1980). He claims (as do others) that the attempts by Descartes and Kant to provide foundations for knowledge and thought have distorted the task of philosophy, which Rorty sees simply as "enlightening discourse," discourse that cannot ultimately be either right or wrong, because there can be no ultimate criteria. For him, as for most current thinkers, a further question is behind every suggested answer.

It is fashionable today to regard philosophy as interpretation or as hermeneutics and built into particular cultural traditions. We might then begin to see our discussion about adult education as highly problematic.

Where Do We Start?

If we start with a concept of adult education, where do we find this concept in the first place? Why are we entitled to believe in this concept and commit ourselves to it?

Many readers of this chapter might respond sympathetically to Burstow and to Knowles, but a person unfamiliar with the liberal tradition might not. But if we do respond to images that are libertarian and if we see adult education as liberating, it is, I suggest, because we operate within liberal democratic societies and within a tradition that has developed and encouraged liberal values. That same tradition has also produced a complementary philosophical tradition that also exerts its influence on subsequent developments within the culture. In my understanding of them, philosophy and education are intertwined with each other and with the cultural values of our society. Each reciprocally influences and is in turn influenced by the others. I believe that the societies in which we live have in part become what they are because of the influence of philosophical thinking, which has in turn been generated in response to problems as they arise within those societies.

This does not mean that philosophy is necessarily conservative. Ideas are produced to contradict and change what already exists as well as to support it. Nevertheless, new ideas are probably accepted because they appeal to some group or other, even though they might be unpalatable to other groups. I doubt whether intellectual development, any more than other development, is in the end independent of political forces. I would therefore argue that adult education is produced by the sum of forces operating within society, and educational thinking is influenced by political philosophy as well as by theories of knowledge, theories of existence, and so on.

But to answer our question, Where do we start with our view of adult education? I suggest that we start from the position in which we find ourselves. Adult education is defined for us by our particular traditions. We may accept or reject what exists, but adult education is what particular people have called adult education in particular places. In this case, we cannot seek a natural phenomenon because we are dealing with a socially constructed concept and its attendant practices (Berger and Luckmann, 1967). This construction is made within a particular social discourse, with its own vocabulary within which there are many subsets. One such subset is the vocabulary of educational discourse. Our understanding of adult education arises from our understanding of the concept of adulthood and the concept of child education. Over time, people—Knowles, for example—draw distinctions that alter our understanding of the concept, and a separate and often unclear concept of adult education has emerged, strongly influenced by our culturally and philosophically conditioned views about society, humanity, knowledge, learning, teaching, and so on. These distinctions become part of our educational vocabulary and in turn our more specialized adult education vocabulary.

The discourse conducted with such a vocabulary reflects our values and our intellectual antecedents, but, over time, additions are made to the vocabulary and the meanings associated with its component terms are modified. The terms do not have fixed immutable meanings; therefore, terms such as *adult education* remain perpetually fluid and systematically ambiguous. We catch their meaning only as snapshots in time, yet they reflect their origins either by retaining some of the original ethos or by reacting radically against it. A large part of adult education in the United Kingdom, for example, grew out of university education, and much of its subsequent history reflects this but also reflects attempts to escape from its origins.

Educational Philosophy as Linguistic Analysis

In the 1960s under the stimulus of Peters (1967) and others, developments in analytical philosophy moved into educational philosophy. Using the concepts developed by Wittgenstein, these thinkers saw educational thought as a part of discourse within a particular form of life and with its own language games in which meaning could be understood only from within a particular game and within a particular form of life. This is one of the roots or foundations of the cultural relativism implicit in my previous argument. This view involves difficulties, because we have to explain how a given game acquired its meaning, and we might have to fall back on the notion of games within bigger games, like Russian dolls enclosed within one another. My emphasis on tradition, derived from Langford (1985), is an attempted solution.

However, for the analytical philosopher, exploration of the use of language in discourse gives clues to what words and concepts mean. Instead of falling back on the observation used in empirical science or the speculative ideas of earlier philosophy, analytical philosophy tries to copy science by looking at linguistic frames of reference. These frames of reference define for us what we look at and what we look for as examples of this or that phenomenon. The study of education thus becomes essentially a linguistic study, and this method has been translated into the adult education field by writers such as Paterson (1979) and myself (Lawson, 1975, 1979).

Instead of looking at adult education per se, the linguistic method of study analyzed what was said about adult education. What was said about it told us what adult education "is," and we deduced the values of adult education from the descriptions given of it and the practices regarded as valid examples of adult education within the terms of the discourse.

Scholars recognized that educational terminology is used flexibly and ambiguously, and they did not seek single, all-embracing definitions. Instead, terms such as *adult education* were seen as having examples at the heart and other examples at the margin of a range of meanings. This led people to say that a given practice was an example of adult education in this or in that sense if it satisfied some of the criteria associated with the concept of adult education. This concept was delineated in terms of a list of criteria, not all of which need be present in every case.

The problem with this approach lay in deciding what constituted central or essential criteria and what were secondary and marginal criteria. There were no clear criteria on which to judge. The accusation can therefore be made that this analysis actually concealed prescription implied by the analyst's selection of relevant criteria. This selection was in turn influenced by the analyst's prior acceptance of criteria associated with concepts such as learning, knowledge, teaching, and so on, that constituted a discourse already accepted as educational discourse. The conceptual terminology of adult education was an extension of that discourse within the same constraining tradition. What was presented as analysis was in fact another prescription within existing values, and it was therefore conservative rather than novel. Such conservatism might not be acceptable to anyone with a radical turn of mind, but as I have argued, all thought emerges within a tradition.

I believe, therefore, that a picture emerged that resembles the one found attractive by the Barstows of the profession and by the supporters of Knowles because they are within the same tradition. Adult education, in other words, emerged as individualistic, libertarian, egalitarian, and democratic in its main outlines. These were the essential criteria to be expected from any example that claimed to be "good" adult education. A normative concept thus emerged as a model to be looked for in practice and a concept to be professionally approved. It was also a concept for those who disapproved to react against.

Substantive Roots or Foundations

The picture that emerged did of course represent a whole series of ideas and values drawn from the tradition that gave it birth. It was a picture uniquely suited to liberal democratic societies as they had then developed. If asked to specify what seem to be the main philosophical roots of adult education, I would reply that they are all of the roots that went into the making of liberal democratic societies and that in turn were produced in those societies at various stages in their development.

I shall now attempt to present the outlines of these roots. Before doing so, I wish to make one point that is related to transatlantic differences. I am not talking about liberal education in a sense that implies a particular content, as in a liberal arts course. I mean any content taught or learned in a liberal manner. In this view, even education on reinforced concrete technology can be included. What is important is the emphasis on such things as student choice, critical judgment, flexibility of curriculum, nonauthoritarian organization, and so on.

I refer to the philosophical tradition that supports such values as the liberal tradition, which has roots as far back as Platonic thought and in Roman, Judaic, and Christian thought. Its more recent emergence can, however, be traced conveniently to Locke in the seventeenth century, to Kant, and to all thinkers who have contributed to what might be called rational empiricism, which presents a political theory of liberalism. Central ideas and values of this philosophical tradition include rights, duties, justice, equality, freedom, and rationality.

Locke's ideas had a practical purpose. He wanted to provide a theoretical defense against absolute monarchy, and he conceived the state as a social contract between individuals for their mutual protection. Such individuals were logically prior to the state and logically independent of it. Central to their protection was the idea of rights. These rights included a right to own property and rights to liberty and the defense of their private self-interest through law and justice. Locke's state is concerned with the establishment and maintenance of justice, and it has no other end. It is a minimal state, as more recently expounded in the writing of Nozick (1974). Individuals are free to decide for themselves what is good. This idea has been taken up by Rawls (1972), who has exhaustively explored a society based on rights, in which no man is entitled to say what is good for another. The right to choose is therefore self-evidently established.

Both Rawls and Nozick draw on the Kantian view that individuals are autonomous centers of consciousness, which both regard as a precondition of their being moral agents. Each person is an end and never a means; therefore it makes no sense to ask, Why is self-development and freedom to choose important? Self-development and freedom to choose are assumed to be worthwhile as part of our normative conception of a mature human being.

For Kant, as for Rawls, choices must be rationally made and not influenced by contingent self-interest. Only if this condition is satisfied can we make moral choices because rationality is the highest moral virtue that we have a duty to observe. In this way morality is rescued from domination by authorities; it is something that derives directly from the consciousness of individuals. We are on the way, therefore, to identifying some of the antecedents of a liberal conception of adult education. Education has to do with the development of rationality and the ability to make judgments. In an individual's pursuit of his or her own version of the good, full scope must be allowed for the individual to choose what shall be learned.

An epistemology, or theory of knowledge, is also required. Here, too, an individualistic theory is provided in the tradition of Descartes, for whom the irreducible "I" that thinks is the source of all knowledge because the existence of a self is the one thing that no one can doubt. The subjective self thinks and has experience, and being able to have sense experiences is the basis of rational empiricism. Experience, rationally ordered, is the source of what we know. The perceptions of individuals become knowledge claims when tested against the experience of others. Knowledge, too, is therefore no longer determined by authorities; it can be tested and established by ordinary people and it enters the free market of public debate. In principle, every knowledge claim is testable. Moreover, in a liberal democracy, equal access to the resources for producing knowledge is also regarded as a right.

Such a philosophical rationale seems to open the way for the kind of adult education to which many people already subscribe. The individual is at the center of this philosophy, and personal development is a primary goal. Adult education, then, as Paterson puts it, is an education that "directly touches us in our personal being, tending our identity at its roots and ministering directly to our condition as conscious selves aspiring in all our undertakings to a greater fullness and completeness of being" (1979, p. 15). In other words, education is a set of processes that help make each person who he or she wants to be. Individual rather than societal aspirations are paramount because, according to existentialist thought, individuals are deemed to be able to choose to be what they are and what they might become. This is an ethical point that begs a number of questions about what is possible, but it emphasizes the principle that the outcomes of adult education should not be prescribed for us and that there should be no compulsion. This brings us to the principle of voluntarism in adult education, a point emphasized by Wiltshire (1964), who regards the goal of adult education as self-discovery and self-development voluntarily undertaken.

We should recognize, therefore, that neither Paterson nor Wiltshire is making statements of fact. They are making ethical claims for a certain kind of status for adults. The autonomous individual is a goal rather than a starting point, but these writers assume, nevertheless, that adults already possess the ability to make choices as they enter adult education. This may or may not be true in individual cases. It becomes almost a normative requirement that adults should choose. This style of thinking includes some tension because the normative element becomes an ideology that prescribes how adults ought to behave rather than a neutral account of how they actually do behave. Such a criticism is also true of Knowles's position on andragogy.

Some Alternative Views

What might be called mainstream philosophies of adult education have been criticized by a number of thinkers, although it is difficult to say how much, if at all, these thinkers have influenced the practice of adult education. I have already mentioned Freire (1970), for whom adult education is essentially a vehicle for making us aware of the oppressive nature of our societies so that we might learn how to change them. His philosophical foundations are derived from Marx and from Christian humanism, but to my mind his program is more interesting than his philosophy. It is as an inspiring teacher rather than as a philosopher that he deserves a reputation.

Some valid criticisms of liberal philosophy are made by Keddie and Thompson. Keddie sees the concept of the liberal person as empty because it "leads to a notion of the learner as an 'abstracted universal individual' rather than as a person situated in a historical and existential context" (1980, p. 47). These writers attack, at the philosophical level, the Kantian tradition of universal abstract categories as the basis of rational thought. In that tradition, we cannot think without a categorical framework, which is brought into education in the form of academic disciplines or bodies of knowledge. Hirst (1974), in his theory of the forms of knowledge, erects these into absolutes. His frameworks correspond roughly to the main academic disciplines, and he believes that they exhaust the possibilities open to us for conceptualizing and comprehending the world. The developed individual, therefore, is one who is versed or educated in forms of knowledge that might not be seen as relevant to real flesh and blood individuals as distinct from a universal abstraction of the individual. For Keddie (1980) the learning needs of real individuals are "socially and politically constituted and understood." A theory of the individual in society as part of a collective or community is therefore the key to a relevant system of adult education.

Somewhat similar points are made by Wain (1987), writing on the philosophy of lifelong education. He sees the rational autonomy of Kant as presented by liberal philosophers as an imposed or predetermined autonomy. It is constrained by the concept of rationalism itself and thus prevents what is called self-realization rather than autonomy. For Wain, liberalism provides a restricted form of individuality that is manifested in the ideal of an educated person, a person knowledgeable within the forms of knowledge or academic disciplines. Wain posits a return to Dewey's pragmatism in a learning society with a system of lifelong education. Learning would then be determined by the concrete needs of a participatory democratic society, and an individual's commitment would be to fellow human beings rather than to abstract ideas about truth generated within academic knowledge.

In a variety of ways, the premises of liberal philosophy and concepts of adult education based upon it are under heavy fire. Bowles and Gintis (1976), Bernstein (1971), and Young (1971) have provided the basis for many of the criticisms by emphasizing the relationship in capitalist societies between knowledge and power. This relationship produced education that favors elites, and it is basically undemocratic. Kuhn is another influential writer. With his theory of scientific revolutions, he explains how science progresses by a series of paradigm shifts (Kuhn, 1970). Each shift, for example, the shift from Newtonian to Einsteinian physics, sets the pattern for normal science until another revolutionary paradigm arises. This idea has been absorbed into the literature on recurrent education, where Houghton and Richardson (1974) argue for a paradigm shift in education. They criticize the model that gives priority to educating children and marginalizes adult education. Their new paradigm is a system in which people move in and out of education in a recurrent way throughout life. This paradigm, too, would require a new epistemology, but apart from condemning curriculum teaching based on academic disciplines, Houghton and Richardson do not provide one.

Conclusion

What I have tried to demonstrate is the interplay between philosophy and education, which occurs in a variety of ways. In some instances, philosophy provides a rationale for existing practices that in turn, on closer examination, also reflect philosophical traditions that have informed our cultures at an earlier stage. Current ideas in various areas of philosophy stimulate or provoke thinking in new ways about adult education and help to generate new practices.

Philosophy, I believe, does not produce absolute foundations that are immutable, but it does provide a meeting point of a more provisional nature. It is in this more limited sense that we can think of philosophical foundations. In my view, the most influential ideas are those drawn from outside adult education, since, I believe, adult education knowledge cannot develop without reference to them. Adult education cannot generate new thoughts from within itself. It is a part of a culture, and it feeds upon ideas from outside adult education. It cannot generate new thinking only from within. My own prescription from my personal reading is to draw upon a wide range of literature reflecting many aspects of philosophy. Some of the greatest stimulus for adult education has come variously from legal philosophy, philosophy of religion, political philosophy, philosophy of language, and partly, of course, from the field of educational philosophy. I do not think that a freestanding philosophy of adult education is possible.

Nevertheless, we can and should continue to make use

of the many kinds of philosophy to provide critical insights that might take adult education in new directions. Much of our current practice is not rigorously thought out and is in need of philosophical justification. The fact that such justification is itself open to criticism and revision should not deter us. Neither should we be afraid of exposing the shortcomings in some of our cherished ideas and practices, as recent studies of Knowles's andragogy have done.

In some quarters, the excessively individualistic thinking behind adult education is giving way to a desire for more communitarian philosophies. There are signs of a move toward the more pragmatically based objectives favored by some writers, and this reflects the current tendency to reject foundational philosophies (although pragmatism is itself a philosophy). An ongoing exploration and discussion of such issues would be entirely consistent with the view that philosophizing is an interpretive process that is endless. Societal change and cultural evolution are equally endless, and they produce new ideologies as well as revive old ones. Philosophy is not value-neutral, but it can be seen as an attempt to produce objective critiques of politically and commercially motivated ideologies. Such activity can be part of the content of adult education programs. It should also be an important activity in the professional lives of adult educators, who have tended to concentrate too much perhaps on techniques without asking in a critical way what the techniques are for and how they might be justified in philosophical terms. A technologically oriented society is a society with an ideology that impinges on adult education. Are adult educators content to let such ideologies determine what they do?

References

Berger, L., and Luckmann, T. *The Social Construction of Reality.* Harmondsworth, England: Penguin, 1967.

Bernstein, B. "On the Classification and Framing of Knowledge." In F. D. Young (ed.), *Knowledge and Control.* London: Collier, 1971.

Bowles, S., and Gintis, H. *Schooling in Capitalist America: Educational Reform & the Contradictions of Economic Life.* New York: Basic Books, 1976.

Burstow, B. "Adult Education: A Sartrean Based Perspective." *International Journal of Lifelong Education,* 1984, *3* (3), 193–202.

Freire, P. *Pedagogy of the Oppressed.* New York: Herder & Herder, 1970.

Hartree, A. "'Malcolm Knowles' Theory of Andragogy: A Critique." *International Journal of Lifelong Education,* 1984, *3* (3), 203–210.

Hirst, P. H. *Knowledge and the Curriculum.* New York: Routledge, Chapman & Hall, 1974.

Houghton, V., and Richardson, K. *Recurrent Education.* London: Ward Lock International, 1974.

Jensen, G., Liveright, A. A., and Hallenbeck, W. (eds.). *Adult Education: Outlines of an Emerging Field of University Study.* Washington, D.C.: American Association for Adult and Continuing Education, 1964.

Keddie, N. "Adult Education: An Ideology of Individualism." In J. L. Thompson (ed.), *Adult Eucation for a Change.* London: Hutchinson, 1980.

Knowles, M. S. *The Modern Practice of Adult Education: Andragogy Versus Pedagogy.* Chicago: Association Press, 1970.

Kuhn, T. S. *The Structure of Scientific Revolution.* (2nd ed.) Chicago: University of Chicago Press, 1970.

Langford, G. *Education, Persons and Society.* New York: Macmillan, 1985.

Lawson, K. H. *Philosophical Concepts and Values in Adult Education.* (Rev. ed.) Milton Keynes, England: Open University Press, 1979.

Nozick, R. *Anarchy, State and Utopia.* Oxford, England: Blackwell, 1974.

Paterson, R.W.K. *Values, Education and the Adult.* Boston: Routledge & Kegan Paul, 1979.

Peters, R. S. (ed.). *The Concept of Education.* Boston: Routledge & Kegan Paul, 1967.

Plecas, D. B., and Sork, T. J. "Curing the Ills of an Undisciplined Discipline." *Adult Education Quarterly,* 1986, *37* (1), 48–62.

Rawls, J. A. *Theory of Justice.* Oxford, England: Oxford University Press, 1972.

Rorty, R. *Philosophy and the Mirror of Nature.* Princeton, N.J.:

Princeton University Press; Oxford, England: Oxford University Press, 1980.

Verner, C. "Definition of Terms." In G. Jensen, A. A. Liveright, and W. Hallenbeck (eds.), *Adult Education: Outlines of an Emerging Field of University Study.* Washington, D.C.: American Association for Adult and Continuing Education, 1964.

Wain, K. *Philosophy of Lifelong Education.* London: Croom Helm, 1987.

Wiltshire, H.C.W. "The Nature and Uses of Adult Education." In A. Rogers (ed.), *The Spirit and the Form.* Nottingham, England: Department of Adult Education, University of Nottingham, 1976.

Young, M.F.D. "An Approach to the Study of Curricula as Socially Organised Knowledge." In M.F.D. Young (ed.), *Knowledge and Control.* London: Collier-Macmillan, 1971.

CHAPTER 12

Relationships with Political Science

Alan M. Thomas

The difficulty of separating any systematic reflection about adult education from political thought is symbolized in a quotation from Kidd and Titmus: "The organization of adult education has been fuelled by faiths, by revolution, by migration, by inventions and renaissances, by nationalist actions, by international actions, and now by the demands of high technology. . . . However since they did not result in permanent institutional forms, they rarely outlasted a particular philosophical or political epoch. Probably the most critical factor in their demise was the fact that these programs were so significant as modes of cultural and political expression they were targets for destruction by any military invader" (1985, p. 94). "In practice adult education has always meant politics and nothing in this respect has changed" (p. 1). Mhaike (1973) notes, "Political education gives meaning to all other subjects" (p. 19).

The purpose of this chapter is to explore the relationships between the two fields of inquiry, political science and adult education. To explore the relationships, it is necessary to examine the content, terminology, and dominant concepts of the two domains. Obviously, given the specific context, more attention will be devoted to the use of "political" concepts in the study of adult education than concepts from adult education in the study of politics. The result may imply that the only significant influence has been one way, from political science to adult education. In fact, the chapter is intended to reveal the existence of a mutual relationship that has been of increasing significance recently and that promises to be an intellectual landmark in the future.

A Mutuality of Interests

In its search for its own intellectual and academic identity, adult education has resisted, so far, being considered a subsection of political science. This appears to be true despite the obvious fact that "adult education research tends to spill out beyond conventional and narrowly defined educational considerations into those which encompass welfare, employment, race and gender issues" (Bryant and Usher, 1986, pp. 16–17). The opening quotation of this chapter by Kidd and Titmus and, indeed, any brief glimpse into the practice of adult education allows a considerable expansion of those areas to include citizenship, cultural identity, economic viability, and national and organizational survival, to name a few.

Nevertheless, the growth of explicit political analysis of adult education of any systematic kind has been slow, especially in North America and Western Europe. The *Handbook of Adult Education* (Knowles, 1960) contains acknowledged references to political matters, although both Bell (1960) and Sheats (1960) make reference to what can be called issues of functional politics.

In the United States, the emergence of adult education and adult educators from or in close association with the existing, largely public, agencies of the child- and youth-centered system of education presumably provoked adult educators to attempt to emulate the "apolitical" character of both these systems. While the same character of adult education was evident in Canada, the United Kingdom, and Western Europe, to varying degrees, the contrast with Eastern Europe, Latin America, and Asia has been dramatic. In the latter areas, adult education has been conceived of as an inescapably political enterprise, either as an unchallenged instrument of the state in the pursuit of "socialist man," for example, or as a major ingredient in the contest of different ideologies for control of the state and political power.

The research and literature of adult education from these areas of the world has been avowedly "political" in its intent and substance: "The owners of the means of production have changed and Marxist philosophy and ideology have been adopted. All of these factors influence the organization of adult education and the areas of training and education at the basis of which is the all-round development of the individual" (Savićević, 1985, p. 136). As this chapter is being written, changes so profound as to affect all aspects of life, especially adult education, are taking place in Eastern Europe. It will be of enormous interest to us to witness what alternations, if any, take place in the political cast of adult education.

Despite the slow development of political analysis of adult education in the West, political considerations now occupy an increasing place in the informed literature of adult education, particularly the international journals. The growth in systematic scholarly and popular interest in this political analysis seems to have paralleled the growth of the role of the state in adult education worldwide. "Programs that were local, often undertaken as a response to specific needs, have become linked with national aspirations, sometimes internationally planned, often based on legislation and directed to broad political, economic, and cultural goals, with consistent and sustained international communications" (Kidd and Titmus, 1985, p. 93). These developments have in turn given rise to increasing numbers of comparative studies, for example, Elsdon (1988), Whyte (1987), Rivera and Dohmen (1985), and Bown (1986). Bown (1986) says that considering the new dominance of the state, too few systematic comparative studies have been launched.

The systematic use of concepts from political science in adult education, however, has been influenced by the ambivalence evident among adult educators about drawing on the resources and "cosmologies" of other disciplines. "Among advocates for a discipline of adult education there is a strong belief that not only is borrowing of little value for adult education, but it is also damaging. . . . This line of reasoning has been criticized. . . . [Rubenson] argues that it is in the effort to understand the structure and the problems of adult education that help from a number of disciplines is needed" (Rubenson, 1985, p. 170). Nowhere is this ambivalence more clear than with respect to the exchange between political science and adult education. Perhaps proximity of these two domains makes cooperation more difficult than in other areas. We can achieve greater clarity about this issue by considering the state of political science as a discipline during the period in which adult education has been trying to forge its own identity.

Easton (1968) describes the development of political science as a discipline in this way: "Political science in the mid-twentieth century is a discipline in search of an identity. Through the efforts to solve this identity problem it has begun to show evidence of emerging as an autonomous, independent discipline with a systematic theoretical structure of its own. The factor that has contributed most to this end has been the reception and integration of the methods of science into the core of the discipline" (p. 282). For a considerable period of time in the last century, political science cohabited intellectually and functionally with economics under the rubric of "political economy." Prior to that, both areas had been subdivisions of philosophy, closely related to history study.

Easton's words, with their emphasis on autonomy, have a familiar ring to anyone aware of the development of the study of adult education during the same period. The use of qualitative instead of quantitative methods of research in political science at that time and the same lingering disputes over the comparative value of the two methods reinforce the familiarity. The struggle to find some unifying theory that would make sense of the accumulation of increasing amounts of descriptive information characterizes the efforts of both fields.

The conceptual building blocks of political theory (groups, power, control and influence, elites, participation, choice and decision making, and so on) refer to individuals acting out their lives in relationship to each other. Adult education has increasingly used the same concepts and terminology and has added the dimension of learning, of transformation, to the concept of the individual. Some evidence suggests that political scientists are beginning to apply the concept of learning to their own explorations (Spencer Foundation, 1989). It would appear, therefore, that the relationship between the two disciplines has been and is more reciprocal than is usually acknowledged and that the potential for such reciprocity is likely to increase.

Throughout the world, the relationship between economic development and adult learning has become relentlessly apparent. The response to that relationship has included particular political developments and increased insights into the relationships of economics and politics. This response is particularly apparent in the Soviet Union and Eastern Europe at the present time. What this outcome points to is the continuing need to maintain the integrity of the study of adult education and the continuing need to maintain close functional and intellectual contact between adult education, economics, and politics, particularly with respect to the preparation of adult educators. Because political science and adult education have the potential to nourish each other, we must consider more precisely the emergence of "political thinking" in adult education.

Political Analysis in Adult Education

We find both functional and structural political concerns in adult education. Functional concerns include primarily concerns of citizenship and its related program area. Structural concerns consist of concerns of administration and finance, legislation and policy, systems analysis, and theories and ideologies. Despite the potential inclusiveness of the latter concerns, a comprehensive theory that would serve to unify, satisfactorily, all of the components of either category has yet to emerge.

Citizenship. Since the time of the transformation of "subjects into citizens," a process that dominated the nineteenth century throughout the world and achieved varying degrees of success, citizenship has been a constant theme of adult education. *Socialization* is another term for this concern, a term arising from the learning needs associated with entry into a group or society (Thomas, 1983). For obvious reasons, countries such as the United States, Canada, Australia, and, to a lesser extent, countries in Latin America that have experienced high levels of immigration during the past century are those countries most preoccupied with citizenship in adult education, as distinct from the education of the young. These countries are concerned with adult "entrants" for whom full-time compulsory attendance in a common school (Cremin, 1951) is not a viable strategy. Other educational mechanisms had to be used or invented. To a considerable degree, these mechanisms, such as the voluntary association, the ubiquitous classroom, and a variety of forms of what is now called "distance education," have become characteristic mechanisms of adult education. Lindeman ([1926] 1961) provided perhaps the grandest conception of citizenship, and Carlson (1987) and Selman (1987), among others, have dealt in more detail with the educational processes involved in citizenship in the United States and Canada. Even in these two neighboring societies, response to this problem, or opportunity, has been quite different.

It is important to acknowledge here a characteristic that permeates all inquiry in adult education: the relevance to adult education of material from essential resources must often be inferred. For example, it would be impossible to imagine a satisfactory examination of citizenship and immigration in North America without consulting such classics as Thomas and Znaniecki (1974), Handlin (1973), or Lysenko (1947). These authors were not writing primarily about adult education, but they were certainly writing about adult learning arising from problems of entry, although they may rarely, if ever, mention the words *adult learning* and *entry*.

Recently, governments have become concerned with issues adjacent to citizenship, such as multiculturalism and literacy. Large numbers of people now move throughout the world as immigrants, refugees, and guest workers, carrying their languages and cultural habits with them apparently more aggressively than in the past. The movements of these people have stimulated interest in the practicability if not the inescapability of "hyphenated" citizenship, resulting in complex educational and political responses. At the same time, literacy, a worldwide mainstay of adult education since the turn of the century, has become a factor of citizenship as well as the subject of more inclusive political analysis both within and outside of adult education. "The modern view of literacy is that it is no longer equated with reading, writing, and arithmetic alone, but is also an element of socio-economic progress, and should aid in the creation of responsible citizens as well as the safeguarding of cultural identity and national interests" (Lazarus, 1985, p. 202). In addition, rapid technological change, with its radical impact on careers, incomes, and gender roles throughout the world, appears to weaken or undermine national and cultural identity among adults. Governments are therefore concerned about "resocialization." This concern has shifted the preoccupation with citizenship onto a lifelong spectrum, making citizenship a problem of continuous renewal rather than a one-time effort associated with childhood or adult entry into a country.

At the heart of all these concerns lies the concept of participation, a concept not only shared by adult education and political science but also shared by all countries, socialist and capitalist, with the claim to be democratic. The concept of participation presents a characteristic problem of adult education theory, based as it must be on some assumptions about learning. Is participation in society to be conceived as the means toward effective or acceptable citizenship? Or is it the end, that is, pure citizenship itself? Or is it both? We are thus confronted with problems of learning about learning. Every learning outcome is accompanied by experience with how it was achieved. Every change in collective behavior, for example, in how a city alters its practices of waste disposal (behavior that is rapidly being identified with citizenship), is accompanied by indicators of how that new behavior was learned. These indicators are frequently difficult to discern. In each case the resultant learning is cumulative and irreversible.

Until recently, the implications of these phenomena had been sensed but rarely articulated either by adult educators or political scientists. However, perhaps for this reason "adult education for participation, despite the mixed feelings it generates, and despite the ever-present danger of merely being a brand of propaganda remains for many adult educators and politicians, the zenith of adult education. Clearly whatever political ideology is involved, it can no longer be the difference between learning and not learning about public matters, or of participating or not participating in them. Any intervention by adult educators is an intervention in learning and participating already taking place, often with very specific objectives in mind" (Thomas, 1985, p. 122).

In the past century, citizenship as an aspect of both theory and practice in adult education seems to have been, with a few exceptions, a matter of maintaining the divisions between one state and another rather than a matter of political divisions within states. As the power of individual states declines, as is surely the case in the contemporary world, we must expect that citizenship and its associated domains along with the associated educational policies and practices will change radically. Undoubtedly, one area of change will arise from people's increasing assertiveness about political identity and sovereignty based on a spoken language. In contrast to such factors as place of birth or skin color, a language can be learned. For that reason, and for others, such as the greater mobility of the world's populations, all education related to citizenship is likely to become similar to the education related to citizenship found in the predominantly immigrant societies. The recent reunification of "East" and "West" Germany is one example of that phenomenon.

Administration and Finance. The political environment of adult education, particularly in the Western industrialized countries, fits within a conventional pattern of the public politics of a multiplicity of organizations within the state — some voluntary and private, some professional, some quasi-nongovernmental, and some, in federal systems, at other levels of government. The pattern involves the establishment of priorities on the local and national agenda. This pattern and "several other factors constitute a spiral: understanding, popularity, support, legislation, funds, beneficial activities, better understanding . . . additional funds, broader benefits" (Bell, 1960, p. 138).

Sometimes independently and sometimes together, adult education agencies have worked at influencing other levels of government with respect to the provision of adult education. North American and British adult educators have tended to envy the greater state support for adult education to be found in European countries, especially Scandinavia and (formerly) West Germany (Elsdon, 1988). They have also admired, with deep reservations, the impressive range of state bodies and programs of the Eastern European countries.

The current research literature (Bown, 1986; Nisbet, 1986) attests to the apparent success of Western educators in influencing the public agenda but at the same time reflects considerable misgivings with respect to the results. "Disagreement as to the extent of national [federal] control of education is fierce. It embraces the entire issue of the centralization versus the decentralization of government. It is perhaps *the* political issue of adult education, although the ultimate question is not that of national versus state policy, but whether or not public policy is even required or desirable" (Rivera, 1982, p. 14). Concern for the results of public policy on education has penetrated to the core of adult education, the conducting of research. "Educational research today is caught between powerful pressure from policy-makers and practitioners . . . and both are imposing pressures toward conformity. . . . It is in danger of becoming a means of reaffirming established or fashionable patterns of thought" (Nisbet, 1986, p. 2).

Systems Analysis. Curiously enough, it is the application of systems theory, or systems analysis, a concept adult education shares with political science, that has tended to bring these underlying concerns into focus. Systems analysis, the careful analysis of the interaction of defined political items, is increasingly being applied to the public development of adult education in the way it is applied to any other dimension of public policy.

Stewart (1981) says, "Systems under study must be truly ob-servable . . . must be large enough so that all relevant concepts can be observed, described, and analyzed" (p. 153). However, he adds, "It is not always easy to study the political dimensions of education, given the traditional suspicion of 'politics' among educators. But the road towards progress in achieving many of the goals of adult education is political and a study of what happens en route, would seem to be a good instrument" (p. 153). Critics are not so sure that adult education should or can be treated in the same way as any other public policy. "Systems analysis in its becoming the major methodology of program and policy analysis is indicative of the trend towards central plan-ning and promulgation of the mechanical method of program development. It reflects the growth of large scale centralized pro-grams and the policy strategies by government agencies towards system in the development of adult education" (Rivera, 1982, p. 17).

Probably, both Stewart's and Rivera's positions are tena-ble. The size of the adult education enterprise in all contempo-rary states, rich and poor, will probably increasingly lead people to analyze adult education through the application of systematic methods of analysis drawn from other and, perhaps, older fields of endeavor. The predominant concern of modern governments with their economies and the now clearly established relation-ship between adult education and the health of those economies ensures that development. Such is the price of success.

Nevertheless, a closer examination of the development of adult education and its supporting theory suggests an internal integrity that justifies resistance to the domination of concepts and systems derived externally. The mix of private, public, voluntary, and nonvoluntary efforts that have so clearly charac-terized the development of adult education in Western coun-tries is not so unique to these countries as is usually thought. Almost all of the Eastern societies have developed and main-tained a form of "voluntary" action in regard to adult educa-tion. The Znanie Society, the major Soviet nonformal adult edu-cation organization, has maintained legal independence from the Soviet government and at its peak was able to boast of more than three million members. The perception of the value of the role of member in the development of adult education, in particular of its organized forms, is the most significant factor in such organizations. In Western societies, organizations with powerful educational potential that were originally established purely as state or commercial organizations, for example, television broadcasting companies, have found it necessary to introduce a voluntary membership aspect to their operations. Organized voluntary behavior is the closest collective approximation of individual learning; it is the best social reflection of that phenomenon. Any organization, public or private, that wishes to attract and stimulate the will to learn among its citizens, members, and so on must develop organizational equivalents for voluntary action and thus for learning. It is hardly necessary to observe that the "information society" obliges all organizations, including states, to stimulate people's will to learn in order to survive.

It is in this regard, perhaps, that we glimpse the outlines of the most fundamental links between politics and adult education. The nurturing of learning requires certain kinds of organization beyond the provision of formal education by the formal agencies of education. These outlines will become clearer when we turn to the examination of the emerging contest of ideologies in adult education. However, first it is necessary to examine the most public and formal domain of interaction between politics and adult education — the domain of legislation.

Legislation and Policy. "The history of adult education in this country cannot be accurately told without referring to the major legislative developments, which have exerted so much influence on the adult education movement" (Whaples and Rivera, 1982, p. v). Despite the obvious truth of this statement, theoretical interest in legislation affecting adult education has been slow to develop, and the area remains relatively unexplored. One reason for this inattention is that legislation explicitly devoted to the education of adults, as distinct from legislation that "enabled adult learning to be included in more sweeping provisions, such as the 'Land Grant Legislation' in the United States has been equally slow to develop. It was not until the mid-1960's that West European countries began to pass laws concerned specifically with adult education. . . . Specific reference in existing education law to the 'rights of adults' is difficult to find" (Stock, 1985, pp. 145–146).

Since the 1960s, a variety of legislation affecting adult education has been enacted, and descriptive accounts of the legislation have been written (Thomas, 1984, 1986, 1988; European Bureau of Adult Education, 1975). In general, the legislation ranges from enabling legislation, to legislation forming agencies explicitly designed for adult education, to detailed acts governing apprentices. Enabling legislation includes that which enables formal agencies of education, such as universities, to take a relatively permissive and benign attitude toward the inclusion of adults. Various agencies explicitly designed for adult education include the Workers' Educational Association in the United Kingdom and Canada's Frontier College. The usually extremely detailed terms of acts governing apprentices found in most industrial societies take their precise formulation from the fact that they are designed and accepted by representatives of three mutually suspicious groups: government, labor, and employers.

My work (Thomas, 1987, 1989; Thomas, Gaskin, and Taylor, 1989) has carried the analysis of legislation further by looking beyond legislation explicitly devoted to adult education to legislation, regulations, and judicial decisions that can be said to apply to the broader sweep of adult learning. In particular, I try to examine the relationship between adult learning and legislation: "Learning is nearly synonymous with human growth and lies at the heart of all social change. When the latter occurs it is safe to conclude that somewhere in a social system someone has learned something that he or she did not know, could not do, or did not understand. When the learning is unexpected, that is in terms of who has accomplished it, or what has been learned, problems of social instability present themselves. In contrast, it is the purpose of the law to define and fix relationships and behavior over periods of time; relationships between groups and individuals, as in contract law; relationships between individuals and the state, as in constitutional law; and relationships between states, as in international law. . . . To a degree all law has implications for learning though, obviously, with differing degrees of specificity" (Thomas, 1989a, p. 105).

Researchers can compare societies based on common law, where procedures are established but goals left undefined, and societies with codes of "normative" law, where ideal human behavior and indeed character are established by law, as a basis for comprehending different climates for adult education. The United Kingdom and most of its former colonies have societies based on common law. France and most socialist societies have normative law as a basis. Roberts's comparison of the development and practice of adult education in two Canadian provinces, Alberta (common law) and Quebec (civil law), is a valuable example of such analysis (Roberts, 1982).

The conceptual shift from education to learning, supported by developments in other areas of research in adult education, allows a broader canvas on which to understand the complexities that legislation explicitly devoted to education or adult education presents. "Thus a dichotomy may be seen between those concerned with the providers and provision of adult education and those focused on learning directed toward the resolution of social problems. . . . Adult education is most often determined and its social direction defined by others than adult educators, by public policy makers for instance" (Rivera, 1982, p. 3). Precisely because legislation may be considered the centerpiece of political science, further examination of its role in and relationship to adult education promises increased clarity about the relationship between the two domains of inquiry and with respect to the internal operating concepts of each domain.

Theories and Ideologies. Since 1965, when Johnstone and Rivera completed their landmark study of adults' participation in education, other researchers have provided statistical summaries of participation in adult education in almost all industrial societies. These studies show that the bulk of publicly provided resources for adult education are used by those individuals who have already succeeded in their initial schooling. Therefore, instead of providing an alternative means of distributing wealth, adult education as it now operates is reinforcing, if not widening, the income divisions in contemporary societies. In these societies, where the ability to manipulate information, the very stuff of education, has become increasingly the basis of wealth and power, the role of adult education has become more and more subject to political analysis and concern.

The most prominent critical analysis has come from adult educators working in or associated with Latin America, that most politicized of all arenas of adult education (Illich, 1970; LaBelle, 1976; Freire, 1970). But there have been earlier and parallel sources of criticism from within the United States and the United Kingdom (Taylor, Rockhill, and Fieldhouse, 1985) and from Europe under the general rubric of critical theory (Gramsci, 1971; Habermas, 1971). The Highlander Research and Education Center in the United States, which plays an exemplary role, must be included in the lexicon of critics. Essentially, all of these critics see adult education as little other than a political phenomenon representing a particular order of society, in this case liberal capitalist, that must be countered by adult education inseparable from other social and economic orders.

The most powerful of these criticisms have been and are Marxist or neo-Marxist in origin, based on a metaphor for learning originally proposed by Hegel. These criticisms conceive of learning as a dialectical process of thesis-antithesis and synthesis, with an underlying implication of conflict, whether it be between an old self and a new one struggling to emerge, within the individual, or between groups competing for power, within a society. The arguments and analyses presented are compelling, and on the surface they reflect the imposition of political philosophies on adult education that have been derived from the analysis of other spheres of activity.

The effect of these arguments has been felt on research in adult education itself, giving rise to such classes of activity as participatory research and action research, activities that are essentially native to adult education. "Current emphasis on action research is no coincidence. It arises from the pragmatics of funding and the priorities of research policy, current models of practice in adult education, and the need for clearer and closer links between research and practice. . . . Indeed one of the characteristics of action research as compared to some other forms is the inherently 'political' nature of the stakeholders' behavior as a feature of the action change dynamic" (Bryant and Usher, 1986, p. 12).

However, here again, it seems more efficacious to shift to learning as distinct from education as a basis for adequate theory: "There is a conceptual distinction to make however between adult learning and the public provision of adult education. . . . In this context, Habermas, Illich, Freire, Gramsci, Gelpi, and so on, are not so much a political analysis as utopian radicalism" (Griffin, 1986, pp. 92, 94). Making this shift reveals the importance of the metaphor for learning contained in the Marxist position and also acknowledges the existence of other such metaphors, such as that contained in the liberal position (Griffin, Chapter Ten).

In the liberal position, political power is lodged at the source of all learning — the individual. The dynamics by which that learning manifests itself are conceived of in individual terms. Further, this position allows us to explore with greater confidence the possibility that learning itself provides the basis for political theory arising from its own data, and, indeed, the basis for the analysis of other traditional political philosophies. There is ground for arguing that critical theory represents an attempt to reconcile classical Marxism with the knowledge of learning, thereby introducing a new dynamic into Marxism. What does seem clear is that political theory or philosophy drawn from the observation of phenomena other than those associated with learning cannot in the future be uncritically applied to adult education.

Conclusion

It can be argued that the functional necessity for the education of adults, as adults, is now established globally. In fact, the necessity has been apparent since the dropping of the atomic bomb in August 1945, when humankind demonstrated the capacity for any generation of adults to effectively render civilized life unrecognizable. Recent fears of environmental collapse have only served to underline the same necessity. Therefore, the argument is no longer about whether adult education is necessary or practical, but about how it should be implemented and, more important, about which adults defined by what criteria should benefit from adult education. The simple fact that adult education cannot be administered or financed in the same manner or by the same means as the education of the young is quite sufficient to ensure argument. We are, at least, no longer obliged to argue that adults do learn and that what they learn or do not learn is of fundamental importance.

In this context, the application of conventional concepts of political science, which defines itself as the study of "that behavior or set of interactions through which authoritative allocations (binding decisions) are made and implemented for a society" (Easton, 1968, p. 285) seems appropriate. Systems theory, concepts of power, influence, and group interaction, as defined by political scientists, are all applicable to adult education. Undoubtedly, we will see more of this kind of analysis in the future. The recent growth of the use of the terms *ownership* and *empowerment* in the practice of adult education is an interesting indication of the likelihood of such analysis with respect to both political science and economics. Though both terms in the context of adult education defy precise definition, the fact that they are being used, apparently to replace such earlier concepts as autonomy, self-realization, and liberation, attests to the continuing growth of an awareness of the political importance of adult education. Nevertheless, it is of equal importance to acknowledge that political science itself is based on unexamined metaphors for learning. It is the task, indeed the obligation, of adult education, or of some more clearly articulated version of "Mathetics" (Faure, 1972) to clarify and elaborate those metaphors. In the future we will be at least as preoccupied with the politics of learning as with the politics of adult education.

At the time that I wrote this chapter, it was impossible to avoid frequent references to the tumultuous events in the Soviet Union and Eastern Europe. Despite the impressive commitment of those societies to formal education and to the education of adults, it seems clear that they have failed in the politics and management of learning. That is to say, they have failed to provide the type of social and political structure that nourishes and supports the will toward lifelong learning that must exist if any contemporary society is to survive economically and politically. What shape the emergent societies will take, particularly with respect to the instruments and climate for adult education, is difficult to determine. A question of singular importance is whether governments in these societies understand the dimensions and significance of learning about learning. In any case, those countries present the most dramatic examples of the evolution of adult education that could be imagined.

For all these reasons it is essential to understand that the relationship between adult education and political science is a two-way street; each field of inquiry has the capacity and the obligation to enrich the other. That understanding may help us find a reasonable balance between the increasing pressure to see adult education only in political terms, which might mean a tacit acceptance of the field's being a subsection of political science, and maintaining the integrity of adult education as, at the very least, a field of practice that involves all the complex facets of human individuals and their cultural aspirations.

With that potential in mind, it seems appropriate to conclude with a statement of an unresolved problem in political science that seems equally germane to adult education: The problem is "what version of science it will choose; the rigorous, fact-minded, anticonceptual view which believes that cumulative knowledge is the result of patient and dogged application of scientific methods, or the view of science as an imaginative undertaking, with its full share of speculation, playfulness, proclivity to error, and its ability to imagine worlds yet undreamed of — an ability which would maintain the critical, projective quality that has enabled past theories to speak meaningfully to the quandaries of political existence" (Wolin, 1968, p. 329).

References

Bell, W. "Finance, Legislation and Public Policy for Adult Education." In M. S. Knowles (ed.), *Handbook of Adult Education in*

the United States. Washington, D.C.: American Association
for Adult and Continuing Education, 1960.

Bown, L. "The State and Adult Education: Suggested Issues
for Comparative Study." Presidential address to the annual
conference of the British Comparative and International Education Society. Glasgow, Scotland: 1986.

Bryant, I., and Usher, R. "Some Tensions in Adult Education
Research." In M. Zukas (ed.), *Standing Conference of University
Teaching and Research in the Education of Adults (SCUTREA)* (16th
annual conference). Leeds, England: Department of Adult
and Continuing Education, Leeds University, 1986.

Carlson, R. A. *The Americanization Syndrome: A Quest for Conformity.* London: Croom Helm, 1987.

Cremin, L. A. *The American Common School.* New York: Teachers
College Press, 1951.

Easton, D. "Political Science." In D. L. Sills (ed.), *Encyclopedia
of the Social Sciences.* Vol. 12. New York: Macmillan, 1968.

Elsdon, K. "Home Thoughts from Abroad on Adult Education
and Politics." *International Journal of Lifelong Learning,* 1988,
7, 3–11.

European Bureau of Adult Education. *Adult Education Legislation in Ten European Countries.* Strasbourg, France: Council of
Europe, 1975.

Faure, E. *Learning to Be: The World of Education, Today and Tomorrow.* Paris: UNESCO, 1972.

Freire, P. *Pedagogy of the Oppressed.* New York: Herder & Herder,
1970.

Gramsci, A. *Selections from the Prison Notebooks.* New York: International Publishers, 1971.

Griffin, C. "A Researchable Politics of Adult Education." In M.
Zukas (ed.), *Standing Conference on University Teaching and Research in the Education of Adults (SCUTREA)* (16th annual conference). Leeds, England: Department of Adult and Continuing Education, Leeds University, 1986.

Habermas, J. *Knowledge and Human Interests.* (J. Shapiro, trans.)
Boston: Beacon Press, 1971.

Handlin, O. *The Uprooted.* (2nd ed.) Boston: Little, Brown, 1973.

Illich, I. *Deschooling Society.* New York: Harper & Row, 1970.

Johnstone, J., and Rivera, W. *Volunteers for Learning: A Study of the Educational Pursuits of American Adults.* Hawthorne, N.Y.: Aldine, 1965.

Kidd, J., and Titmus, C. J. "Adult Education: An Overview." In T. Husen and T. Postlethwaite (eds.), *The International Encyclopedia of Education.* Vol. 1. Oxford, England: Pergamon Press, 1985.

Knowles, M. S. (ed.). *Handbook of Adult Education in the United States.* Washington, D.C.: American Association of Adult and Continuing Education, 1960.

LaBelle, T. *Non-Formal Education and Social Change in Latin America.* Los Angeles: Latin America Center Publications, University of California, 1976.

Lazarus, R. "Adult Literacy: Second Stage." In T. Husen and T. Postlethwaite (eds.), *The International Encyclopedia of Education.* Vol. 1. Oxford, England: Pergamon Press, 1985.

Lindeman, E. *The Meaning of Adult Education.* Norman: Oklahoma Research Center for Continuing Professional and Higher Education, 1961. (Originally published 1926.)

Lysenko, V. *Men in Sheepskin Coats: A Study in Assimilation.* Toronto: Ryerson, 1947.

Mhaike, P. "Political Education and Adult Education." *Convergence: Journal of the International Council for Adult Education,* 1973, *6* (1), 15-21.

Nisbet, J. "The Politics of Educational Research." In M. Zukas (ed.), *Conference on University Teaching and Research in the Education of Adults (SCUTREA)* (16th annual conference). Leeds, England: Department of Adult and Continuing Education, Leeds University, 1986.

Rivera, W. "Reflections on Policy Issues in Adult Education." In G. Whaples and W. Rivera (eds.), *Policy Issues and Process: Issues in Education for Adults.* College Park: Department of Agriculture and Extension Education, University of Maryland, 1982.

Rivera, W., and Dohmen, G. "Political System, Educational Policy, and Lifelong Learning: The Experience of Two Federally Constituted Nations, the United States and the Federal Republic of Germany." *International Journal of Lifelong Education,* 1985, *4* (2), 135-148.

Roberts, H. *Adult Education and Culture: A Comparative Study of*

Alberta and Quebec. Edmonton, Canada: University of Alberta Press, 1982.

Rubenson, K. "Adult Education Research." In T. Husen and T. Postlethwaite (eds.), *The International Encyclopedia of Education.* Vol. 1. Oxford, England: Pergamon Press, 1985.

Savićević, D. "Adult Education in Eastern Europe." In T. Husen and T. Postlethwaite (eds.), *The International Encyclopedia of Education.* Vol. 1. Oxford, England: Pergamon Press, 1985.

Selman, G. "Adult Education and Citizenship." In F. Cassidy and R. Ferris (eds.), *Choosing Our Future: Adult Education and Public Policy in Canada.* Toronto: OISE Press, 1987.

Sheats, P. "Present Trends and Future Strategies in Adult Education." In M. Knowles (ed.), *Handbook of Adult Education in the United States.* Washington, D.C.: American Association for Adult and Continuing Education, 1960.

Spencer Foundation. "Some Recent Studies of Political Learning." *Newsletter of the Spencer Foundation,* 1989, *4* (2), 1–4.

Stewart, D. "Systems Theory as a Framework for Analysis of the Politics of Adult Education." *Adult Education,* 1981, *32* (3), 142–154.

Stock, A. "Adult Education: Legislation in Western Europe." In T. Husen and T. Postlethwaite (eds.), *The International Encyclopedia of Education.* Vol. 1. Oxford, England: Pergamon Press, 1985.

Taylor, R., Rockhill, K., and Fieldhouse, R. *University Adult Education in England and the USA: A Reappraisal of the Liberal Tradition.* London: Croom Helm, 1985.

Thomas, A. *Learning in Society: Toward a New Paradigm.* Symposium on Learning in Society Conference Proceedings, Occasional Paper no. 51. Ottawa, Canada: Canadian Conference for UNESCO, 1983.

Thomas, A. *Registers of Legislation Governing the Practice of Adult Education in Canada.* Toronto: Department of Adult Education, Ontario Institute for Studies in Education, 1984.

Thomas, A. "Adult Education for Participation." In T. Husen and T. Postlethwaite (eds.), *The International Encyclopedia of Education.* Vol. 1. Oxford, England: Pergamon Press, 1985.

Thomas, A. *Registers of Legislation Governing the Practice of Adult Education in Canada.* Toronto: Department of Adult Education, Ontario Institute for Studies in Education, 1986.

Thomas, A. "Government and Adult Learning." In F. Cassidy and R. Faris (eds.), *Choosing Our Future: Adult Education and Public Policy in Canada.* Toronto: OISE Press, 1987.

Thomas, A. *Registers of Legislation Governing the Practice of Adult Education in Canada.* Toronto: Department of Adult Education, Ontario Institute for Studies in Education, 1988.

Thomas, A. "Legislation and Adult Education in Canada." *International Journal of Lifelong Education,* 1989, *8* (2), 103–125.

Thomas, A., Gaskin, C., and Taylor, M. "Federal Legislation and Adult Basic Education in Canada." In M. Taylor and J. Draper (eds.), *Adult Literacy Perspectives.* Toronto: Culture Concepts, 1989.

Thomas, W., and Znaniecki, F. *The Polish Peasant in Poland and America.* Urbana, Ill.: University of Illinois Press, 1974.

Whaples, G., and Rivera, W. (eds.). *Policy Issues and Process: Issues in Education for Adults.* College Park: Department of Agriculture and Extension Education, University of Maryland, 1982.

Whyte, A. "Educational Trends in the Development of Adult Education in OECD Countries." *Australian Journal of Adult Education,* 1987, *27,* 4–8.

Wolin, S. "Political Theory: Trends and Goals." In D. L. Sills (ed.), *Encyclopedia of the Social Sciences.* Vol. 12. New York: Macmillan, 1968.

CHAPTER 13

Learning from
the Discipline
of History

Harold W. Stubblefield

History as a discipline directed toward the study of past events has an ambiguous status within the professional study of adult education in the United States, and that status is long-standing. Although the importance of history is sometimes briefly recognized (Long, 1983), history has usually been conspicuous by its absence in books on research (Brunner, Wilder, Kirchner, and Newberry, 1959) and foundations of practice (Darkenwald and Merriam, 1982) and in handbooks (Ely, 1948; Smith, Aker, and Kidd, 1970). The exceptions are the 1960, 1980, and 1989 handbooks (Knowles, 1960; Peters and Associates, 1980; Merriam and Cunningham, 1989). Adult education scholars explain the neglect of history by saying that they have been too busy "doing" adult education to write about its past.

The neglect of history in American publications stands in marked contrast with the situation in England, Germany, and the Scandinavian countries, which have valued historical research to illuminate their traditions of adult education. In these countries, though, adult education has been narrowly defined, directed toward specific subpopulations, conducted through an institutional form, and designed to serve a broad national purpose.

Certain characteristics among adult education professors and graduate education programs in the United States partially account for this neglect of history. Many doctoral programs that are more practitioner oriented than research oriented neglect the foundation disciplines. Moreover, few adult education professors are trained in history. In colleges of education, quantitative research methods are valued as the principal instrument to advance knowledge. Although historians of education and social history often study adult education, they usually study events in this field as part of their broader scholarly interests and not as an agenda of research in adult education. As a result, the history of adult education as a subject of inquiry lacks a clear definition and is not recognized as a specialization.

In the 1980s, several adult education scholars in the United States began constructive work on the history of adult education that makes it possible for me to write a different kind of chapter than Whipple (1964) could write a quarter of a century ago or Carlson (1980) a decade ago. Even now, history's role as a foundation in adult education graduate studies is not fully understood, much less secured. This chapter offers a rationale for including history in these graduate programs based on the nature of history as a discipline and its value as a way of learning. The chapter analyzes the historiography of adult education, explains the new developments relating to history among adult education scholars, and shows how the history of adult education is related to the larger fields of educational, intellectual, social, and cultural history. I close the chapter with suggestions about the teaching and study of history in adult education graduate programs and speculate about the problems and possibilities of securing the future of the history of adult education.

History as a Foundation

The inclusion of the discipline of history as a foundation for the study of adult education as a social practice goes beyond any practical consideration — past and present are inseparably connected. Edward Shils (1981) explains it in more technical language: "Every human action and belief has a career behind it, it is the momentary end-state of a sequence of transmissions and modifications and their adaptation to current circumstances. Although everyone bears a great deal of past achievement in his belief and conduct, there are many persons who fail to see this" (p. 43).

History as a Discipline. History, simply put, is "the study of a subject by analysis of its record" (Colson, 1976, p. 11). History's subject matter is any past event, but for that event to be studied there must be records. Unlike researchers in other disciplines who study ongoing or repeated events, historians study events that have already occurred, events that cannot be repeated. But what they study are the records of the events and not the events themselves. The product of their research is a written report.

The historian's task is not to chronicle past events but to explain, understand, and evaluate these events. History is "a problem-solving discipline," in which a historian — or anyone interested in the past — performs several tasks: asks questions about past events, examines records, uses selected facts to answer the questions, and arranges the facts into an explanation (Fischer, 1970, p. xv).

Historians, like researchers in other disciplines, are guided by canons of research appropriate to their field. They find facts, verify the facts, assess the evidence for the conditions under which the event emerged, and fit that event into a pattern (Barzun and Graff, 1985). Because historians evaluate human behavior and its consequences, the historian's knowledge is "value-charged" (Leff, 1971). In analyzing some aspect of a subject through study of its record, historians bring knowledge, ideas, and questions to the record. They approach the record after having read the previous works and interpretation: historians work in light of previous historical explanations. And as do other disciplines, history has its branches of specialization.

Value of History. Two beliefs about history must be challenged before its value in adult education can be realized. The first is the incorrect belief that the study of history can help us avoid the mistakes of the past. A study of adult education history will yield neither lessons that are applicable to present conditions nor "laws" that can create a science of adult education. The second belief is that a history of adult education is waiting to be discovered through reading and reporting the records. Researchers who hold this second belief produce reports describing how an institution or program developed or a person's contribution to adult education, often interpreting that event or contribution in light of some theory. Such reports do not contain new insights because the researchers ignore both the historiography and context of their subject.

The value of history — its unique task in the professional study of adult education — is evident when we view history as a way of learning. History as a way of learning, Williams (1973) says, begins by describing the realities — the structures and circumstances — of society at different periods, characterizing the beliefs that Americans held at different times and explaining how these beliefs were incorporated into current explanations of the past. Going to the past permits people to see what they once were, how they have changed, and how the changes took place. Aware of the restrictions imposed by their former outlooks, they can be more aware of their alternatives in the present and thus be better able to make choices.

Historical research in adult education is entirely relevant to the present. By connecting adult educators with their past, historical research provides these educators with a rudder for the present. Applying Simon's (1983) ideas to adult education, we can think of history's unique tasks as (1) to explicate why the present arrangements, structures, and provisions exist, (2) to probe into the social and ideological movements of the past that are expressed in present activities, and (3) to seek to understand the origins, processes, and dynamics of educational change.

History can "clarify contexts in which contemporary problems exist" (Fischer, 1970, p. 315). Consider, for example, the problem of adult illiteracy, which was discovered in the early 1900s and has resisted many solutions. The responses to the problem have usually been responses to a perceived crisis. Programs

have been too short, have included too little material and personnel resources, and have been driven by ideological conflict.
Why has a problem of such recognized national importance
resisted resolution? Simply, we seem to repeat the mistake of
applying old solutions to new and distinctly different problems
of the present day.

Refining the logic of historical thinking and extending it
to the everyday world would help adult educators avoid making the historical error of conceptualizing present problems in
terms of prior eras and applying past solutions to the present
(Fischer, 1970). Approaches to adult illiteracy, immigrant education, and industrial worker training around the turn of the
century — though meriting more study than they have received —
cannot be transposed on to similar contemporary problems.

Although history does not yield scientific laws, history can
help refine theoretical knowledge when past events are analyzed
as case studies. Researchers can make generalizations if the past
and present situations are similar. They can answer questions
like these: Under what conditions are innovations in adult education diffused within American culture? Under what conditions
do innovations in adult education change or disappear? Why
did an oppositional educational institution such as the Highlander Research and Education Center survive while other institutions founded at the same time did not?

Old Practices and New Developments

When adult education scholars write adult education history and
debate how history should be written, they are concerned about
disciplinary history (the history of a science or discipline). Their
purpose is to legitimate adult education. The functions of legitimation include gathering support of the lay public, government,
and foundations; socializing novices in the field; and advancing scholarly interests (Graham, 1983; Lepenies and Weingart,
1983).

Creating a History. The first historical interpretations of adult
education in the United States were written between the 1930s

As stubblefield states, the first historical interpretations of adult education were written ≠ 1930 1960 a second phase 327 began 1970

Learning from the Discipline of History

and 1960s in a period of intense effort by organizations and individuals to create a national interest in adult education, to impose a dominant purpose on the field, and to organize institutional components of the field. The adult education movement was born in the aftershock of World War I and the Depression and grew to maturity after World War II. For those people trying to promote and organize adult education, the field in its diversity appeared to be a social force in its own right that could provide cohesiveness and direction to a society they believed to be divisive.

Attempts to interpret the efforts of these people began with the interpretation by Morse Cartwright (1935), the executive director of the American Association for Adult Education. In his interpretation, the Carnegie Corporation's efforts through the AAAE ushered in a new era of national acceptance of educational activities for adults. Lyman Bryson's (1936) textbook on adult education stressed the continuity of this new recognition of the field with the previous efforts to promote and organize the field, but he emphasized adult education's new importance in a time of rapid change. To provide evidence of the social significance of adult education, the Carnegie Corporation commissioned James Truslow Adams (1944), a well-known historian of American life, to write a history of adult education in the United States. Adams, who knew little about adult education, relied upon his own previous work and Carnegie Corporation studies. His work, published in 1944, proved disappointing.

After the war, the Ford Foundation created the Fund for Adult Education (1951–1961) to promote liberal adult education. It commissioned C. Hartley Grattan, a historian specializing in the South Pacific, to write a history of liberal adult education. Grattan produced a readable and still useful history. He approached adult education as an instrument for the diffusion of knowledge and interpreted adult education as it developed in Western history and in England and the United States. Grattan saw adult educators who promoted liberal education as engaging in a human drama.

In 1951, the Adult Education Association of the U.S.A. replaced the AAAE as the national umbrella organization of adult education. It concentrated on providing membership services to workers in various segments of the field and organizing the institutional components of the field. By 1959, when Knowles resigned as executive director of the organization, there were signs that this strategy had failed. For almost thirty years, Knowles's *The Adult Education Movement in the U.S.* (1962), the 1977 revised edition of the book, and chapters in the Knowles (1960) and Peters and Associates (1980) handbooks of adult education have been practically the only accessible materials about the history of adult education in the United States. Knowles interpreted adult education as an entity responsive to changing societal conditions and progressive in its expanding outreach but one searching unsuccessfully for a national organization to unify the institutional segments of the field. Knowles found a new rationale for learning in adulthood in the threat of obsolescence and the unifying principle in method, which he later called andragogy. As he put it in 1962: "The highest priority subject matter for adult education in the immediate future is education about education. If that succeeds, then all education would become unified into a 'lifelong education movement'" (p. 280).

Hallenbeck and Verner both advocated sociological approaches to adult education but did not themselves write a history. Hallenbeck (1938) cautioned against reducing adult education history to the study of programs, precisely the problem that plagued Adams, Knowles, and, to some extent, Grattan. The historian's task at that time, according to Hallenbeck, entailed analyzing "events, persons, social changes, and discoveries that have contributed essential factors to the process now known as adult education" (p. 169). The historian who wanted to write the history of adult education would have to study adult education movements devoted to furthering knowledge and progress and the social movements that accompanied them. Verner (1961) warned against making sweeping generalizations about the national experience without evidence from local, state, and regional studies.

In the black book Whipple (1964), a professionally trained historian, wrote the first statement about the use of history as a foundation for adult education. He said that history as applied to adult education and graduate study provided knowledge about adult education and a supplementary research tool for adult education practitioners that would enhance their effectiveness by providing "a method in the conduct of practical affairs" (p. 212). Whipple felt that as a discipline history was neither scientific nor humane but a link between science and humanism. Nevertheless, Whipple believed that concepts from social science could be applied to historical research and that most issues that concerned adult educators could be studied historically.

Reappraisal and New Directions. A second phase of research into the history of adult education began in the 1970s and continues to the present. It is fueled partly by the revisionist movements in history, concern about what the older approach to history omitted, dissatisfaction with institutional responses, social reform concerns, and renewed interest in discovering a usable past for a contemporary adult education driven more by economic market concerns than by a social mission. One emphasis of this second phase is critical (radical) history, that is, history as the critique of ideology. Carlson (1975) challenges the accepted position that "Americanization" was a one-time activity directed toward the immigrants from eastern and southern Europe from the 1890s through World War I. Tracing the idea of Americanization from the colonial period to the present, he argues that education has been used to force both American Indians and immigrants to conform to white Protestant middle-class values. These attempts to induce conformity were acts of "cultural genocide" (p. 15).

A bicentennial issue of *Adult Education* on the history of adult education reexamined how histories of adult education had been written. The federal government initiatives in adult education in the 1960s provided the background for Rockhill's (1976) indictment of the history of adult education as written from a national policy perspective; that is, based on a formal public school model that emphasizes academic and vocational ends and middle-class values. Other approaches to adult education can be found in American history, but Rockhill feels that for historical research to influence policy several aspects of the past, previously ignored, had to be addressed. Her list of needed historical research constitutes the only published agenda for the history of the field. It greatly expands the domain of historical research to include such topics as how socializing agencies of adulthood function as adult education, the importance of voluntary associations in adult education, what people experience when they participate in adult education, and the effect of that experience on their lives.

In 1983, Rockhill examined the conflict within universities, especially the University of California, between the mission of knowledge production and cultural transmission to an elite and the popular mission of disseminating knowledge to all people. She found that the popular mission has been subordinated to academic excellence. In a later book, Taylor, Rockhill, and Fieldhouse (1985) critique the liberal tradition in university adult education through an analysis of the conflict between elite and equalitarian goals and the epistemological question of who gets access to knowledge.

Using the perspective of social policy, Griffin (1987) located the origin of modern adult education in nineteenth-century social movements. He says that as the field developed, its focus changed from adult education as applied sociology, associated with societal development and progress, to adult education as adult learning applied to social contexts.

Carlson (1980), in contrast to Whipple's emphasis on history as a social science and its potential use in producing knowledge, argues for "humanistic historical research." By humanistic, Carlson means the study of the motives and actions of adult educators in a specific context that are reported as a narrative. Through the form of a story, the historian interprets a person's action or an event in the past. Carlson claims that such study does more than produce knowledge; it may serve as a critique of past practices and thought.

Other researchers focused on finding a usable past: a tradition of adult education to provide direction for present efforts. Cotton's (1968) description of the purposes of adult education based on an analysis of the literature from the 1920s to the 1960s was the first attempt to find such a tradition.

In the 1980s, adult education scholars wrote about the theorists and innovators in adult education. Morehead and Goldenstein (1985) portrayed the pioneer innovators of adult education. Jarvis (1987) presented the contributions of various adult education theorists in the twentieth century in Great Britain and the United States. My work (Stubblefield, 1988) examined several important theorists and their ideas about adult education in the formative period of American adult education, the 1930s–1950s.

In this sifting of the contributions of early leaders, Eduard Lindeman has emerged as the most important American theorist of adult education, even though adult education was only one of his many interests (Brookfield, 1984; Stewart, 1987). Stewart's (1987) biography of Lindeman traces his career in adult education and tells how in the 1920s and 1930s he developed his conception of adult education. From Lindeman's philosophy, Stewart derives principles of practice as the charter for the learning society.

Houle (1984) used biographical studies to reveal how learning had been of central importance to several persons in history. He felt that historical study of such cases could help free adult educators from the limitations of present-day conceptions and place life-span learning in broader context. Houle uses these cases to show that adults used processes of learning long before adult education as a practice emerged in the 1920s.

The scholars discussed above treated history within the domain of general adult education history. Another aspect of the history of adult education is the history of specialized segments of the field. Researchers have concentrated on such specialized areas as the Cooperative Extension Service, the library, and workers' education. Recently, books on human resource development, educational gerontology, continuing professional education, and community education have included chapters on history, but the approach to history in these chapters tends to be unsophisticated and celebratory. The *Handbook of Adult and Continuing Education* (Merriam and Cunningham, 1989) is distinguished from its predecessors by how several authors treat the historical development of major providers, program areas, and special clienteles.

The Larger Context. Adult education scholars and practitioners who believe adult education has an impoverished and incomplete history have not gotten beyond their own literature. Adult education as a societal agency in American life since the colonial period has scarcely been ignored by historians. Under such topics as agencies of cultural transmission, forms of popular education, and the educative component of social movements, historians have woven adult education into the very fabric of American history, as a cursory survey of the old standard intellectual and cultural histories shows (Curti, 1964; Wish, 1962). Now new emphases in social history and a revisionist historiography in education bring new opportunity for an expanded history of adult education.

Revisionist views of educational historiography in the 1960s expanded the domain of educational history beyond schooling and its celebration as the door of opportunity for all classes. The focus expanded in one direction to include all societal institutions as educative agencies, greatly broadening the study of education to include people of all ages and the societal context in which institutions educated people. The focus shifted in a second direction to examining the political character of schools and the participation of the economic system in determining the curricula and the purposes of education.

General historiography also included new emphases (Kammen, 1980). The new social history addressed the everyday life of ordinary people, broadening to study the experiences of laborers, women, minorities, and urban dwellers. The social history approach also included examinations of the actual operation of institutions and the interaction of practitioners in institutions with their clients (Stearns, 1980).

The history of education has moved closer to becoming a form of social, cultural, and intellectual history. This change is apparent in Cremin's (1970, 1980, 1988) encyclopedic trilogy of American education from the colonial period to the present and in Best's (1983) *Historical Inquiry in Education: A Research Agenda,* an interpretive and prescriptive work. Cremin's and Best's view of education as occurring outside of and beyond schooling encompasses adult education.

These developments in general and educational historiography provide an enlarged context for the study of adult education history. In its largest context, adult education must be regarded as part of a system for the diffusion of knowledge. Two recent works edited by Oleson and Brown (1976) and Oleson and Voss (1979) focus on the organization of knowledge and the principal institutions involved in the production and diffusion of knowledge from the colonial period to World War I. These works depict adult education as the "underside" of learned societies and as imitative of the higher order of learning. Brown (1989) examines the diffusion of information in the colonial and national periods from the perspective of individual experience and public communication. Burnham (1987), focusing on the dissemination of science to the lay public as a particular form of the diffusion of knowledge — popularization — traces the popularization of science and health in the United States from the 1830s to the present. Jacoby (1987) treats the problem of popularization from another perspective in his description of the loss to the educated reading public in the disappearance of the public intellectual, now replaced by the academic specialist.

The insights that emerge when the history of adult education institutions is written as social and cultural history are demonstrated in studies of the New School for Social Research (Rutkoff and Scott, 1986), the Highlander Research and Education Center (Glen, 1988), and the John C. Campbell Folk School (Whisnant, 1983). Studies of the Great Books program and the Chautauqua Institution show how specific curricula of adult education are advanced as solutions to societal disruptions. Allen (1983) and Purcell (1973) show that the Great Books reading and discussion program, on the surface an inoffensive studying of classical texts, had its roots in a revival of general education in World War I to counter threats to the unity of knowledge and cultural absolutism by the specialization of knowledge. Alan Trachtenberg's (1984) interpretation of the Chautauqua Institution's place in American culture resists easy classification. He contends that Chautauqua sought to sacralize culture and through culture to create a homogeneous America that was not divided by immigration, industrialization, and class conflicts.

Perhaps the most important contribution of recent scholarship has been to illuminate the role of education in the origin and rise of democratic social movements. Using the metaphor of "free space," Evans and Boyte (1986) demonstrate the power of people — women, blacks, workers, and farmers — to challenge their consigned space in the social, political, and economic order through collective action. Paulston's (1980) study of the folk schools in social and ethnic movements offers a more sophisticated theoretical analysis. He says that learning processes in which people create their own indigenous culture, challenging the economic and political assumptions of the dominant culture, are central to these movements.

The educational component of social movements is sometimes hidden in their written histories and the biographies of their leaders, but several writers have made the educational processes in these movements explicit. Mitchell (1987) explains the political education program of the Southern Farmers' Alliance, its underlying ideology and formal pedagogy, in the framework of the larger populist movement. Blair (1980) interprets the women's club movement of the post–Civil War period and similar organizations as an instrument of and for women to form and express their self-identity, first through literary study and then through social reform.

Recent scholarship on race, class, and gender has further expanded the boundaries of adult education history, as shown in the works of Neufeldt and McGee (1990) on the history of African American adult education, Altenbaugh (1990) on the American labor colleges of the 1920s and 1930s, and Antler and Biklen (1990) on the informal contexts of women's education.

Even this rich treasure of resources will not give adult educators a ready-made history of their field. The questions necessary to guide and order the development of adult education history are still to be formulated.

History and the Professional Study of Adult Education

The inclusion of history in graduate professional study in adult education rests on the assumption that the adult education practitioner is more than a craftsperson operating programs from apprenticeship learning and commonsense assumptions. In their work, practitioners make decisions that are influenced by economic and social conditions and by the expressed aims of adult education and policy issues.

Role of History in Curriculum. History has several roles to perform in the adult education curriculum. In its most elementary role, history socializes novices in the field. In their first exposure to the field's history, novices experience their field as one of heroic achievement, see its larger tradition, and enlarge their narrow vision beyond their specific institutional orientation. This "landmarks and heroes" experience is best described in Knowles's *The Making of an Adult Educator* (1989). The socialization function of history should not be minimized, but it should not be considered sufficient in the training of adult educators.

Beyond its socializing function, history in a professional program can be viewed as various kinds of study: functional (Anderson, 1984), liberal arts (Noble, 1984), existential (Greene, 1984), and critical (Zinn, 1984). When approaching history as liberal arts study, adult education students examine the evolution of adult education — its continuity and discontinuity — in its social, cultural, intellectual, political, and economic context. Only historical study shows how adult education in its many forms came to be, how its conceptions changed, the social functions it served, its relationship to class structure, and what intellectual foundations supported its practice.

As existential study, history in professional study programs for adult educators focuses on educators as decision makers. In this view, history has significance to adult educators insofar as it is relevant to their work. History, then, is used the same way that other disciplines are used: to help educators make informed decisions about the teaching-learning process, the organization of education, and the aims of education and its relationship to society. Adult educators study history and other disciplines and use their concepts to address educational tasks. History, as Greene (1984) points out, helps educators search for meaning. Inquiry as a search for meaning — historical and other kinds — is best done if it begins with questions arising from the educator's responsibility. Educators go to the relevant social science disciplines or academic history for concepts to organize their choices, recognizing that any choice is but an alternative among choices that they could make.

History as critical study goes to the roots of historical and contemporary adult education practices and examines the belief systems that support these practices. This type of study is particularly concerned with social, economic, political, and educational inequality (Walton, 1986). Critical (radical) history, as Zinn (1984) stated, studies the victims of society, lifting the veil off their condition and exposing the limitations of governmental and other societal institutions in redressing their condition. In the process, critical history shows how some people have acted to create a more humane and democratic community and unearths ideals from previous periods that give strength to people in their present struggles.

Engaging Students in Study. The study of history included in an introductory course can, perhaps, serve only a socializing function. But when history is made a foundation in graduate professional programs, then more stringent conditions must apply. Both history as "the character and significance of past events" and historiography as "the writing of history, the written product," must be included (Clifford, 1986, p. 218). The history of adult education should not be taught as only disciplinary history that excludes social and intellectual history. Often, students taking a course on the history of adult education read a standard work to learn the "facts" of adult education history and read other disciplinary histories to learn how the problems of adult education as a social practice have been identified and interpreted historically. A course that includes these sources and no more is grossly insufficient. Students must also read the best historical scholarship to understand history as a method of research and history as knowledge.

Students should also conduct a historical research project, using primary sources when possible or "good" histories when only secondary sources are available. Only by engaging directly in the historical research process will students become competent in such research.

The Future

The discipline of history as a foundation in professional study programs has an ambiguous status. It is also true, as foreign observers of American adult education are quick to note, that the narrative-outline histories attempted by Grattan ([1955] 1971) and Knowles (1962, 1977) fall short of the comprehensiveness and style of Kelly's (1970) work on Great Britain. These observations notwithstanding, research in the history of adult education in the United States has a future, and certain past and present events presage what it will be.

The apparent poverty of historical research in adult education is just that, more apparent than real. The first task for future researchers will be to identify and classify the existing historical research in adult education. Doctoral dissertations are examples of neglected literature. From the 1950s to the present, graduates of adult education programs have produced an impressive number of doctoral dissertations on the history of adult education, some of which are of high quality, but unfortunately only a few have been published in any form. Even listings of books and journal articles are not available. The historical studies exist, they are just not known.

Bibliographies will permit a second task — the historiographical task — to be accomplished. Existing historical studies have to be evaluated and interpreted: What are the lines of research? What interpretations have emerged? Where are the gaps in the research? What are the conflicting opinions?

Obviously, we can only speculate about future research. One set of research activities will probably cluster around general adult education theory. Researchers will attempt to produce a more adequate narrative-outline history of adult education in the United States, that is, a national history. Adult education as an occupational practice, particularly attempts at professionalization, will also be examined. Researchers concerned about the mission of adult education — its social purpose and unity —

will return to the past to recover a heritage appropriate for a diverse field driven by market concerns. Other researchers will probe more deeply into the ideology of adult education.

A second set of research activities will probably focus on history from the "bottom up," that is, social movements with an educational base and the participation of ordinary people in adult education. A third area of research might be the study of the occupational specializations in adult education. Several conditions of the economic sector—global competition, educational requirements for the work force, quality of life issues, and the emergence of human resource development as an occupational practice—will motivate researchers to study the history of work-related education.

A fourth area of research may examine policy formation and implementation in adult education. Legislative acts in the past will be one focus, but another focus will be the origin and consequences of the historical division of responsibility among the public, for-profit, and independent sectors for adult education.

Historians—the professionally committed and those merely interested in past events—have many motivations. History opens a door for adult education scholars and students to break out of narrow specializations and to view their work as knowledge diffusers in a long-term perspective. Viewing their chosen work through the perspective of history, they will observe the consequences of the adult education interventions of their forebears and be sobered by the potential of adult education to liberate and oppress, to change and to conserve.

References

Adams, J. T. *Frontiers of American Culture: A Study of Adult Education in a Democracy.* New York: Scribner's, 1944.

Allen, J. A. *The Romance of Commerce and Culture: Capitalism, Modernism, and the Chicago-Aspen Crusade for Cultural Reform.* Chicago: University of Chicago Press, 1983.

Altenbaugh, R. J. *Education for Struggle: The American Labor Colleges of the 1920s and 1930s.* Philadelphia: Temple University Press, 1990.

Anderson, A. W. "Is There a Functional Role for the History of Education in the Training of Teachers?" In R. R. Sherman (ed.), *Understanding History of Education.* Cambridge, Mass.: Schenkman, 1984.

Antler, J., and Biklen, S. K. (eds.). *Changing Education: Women as Radicals and Conservators.* Albany: State University of New York Press, 1990.

Barzun, J., and Graff, H. F. *The Modern Researcher.* (4th ed.) San Diego, Calif.: Harcourt Brace Jovanovich, 1985.

Best, J. H. (ed.). *Historical Inquiry in Education: A Research Agenda.* Washington, D.C.: American Educational Research Association, 1983.

Blair, K. J. *The Clubwoman as Feminist: True Womanhood Redefined, 1868–1914.* New York: Holmes and Meier, 1980.

Brookfield, S. "The Contribution of Eduard Lindeman to the Development of Theory and Philosophy in Adult Education." *Adult Education Quarterly,* 1984, *34,* 185–195.

Brown, R. D. *Knowledge Is Power: The Diffusion of Information in Early America, 1700–1865.* New York: Oxford University Press, 1989.

Brunner, E. de S., Wilder, D. S., Kirchner, C., and Newberry, J. S., Jr. *An Overview of Adult Education Research.* Washington, D.C.: American Association for Adult and Continuing Education, 1959.

Bryson, L. *Adult Education.* New York: American Book, 1936.

Burnham, J. C. *How Superstition Won and Science Lost: Popularizing Science and Health in the United States.* New Brunswick, N.J.: Rutgers University Press, 1987.

Carlson, R. A. *The Quest for Conformity: Americanization Through Education.* New York: Wiley, 1975.

Carlson, R. A. "Humanistic Historical Research." In H. B. Long, R. Hiemstra, and Associates (eds.), *Changing Approaches to Studying Adult Education.* San Francisco: Jossey-Bass, 1980.

Cartwright, M. A. *Ten Years of Adult Education: A Report on a Decade of Progress in the American Movement.* New York: Macmillan, 1935.

Clifford, G. J. "On Historiography." In J. Hannaway and M. E. Lockheed (eds.), *The Contributions of the Social Sciences to*

Educational Policy and Practice: 1965–1985. Berkeley, Calif.: McCutchan, 1986.

Colson, J. C. "The Writing of American Library History, 1876–1976." *Library Trends,* 1976, *25* (1), 7–21.

Cotton, W. E. *On Behalf of Adult Education: A Historical Examination of the Supporting Literature.* Boston: Center for the Study of Liberal Education for Adults, 1968.

Cremin, L. A. *American Education: The Colonial Experience: 1607–1783.* New York: Harper & Row, 1970.

Cremin, L. A. *American Education: The National Experience: 1783–1876.* New York: Harper & Row, 1980.

Cremin, L. A. *American Education: The Metropolitan Experience: 1876–1980.* New York: Harper & Row, 1988.

Curti, M. *The Growth of American Thought.* (3rd ed.) New York: Harper & Row, 1964.

Darkenwald, G. G., and Merriam, S. B. *Adult Education: Foundations of Practice.* New York: Harper & Row, 1982.

Ely, M. L. (ed.). *Handbook of Adult Education in the United States.* New York: Teachers College, Columbia University, 1948.

Evans, S. M., and Boyte, H. C. *Free Spaces: The Sources of Democratic Change in America.* New York: Harper & Row, 1986.

Fischer, D. H. *Historians' Fallacies: Toward a Logic of Historical Thought.* New York: Harper & Row, 1970.

Glen, J. M. *Highlander: No Ordinary School, 1932–1962.* Lexington: University Press of Kentucky, 1988.

Graham, L. "Epilogue." In L. Graham, W. Lepenies, and P. Weingart (eds.), *Functions and Uses of Disciplinary Histories.* Boston: Reidel, 1983.

Grattan, C. H. *In Quest of Knowledge: A Historical Perspective on Adult Education.* New York: Arno Press and The New York Times, 1971. (Originally published 1955.)

Greene, M. "The Professional Significance of History of Education." In R. R. Sherman (ed.), *Understanding History of Education.* Cambridge, Mass.: Schenkman, 1984.

Griffin, C. *Adult Education as Social Policy.* London: Croom Helm, 1987.

Hallenbeck, W. C. "Historical Antecedents." *Journal of Adult Education,* 1938, *10,* 168–170.

Houle, C. O. *Patterns of Learning: New Perspectives on Life-Span Education.* San Francisco: Jossey-Bass, 1984.

Jacoby, R. *The Last Intellectuals: American Culture in the Age of Academe.* New York: Basic Books, 1987.

Jarvis, P. (ed.). *Twentieth Century Thinkers in Adult Education.* London: Croom Helm, 1987.

Kammen, M. (ed.). *The Past Before Us: Contemporary Historical Writing in the United States.* Ithaca, N.Y.: Cornell University Press, 1980.

Kelly, T. *A History of Adult Education in Great Britain.* (2nd ed.) Liverpool, England: Liverpool University Press, 1970.

Knowles, M. S. *Handbook of Adult Education in the United States.* Washington, D.C.: American Association for Adult and Continuing Education, 1960.

Knowles, M. S. *The Adult Education Movement in the U.S.* New York: Holt, Rinehart & Winston, 1962.

Knowles, M. S. *A History of the Adult Education Movement in the United States.* Melbourne, Fla.: Krieger, 1977.

Knowles, M. S. *The Making of an Adult Educator: An Autobiographical Journey.* San Francisco: Jossey-Bass, 1989.

Leff, G. *History and Social Theory.* New York: Doubleday, 1971.

Lepenies, W., and Weingart, P. "Introduction." In L. Graham, W. Lepenies, and P. Weingart (eds.), *Functions and Uses of Disciplinary Histories.* Boston: Reidel, 1983.

Long, H. B. *Adult Learning: Research and Practice.* New York: Cambridge Books, 1983.

Merriam, S. B., and Cunningham, P. M. (eds.). *Handbook of Adult and Continuing Education.* San Francisco: Jossey-Bass, 1989.

Mitchell, T. *Political Education in the Southern Farmers' Alliance, 1887–1900.* Madison: University of Wisconsin Press, 1987.

Morehead, W. D., and Goldenstein, E. H. *Pioneers in Adult Education.* Chicago: Nelson-Hall, 1985.

Neufeldt, H. G., and McGee, L. (eds.). *Education of the African American Adult: An Historical Overview.* Westport, Conn.: Greenwood Press, 1990.

Noble, S. G. "The Relevance of the History of Education to Current Problems." In R. R. Sherman (ed.), *Understanding History of Education.* Cambridge, Mass.: Schenkman, 1984.

Oleson, A., and Brown, S. C. (eds.). *The Pursuit of Knowledge in the Early American Republic*. Baltimore, Md.: Johns Hopkins University Press, 1976.

Oleson, A., and Voss, J. (eds.). *The Organization of Knowledge in Modern America: 1860–1920*. Baltimore, Md.: Johns Hopkins University Press, 1979.

Paulston, R. G. *Other Dreams, Other Schools: Folk Colleges in Social and Ethnic Movements*. Pittsburgh: University Center for International Studies, University of Pittsburgh, 1980.

Peters, J. M., and Associates. *Building an Effective Adult Education Enterprise*. San Francisco: Jossey-Bass, 1980.

Purcell, E. A., Jr. *The Crisis of Democratic Theory: Scientific Naturalism and the Problem of Value*. Lexington: University Press of Kentucky, 1973.

Rockhill, K. "The Past as Prologue: Toward an Expanded View of Adult Education." *Adult Education,* 1976, *26* (4), 196–207.

Rockhill, K. *Academic Excellence and Public Service: A History of University Extension in California*. New Brunswick, N.J.: Transaction Press, 1983.

Rutkoff, P. M., and Scott, W. B. *New School: A History of the New School for Social Research*. New York: Free Press, 1986.

Shils, E. *Tradition*. Chicago: University of Chicago Press, 1981.

Simon, B. "History in Education." In P. H. Hirst (ed.), *Educational Theory and Its Foundation Disciplines*. London: Routledge & Kegan Paul, 1983.

Smith, R. M., Aker, G. F., and Kidd, J. R. (eds.). *Handbook of Adult Education*. New York: Macmillan, 1970.

Stearns, P. N. "Towards a Wider Vision: Trends in Social History." In M. Kammen (ed.), *The Past Before Us: Contemporary Historical Writing in the United States*. Ithaca, N.Y.: Cornell University Press, 1980.

Stewart, D. W. *Adult Learning in America: Eduard Lindeman and His Agenda for Lifelong Education*. Melbourne, Fla.: Krieger, 1987.

Stubblefield, H. W. *Towards a History of Adult Education in America*. London: Croom Helm, 1988.

Taylor, R., Rockhill, K., and Fieldhouse, R. *University Adult Education in England and the USA: A Reappraisal of the Liberal Tradition*. London: Croom Helm, 1985.

Trachtenberg, A. "'We Study the Word and Works of God': Chautauqua and the Sacralization of Culture in America." *Henry Ford Museum and Greenfield Village Herald,* 1984, *13,* 3–11.

Verner, C. "Adult Education and History." *Adult Education,* 1961, *11,* 181–182.

Walton, J. *Sociology and Critical Inquiry.* Homewood, Ill.: Dorsey Press, 1986.

Whipple, J. B. "The Uses of History for Adult Education." In G. Jensen, A. A. Liveright, and W. Hallenbeck (eds.), *Adult Education: Outlines of an Emerging Field of University Study.* Washington, D.C.: American Association for Adult and Continuing Education, 1964.

Whisnant, D. E. *All That Is Native and Fine: The Politics of Culture in an American Region.* Chapel Hill: University of North Carolina Press, 1983.

Williams, W. A. *The Contours of American History.* New York: New Viewpoints, 1973.

Wish, H. (1962). *Society and Thought in Modern America.* (2nd ed.) New York: McKay, 1962.

Zinn, H. "What Is Radical History?" In R. R. Sherman (ed.), *Understanding History of Education.* Cambridge, Mass.: Schenkman, 1984.

PART THREE

FORCES AND TRENDS
SHAPING THE FUTURE

This part of the book deals with special issues and forces that help shape the academic study of adult education. It begins with a discussion of the special influence that international developments have on study in North America. Cunningham's treatment of this topic in Chapter Fourteen is provocative and informative. She highlights the special role that influences from the Third World have on the field. She also draws attention to the changes in the body of knowledge of adult education since 1964, changes that reflect work done within alternative research paradigms and different ideological systems. In fact, her chapter will be interpreted by many readers as a strongly ideological one, but her passion for the subject is a plus for this topic and the book as a whole. Following a review of people who have made global contributions to the study of adult education, she turns to a discussion of non–North American theories that have had special influence on North American thought. A review of graduate programs that are particularly active in international education and a discussion of international publications are followed by some speculations about future directions.

Deshler's Chapter Fifteen is a treatment of issues that help shape the field of study. Deshler divides the issues into three areas: social, professional, and academic. He spots trends, disruptions, and possible future events that he considers of special importance to those people who spend time studying the field. Deshler's chapter is filled with interesting questions about the field's role in shaping society or being shaped by it. Deshler is not reluctant to give his own opinion, shaped by years of experience in academe and in international and community education.

Peters wraps up Part Four by reflecting on the book as a whole in Chapter Sixteen. He identifies and discusses six themes: the knowledge base, the relationship between the field of study and related disciplines, changing research paradigms, the relationship between theory and practice, the development of graduate programs, and the internationalization of the field. Each theme is addressed in terms of future directions suggested by the contents of this book.

That finishes the chapters, but not the book. Malcolm Knowles's epilogue does that.

CHAPTER 14

International Influences
on the Development
of Knowledge

Phyllis M. Cunningham

When the black book was published in 1964, the predominant social science paradigm was positivistic; a systematic study of the social world was said to be able to yield an objective and objectifiable knowledge base. It was thought that in time this knowledge base would allow us to discover the laws that govern social behavior. Positivism is intrinsic to the rhetoric of the black book (Jensen, Liveright, and Hallenbeck, 1964), particularly in its discussion of the need for rigorous research, its debate on the developing discipline of adult education, its alignment with university social science disciplines, and its uncritical promotion of professionalism. If we turn to the major research journal of that time, *Adult Education,* we can see that the editorial policy that became explicit with Robert Boyd's editorship was also organized around the positivist paradigm.

In 1966, *The Social Construction of Reality,* a seminal work by Berger and Luckmann, challenged the prevailing hegemony of a single objective social reality that had become a fixed concept in the consciousness of most North American adult education theorists and practitioners. Drawing from conflict theory in sociology and interactionism in social psychology, Berger and Luckmann and other writers like them helped to create ideological space for the development of alternative approaches to the creation of a knowledge base by staking out the claim that there are many knowledges. On some North American campuses and with some adult educators, the sociology of knowledge became identified with the works of people such as Franz Fanon, Herbert Marcuse, Eldridge Cleaver, and Paulo Freire. These writers were not speaking from the dominant ideology. Michael Law, a New Zealander, suggested (in a lecture to a Radical Adult Education class at Syracuse University in June 1987) that the revolution in paradigmatic thought on university campuses in the late sixties left most North American professors of adult education untouched. But he believes that the seeds of multiple realities were sown in the hearts and minds of some graduate students, who in the eighties opened up the intellectual landscape of North American adult education. These intellectuals, some of whom are now faculty members, are concerned with changing the frame for looking at the world to one that the Frankfurt school of critical theory called "possibility."

In the confrontation in North American adult education between the discourse on prediction and the discourse on possibility, clearly the "American" view, that is, positivism (which more strongly characterized adult educators from the United States than from Canada) has been challenged by several strongly competing "global" views within the study of adult education. In other words, in the twenty-seven years since the black book appeared the knowledge base on which studies of adult education are built has expanded. "Official" knowledge has had to move over to allow room for alternative research paradigms and their methodologies, ideologies, and practices (see Merriam, Chapter Three). Many of these challenges are the result of international influences, and it is these influences that are central to this chapter's discussion.

In order to trace international influences on the knowledge base of North American adult education, I will map the territory by asking questions that define borders: Who has stimulated global influences on the development of adult education knowledge? What non–North American theories have influenced the intellectual thought of North American adult educators? In what institutions of higher education has this influence been concentrated? What organizations or publications have contributed to this globalized view? What might be the future of these influences? This chapter is centered on changes in the adult education knowledge base, not merely on who has had international experiences or the import or export of existing knowledge or technology. This discussion of changes in the knowledge base is followed by a chronology of the internationalization of the knowledge base, located at the end of this chapter.

Knowledge Base in 1964

The major purpose of the black book was to define the emerging field of adult education in the United States, although passing references to the Canadian scene were included. Few Canadian professors were in the CPAE at that time, and only one Canadian university, the University of British Columbia (UBC), had a graduate program in adult education. The Ontario Institute for Studies in Education at the University of Toronto began its graduate program in 1966. The fact that the CPAE membership was almost exclusively from the United States may be one reason that the commission ignored the global context for viewing adult education.

Other reasons for this narrow focus may be found in the professors' emphasis on professionalism, with its corollary dependence on knowledge emanating from the traditional academic disciplines, particularly those marked by "scientific rigor." For it is the black book that has served as the benchmark for judging the health of "the field of study" (now separated from the "field of practice"). This professionalization meant the defining of adult education predominantly by its institutional sponsorship, thereby moving it away from its broader history and the part adult education has played in social movements as well as the role of voluntarism in its history. The emphasis on scientific legitimation was strongly felt in Western thought, and the proclivity to objectify and remove the object of study from its social history and cultural context perhaps exemplifies not only the character of the black book but also the boundaries of the North American adult educator's knowledge base, at least as defined by academicians in the 1960s and 1970s.

Although the 1934 handbook of adult education (Rowden, 1934) does not mention international adult education, the 1936 edition details the importance of a worldview, quoting from the May 1933 *International Quarterly of Adult Education* (Rowden, 1936, p. 76). Then in its second year of publication, this journal was a product of the short-lived World Association for Adult Education, founded in 1919, which held the first world conference for adult educators in Cambridge, England, in 1929. References to international adult education in the 1948 and 1960 handbooks (Ely, 1948; Knowles, 1960) concentrated on UNESCO (which had been founded in 1946) and on the elaboration of international organizations and networks that had been formed by 1960. More recent handbooks (Smith, Aker, and Kidd, 1970; Charters and Associates, 1981; Merriam and Cunningham, 1989) provide strong support for international adult education by providing either a chapter or a complete volume for its explication. Thus, a well-established rhetoric of a worldview within North American adult education can be seen from the very early years of formal associations. Some adult education forms and practices from abroad, almost entirely defined as European, have also been acknowledged.

United States historians of adult education have usually acknowledged the influences of the British 1919 Report, the Danish folk schools, British extramural study, and the Mechanics Institutes (Knowles, 1977). At the same time, these historians said little, if anything, about European socialist influences such as the Labour colleges, cooperatives, and workers' education. Nor did they take any notice of the work of Jamaican Marcus Garvey, who launched one of the largest adult education movements ever undertaken among African Americans and provided a link between members of the African diaspora around the world (Colin, 1988). Similarly, the black book shows a selective use of history and international practices that demonstrates the Eurocentric roots of North American practice of adult education, but it shows little concern with the then current developments outside of the United States. These selective histories and philosophies were compatible with the structural functionalist analyses that informed the day-to-day activities of North American adult educators (see Stubblefield, Chapter Thirteen).

The technology of adult education, as exhibited in graduate curricula, includes program planning, program evaluation, adult learning (andragogy, mathetics), institutional marginality and its consequences, and program administration (Rubenson, 1989a; Cunningham, 1988; Long, Chapter Four). The adult education field in North America has progressively moved into institutions. With institutionalization, the field has become more and more like schooling in practice while claiming in theory to be more and more distinct from schooling. In other words, adult education as a field of practice in the United States and most developed countries has increasingly been used by the state and professionals to reproduce the existing social, cultural, and economic relationships. Accordingly, discourse in adult education has been dominated by theories of individualism; market-oriented promotional strategies; deficit models for defining the adult learner; devaluation of volunteerism and voluntarism; exhortations to professionalism; and increasing concern with a close relationship of adult education, work, and the workplace. Gender, race, and class have tended to be nonissues (see Deshler, Chapter Fifteen).

The study of adult education in North America thus generated theories from a very narrow and highly framed ideological stance. Research on motivational explanations of participation was widely reported at research conferences. Self-directed learning, learning styles, learning how to learn, distance learning, and collaborative learning were also high-priority areas on the research agenda (see Long, Chapter Four).

When the Canadian and U.S. governments took an interest in literacy, for the purpose of removing people from the welfare rolls or the streets and placing them in the work force or at the least in public educational programs, adult educators readily obliged. Many graduate programs were started and made

viable through the use of federal funds for adult basic education training (see Peters and Kreitlow, Chapter Seven). As literacy leaders were trained, graduate study incorporated the language of individual inadequacy, terms such as *learning disabilities,
low self-esteem, lack of efficacy, poor motivation,* and *cultural and educational deprivation.* It also developed conceptualizations with such
labels as coping skills, functional literacy, and learning disor-
ders on which to base literacy training. Literacy became wed-
ded to the workplace and, more recently in the United States,
to family literacy, as the government used adult education as
a means for social engineering. Many adult educators involved
in the field of study turned like lemmings to the sea, their direction determined by public policy decisions in which they rarely
were involved.

The type of literacy education developed to train working class and underclass people in literacy has been repeated
for people in the technical and professional class. Many graduate programs, at least in the United States, became more and
more defined by human resource development, or continuing
professional education. This specialization was apparently undertaken by adult educators uncritically and with a strong sense
of pragmatism. Powerful forces of adaptation and accommo-
dation pushed adult education into the form of graduate study
in the university. In Gramsci's (1971) terms, professors became
organic intellectuals for the state, mentoring and producing
graduate students who were prepared to develop intellectual concepts to rationalize those policies that stabilized the existing
power relations in the state.

The internationalizing of the field of study of adult education has provided, complemented, or nurtured alternative
paradigms for the intellectual landscape of adult education. International influences were present twenty-seven years ago, but
their impact on the field of study and the field of practice was
minimal. This is no longer true. Now a strong platform of ideas
and theories from outside North America exists, and in combination with ideas and theories from inside North America, it
challenges the former narrowly conceived ideology based on

positivism. I now turn to the people, the structures, and the institutions who have created this challenge.

North Americans with Worldviews

Comparatively few professors over the last twenty-seven years have consistently been internationalists and have influenced adult education: J. Roby Kidd, Alexander N. Charters, A. A. Liveright, and Paul Sheats are such persons. J. Roby Kidd unequivocably has been the most influential of these professors (see Griffith, Chapter Five).

Kidd was the first Canadian to receive his doctorate in adult education (at Columbia University in 1941). He established the first comparative studies program in Canada at the Ontario Institute for Studies in Education in 1966, organized and was made secretary general of the International Council for Adult Education in 1973, and in 1968 established *Convergence,* an international journal of adult education. With his broad, progressive worldview, Kidd was constantly sought out for international activities. He served as president of UNESCO's Second World Conference on Adult Education in Montreal and chairperson of the UNESCO Evaluation Committee on the Experimental World Literacy Project. His work was characterized by internationalism; his concern for peace, justice, and quality of life for all persons in all nations was a driving force in his life. As Dutta (1986) said in a personal reference to Kidd's influence, "The greatest lesson I learned from him was 'that we must break barriers within our own country, and we must build bridges with other countries,'" (p. 99).

Kidd was an active participant in establishing what he called comparative studies in adult education. Noting that systematic efforts at comparison began in the field of adult education in June 1966 with the Exeter Conference and the subsequent *Exeter Papers* (Liveright and Haygood, 1968), Kidd rejected the term *comparative education* because "our concerns go far beyond the field of education. We are interested in that which can be applied from comparative history, comparative sociology, or any other discipline; we are concerned with the impact of events and happenings and circumstances — activities that are rarely considered in a course in education — upon the learning of people" (Bennett, Kidd, and Kulich, 1975, p. 8). His view on adult education was broad and it was contextualized in history and in the social fabric of adult education.

Kidd's (1974) ideological view of the production of knowledge can be seen in the following discussion on method in comparative studies of adult education: "Until recently there has been little discussion about method in comparative adult education, except by those who decried efforts to identify suitable methods and regarded such efforts as academic gamesmanship. This is perhaps because to many people, the need for action seems so urgent — They are too well aware that adult education, even their own efforts, has aided most those who are already in an advantaged position, has provided least to the disadvantaged, and may have broadened and deepened the fissure separating the 'two solitudes.' They are wearied of debate about esoteric educational theories and concepts, which they perceive as intellectual diddling while millions of people are burning with frustration and hatred because their legitimate aspirations seem no nearer to achievement" (p. 9).

Kidd's influences are in many ways remarkable. He organized international structures and publications that provided a means to disseminate ideas and competing theories from many parts of the world. Further, he himself challenged the prevailing ideology, thus intellectually as well as organizationally affecting adult education.

Another Canadian (transplanted to the United States) who as a professor of adult education has made a contribution to internationalizing university graduate programs is Alexander N. Charters (see Griffith, Chapter Five). Charters, now professor emeritus at Syracuse University, was a founder and an executive committee member of the International Congress of University Adult Education (ICUAE). The ICUAE got its start following the Second UNESCO Conference on Adult Education held in Montreal and obtained UNESCO consultative status (category B, nongovernmental) in 1963. Charters hosted the first organizational meeting of the ICUAE in 1961, at which the first World Conference on University Adult Education was planned. This conference was held in Humelback, Denmark, in 1965, and 180 people from thirty-eight different countries attended.

Members of the ICUAE who were interested in research, under the leadership of A. A. Liveright, organized the Exeter Conference on Comparative Study of Adult Education held in 1966. That conference was followed by similar ones sponsored by the ICUAE at Nordberg, Norway (1972); Oxford, England (1987); and Frascati, Italy (1988). An international Committee for Study and Research in Comparative Adult Education, cosponsored by the ICUAE and the ICAE, was organized following the Frascati conference.

Charters, who represented the United States at three UNESCO world conferences on adult education, was appointed the U.S. representative to the UNESCO International Conference on Documentation in 1972. Both Charters and Liveright were able to influence the field in terms of international publishing and comparative studies in adult education (Liveright and Haygood, 1968).

Paul Sheats (University of California, Los Angeles), who spent almost thirty years in the professoriate, was a member and vice chairman of the U.S. national commission for UNESCO from 1950 to 1956. He attended the UNESCO conference at Elsinore, Denmark (1949), and chaired the United States delegation in Montreal (1960). He traveled widely throughout the world, sponsored by the Fund for Adult Education and later World Education, consulting primarily on literacy and family planning. He also was an evaluator for the Agency for International Development. His strong interest in international education started while he was working on his doctorate at Yale, when he spent time in Germany studying the Hitler youth movement and the work camps.

Sheats wrote, "As a practitioner for many years in the field of adult continuing education, I have lived long enough to see lifelong education accepted as a necessity by countries with many political systems and cultural heritages. I have become more and more convinced that in a free society intent on remaining free, lifelong learning must be embraced as a major instrument through which the process of self-government can be maintained" (*Who's Who in America,* 1980–1981, p. 3002). Sheats was president of the Adult Education Association of the United States of America (AEA-USA), statewide director of the University of California Extension, president of the National University Extension Association, and a professor of adult education. Through his leadership, Sheats was able to promote his international perspective and infuse it into the organizations of which he was a member and into the consciousness of his students and staff.

A new generation of professors has also helped to internationalize the CPAE and the adult education knowledge base. The Swede Kjell Rubenson, who holds both a chair at Linköping University and an appointment at the University of British Columbia, has helped to initiate a strong socialist and sociological approach to research and knowledge. Prior to the 1980 Adult Education Research Conference in Vancouver, when Rubenson and a delegation of Swedish adult educators presented their research, very few social policy issues and little application of sociological thinking to participation research had been discussed in the United States (Höghielm and Rubenson, 1980). Later, Sean Courtney (University of Nebraska), who had come to the United States from Ireland and who had worked with Tom Lovett, a community-oriented, working-class adult educator, extended that discourse (Courtney, 1984). Courtney's ideas, along with Rubenson's, present a major challenge to the psychological orientation to the field as well as to functionalist sociological interpretations. Both Courtney and Rubenson use a sociological perspective that emphasizes conflict theory (Courtney, 1984; Rubenson, 1989a). This theoretical approach to conceptualizing adult education links up with and is closely related to the emphasis by some adult educators on the capacity of the poor to create their own knowledge collectively, direct their own learning, and be self-reliant (Tandon, 1981; Freire, 1970; Nyerere, 1968; Bell, Gaventa, and Peters, 1990).

This sociological perspective also informs the viewpoints of other researchers, including those researchers in the Organization for Economic Cooperation and Development who have concentrated on social policy and have developed schemes for recurrent education (Organization for Economic Cooperation and Development, 1973). These researchers have affected North American adult education, especially in examining policies on paid educational leave.

A strong impact on North American adult education was also made by Edgar Faure and the UNESCO report *Learning to Be* (1972). The concept of *education permanente* is similar to the North American concept of lifelong learning, and the emphasis of his book on rationalizing adult education throughout life and through institutional provision put adult education into the mainstream and legitimized it. Accordingly, the book was highly regarded in North America.

Roger Boshier (a New Zealander at the University of British Columbia), along with the North American futurists, popularized both of the Club of Rome reports, *Limits to Growth* (Meadows, Meadows, Randers, and Behrens, 1972) and *No Limits to Learning* (Botkin, Elmandjra, and Malitza, 1979), within the professoriate. People such as Boshier, speaking out on the appropriateness of technology and the fragility of our planet, have been persistent challengers of the ethical choices of educators. The content of adult education was also challenged by Helen Kekkonen from Finland, who was introduced to the CPAE by Budd Hall of the ICAE. She raised the question of the responsibility of adult educators toward promoting peace and the peace movement. Canadian adult educators appear to be much closer to the ecology and peace movements than professional adult educators in the United States, but to see the role of adult education in such movements. North American and international activists continue to pressure adult educators.

Jack Mezirow (Columbia University), who utilized Habermas (1978) as the base for his concept of perspective transformation, disseminated new philosophical expressions from abroad. His work was later complemented by Victoria Marsick, an internationalist with experience in the Third World who trained at Berkeley under Jack London prior to coming to Columbia University. Marsick's work (1988) applies action learning and participatory research to the training of adult educators.

Phenomenological study linking Husserl and the German philosophers to Charles Sanders Peirce (a teacher of Dewey) was introduced into adult education by Sherman Stanage (1987) of Northern Illinois University (NIU). He contends that the phenomenological traditions are fundamental to critical theory approaches to the development of adult education in a postmodern world or the development of a postmodern adult education. Michael Collins (University of Saskatchewan), trained by Stanage, based his original work on Shutz (Collins, 1980), but also emphasizes a concern for inductively derived social change and critical practice. Paul Ilsley (NIU), also trained by Stanage, has sought like Collins to ground his concern in social change; futurism and the "new sociology" inform his work on voluntarism (Ilsley, 1990).

It was David Little, University of Regina, who in a practical way helped to consolidate the influence of critical theory in North American thought. He started a critical theory network that became formalized in the commission of professors as a task force in 1988. He organized a travel forum to debate critical theory. The forum culminated in a miniconference prior to the 1988 meeting of the AERC that included Steven Kemmis (Deakin University, Australia), Sherman Stanage (NIU), Michael Welton (Dalhousie University), Susan Collard (University of British Columbia), Carmel Chambers (University of British Columbia), and Michael Collins (University of Saskatchewan). Little provided the platform for the debate and dissemination of critical theory, critical social science, and critical thinking into the consciousness of the North American professoriate.

The role of women in the North American professoriate was minimal until after the civil rights struggle in the late sixties. Even though the number of women within the CPAE increased at that time, a feminist discourse was lacking. Adult educators were more interested in attracting women as consumers of continuing education and as applicants to returning students' programs than in establishing a feminist discourse.

The University of Montreal offered the first university course dealing with feminism in 1969, but the progressive work that followed did not find its way into the mainstream. Although

Kathleen Rockhill (OISE) and Susan Davenport (NIU) attempted to initiate a feminist discourse within the AERC in Montreal, there was no strong support for their efforts. Jane Hugo (Syracuse University) has reported on her feminist research prior to the dissertation at a CPAE meeting in 1988, and Wendy Luttrell (Duke University and Highlander Research and Education Center) introduced her feminist research findings at the 1988 Leeds conference. But for the most part, it has been women from the United Kingdom such as Jane Thompson (University of London), Sallie Westwood (University of Leicester), and Miriam Zukas (University of Leeds), who through their writing or as visiting scholars, have promoted the feminist discourse in adult education. Recently, Susan Collard (from England) and Carmel Chambers, both at the University of British Columbia, have developed a strong feminist critique of the social theories that inform adult education.

Adult educators promoting critical theory, such as conflict sociology, have attacked the dominant paradigms of positivism and structural functionalism that still have a grip on much of the field of adult education today. The links and conceptual contributions in critical thought from Australia, Europe, and Ireland have been noted. It is doubtful, though, how effectively these intellectual challenges could have permeated the psychologically informed "science" paradigms that held a relentless grip on the field of North American adult education if it were not for the primary assault on these paradigms that came earlier. This early assault came directly from the Third World or through the influence and work of the ICAE. It is to these voices from the Third World that I now turn.

Challenges from the Third World

Paulo Freire's and other Latin American thinkers' concepts of liberatory pedagogy provided some of the strongest intellectual challenges to the prevailing hegemony of scientific rationality in North American thought. In the early seventies, the effect of Freire's ideas was perhaps stronger on adult education graduate students in the universities (under siege at that time by the

civil rights and Vietnam resistance movements) and on marginalized groups in the field of practice than on professors of
adult education (Freire, 1970; Grabowski, 1972). Graduate students who were radicalized by the Vietnam war were open to
hearing the debate. North American indigenous peoples, racial and ethnic minorities, women, and older people who had
experienced oppression could more easily understand the discourse on oppression. Their consciousness was awakened out
of their own activity (their praxis), and they applied pressure
to the weakness within the predominant theories that characterized if not dominated the university. Thus we see the field
of practice influencing the field of study, as it is dichotomized
in much of North American thinking.

The participatory researchers accomplished a second in-
vasion of the North American intellectual terrain (Tandon, 1981;
Hall, 1977). Participatory research, legitimated in North American adult education in 1979 by an ERIC publication (Niemi,
1979) was a shock to the established order of things. Participatory research and its bold attack on scientific rationality would
not go away. It was supported, encouraged, and nurtured by
the ICAE, the Participatory Research Network, and *Convergence*.
The ICAE encouraged the dissemination and application of participatory research, and through Budd Hall, secretary general
of the ICAE, the voices of Tanzania and India were heard. The
stronger the resistance from the established professoriate the
more the newer professors and professors-to-be recognized the
legitimacy of the claims of this research. They felt that surely
knowledge was socially constructed and that surely such a construction was possible for all people, not simply university professors. This discourse accelerated the quantitative-qualitative research debate and helped force changes in the approaches to
the production of knowledge sanctioned by the university and
the journals.

North American Social Activists

The legitimation in North America of critical pedagogy, liberatory education, and participatory research, concepts flowing

from the Third World, was assisted by links between the architects of the concepts and social critics in the United States such as Myles Horton (Highlander Education and Research Center) and John Ohliger (Basic Choices). Horton, who had worked with the ICAE, had international connections and was well known among Latin American and Indian adult educators. The ICAE does its work through networks, and the Society for Participatory Research in Asia, located in New Delhi, is one of the more active networks.

John Gaventa, associate professor at the University of Tennessee, director of the Highlander Education and Research Center, and head of the North American Participatory Research Network, worked with the ICAE to promote scholarship arising out of praxis. He initiated research linking Appalachian and British coal miners in their similar struggles. He facilitated meetings of Appalachian people and Latin Americans who, with their own research, documented their related oppression by transnational companies (Gaventa, 1990). Gaventa and his spouse, Juliet Merrifield, as codirectors of research at Highlander, brought together Indians from the Bhopal Union Carbide disaster with people from West Virginia battling Union Carbide in Institute, West Virginia. The two groups learned from each other's struggles and strategies. The facilitation and building of international discourse to help ordinary citizens expose and intervene in transnational exploitation is a major advance forward in international adult education. Merrifield, who now directs the Center for Literacy Study at the University of Tennessee, now concentrates her attention on literacy in its international contexts.

Joining these escalating voices of opposition was John Ohliger, from his small intellectual center for alternatives, Basic Choices, in Madison, Wisconsin. Ohliger, who battled self-serving professionalism and the mandatory education of adults, was a cause célèbre in the history of the CPAE. Ohliger left a tenured position at Ohio State University partly because of his conviction that adult education was becoming adult schooling. Influenced by Everett Reimer and Ivan Illich, Ohliger arrived at an intellectual position on schooling, similar to their position. He was joined at Basic Choices by people influenced by the reproduction theorists working out of the new sociology and by the voluntarists who were resisting the professionalization and institutionalization of adult education.

He was one of the few people who challenged Faure's report for promoting what Ohliger termed lifelong schooling. His commitment to the freedom of people from state-mandated education was well known in UNESCO (Ohliger, 1983). Through his newsletter, *Second Thoughts,* Ohliger linked social activists who mounted an attack on the lack of social critique within the profession in the Adult Education Association of the United States. Typical of these activists were William Draves, Thomas Heaney, Ronald Gross, and Larry Olds. Draves had established the University of Man and written *The Free University* (Draves, 1980). Heaney, working on critical social change in Chicago, had established what was to become the Lindeman Center. Gross was a deschooler and a proponent of community or independent scholarship. Olds, who worked in the College for Working Adults (Minneapolis), was a leader in international peace education.

About twenty people, including those mentioned above, met at Highlander in spring 1979 to discuss mutual social concerns. Selecting the issue of mandatory continuing education on which to concentrate, the participants decided to form an association and to mount political action at the 1979 AEA-USA national conference being held in Boston. This group, the National Alliance for Voluntary Learning (NAVL), forced the AEA-USA and the CPAE to take notice of voices coming from outside the "profession." A task force was appointed by the AEA executive committee to report to the AEA-USA on mandatory continuing education.

The National Alliance for Voluntary Learning published two monographs: *Task Force Report: AEA/Task Force on Voluntary Learning* (Heaney, 1980) and *Compass: A Resource Directory* (Cunningham and Associates, 1982). *Compass* linked activists in North America with international networks of like-minded adult educators. NAVL was a cooperation of equals. Increasingly, some professors of adult education recognized the legitimacy of knowledge produced outside the university.

Highlander continues to be the site at which adult educators fostering a sense of social concern in their work meet and organize. In March 1990, Jack Mezirow (Columbia) and Aimee Horton (Lindeman Center, NIU) organized a meeting at Highlander for North American adult educators concerned that popular educators in North America were being excluded from the agenda of the national association, the AAACE. From this meeting, French-, English-, and Spanish-speaking people representing workers' education, peace education, community-based education, and church educators and activists as well as people of diverse races and ethnic backgrounds from the United States, Canada, and Puerto Rico established the North American Educators of Adults for Democratic Social Action. This association has as its mission the building of a community of popular educators and university academicians who can share equally and reflect critically on their praxis as well as constitute a group that can relate with popular educators internationally.

University Centers of Alternative Knowledge

The importance of the Ontario Institute for Studies in Education as the base for the International Council for Adult Education and Syracuse University as a base for the work of Charters has been mentioned earlier. International work and ideological challenges to dominant paradigms developed at other campuses as well.

One university that has systematically developed a strong international program is the University of the District of Columbia (UDC), under the direction of Beverly Cassara. Cassara, who was awarded a Fulbright scholarship to examine women in education in Germany, has played a central role in developing international concerns within adult education. With a United States Information Agency grant, she created a three-year exchange program with the University of Nairobi, Kenya, in which UDC professors taught in Kenya and University of Nairobi professors taught UDC students in Washington. Along with her African American graduate students, she organized three different study tours to eastern Africa. She also developed three international conferences at UDC and, with this stimulus, created the *Graduate Journal* to publish the conference proceedings and other international articles. Along with Peter Cookson (Pennsylvania State University) and Richard Henstrom (Brigham Young University), Cassara systematized cooperative activity among the International Associates, the international task force of the CPAE, and the international section of the then AEA-USA. Together, these groups sponsored a directory of people interested in international networking on adult education concerns (Cookson, 1984).

Another university that has systematically promoted an international agenda is the University of British Columbia. UBC has developed a diploma program with an international focus, a program that is suitable for other countries to adopt. Accordingly, UBC faculty members have established cooperative programs in Brazil, Singapore, and China. They have also regularly brought international professors (both visiting and permanent) and graduate students to the UBC campus. Many of these professors, including Stephen Brookfield (United Kingdom), Roger Boshier (New Zealand), Kjell Rubenson (Sweden), now hold positions in North America and are prolific writers affecting North American thought. Paz Butterdahl (Chile), another professor brought to North America by UBC, was key in helping to develop the diploma program of UBC in Brazil. UBC graduates such as Michael Law (New Zealand), Philip Candy (Australia), and Susan Collard (United Kingdom) have made substantive contributions to the thinking of adult educators in North America.

The University of Montreal, under Claude Touchette, created a Department of Andragogy in the early seventies, a time of much intellectual ferment and social organizing. Adult education in Quebec was rooted in the political process of liberation and the elaboration of a social project of democracy. Students' research at the university in feminist studies, literacy for empowerment, and popular education reflected and illuminated these social movements. As these movements grew, Quebec developed strong relationships with Africa, Europe, and Latin America.

The University of Montreal's graduate program was the only francophone graduate program in adult education in Canada and was characterized by voluntarism (50 percent of its students work in voluntary agencies). The university allocated spaces in the program for students from other countries. International students now represent 5 percent of some 550 students in the program (80 doctoral students, 35 master's degree students, 280 professional master's students, and 150 undergraduates). The university has formal agreements with the University of Simón Rodriguez (Venezuela), the National University (Zaire), the National University (Cameroons), the National Institute for Alphabetization (Guinea), the National Institute for Sport and Popular Education (Ivory Coast), and the Paris Conservatory of Arts and Trade Exchange (Paris). Students representing one Asian, one Middle Eastern, five South American, one Caribbean, twelve African, and two European countries turned this program into one of the strongest international programs in North America. The exchanges with these countries were developed in ways to avoid neocolonialism and in a spirit of sharing. They emphasize cultural distinctions within groups and feature cooperative projects.

Perhaps it is no surprise that the professors and students at Columbia University, home of a number of social reconstructionists and the first university to establish an adult education program, became a campus of resisting professors. Mezirow, working with World Education, raised a critical voice toward much of what passed as adult basic education, noting that it was rooted in the concept of social control (Mezirow, 1978; see Griffith, Chapter Five). But it was Harold Beder, one of Mezirow's students and a professor at Rutgers University, who, along with the support of Robert Höghielm from Sweden, instituted the International League for Social Commitment in Adult Education (ILSCAE). The league challenged the professoriate to acknowledge international concerns, to put peace and justice on the agenda, and to adopt a global consciousness. Until 1989, the league, with its strong international vision, held a small annual conference that was attended by 100 or more mostly European and North American adult educators who introduced and socialized students, practitioners, and some professors into progressive international relationships. In 1989 and in 1990, the league moved its annual meeting to Nicaragua and began to build bridges with the Third World. Accordingly, its internationalizing influence may be increased.

An unlikely candidate as a center of resistance was the new doctoral program approved at Northern Illinois University in 1976. This program has, in fifteen years, become large (300 graduate students), diverse (20 percent minorities), and international (14 percent international students). It has done more than most graduate programs to develop curricular alternatives in the areas of public policy, sociology, phenomenology, oppressed people, popular education, and participatory research. International faculty members include Marcelo Zwierzynski, an Argentine expatriate, political activist, and popular educator with extensive experience as an employee of the United Nations. He is a friend of Freire and is familiar with Freire's work in Latin America and Africa. This background has helped him to challenge and change the students and faculty and the curriculum as he works among Hispanic communities through the university's community services office. In 1989, Jorge Jeria, a Chilean expatriate, continued the South American influence on the university's doctoral program.

Faculty member Thomas Heaney, committed to popular and liberatory education, developed the small community services office that assists the community in creating and carving out their educational agendas and gives graduate students the opportunity to interact with critical pedagogy. Graduate students from marginalized groups are encouraged to write their own histories, and they have initiated scholarship in such areas as revisionist labor history, immigrant history, African American contributions to adult education, Latin American feminism, critical theory as applied to the silencing of women, and inclusive language in the church. The university has established international exchanges, especially with China and Latin America, with a clear ideology of an exchange among equals avoiding any semblance of neocolonialism and with a critical view of the concept of development. Faculty member Robert Smith has led two international conferences on learning to learn and headed a team that collaborated on two books on this topic (Smith 1987, 1990). Further, the *International History of Adult Education Bulletin* (started by NIU students) and the *Participatory Formation Newsletter of Adult Education* were initiated, given financial support, and are currently edited on this campus.

Other universities that have established links with the Third World are Florida State University (linked with South and Central America), the University of New Mexico (linked with Central America and offering the only Spanish bilingual degree for adult educators in the United States), Pennsylvania State University (linked with South and Central America), and the University of Tennessee (affiliated with the Highlander Education and Research Center). Particularly noteworthy was the work of George Aker at Florida State University. In the midst of establishing a major network among universities in Latin America with Florida State, Aker was killed in an auto accident while traveling in Central America. This caused a premature cessation of what appeared to be a robust international exchange.

Links Between Associations

In 1978, the ICAE began forming links between professional associations. At the 1978 meeting of the AERC in San Antonio, Texas, ICAE sponsored a representative (Paul Fordham) from the Standing Committee on University Teaching and Research on the Education of Adults. The next year an AERC representative (Phyllis Cunningham) was sent to SCUTREA. Progressively, researchers began to move back and forth between these annual meetings.

At least two study groups from the United States (NIU and Rutgers) have gone to the United Kingdom. Gerald Normie, from the British Open University, was connected with these groups and, perhaps more than any other person from the United Kingdom, worked to forge an alliance between SCUTREA, CPAE, and AERC. Through international research conferences held at Oxford University on subjects such as the history of adult education, corrections education, and international adult education, Normie provided a place for cross-fertilization of ideas from a number of countries. Normie also developed a comparative adult education newsletter that joined North American professors to mostly European adult educators.

In the same year that the ILSCAE was launched, a proposed exchange between SCUTREA and the CPAE, initiated by Beder, Normie, and David Jones (Nottingham University), was implemented by the CPAE's international task force. The task force, working with Normie and under the leadership of Phyllis Cunningham, expanded the exchange to include the Canadian Association for the Study of Adult Education and defined the exchange program as directed toward the professional development of young or new professors. It opened the gates to all who qualified by selecting participants on a competitive basis from the CPAE members.

During the years 1984–1986, grants from the Kellogg Foundation ($50,000) and the British Consul helped to fund an exchange program of nine North American and twelve British professors. Members of the exchange group spent two weeks in each other's countries on a study visit at two to three universities, attended the annual research conference or national meeting of practitioners, prepared and gave papers that were circulated in a monograph (Conti and Fellenz, 1985), and developed some international contacts to apply to their research interests. The use of the cadre concept and the emphasis on less-experienced persons in the exchange unleashed the collective energy of the young, who were eager for new experiences and welcomed the bond with fellow neophytes in thinking through their views of the profession. This exchange broadened the support within the CPAE and the AERC for competing viewpoints to the dominant research paradigms and for a global perspective.

One activity pursued by this group of professors, known as the Kellogg Exchange Fellows, was the development of a Trans-Atlantic Dialogue Research Conference under the joint auspices of the AERC, CASAE, and SCUTREA. A proposal from this group resulted in a five-year grant from the W. K. Kellogg Foundation to help fund the conference and to find new initiatives to broaden the exchange. The proposal, granted to the ICAE, called for the new initiative to represent a North-South dialogue between university researchers and participatory researchers. The process was open to any person giving a research paper at the Trans-Atlantic Dialogue Conference who shared the North-South vision for framing international dialogue.

In July 1988, 55 researchers from nine countries assembled in Great Britain at Leeds to have their first meeting about the Trans-Atlantic Dialogue Research Conference (at which over 200 people later gathered). During the three-day meeting, strong differences in views emerged as the participants discussed ideological differences and the varying conceptions of the production of knowledge. The participants decided, with the dissent of a vocal minority, to form the Transformative Research Network, with the term *transformative research* yet to be defined (see Chapter Fifteen). However, it was clear that this group saw comparative research in adult education as research designed to help produce social transformation. The objectives of the Transformative Research Network and the newly formed Committee for Study and Research in Comparative Adult Education organized at the Frascati conference did not overlap. The latter group was seen to be organized around the more traditional modes of scientific rationalism. The Transformative Research Network took the position that neutrality was not an option, and that adult education researchers were responsible for the values that their research represented.

Adult educators have also learned about international viewpoints through the Fulbright scholars program. Alan Knox (University of Wisconsin) and John Niemi (Northern Illinois University) used their Fulbright study to affect the North American knowledge base. Knox developed a cadre of researchers in over thirty countries to develop case studies of adult education within a given set of parameters. These researchers have assembled a mass of material that is disseminated through ERIC and is now in the process of being analyzed comparatively. Niemi acted as a consultant in the development of graduate programs at the Universities of Tampere and Helsinki. He then was invited to link NIU with the Lahti [Finland] Research

Center and six other universities in the United Kingdom, the Soviet Union, Canada, Sweden, and Ireland.

By the late eighties, more and more opportunities were available for professors and many graduate students of adult education to go abroad or be involved with researchers from abroad or to participate in an international conference. The number of formal exchanges has increased. These opportunities continue to establish and broaden the knowledge base.

International Publications

The flow of ideas from outside North America into literature that is easily accessible by professors, graduate students, and critically reflective practitioners has also facilitated changes in as well as developed and disseminated the knowledge base. Adult education literature from outside North America has appeared in journals, newsletters, conference proceedings, and books (see Brockett, Chapter Six). *Convergence* has already been discussed as a primary resource for introducing ideas from a truly global perspective to North American readers. Published quarterly by the ICAE since 1966, *Convergence* currently has a readership of about 800 in North America.

The ICAE also publishes or facilitates the publication of several newsletters that contain substantive critiques of adult education in North America. Among those publications that have presented strong alternative views are *Voices Rising* (Women's Network), *Participatory Research* (the Participatory Research Networks in Asia and Africa), and *Participatory Formation* (the Training Network). The ICAE also maintains a publications program of its own, cosponsors publications in the international arena, and disseminates publications from its regional networks. Monographs on Comparative and Area Studies in Adult Education is a cooperative effort of the Centre for Continuing Education of the University of British Columbia and the ICAE. Jindra Kulich, editor of the series, is the North American adult educator who has done the most to introduce his colleagues to and keep them informed about adult education in Eastern Europe. The series has produced eleven monographs that focus on, but are not limited to, European adult education.

The ICAE regional networks have become a growing source of adult education literature. The African Association for Literacy and Adult Education edits a quarterly newsletter, *The Spider,* and publishes monographs and occasional papers. The Asian South Pacific Bureau of Adult Education edits a newsletter, *ASPBE News,* and has a strong publication program. The Council for Adult Education in Latin America has a major publishing program, but their materials are not yet available in English.

The Croom Helm Series: International Perspectives in Adult and Continuing Education, another source of international information, was started in 1984. Twenty books have been published in the series under the editorship of Peter Jarvis (University of Surrey), who also established and coedits with J. E. Thomas (Nottingham University) the *International Journal for Lifelong Education.* This journal, launched in 1981, *Convergence,* and the *International Journal of University Adult Education* (edited by Chris Duke at the University of Warwick) are the only three international journals committed to adult education. The latter two provide more space to Third World experiences and research than does the first. It is not clear how many North American professors regularly read any of these journals, but readership in terms of subscriptions is reported to be steadily, if slowly, rising.

It is worth noting the impact of Peter Jarvis and the book series called Theory and Practice of Adult Education in North America, even though all but two authors in the series are from North America and Europe (see Chapter Five). European authors have had a considerable impact on North American thinking, as measured by the increasing number of citations of European authors by North American professors and research ideas derived from European authors. Especially important among these authors is Jarvis, who appears intrigued with the idea of a knowledge base. His book *Twentieth Century Thinkers in Adult Education* (1987b) takes the knowledge base as its subject and limits itself to English and North American males who have been the "thinkers" who have shaped the knowledge base. Jarvis's book *Adult Learning in the Social Context* (1987a) earned the Houle award in 1988. His sociology book is perhaps the only one available that addresses the sociology of adult education (Jarvis, 1985).

Thus, Jarvis's writings have had a direct effect on North American thinking, and his role as gatekeeper in the Croom Helm and Routledge series has resulted in some indirect effects on the dissemination of ideas. The Leirman and Kulich book (1987), published in the Croom Helm series, introduced North Americans to a number of European authors and their adult education agendas. Chapters on environmental education, peace making, peace education, multiculturalism, and development and dialogue press these global concerns on a process-oriented North American audience. Duke's book on national development (1985) introduced very distinct strategies of adult education, such as Sri Lanka's Sarvodaya movement, Saemoul education in the Republic of Korea, and the Nicaraguan Literacy Crusade. Gelpi (1985), from his post as head of the lifelong learning unit at UNESCO, provided an international perspective on major adult education issues confronting the field in international arenas. Mark Tennant (1990) edited a book surveying Australia's practice of adult education that gives the North American reader a good overview of that continent's practice. Finally, Collin Griffin's work on social policy (1987) has created a renewed interest in this subject, and Griffin's orientation to a more societally organized and historically grounded adult education challenges the individual, ahistorical orientation of many North Americans (see Chapter Ten).

The Routledge series of books on adult education, the Radical Forum on Adult Education Series, edited by Jo Campling and published in England, has also made an impact on North American thinking. This series presents in a systematic way radical and bottom-up approaches and concepts of adult education that cannot be found in books published in North America. Bergin and Garvey publish the Critical Studies in Education series, some books of which are directed toward adult education. To date, the authors in these two series, with the exception of Paulo Freire, are North Americans. Nevertheless, these two series of books have helped to extend the knowledge base of the field. Progressive professors now have a choice in textbooks in which the official knowledge and the dominant culture are challenged.

The Prague series of a dozen proposed volumes published by the European Centre for Leisure and Education, funded by UNESCO, provides descriptive and sometimes theoretical accounts of adult education systems in various European countries. This series is not well known in North America and thus has had little influence on the exchange of international knowledge. *Lifelong Education for Adults: An International Handbook* (Titmus, 1989) is a recently published reference work that along with *The International Encyclopedia of Education* (Husen and Postlethwaite, 1985) has the potential to broaden the adult education knowledge base in North America. In *Lifelong Education for Adults,* Rubenson, representing a European viewpoint, critiques North American adult education as being dominated by psychologism. He asks two questions when analyzing territorial maps of the production of knowledge: "(a) which assumptions and perceptions of the territory govern the efforts to accumulate knowledge within adult education, that is which questions are regarded as legitimate within the field? (b) which research traditions (scientific ideals and perceptives) govern research in adult education?" (Rubenson, 1989a, p. 508).

Rubenson (1989b) suggests that in North America the premise seems to be people over society while the European adult educator conceptualizes research problems around people in society. Accordingly, Rubenson believes that North American research can be characterized by psychological reductionism. His criticism is no less severe of research from Western Europe. He says that adult education in this area is so closely aligned with public policy that it suffers from sociological deductionism. Further, he criticizes the newer interpretive approaches in the United States as an extension of the emphasis on individualism. Titmus, whose earlier book on European adult education (1981) has been widely read by North Americans, shares Rubenson's concerns regarding the sociological emphasis in Europe vis-à-vis the psychological orientations found in the United States in his discussion of present-day adult education research in Western Europe (Titmus, 1989).

Two newsletters on critical theory provided for an exchange of information. David Little, mentioned earlier, puts out information in photocopied form to a North American audience in the *Critical Theory Network*. The *Critical Pedagogy Networker: A Publication on Critical Social Issues in Education* is published quarterly by John Smyth and is read by a growing number of North American professors.

Sweden, Germany, and Finland have initiated activities that have made inroads into adult education thought in North America. Sweden has provided funds for an exchange of individuals with the United States. The New Sweden program, launched in 1988, celebrated the 350 years of friendship between the United States and Sweden with an exchange program involving twenty-four people. Sweden and Germany distribute English-language publications developed by each state's department of adult education free of charge in North America. The German monograph series *Adult Education and Development* has focused on adult education in the Third World and has had fairly wide dissemination in North America. The Finnish journal *Adult Education* is also available in English.

Internationalization in the Future

In the preceding discussion, I have argued that increased international contact and interaction have changed the nature not only of the knowledge base of American adult educators but the ideological spaces in which educators operate. These changes reflect the larger social world in which adult education exists. This book is being written and edited by an international team of writers and editors. The content has been internationalized. There is no question about the increased international influences and increased interaction between North Americans and adult educators from around the world. Only the nature of that interaction remains unclear.

It would appear that to the degree that North American adult educators strengthen their theoretical exchanges with Africa, Asia, and Latin America, adult education will become more diverse. To the extent that most universities and groups maintain and strengthen a Eurocentric orientation, the nature of adult education may change but be increasingly isolated from the most populous countries of the world and their discourses.

The adult educators in the United States must lose the parochial nature and naivete which many people say characterize us. To the extent that we remain monolingual and predominantly monocultural we will be limited in understanding the diversity one can experience internationally. To the extent that we ignore our own marginalized populations — indigenous persons, non-European populations, persons of color — we will experience difficulties in being accepted as internationalists.

The issues with which we are concerned will probably change. Concepts such as peace education, sustainable development, and transnational exploitation may have to become a part of our discourse depending on which areas of the world we make our links with and how we contextualize our experience. Literacy may have to be reconceptualized as more than reading and writing; analyses that contextualize literacy as a political and socially embedded construct on which power relations turn will be necessary assuming we desire to decrease the gap between the rich and poor. To address the inequity in our society, we would have to contextualize our practice and encourage the democratization of the production of knowledge. It could mean that we must try to democratize our emerging field, if not deprofessionalize it. Without overselling what education can do, we must promote a growing awareness of the importance of the education of adults as a social force for increasing equity and equality of opportunities. Accordingly, we would have to emphasize adult educators as policy makers prepared to negotiate the formal and the unwritten policies that operate locally, nationally, and internationally.

At issue for North American adult educators will be the struggle as to the worldview that will prevail. It remains to be seen on which paradigm the critical mass will be built.

Chronology of the Internationalization
of the Knowledge Base of
North American Adult Education
1949–1990

1949   First World Conference on Adult Education (UN-
         ESCO), Elsinore, Denmark. Twenty-nine countries
         represented.

1960   The Second World Conference on Adult Education
         (UNESCO), Montreal, Canada. Fifty-one countries
         represented.

1960   International Congress of University Adult Education
         founded (UNESCO consultative status, to become
         Category B in 1963).

1965   First International Conference on the Comparative
         Study of Adult Education, Exeter, United States.

1966   *International Journal of University Adult Education* founded.
         C. Duke, ed.

1967   First graduate course in comparative adult education
         offered by the Ontario Institute for the Study of Edu-
         cation.

1968   *Convergence* initiated.

1972   International Experts' meeting, "An Agenda for Com-
         parative Studies in Adult Education," Nordberg, Den-
         mark.

1972   *Learning to Be* published by UNESCO.

1972   Third International Conference on Adult Education
         (UNESCO), Tokyo, Japan.

1973   Founding of the International Council for Adult Education. Twenty-two national and regional members. UNESCO consultative status.

1975   Publication of *Comparative Studies in Adult Education: An Anthology,* by C. Bennett, J. Kulich, and J. R. Kidd.

1976   First World Congress on Adult Education, International Council for Adult Education, Dar es Salaam, Tanzania. Forty-five national and regional members.

1977   Publication of series by J. Kulich of annotated bibliographies on adult education in Europe begins.

1977   ICAE sponsors exchange between AERC and SCUTREA.

1981   *International Journal of Lifelong Education* founded, P. Jarvis, ed., in association with Michael Stephens of Nottingham University.

1981   Publication of *Comparing Adult Education Worldwide,* by A. Charters and Associates.

1982   Second World Congress on Adult Education, International Council for Adult Education, Paris, France. One hundred and twenty-two countries represented.

1983   Publication of the monograph series *Adult Education in Continental Europe,* by P. Maydl and others.

1983   Croom-Helm international adult education series initiated, P. Jarvis, ed.

1984   International League for Social Commitment in Adult Education founded.

1984   Publication of *Directory of International Adult Education Exchange and Cooperation,* P. Cookson, ed.

1985   Fourth International Conference on Adult Education (UNESCO), Paris, France. One hundred and twenty-two countries represented.

1985   Third World Congress on Adult Education, International Council for Adult Education, Buenos Aires, Argentina. Ninety-seven countries represented.

1985–
1987   Kellogg British and North American professorial exchange.

1987   Comparative Adult Education Conference (Open University), Oxford, United Kingdom.

1988   International Seminar on Comparative Research in Adult Education organized by Centro Europeo Dell' Educazione, Frascati, Italy. Cosponsored by ICAE and ICUAE.

1988   Trans-Atlantic Dialogue Research Conference, cosponsored by AERC, CASAE, and SCUTREA, University of Leeds, England.

1988   Formation of the Transformative Research Network by an international gathering of professors, Leeds University. Affiliated with ICAE.

1990   Fourth World Congress on Adult Education, International Council for Adult Education, Bangkok, Thailand.

References

Bell, B., Gaventa, J. P., and Peters, J. M. (eds.). *We Make the Road by Walking: Conversations on Education and Social Change*. Philadelphia: Temple University Press, 1990.

Bennett, C., Kulich, J., and Kidd, J. R. *Comparative Studies in Adult Education: An Anthology*. Syracuse, N.Y.: Syracuse University Publications in Continuing Education, 1975.

Berger, L., and Luckmann, T., *Social Construction of Reality: A Treatise in the Sociology of Knowledge*. New York: Doubleday, 1966.

Botkin, J., Elmandjra, M., and Malitza, M. *No Limits to Learning: Bridging the Human Gap*. Oxford, England: Pergamon Press, 1979.

Charters, A. N., and Associates (eds.). *Comparing Adult Education Worldwide*. San Francisco: Jossey-Bass, 1981.

Colin, S.A.J., III. "Voices from Beyond the Veil: Marcus Garvey, the Universal Negro Improvement Society and the Education of African Ameripean Adults." Unpublished doctoral dissertation, Leadership and Educational Policy Studies Department, Northern Illinois University, 1988.

Collins, M. "Competency in Adult Education: Applying a Theory of Relevance." Unpublished doctoral dissertation, Leadership and Educational Policy Studies Department, Northern Illinois University, 1980.

Conti, G. J., and Fellenz, R. A. *Dialogue on Issues of Lifelong Learning in a Democratic Society*. College Station, Tex.: Department of Interdisciplinary Studies, Texas A&M University, 1985.

Cookson, P. S. (ed.). *Directory of International Adult Education Exchange and Cooperation*. Washington, D.C.: Commission of Professors of Adult Education, American Association of Adult and Continuing Education, 1984.

Courtney, S. "Visible Learning; Adult Education and the Question of Participation." Unpublished doctoral dissertation, Leadership and Educational Policy Studies Department, Northern Illinois University, 1984.

Cunningham, P. M. "The Adult Educator and Social Responsibility." In R. G. Brockett (ed.), *Ethical Issues in Adult Education*. New York: Teachers College Press, 1988.

Cunningham, P. M., and Associates. *Compass: A Resource Directory*. DeKalb, Ill.: National Alliance for Voluntary Learning, Leadership and Educational Policy Studies Department, Northern Illinois University, 1982.

Draves, W. *The Free University*. Chicago: Follett, 1980.

Duke, C. (ed.). *Combating Poverty Through Adult Education: National Development Strategies*. London: Croom Helm, 1985.

Dutta, S. C. "International Outreach." In N. J. Cochrane and Associates (eds.), *J. R. Kidd: An International Legacy of Learning*. Vancouver, Canada: Centre for Continuing Education, University of British Columbia, 1986.

Ely, M. L. (ed.). *Handbook of Adult Education in the United States*. Washington, D.C.: American Association for Adult Education, 1948.

Faure, E., and others. *Learning To Be: The World of Education Today and Tomorrow*. Paris: UNESCO, 1972.

Freire, P. *Pedagogy of the Oppressed*. New York: Herder & Herder, 1970.

Gaventa, J. P. "From the Mountains to the Maquiladoras: A Case Study of Capital Flight and its Impact on Workers." In J. P. Gaventa and Associates (eds.), *Communities in Economic Crisis*. Philadelphia: Temple University Press, 1990.

Gelpi, E. *Lifelong Education and International Relations*. London: Croom Helm, 1985.

Grabowski, S. M. (ed.). *Paulo Freire: A Revolutionary Dilemma for the Adult Educator*. Syracuse, N.Y.: Syracuse University Publications in Continuing Education, 1972.

Gramsci, A. *Selections from the Prison Notebooks*. New York: International Publishers, 1987.

Griffin, C. *Adult Education as Social Policy*. London: Croom Helm, 1987.

Hall, B. L. "Participatory Research: Expanding the Base of Analysis." *International Development Review/Focus*, 1977, 23–28.

Heaney, T. W. (ed.). *Task Force Report: AEA/USA Task Force on Voluntary Learning*. Chicago: Lindeman Center, Northern Illinois University, 1980.

Höghielm, R., and Rubenson, K. (eds.). *Adult Education for Social Change*. Stockholm: Gleerun, 1980.

Husen, T., and Postlethwaite, T. N. (eds.). *The International Encyclopedia of Education.* Elmsford, N.Y.: Pergamon Press, 1985.

Ilsley, P. J. *Enhancing the Volunteer Experience.* San Francisco: Jossey-Bass, 1990.

Jarvis, P. *The Sociology of Adult and Continuing Education.* London: Croom Helm, 1985.

Jarvis, P. *Adult Learning in the Social Context.* London: Croom Helm, 1987a.

Jarvis, P. (ed.). *Twentieth Century Thinkers in Adult Education.* London: Croom Helm, 1987b.

Jensen, G., Liveright, A. A., and Hallenbeck, W. *Adult Education: Outlines of an Emerging Field of University Study.* Washington, D.C.: American Asociation for Adult and Continuing Education, 1964.

Kidd, J. R. *A Tale of Three Cities: Elsinore-Montreal-Tokyo: The Influence of Three Unesco World Conferences upon the Development of Adult Education.* Syracuse, N.Y.: Syracuse University Publications in Continuing Education, 1974.

Knowles, M. S. *A History of the Adult Education Movement in the United States.* Melbourne, Fla.: Krieger, 1977.

Knowles, M. S. (ed.). *Handbook of Adult Education in the United States.* Washington, D.C.: American Association for Adult and Continuing Education, 1960.

Leirman, W., and Kulich, J. (ed.). *Adult Education and the Challenges of the 1990s.* London: Croom Helm, 1987.

Liveright, A. A., and Haygood, N. (eds.). *The Exeter Papers: Report of the First International Conference on the Comparative Study of Adult Education.* Boston: Center for the Study of Liberal Education for Adults, Boston University, 1968.

Marsick, V. J., and Cederholm, L. "Developing Leadership in International Managers—An Urgent Challenge!" *Columbia Journal of World Business,* 1988, *23* (4), pp. 3-11.

Meadows, D. H., Meadows, D. L., Randers, J., and Behrens, W. W. *The Limits to Growth.* New York: Universe Books, 1972.

Merriam, S. B., and Cunningham, P. M. (eds.). *Handbook of Adult and Continuing Education.* San Francisco: Jossey-Bass, 1989.

Mezirow, J. "Perspective Transformation." *Adult Education,* 1978, *28* (2), 100–110.

Niemi, J. A. *Viewpoints on Adult Education Research.* Information Series, no. 171. Columbus: ERIC Clearinghouse on Adult, Career, and Vocational Education, 1979.

Nyerere, J. K. "Education for Self-Reliance." In J. K. Nyerere, *Ujamaa: Essays on Socialism.* London: Oxford University Press, 1968.

Ohliger, J. "Reconciling Education with Liberty." *Prospects: UNESCO Quarterly Journal of Education,* 1983, *13* (2), 161–179.

Organization of Economic Cooperation and Development. *Recurrent Education: A Strategy for Lifelong Learning.* Paris: Organization of Economic Cooperation and Development, 1973.

Rowden, D. (ed.). *Handbook of Adult Education in the United States.* American Association for Adult Education, 1934.

Rowden, D. (ed.). *Handbook of Adult Education in the United States.* Washington, D.C.: American Association for Adult Education, 1936.

Rubenson, K. "Adult Education Research: General." In C. J. Titmus (ed.), *Lifelong Education for Adults: An International Handbook.* Oxford, England: Pergamon Press, 1989a.

Rubenson, K. "The Sociology of Adult Education." In S. B. Merriam and P. M. Cunningham (eds.), *Handbook of Adult and Continuing Education.* San Francisco: Jossey-Bass, 1989b.

Smith, R. M. (ed.). *Theory Building for Learning How to Learn.* Chicago: Educational Studies Press, 1987.

Smith, R. M., Aker, G. F., and Kidd, J. R. *Handbook of Adult Education.* New York: Macmillan, 1970.

Smith, R. M., and Associates. *Learning to Learn Across the Lifespan.* San Francisco: Jossey-Bass, 1990.

Stanage, S. *Adult Education and Phenomenological Research.* Melbourne, Fla.: Krieger, 1987.

Tandon, R. "Participatory Evaluation and Research: Main Concepts and Issues." In W. Fernandes, and R. Tandon (eds.), *Participatory Research and Evaluation.* New Delhi: Aruna Printing Press, 1981.

Tennant, M. (ed.). *Adult and Continuing Education in Australia.* New York: Routledge, Chapman & Hall, 1990.

Titmus, C. J. *Strategies for Adult Education: Practices in Western Europe.* Chicago: Follett, 1981.

Titmus, C. J. (ed.). *Lifelong Education for Adults: An International Handbook.* Oxford, England: Pergamon Press, 1989.

Who's Who in America. (41st ed.) Vol. 2. Chicago: Marquis' Who's Who, 1980–1981.

CHAPTER 15

Social, Professional, and Academic Issues

David Deshler

The primary thesis of this chapter is that the field of study of adult education in North America has emerged within a context of social, professional, and academic issues. Sometimes the field has been shaped by its passive reaction, avoidance of conflict, and co-optation. In other instances, it has acted directly to shape issues and their effects on graduate programs, the field of practice, and society. A critical reflection on major social, professional, and academic issues and their relationship with the field of study may increase our capacity to take charge of our destiny rather than be shaped by external forces. The purpose of this chapter is to discuss selected issues in these three areas and their relationship to the field of study.

The term *issue,* as used in this chapter, refers to a dispute; a contention; or a lack of clear consensus regarding values, means, or ends concerning a matter about which multiple decisions can be made. I selected issues for this chapter based on their emergence historically and on the strength of the controversy that they have evoked as viewed from a North American perspective. The list of issues is not intended to be exhaustive but rather a starting point for future questions for discourse among students and scholars in the field. For each issue, I describe the nature of the conflict and the way the issue has been joined or could be joined by the field of study.

Social Issues

Major controversies in human society are usually associated with social movements. These movements provide the context for understanding our past and present values. Adult education emerged historically out of social movements. During the twenty-seven years since the black book was published, the field of practice, the field of study, and the body of knowledge of adult education have existed within the economic, social, and political context of the cold war, racism and human rights, the role and status of women, the arms race and the peace movement, technological change and obsolescence, internationalization and development, and environmental survival. Practitioners, some of whom have participated in our graduate programs, have been involved in social issues. Our professional associations have been actively involved in some of these issues and have ignored others. Social issues have often defined the types of program that we have offered, the content of our academic studies, and the focus of research we have or have not undertaken.

Cold War. Following World War II, the Red scare of 1919 returned in the McCarthy era, a wave of national hysteria about communism. By 1964 when the black book was published, McCarthy had been discredited, but his legacy of commyphobia has continued to define the notions of loyalty and dissent (Law, 1988). After the Cuban revolution of the early 1960s, a wave of anticommunist schools and study groups and the rise of the John Birch Society continued the attack on the United Nations, liberal religion, labor unions, and institutions of higher education.

This anticommunist era defined the nature of what constituted acceptable patriotic loyalty of adult education in the

United States. Even what had previously been considered liberal was suspect, especially the social reformism of the 1930s. From 1919 on, radical adult educators in the United States were frequently accused of being communist or being communist sympathizers. Those educators who advocated social change usually proclaimed that they hated communism and supported individualistic democratic approaches to change. During this period, colleges and universities played down the study of Russian history for fear that they would be accused of being infiltrated by communists or that their professors would be accused of being soft on communism — accusations that meant a decrease in alumni and corporate giving. Teachers and professors were required to sign loyalty oaths. The Highlander Research and Education Center in Tennessee was frequently accused of being communist (Adams, 1975). These conflicts dampened adult education aimed at radical social reform. Graduate programs gave less and less attention to community development and tended to ignore adult education in the People's Republic of China and the Soviet Union until early in the 1980s.

Although Verner, Coit, Lindeman, Hutchins, and Kaplan were forthright in their attacks on McCarthyism, Higham (1960) claims that during the McCarthy era adult educators hid in their specializations. Law (1988) claims that McCarthy succeeded in isolating mainstream adult educators from their impulse toward social movements and forced them to define themselves within the cold war consensus. The community development section in the Adult Education Association (AEA), the national organization, ceased to exist after 1978. The social philosophy section became weak and almost nonexistent. And a few U.S. professors each year have lamented the loss of social commitment in adult education.

The authors of the black book did not specifically mention the anticommunist attack that was flourishing at the time in which they wrote the book (Jensen, Liveright, and Hallenbeck, 1964). They did, however, reaffirm adult education's commitment to liberal democratic enlightenment, but they carefully avoided support of radical adult education that called for collective social action and criticism of U.S. social institutions and they tended to ignore community development. With the fall of the Berlin Wall, the end of the cold war, and the unrest in the Soviet Union, a new historical era is emerging, with potentially new definitions of what is acceptable collective social action for adult educators in North America. The debate over acceptable collective action will be mentioned later in relationship to other social issues.

Racism and Human Rights. When the black book was published, President Kennedy had just been assassinated, and Lyndon Johnson was in the White House. Civil rights legislation, the Adult Basic Education Act, and the Economic Opportunity Act had just been passed. The War on Poverty legislation, in which adult education was viewed as an instrument of national policy, provided funds for community action programs. These programs were initiated partly in response to the civil rights movement and partly in response to poverty and racial unrest (Stubblefield and Keane, 1989). An immediate effect of these programs on adult education was an influx of teachers into the public adult education system. Many administrators and adult education teachers that benefited from this new funding eventually pursued graduate degrees, thereby expanding the number and size of graduate programs. A secondary effect was an increase of applications for membership into the Commission of Professors of Adult Education. The National Association of Public School Adult Education grew rapidly and eventually merged with the AEA to form the American Association of Adult and Continuing Education (AAACE).

Although some nonwhites have enrolled in graduate programs in adult education in the United States, they are still underrepresented in proportion to their presence in the general population. Nonwhites are very scarce among professors of adult education in spite of affirmative action in higher education. For the most part, whites are the predominant group teaching nonwhites in adult education in the United States and in Canada. Race is still an unacknowledged and invisible variable in adult education research in North America. Examples of research on the nature of racism in the provision of adult education (Darkenwald, 1975; Ross, 1989) are few and far between.

Also at issue in adult education's response to the civil rights movement was the type of adult education that should be offered to the nation's poor: skill training to help people enter the labor market or education for social and structural transformation. The legislation funding adult education made sure that radical adult education, with its critique of social structures, would not occur by giving authority for adult education programs to state education departments, the public school system, and poverty boards appointed by local governments and existing human service agencies. The poor, clearly, were not to be in control of their own adult education programs as part of the War on Poverty.

During the last twenty-seven years, racial and human rights issues have arisen in many parts of the world (Blaustein, Clark, and Sigler, 1987). In Canada, conflicts over French identity and language have given rise to a separatist movement in Quebec. In Europe, increasd emigration of guest workers from former colonies has exacerbated racial tensions. Islamic cultural assertiveness has caused human rights tensions in many countries. Racism is still legally defended in South Africa. The class struggle in Latin America is also a struggle of indigenous people against racism. In Central and South America, many adult educators working with indigenous people have been accused of promoting communism, have been abducted, and, in some cases, have been assassinated. Resettlement programs in Southeast Asia and Latin America, with their accompanying adult education programs, often destroy rain forests upon which indigenous people depend for survival. In other parts of the world, the rights of indigenous people have been increasingly contested and violations have been cited. What is emerging out of these conflicts is a growing movement toward universal human rights, a movement in opposition to all forms of political oppression and racism (Donnelly, 1989). The prodemocracy uprisings in Eastern Europe, the Baltic states, and China are, in part, due to protests against abuses of human rights.

Adult education to address human rights issues struggles to exist in the United States through community-based programs. Racial and human rights issues in Latin America, however, have given rise to "popular education," with its emphasis on collective social action. In South Africa, the people's education movement, with its human rights curriculum, is gaining boldness. Adult education in ethnic languages that is designed to preserve native and national cultures is flourishing all over the world. The choice between teaching literacy in dominant official languages or in native languages is often a bitter political choice (Wagner, 1987; Fry and Thurber, 1989). Is the purpose of adult education to assimilate nondominant cultures, or is it to increase appreciation and preservation of minority cultures among dominant cultures?

The human rights movement and its knowledge base have grown over the last twenty-seven years. This movement presents adult educators with many questions: Does the knowledge base of adult education incorporate this universal challenge? Should adult education be actively engaged in confronting human rights injustices? Is our curriculum intended to combat racism by empowering the oppressed? Should our graduate programs prepare professionals to work for human rights? Should our research contribute to the reduction of racism? Do we know what kind of adult education will reduce racism and human rights violations? Do we intend to use adult education to confront those who maintain racism and deny human rights? Should there be a curriculum against oppression for the nonoppressed? These questions are likely to become more intense in our future debate.

Role and Status of Women. Another aspect of human rights is the fundamental challenge to patriarchy presented by the feminist movement, especially during the last ten years. Today, various parts of this movement are expressing root arguments that challenge traditional views of sexuality and identity, gender and work, culture and religion, moral development, economics and the division of labor, and science and the creation of knowledge. The feminist movement involves more than the massive influx of women into the labor force during World War II or women's reentry into higher education during the 1970s and 1980s. It involves more than an equal rights amendment or specific laws to prevent gender discrimination. The feminist movement is concerned about childhood socialization and educational reproduction of the dominant cultural patriarchy. It is concerned about identity and consciousness and the social construction of knowledge (Belenky, Clinchy, Goldberger, and Tarule, 1986) as well as gender-offensive language and sexual harassment. It is concerned about the different levels of power that operate in the concrete practices of women's everyday life (Smith, 1987). It struggles against the prevailing notions that women are knowledge receivers rather than knowledge producers; against unequal career opportunities and pay; against the disproportionate power that society gives to men who invest themselves in activities carried out independently as opposed to women who invest themselves in relational activities carried out in the service of others as wives and mothers (Luttrell, 1988). The feminist movement is concerned about the different meanings of patriarchal hierarchies as well as gender meanings among people in different classes and ethnic traditions and about the increasing burdens of women in subsistence agriculture among the world's poor. Adult education, which challenges women and men to reflect on the social, cultural, economic, and political reproduction of debilitating and constraining gender-conscious thought and action, is central to the feminist movement. The movement is critical of adult education that contributes to the reinforcement of the dominant culture and the reproduction of women's subjugation.

Reading with the contemporary eyes of the feminist movement, we can see the black book, whose authors are all male, as a product of its time. It includes what is now considered gender-offensive language by the authors, sanctioned by the publisher. Twenty-seven years ago, few males anticipated the feminist movement's criticism of adult education practice, research and, above all, male consciousness.

Since the publication of the black book, women have become the majority of students in higher education (U.S. Department of Education, 1987). Most universities have women's study programs, and some have undertaken a feminist curriculum transformation (Aiken and others, 1988). Women students and teachers of adult education have interjected feminist issues into the field of practice and have made significant contributions to the body of knowledge, especially on the struggles of women reentering school and the barriers to their participation (Scott, 1980). The number of female professors of adult education has increased. The quality of their leadership in the AAACE and the CPAE and their research contributions have been exceptional. They have produced a new body of literature, mostly from outside of the mainstream of adult education. Women researchers have documented the reproduction of limited female roles through education (Connel, Ashenden, Kessler, and Dowsett, 1982; Deem, 1980), questioned assumptions underlying adult development (Gilligan, 1982; Belenky and others, 1986), and challenged science's male bias (Keller, 1982).

However, the focus on women as a separate group has also encouraged identification of gender issues as a "woman's problem," enabling men to avoid dealing with gender as a mainstream issue. Recently, astute men have recognized that the feminist movement is not only about the role and status of women but also about the profound rethinking of gender roles for men. Male liberation from counterproductive gender socialization, which limits male psychological, social, and moral maturity, has also become an issue. Research by women social scientists has brought to our awareness the interconnection of gender issues with other root causes of poverty, racial discrimination, militarism, and environmental deterioration (McHale and Choong, 1989; Bordo, 1986).

Although the points of view mentioned above are expressed in a few papers at adult education research conferences and in some of the research journals, can we say that these issues are now mainstream? We must ask ourselves: Is this content integrated into graduate curricula? Are these concerns equally espoused by male and female adult educators and scholars? Are adult educators repelled enough by sexist language to challenge it rather than to ignore it politely? Are scholars of the field sensitive to gender issues in the selection of faculty members, in admissions to graduate programs, in male research bias, in their own socialization, and in their consideration of dual careers? Are we willing to address the fact that females earn only 60 percent of what males earn in the practice of adult education?

We are undoubtedly on the threshold of uncovering how we take for granted our assumptions regarding gender. Will professors and students of adult education actively participate in reflecting on the meaning of gender, and will they recognize that they can construct more liberating and expanded roles for themselves and for the practice of adult education?

Arms Race and Peace Movement. During the last twenty-seven years, the world has experienced the largest arms buildup in the history of civilization. The nuclear arms race between the Soviet Union and the United States reached an all-time high. Military expenditures of the superpowers and developing countries have strained national budgets and have limited investment in education, domestic programs, and development. The effects of the arms race on adult education have been mixed and controversial. They include the rise of the peace movement, increased funds for military adult education, and the addition of programs in peace studies in higher education.

The U.S. involvement in the United Nations peacekeeping action in Korea did not spark much of a peace movement. However, the U.S. involvement in the Vietnam War gave rise to a massive peace movement in North America, with teachins; study circles; public affairs debates; and mass media educational efforts by religious groups, student groups, and many other voluntary associations. Many adult education professionals participated in these activities as individuals. However, there is little evidence that the Adult Education Association and its successor, the AAACE, devoted much effort to the debate that rent the public fabric of North America. The antinuclear movement in Europe also reached North America in the form of Nuclear Freeze and Sane-Freeze, and some adult educators were involved in the movement as individuals. Again, little formal debate about the antinuclear movement took place in professional associations, with the exception of one meeting of the commission of professors at AAACE in 1981. At this meeting in Anaheim, California, a plenary session was devoted to the work of Kekkonen (1989), the Finnish adult educator who won the United Nations Peace award.

One legacy of the Korean and Vietnam Wars was an increase of funds for military adult education and veterans education benefits. In addition, with the advent of the all-voluntary military in the United States, the promise of training and continuing education became the primary argument used by the military to encourage recruitment and retention. The military arranged for military personnel to take courses at community colleges and universities near military bases for academic credit through the Servicemembers Opportunity College (Veeman and Singer, 1989). The Veterans Administration also provided educational benefits. Military adult educators began to participate in large numbers in AAACE, making the Armed Forces section one of the largest groups of adult educators attending national conferences.

Another response to the military buildup has been a sporadic increase in peace studies programs in schools and in some universities (Reardon, 1988). The curricula of these programs are far from homogeneous. They emphasize nuclear disarmament issues, international relations, political science, economic analysis, religious pacifism, international terrorism, racial and ethnic strife, interpersonal peacekeeping, and conflict resolution.

Although increased military spending has meant an increase in adult education military practitioners and additional graduate students in adult education programs, the indirect impact of this spending has been decreased support by the federal government to higher education and social science research. With the dramatic uprisings in Eastern Europe and the Baltic states, the unrest in the Soviet Union, and the military euphoria of the Gulf War, there appears to be little hope that a "peace dividend" from reduction of the military and the cold war will make possible increased government funding for adult education.

Those people who study international development issues in adult education view military budgets of developing countries as major governmental expenditures that displace funding for adult education and other efforts at development. The military in some countries threatens and oppresses adult educators working on behalf of the poor, particularly if their programs are directed toward political action for social justice. The relationship of the arms race to adult education has yet to be debated vigorously among scholars of adult education. Research on the relationship would be helpful and potentially transformative to our field of study.

Technological Change and Obsolescence. Technological obsolescence has been for many years a major rationale for educational reform and advocacy for what is now referred to as human resource development (HRD). The reports committee of the Commission of Professors of Adult Education, which commissioned the black book, stated in their introduction to the book that adults must continue to learn because learning is a requirement for survival in our age of social and technological change. The danger of becoming obsolescent served as the primary rationale for the promotion and study of adult education. It was the reason "why adult education was shifting rapidly from a marginal to a central concern for many educational statesmen; why legislators and educational policy-makers recognize that society now has as great a stake in the continued learning of adults as it ever had in the education of children" (Jensen, Liveright, and Hallenbeck, 1964, p. v).

Technological change and the threat of obsolescence have accelerated during the last twenty-seven years. We are now well into the third industrial revolution, based on computers and information sciences (Bezold and Olson, 1986). We are examining the political economy of information (Mosco and Wasco, 1988), and the impact of ideology and the mass media (Compaine, 1988; Slack and Fejes, 1987; Klapp, 1986). Science 'infoglut' is growing; more than 40,000 scientific journals publish more than one million new articles each year, and experts estimate that the scientific literature doubles every ten to fifteen years (Broad, 1988). Technology has changed the global economy (Guile and Brooks, 1987). Biotechnology will further complicate issues of law, economics, and ethics (Fowle, 1987).

Rachal (1989, p. 7) points out that "without question, the

workplace is the engine that is changing the nature of adult education, and technology is its fuel." About 80 percent of American adult education in 1984 was job related. Businesses and industries in the United States spend well over $30 billion a year on formal training of employees (American Society for Training and Development, 1986). The American Society for Training and Development has over 50,000 members in its national and local chapters, making it by far the largest adult education organization of professionals in North America (American Society for Training and Development, n.d.).

Proliferation of instrumental adult education in North America, in service of the state and of business and industry, has injected values and interests into adult education that are external to its historical interests. Universities are adding graduate programs in human resource development in combination with or distinct from adult education. More graduate students with interests in HRD are entering both adult education and HRD programs (see Chapter Seven). We are told that a failure to increase and improve human resource development in the United States will jeopardize our technical competitiveness with Japan and Europe. The commercialization of adult education has arrived.

Graduate courses in HRD address many professional issues, including (1) the difficulty of justifying training through program evaluation, (2) the problem of increasing students' commitment to the career as well as to the organization, (3) the challenge of providing efficient learning methods appropriate to the workplace, (4) the challenge of relating theory to practice, and (5) the task of balancing human relations and people skills with technical skills. These issues are important. However, four issues go beyond these internal matters.

The first issue concerns the relationship of human resource development with the rest of adult education. Some people do not consider training to be genuine adult education. Others base their definitions of adult education on its voluntariness. HRD practitioners have not traditionally viewed themselves within the broader adult education movement. What or who contributes to this viewpoint, and should it be changed? Several programs at the commission of professors annual meetings of the AAACE have addressed these issues but have found few conceptual or practical solutions.

The second issue concerns the term *human resource development*. This relatively new term has replaced the earlier terms *manpower* and *vocational education* or *vocational training*. *Human resource* is a capitalistic term that is a sister to the idea of human capital investment, which is a cousin to investment for a profitable return. The term makes humans merely one type among other types of resources that are used for production in business and industry. The term blurs the distinction between people as subjects and things as objects, thereby making people objects to be used. The term means that business and industry uses people and that adult education prepares them to be used effectively. I doubt that workers dreamed up this term to refer to themselves. The fact that most human resource training is mandatory rather than voluntary and is initiated by employers rather than employees further confounds the dimensions of the learner as a person. Human resource is probably preferable to the earlier term *manpower,* which was sexist. However, replacing the term *vocational education* with *human resource development* is unfortunate because the earlier concept of "vocation" had a sacred dimension of commitment and calling that helped to link the specific job in the world of work with one's religious values.

The third issue concerns the breadth of purpose of HRD. Its content is driven by organizational productivity goals. Where will adult education take place that can assist in generating critical social perspectives on technology itself (Benne and Tozer, 1987)? Can we expect business and industry to sponsor learning that helps people to reflect on the purposes and practices of the organizations themselves in relationship to public interest and global concerns? For instance, is HRD likely to assist workers in a plant in addressing company policies for disposal of hazardous waste? If it is unreasonable to expect HRD in the workplace to include educating adults to think critically, then where will this type of education occur? The primary problems in our world, even in business and industry, are not rooted in technical matters. Is it possible to detrivialize technical training by adding critical moral and spiritual dimensions to it? Purpel (1989) has suggested that what education in the United States needs is a curriculum for justice and compassion. Education that is merely technical training can make us rich and smart, but not free and wise.

The fourth issue concerns the equality of access to new technologies through adult education. Will rapidly changing technologies increase the abyss between rich and poor nations, between the educated and uneducated? Easy access to global mass media will radically change people's levels of aspiration and feelings of subjective deprivation (Dror, 1988). Human resource development may well be an instrument for widening the technical knowledge gap. Technical obsolescence may be an engine that drives HRD. However, we may need to ask ourselves, through research and the knowledge base, if adult education that is reduced to pragmatism in the service of government and business and industry is sufficient for the survival of human civilization.

Internationalization and Development. Few people would dispute the notion that internationalization and global interdependence have rapidly accelerated during the last twenty-seven years (see Chapter Fourteen). Multinational corporations, international agribusiness, the International Monetary Fund, the World Bank, the European Common Market, the Japanese stock market, instant global news via satellite communications, and international debt crises are all symbols of international interdependency and contention. However, this interdependency has not fulfilled the high hopes following World War II for both democracy and development in poor countries. Twenty-seven years ago people assumed that poverty would be alleviated and democracy would be secured around the world by (1) the transfer of technology to poor countries through extension programs, (2) industrialization and training through Western capital investment, and (3) community development, funded by the United States as a strategy against international communism, that involved local participation without challenge to political structures. The poor nations built up numerous development-related institutions and trained thousands of people in development-related skills, many of them in U.S. and European universities and adult education graduate programs. Yet after a quarter of a century of economic growth, human resource development, and foreign aid, 800 million people live in absolute poverty, the gap between the rich and poor countries has increased (Steidlmeier, 1987), poor countries are in greater debt than ever before (George, 1988), world topsoil is being eroded at about 7 percent per decade, forest area is declining, deserts are expanding, and world hunger is still a problem in spite of the green revolution. What is at issue for the field of study is the nature and purpose of adult education when linked to international development.

The major thesis of Cunningham in Chapter Fourteen is that the ideology of North American adult education has been challenged by competing views, including those of popular education, participatory research, phenomenology, critical theory, critical pedagogy, critical social science, and conflict sociology (see also Chapter Three). All of these theories, many flowing from the South to the North, are relevant to the analysis of the failure of international development.

What should we teach our students, both foreign and domestic, about why development efforts, for the most part, have failed? Some people, particularly those with agricultural backgrounds, tend to hold that what is needed is the transfer of appropriate technology through agricultural cooperatives or investment in nongovernmental organizations (Hanks, 1987). Others think that the training and visit system of the World Bank or research on farming systems will rescue the failing bureaucratic extension systems, which, in the past, have tended to make the rich richer while failing to assist subsistence farmers (Selener, 1989). Still other people believe that popular education and integrated community-based development should be emphasized (Hamilton and Cunningham, 1989; Duke, 1985; Ewert, 1989; Lappe, Schurman, and Danaher, 1987). In addition, some people are questioning the vision of development as modernization in the light of the ethic of sustainability.

A consensus is growing in the international development

literature that the unhappy state of international development is not the result of technological problems but rather political ones. Only a few people in most developing countries have access to resources, public organizations, and legal protection. Creating access for the multitudes requires political change rather than an increase in a country's gross national product, which may benefit only a small group of people. Development should be first and foremost a process of political reform. Agricultural development without land reform is cosmetic (Prosterman, 1987). Community development that fails to redistribute power only reinforces an unjust status quo (Holdcroft, 1982). What the poor need is release from centuries of coercion, condescension, and corruption. People working in development have heretofore ignored the political issues implicit in their work, seeking to substitute technology, capital investment, and trickle-down economic growth for genuine economic and political democracy (Owens, 1987).

The idea that adult education is political is still controversial in North America. Many North American adult educators still think that popular education is for Latin Americans and not for North Americans because it emphasizes social and political analysis and group action rather than individual enlightenment and personal action. Individual versus collective action is also at issue in the distinction between critical thinking and critical theory (Griffin, 1988). Critical theory proponents (Habermas, 1984, 1987) maintain that in order for reflection to be critical, it must be within the larger social political context and must require social action, not just personal theory or organizational renewal. Cunningham in Chapter Fourteen further describes philosophical expressions that have challenged North American political assumptions.

Participants in the meeting at Leeds in 1988 at which the Transformative Research Network was formed disagreed intensely over whether adult education research should be directed toward political, cultural, and social transformation. A majority of researchers there voted that it should be so directed, but a minority felt quite uncomfortable with that stand as well as with the name of the network. The network promotes and funds international research teams that undertake research that can be used for social and political action for social transformation. Examination of the political nature of adult education practice and the creation of knowledge in adult education, with its concomitant controversies, is the result of the internationalization of the field. The internationalization of adult education has brought with it many controversies that were not addressed twenty-seven years ago, including challenges to national parochialism and even the tendency of professors to read only literature produced in their own countries.

Environmental Survival. Since the time in which the black book was published, many changes have occurred in our natural environment and in our consciousness about environmental destruction. Most futurists now acknowledge that environmental concerns top the list of global fears, trends, and plausible cause for pessimism (Marien, 1989). Environmental concerns include the greenhouse effect, climate change, ozone loss, deforestation, species loss, acid rain, toxic waste, trash disposal, drinking water pollution, water salinization, ocean pollution, soil erosion, and indoor air quality (Smil, 1987; Ehrlich and Holdren, 1988; Wilson, 1988; World Commission on Empowerment and Development, 1988; Brown, 1990). The environmental movement has grown steadily as a grass-roots phenomenon on a worldwide basis (Emmelin, 1989).

The environmental movement embraces adult education as the essence of the movement and not just a means to political ends. Environmentalists assume that nothing less than global mind change, including personal as well as social action, is necessary for planetary survival. Consciousness-raising is their primary focus. Poster (1989) claims that the most important changes in contemporary society are taking place not at the level of social action but at the level of language. Harman (1988) states that throughout history the most fundamental changes in societies have come not from the dictates of governments and the results of war but through vast numbers of people changing their minds — sometimes only a little bit. The rapid political changes in Eastern Europe present an example of this theory. Environmentalists usually assume that adult education is central to combining change in consciousness with personal and social action.

Habermas (1984, 1987) has suggested that Western civilization's overemphasis on rational-purposive material success to the exclusion of the moral-interpretive, aesthetic-expressive, and explicative discourse (communication directed toward language itself) has contributed to the environmental crisis. He states that social integration and system reproduction become dysfunctional when rational-purposive discourse and related instrumental action crowd out moral-interpretive discourse, aesthetic-expressive critique, and explicative discourse. The implication of this for adult education is that education must be more than HRD and information transfer from technical elites. That is why the familiar decide-announce-defend process of planners, engineers, and scientists in environmental public affairs cases, a process based on scientific rationality, is dysfunctional.

Environmental conflicts obviously are value-laden and political. Solutions to environmental problems call for individual, organizational, governmental, and international understanding and action. Different solutions reflect different social goals. "Hard research" solutions and degrees of tolerable risk turn out to be political. The capacity of scientists and technological elites to communicate with those who are most likely to benefit and suffer from technological applications is also central to environmental education.

Students with concerns about the environment and aspirations to careers related to these concerns are entering graduate programs in large numbers. New careers in voluntary environmental associations, international development and environment organizations, natural resource management, solid waste management and recycling, energy conservation, social forestry, and low-input agriculture involve adult education and public policy education roles and skills. Will students with concerns about the environment be drawn into graduate programs in adult education? Will adult education be included in their technical higher education? Today, adult education knowledge on environmental public policy education is quite limited and so are the graduate courses that are specific to environmental adult educators and researchers.

There is a crisis in Western society's vision of the future. The demise of colonialism, the domination of international capitalism, the disillusionment with rigid communism, the distrust of technology and industrialization's effect on the environment, the continuation of racism, and the rise of religious fundamentalism have not brought about a cohesive and inspiring image of the future. Is adult education merely an instrumental device in service of and training people for the reproduction of social injustice, inequities, unbridled development, and uncritical modernization? Some of the contemporary social issues that I have mentioned are disturbing, but they provide a starting point for the dialogue essential for the creation of a new vision that can inform the direction of practice, graduate instruction, and the creation of knowledge.

Professional Issues

The authors of the black book tended to assume that the goal of the field of study was a movement toward further professionalization of adult education practice, a trend unquestioned at that time in education, social services, and health services. Graduate programs were to contribute to the definition of the responsibilities of adult educators, establish criteria for the selection of personnel, and provide adequate in-service training so that personnel could develop professional competencies. After twenty-seven years, at least four questions related to professionalization of the field remain: Is professional identity a foundation for the study of adult education? Should the study of adult education promote further professionalization? Should there be general professional standards for the provision of academic instruction in adult education? How is the body of professional knowledge related to practice?

Professional Identity. In spite of enormous efforts on the part of national and international organizations to espouse a common identity under the term *adult education,* the lack of identity under that term persists among practitioners and administrators. For instance, the American Association for Adult and Continuing Education must include two terms in its title in order to accommodate a membership that is quite diverse and for which the meanings of *adult education* and *continuing education* are important distinctions. As discussed earlier, in North America the term *human resource development* has a meaning that is quite different from the meaning of the term *adult education,* which the lay public tends to associate with remedial education.

Titmus (1989) questions the politics of the term *adult education* and questions the global applicability and adequacy of the term. His point is that *adult education* is an academic term created by academics in Europe and North America in a world in which practitioners refer to themselves by many names — trainers, human resource developers, extension agents, labor educators, popular educators, adult basic educators, second language teachers, literacy tutors, health educators, armed forces trainers, public policy educators, community-based educators, gerontology educators, and continuing educators. The field of study assumes inclusivity, while the field of practice assumes diversity of identity by virtue of different subject matter, sponsorship, types of learners, methods, purposes, and contexts.

Merriam and Cunningham (1989, p. 1), at the beginning of the *Handbook of Adult and Continuing Education,* state that "despite the enormous diversity characteristic of the field of adult education, numerous areas of common interest and concern provide a foundation for professional practice." This handbook itself describes far better the diverse identity of adult education than the common elements. Long, in Chapter Four of this book and Griffith in Chapter Five decry the undisciplined nomenclature of adult education as an inhibitor to research. However, the issue is whether the study of adult education can be based on a foundation that lacks common professional identity or whether the substance of the study of adult education as a distinct field is too diverse to be an inclusive field of professional practice. Perhaps adult education is a diverse human activity and not a profession.

Another related question of identity is whether the distinction between adult education and the rest of education, which includes schooling from primary through higher education, is essential for the study of adult education or is just a distinction made for political and organizational purposes. Independence from the rest of education may have been necessary at one time to justify the field of study of adult education. In our efforts to survive in academia, have we created an academic ghetto? Can the field now benefit from addressing common issues faced by the study of education as a whole? Can adult education knowledge now benefit from knowledge about schooling?

Further Professionalization. The debate about further professionalization of the field has its roots, on the one hand, in the idea that the best adult education is a "friend teaching a friend," and, on the other, in the idea that the best adult education must be assured through professionalization. One of several roads to professionalization is the assurance of competence that certification is supposed to bring. Professionalization has many aspects or ingredients, including a code of ethics, a consensus on professional standards consecrated by society, legal protection through licensure, and certification through professional study of the field (Vollmer and Mills, 1966). Graduate programs in adult education, particularly when they are used to further certification, constitute part of the professionalization of the field.

People who oppose the professionalization of the field of adult education declare that increased professionalization increases the gap between the teacher and the learner, thereby reducing the quality of the learning experience rather than increasing it. Part of this gap is caused by the increased use of jargon that accompanies professionalization, mostly through the study of the knowledge of the field. In addition, volunteerism, the heart of the earlier adult education movement, is weakened with increased professionalization.

It can be argued that professionalization increases the costs of adult education and protects the financial interests of the educator rather than protecting the learner from incompetent educators. The control of quality through professionalization has not been well demonstrated. Self-regulation to reduce incompetence and bad practice on the part of professionals such as doctors and lawyers has not worked well. On the contrary, self-regulation has increased the means for professionals to protect themselves from consumer, client, or learner protests (Illich, 1971). Self-regulation has resulted in increased litigation against professionals, which drives up the cost of malpractice insurance and makes lawyers rich. It appears that the lack of professionalization in adult education has saved us from this fate.

Salaries for human service professionals (health, welfare, criminal justice, and education) have increased dramatically, and public criticism about the effectiveness of these professionals has mounted. The latest remedy for these criticisms is called coproduction of services — the community, including volunteers, working with professionals to address community situations. Coproduction is a concept that suggests that professionals alone will always be inadequate to solve community problems. In fact, to depend on them alone condemns them to an impossible responsibility. The police and criminal justice system will never be adequate without coproduction with citizens to prevent criminality and to rehabilitate criminals. Social workers will always be burned out without volunteers to address not only people's immediate needs but to work to prevent structural poverty. The medical profession needs the public to practice preventive health care in order to reduce its emphasis on an illness response system. Schools will always be inadequate without a school-home-work connection. Professionals need to coproduce with each other in partnership. Some people claim that it is the professionals themselves, trying to protect their own turf, that prevent coproduction. Will professionalism in adult education lead toward or away from coproduction?

The trend toward professionalization of adult education has marched on in spite of the opposition. In the United States, many states require that educators have adult education teaching credentials to teach in public adult education systems (Howe, 1978). More continuing education is being mandated by government for various professions. Several years ago a movement to oppose lifelong education and mandated continuing education was launched in the United States (Ohliger, 1974, 1985; Phillips, 1987). Adult educators still lack consensus regarding credentialing and mandatory continuing education.

The role of graduate programs in adult education as part of the process of professionalization has received the attention of the Commission of Professors of Adult Education on several occasions during the last twenty years (Wright, 1970; Knox, 1973; Griffith and Marcus, 1976; Carlson, 1977; Cameron, Rockhill, and Wright, 1978). At least two CPAE task forces have brought reports on the topic to annual meetings and at least three opening sessions at these meetings have featured the topic. These discussions have always been filled with disagreement on the desirability of graduate programs contributing to further professionalization, although the majority of those who speak appear to favor more professionalization. Perhaps the group in favor of professionalization may feel that increased professionalization could boost the status of adult education graduate programs within colleges of education in the United States. Is the effort toward further professionalization on the part of adult educators self-serving or a genuine movement toward protecting the public and improving practice? Most people agree that adult education has not yet reached the status of a profession. Some see this as a blessing in disguise.

Professional Standards. Applications for membership into the CPAE increased rapidly, particularly in the 1970s, from the growth of new graduate programs in adult education. The question of whether there should be professional standards for graduate programs in adult education became an issue at annual meetings. Some members alleged that colleges of education with decreasing graduate enrollments were creating adult education graduate programs to attract students for underutilized education professors. The perceived lack of quality of faculty for these new programs was at issue; were the programs being staffed only with education faculty with little former interest or preparation in adult education and who were not in demand for other education graduate degrees? Peters and Kreitlow, in Chapter Seven, describe the action taken by the CPAE to initiate standards. The CPAE also offered to provide consulting services to universities in the process of starting new programs. The essential nature of content of graduate programs and whether graduate education prepares practitioners any better than ad hoc apprenticeships is at question. It has yet to be seen whether these standards will have any effect on the quality of graduate programs in adult education through department self-study or external accreditation teams.

Professional Knowledge and Practice. At present, scholars do not agree about the relationship between professional knowledge or theory and practice. In Chapter Two, Cervero described four viewpoints. In the first viewpoint, adult education is carried out without references to an organized body of professional knowledge and theory. The second view holds that a body of knowledge developed through the scientific process should be applied to practice so that practice can be improved. The third view holds that the best way to improve practice is to uncover and critique the informal theory that practitioners use in their work. The fourth view sees a fundamental unity between theory and practice, highlights the ideological character of all knowledge, and argues that adult education can be improved by fostering emancipation. These positions parallel the conflict about research paradigms in social science. The empirical-analytic group favors application of theory to practice. The interpretist group favors the uncovering of informal theory within practice. The critical theorists favor emancipatory creation of knowlege through participatory research by practitioners (Merriam, Chapter Four).

Academic Issues

Before 1950, few universities recognized the field of adult education. The majority of universities, from all areas of the world, that offer degrees in this field did not do so until after 1969. According to Touchette (1989, p. 1), status and "recognition by universities of adult education as a field of academic study was preceded: (1) by the creation of associations of adult education; (2) by the constitution of consultative bodies; (3) by the establishment of governmental administration division; and it is consecrated: (4) by the creation of professional associations of adult educators; (5) by the creation of scientific associations of research workers; and (6) by the publication of research journals." Much of this work outside the universities had been well under way by the time the black book was published. Historically, the black book provided adult educators with the justification for strengthening the emerging adult education graduate programs within universities. According to Touchette (1989, p. 2), "In many instances, universities begin to offer a single course in the new field of study. Academic recognition occurs with the creation of a specific degree and is consecrated with the establishment of an independent unit. The evolution of the new field of study is represented by the number of universities from every area of the world who offer a degree in the field and by a certain consensus on the specific contents of the courses and the domains of research." In Chapter Seven, Peters and Kreitlow describe the stages of evolution of graduate study of adult education and some of the setbacks that some of the programs have suffered. However, how graduate programs achieve these goals is still at issue: Which organizational survival strategies are most effective for adult education graduate programs? What constitutes the domain of knowledge of the study of adult education? How can research legitimacy be achieved for adult education?

Organizational Survival in Academia. There are four general arguments or strategies that adult educators use to politically justify the inclusion of adult education graduate study within higher education. The first strategy, called *survival by political constituency,* justifies adult education graduate programs by referring to political support (that is, continuing education of the professions) from a growing constituency outside academia. This strategy may be effective, based on how much the university depends on outside political constituencies and the mission of the university in responding to these constituencies. This strategy also can attract graduate students from an influential constituency. These graduate students tend to be part-time students, often residing large distances from the university, and they tend to be middle and upper-middle class. Some programs have initiated distance education to expand this political base.

Would the field have been different if it had included more graduates with less political power from lower socioeconomic status or a greater cultural and racial diversity? Will more diverse students be included in the future?

The second strategy, called *survival by specialization,* is based on a claim of specialized knowledge for specific forms or program areas of adult education, thereby attracting graduate students who want career specializations that are congruent with faculty expertise. This strategy has worked for some institutions, which have focused on adult basic education, extension education, educational gerontology, or other program specializations. Peters and Kreitlow ask in Chapter Seven whether graduate programs are driven by the laws of supply and demand for specializations or by scholarly values.

The third strategy, called *survival by age domain,* seeks to legitimize adult education graduate programs by claiming that the domain of adult learning and the provision of nonschool education is as important as child learning and schooling. One less than persuasive aspect of this argument is that occupational, agricultural, home economics, environmental, and science education, as graduate program areas, also claim both child and adult domains, based on the application of their subject matter area to both child and adult constituencies through provider organizations.

Justifying graduate programs on the basis of nonschool providers puts adult education at a disadvantage in comparison to schooling, which is much more standardized and universally recognized as a societal function. The andragogy versus pedagogy argument has tended to be persuasive with only some educators. The notion of self-directed learning as the domain of adulthood is weak as an age domain argument because children can also engage in self-directed learning. Titmus (1989) points out that the organization of adult education according to age is not as helpful as distinctions according to social situations that transcend age divisions, such as special provision for women, ethnic minorities, parents, workers, and communities. He asks if it would be helpful to give more attention to roles, situations, tasks, and purposes, all socially defined phenomena.

The fourth strategy, called *survival by merger,* is evident in academic institutions in which adult education programs have not achieved independence. For instance, some programs will be called agriculture-extension education, occupational-adult education, higher-continuing education, community college–continuing education, and educational administration–adult education, to name a few. These names may represent the expansion of an existing program to include adult and continuing education as a new or marginal program, or they may be the result of co-optation. Some of these mergers turn out to be unhappy marriages with an unequal distribution of power, resources, and responsibilities. These programs are often unattractive to potential graduate students, and sometimes the student advisers do not know the literature of adult education. Institutional contexts have surely shaped our field.

Are there some academic homes that are better for adult education than others, such as colleges of education, arts and sciences, or agriculture? Touchette (1989, p. 15) states that "One of the most pressing questions now asked of the field is where are its natural links, in the social sciences (politics, economics, sociology, industrial-relations, social services, anthropology) or in education? The political consequences of the answer to this question, for the growth of the field are crucial." Touchette, in his worldwide survey of ninety-four graduate programs in adult education (Europe, North America, Africa, Central and South America), found that 63 percent had achieved self-sustaining administrative independence by 1982. He comments that "It is only in the U.S. that such status was not granted by the majority of universities. This characteristic is more evident when adult education has a link with a school of education" (1989, p. 13). It is clear that strategies for achieving relative autonomy and interdependence are still at issue, especially in the United States.

Body of Knowledge. Generating a consensus about what constitutes the domains of knowledge of a field of study is essential to the field's status and recognition in academia. The black book provided a vision of that consensus twenty-seven years ago. Is there a consensus today concerning the major categories of knowledge of adult education? Touchette (1989) claims to have found considerable consensus about the boundaries of the contents of adult education as an academic field of study in his analysis of 654 courses offered in 1982 by 81 universities throughout the world. He grouped the contents of the courses into the following six domains of knowledge, which are research categories: "(1) society, adult education and social change, (2) nature, orientations, theories, research, problems and trends of adult education, (3) domains of adult education, (4) organization and administration of adult education, (5) elaboration and evaluation of adult education activities, and (6) instrumentation, didactics, adult learners and adult learning, and adult educators" (Touchette, 1989, p. 9). The degree of consensus that Touchette found should be debated, since he claimed that a certain consensus was achieved if between 35 percent and 67 percent of the universities reported congruent content.

The curricula in graduate programs also differ in emphasis. The areas of emphasis include (1) practical skills versus analytical research orientations; (2) extent of use of the disciplines of psychology, sociology, economics, political science, history, anthropology, and philosophy; (3) flexibility or rigidity of course and degree requirements; (4) extent of the internationalization of the curriculum; (5) degree of commitment to social reconstruction through community-based adult education, community development, or popular education; (6) degree of commitment to human resource development; and (7) degree of participation and control on the part of graduate students in their own learning decisions.

Another important question about the body of knowledge is who determines and creates it. How much influence do the host university's academic research tradition, culture, and degree requirements exert? Is the body of knowledge driven by the demands of domestic or international graduate students? Is it the product of the special interests of professors? Is it the product of research? Is it the result of miscellaneous ingredients borrowed from the disciplines from which professors have migrated? Is it the product of publications and their selectivity? Or is the body of knowledge the product of external funding of projects and research? Different mixtures of the above would probably account for some of the variation among university programs. Again, it is the variation that should be debated for the sake of reshaping the body of knowledge.

Another area of tension in regard to the body of knowledge is the relationship of the body of knowledge to other disciplines. Is adult education a discipline among disciplines, or is the body of knowledge a field of practice that borrows from other disciplines similar to the way that medicine is informed by several disciplines? This situation would strengthen the links between a field of practice and the disciplines. Almost all of the founding professors of adult education came from disciplines other than education, which explains the strong emphasis on borrowing from other disciplines in the black book (Jensen, Liveright, and Hallenbeck, 1964). Do the current professors with majors in adult education have the same links with the other disciplines? Do these links affect the nature of the body of knowledge?

Still another point of tension is over the degree to which the body of knowledge of adult education is dominated by Western cultural and academic ways of thinking and styles of academic research. This issue is most in evidence at international conferences and sometimes in graduate courses when non-Western students participate. The body of knowledge will undoubtedly change through adult educators' greater international discourse, travel, and consultation (Fry and Thurber, 1989).

Research Legitimacy. One of the most crucial ways to establish a field of study is to legitimize its field of knowledge through research. When the black book was published, Campbell and Stanley (1963), the "Bible" of positivist social science research had just been published. Long, in Chapter Four, complains that the body of knowledge of adult education in North America, in many ways, failed to live up to this positivist paradigm. He states that it has lacked coherence, accumulative effort, and theoretical testing. His positivist perspective reflects the dominant research position in North America over the last twenty-seven years. That position is currently being challenged. Merriam, in Chapter Three, presents the interpretive (historical-hermeneutical) paradigm and the critical theory paradigm as alternatives to the positivist paradigm.

It is apparent that the authors in this book do not agree on the best paradigm. Long declares that a phenomenological subject orientation (that is, interpretive paradigm) defeats the development of knowledge. In contrast, Cunningham praises the advent of phenomenology and critical theory (Habermas, 1984, 1987).

Kemmis (1989) suggests that each paradigm has implicit differences in social relations. Positivist research is third-person research. Interpretive research is second-person research. And Critical theory is first-person research. Those people who work from each of these paradigms also differ in their views regarding the nature of education as an object of research, educational philosophy, the purposes of research, the forms of research knowledge, educational values, goals of educational reform, forms of reasoning, and human nature. The dispute is not just over methods. It is fundamental, and it is unlikely to dissipate soon.

The following questions are just a few that provoke dialogue among those people who believe in these different paradigms: Does scholarship follow market demand, or does it have a life of its own independent from practice? Who should determine the focus and methodology of research? Should research be put to the task of social transformation or to the task of exploring whatever the individual researcher values? Who produces, controls, and benefits from research. Is participatory research legitimate for doctoral research? To whom is the researcher accountable—to academic colleagues in the field of study through peer review, to the institution of higher education, to external funders, to practitioners, to the demands of social and historical circumstances, or to himself or herself? What are the rights of students in the selection of the focus and methodology of research? Do faculty members have a right to require students to research what serves the faculty members' interests?

A Fundamental Future Issue

This chapter has presented for critical reflection selected social, professional, and academic issues, which have formed much of the debate in adult education since the black book was published.

To forecast or project the substance of future debate is always precarious. However, the most fundamental issue that has yet to be vigorously joined, and that is likely to be debated in the future, is the use of adult education as a tool of social policy to reproduce instrumental goals set by government and business and industry to primarily serve the ends of people who have power and wealth. The other side of this issue is the use of adult education as a major force in service of social movements for justice, peace, human rights, ecological sustainability, and empowerment, particularly among those who at present lack political and economic privilege. In short, to what extent will adult education serve democratic purposes? If the field of study takes a critical perspective on this debate and takes charge of its own destiny for the sake of its practitioners and for those it is serving, it will avoid becoming an unwitting accomplice to the reproduction of social values and purposes that are not its own.

References

Adams, F. *Unearthing Seeds of Fire.* Winston-Salem, N.C.: Blair, 1975.

Aiken, S. H., and others. *Changing Our Minds: Feminist Transformations of Knowledge.* Albany: State University of New York Press, 1988.

American Society for Training and Development. *Facts About Training and the American Society for Training and Development.* Alexandria, Va.: American Society for Training and Development, n.d.

American Society for Training and Development. *Serving the New Corporation.* Alexandria, Va.: American Society for Training and Development, 1986.

Belenky, M. F., Clinchy, B. M., Goldberger, N. R., and Tarule, J. M. *Women's Ways of Knowing: The Development of Self, Voice and Mind.* New York: Basic Books, 1986.

Benne, K. D., and Tozer, S. (eds.). *National Society for the Study of Education, 86 Yearbook.* Part 2: *Society as Educator in an Age of Transition.* Chicago: University of Chicago Press, 1987.

Bezold, C., and Olson, R. L. *The Information Millennium: Alter-*

native Futures. Washington, D.C.: Information Industry Association, 1986.

Blaustein, A. P., Clark, R. S., and Sigler, J. A. *Human Rights Sourcebook.* New York: Paragon House, 1987.

Bordo, S. "The Cartesian Masculinization of Thought." *Signs: Journal of Women in Culture and Society,* 1986, *11* (3), 16–28.

Broad, W. J. "Science Can't Keep Up with the Flood of New Journals." *New York Times,* Feb. 16, 1988, p. 61.

Brown, L. R., and Associates. *State of the World 1989: A Worldwatch Institute Report on Progress Toward a Sustainable Society.* New York: Norton, 1990.

Cameron, C., Rockhill, K., and Wright, J. "Certification: An Examination of the Issues by and for Adult Educators." Paper presented at annual meeting of the Commission of Professors of Adult Education, San Antonio, Oct. 1978.

Campbell, D. T., and Stanley, J. C. *Experimental and Quasi-Experimental Designs for Research.* Skokie, Ill.: Rand McNalley, 1963.

Carlson, R. A. "Professionalization of Adult Education: An Historical-Philosophical Analysis." *Adult Education,* 1977, *28* (1), 53–63.

Compaine, B. M. (ed.). *Issues in New Information Technology.* Norwood, N.J.: Ablex, 1988.

Connel, R. W., Ashenden, D. J., Kessler, S., and Dowsett. *Making the Difference: Schools, Families and Social Division.* London: Allen & Unwin, 1982.

Darkenwald, G. G. "Some Effects of the 'Obvious Variable': Teacher's Race and Holding Power with Black Adult Students." *Sociology of Education,* 1975, *48* (4), 420–431.

Deem, R. (ed.). *Schooling for Women's Work.* London: Routledge & Kegan Paul, 1980.

Donnelly, J. *Universal Human Rights in Theory and Practice.* Ithaca, N.Y.: Cornell University Press, 1989.

Dror, Y. "World Politics Toward the 21st Century." *Futures* 1988, *20* (1), 46–53.

Duke, C. (ed.). *Combating Poverty Through Adult Education: National Development Strategies.* London: Croom Helm, 1985.

Ehrlich, P. R., and Holdren, J. P. (eds.). *The Cassandra Conference:*

Resources and the Human Predicament. College Station: Texas A&M University Press, 1988.

Emmelin, L. "Environmental Education." In C. J. Titmus (ed.), *Lifelong Education for Adults: An International Handbook.* Elmsford, N.Y.: Pergamon Press, 1989.

Ewert, D. M. "Adult Education and International Development." In S. B. Merriam and P. M. Cunningham (eds.), *Handbook of Adult and Continuing Education.* San Francisco: Jossey-Bass, 1989.

Fowle, J. R. (ed.). *Application of Biotechnology: Environmental and Policy Issues.* Boulder, Colo.: Westview Press, 1987.

Fry, G. W., and Thurber, C. E. *The International Education of the Development Consultant: Communicating with Peasants and Princes.* Elmsford, N.Y.: Pergamon Press, 1989.

George, S. *A Fate Worse than Debt: The World Financial Crisis and the Poor.* New York: Grove Press, 1988.

Gilligan, C. *In a Different Voice: Psychological Theory and Women's Development.* Cambridge, Mass.: Harvard University Press, 1982.

Griffin, C. "Critical Thinking and Critical Theory in Adult Education." In M. Zukas (ed.), *Transatlantic Dialogue.* Leeds, England: School of Continuing Education, University of Leeds, 1988.

Griffith, W. S., and Marcus, E. E. "Accreditation, Certification and Licensing for Adult Education Teachers." Chicago: University of Chicago, 1976. (Mimeographed.)

Guile, B. R., and Brooks, H. (eds.). *Technology and Global Industry: Companies and Nations in the World Economy.* Washington, D.C.: National Academy Press, 1987.

Habermas, J. *The Theory of Communicative Action.* (T. McCarthy, trans.) Vol. 1. Boston: Beacon Press, 1984.

Habermas, J. *The Theory of Communicative Action.* (T. McCarthy, trans.) Vol. 2. Boston: Beacon Press, 1987.

Hamilton, E., and Cunningham, P. M. "Community-Based Adult Education." In S. B. Merriam and P. M. Cunningham (eds.), *Handbook of Adult and Continuing Education.* San Francisco: Jossey-Bass, 1989.

Hanks, S. H. (ed.). *Privatization of Development.* San Francisco: Institute for Contemporary Studies, 1987.

Harman, W. *Global Mind Change: The Promise of the Last Years of the Twentieth Century.* Indianapolis, Ind.: Knowledge Systems, 1988.

Higham, H. H. "Comments to Liberal Adult Education Workshop, 1960 AEA Conference." *Adult Leadership,* 1960, *9* (7), 229.

Holdcroft, L. E. "The Rise and Fall of Community Development in Developing Countries, 1950–1965: A Critical Analysis and Implications." In G. E. Jones and M. J. Rolls (eds.), *Progress in Rural Extension and Community Development.* Vol. 1. New York: Wiley, 1982.

Howe, P. A. "Certification Practices in Adult Education." Unpublished master's thesis, Department of Education, Cornell University, 1978.

Illich, I. *Deschooling Society.* New York: Harper & Row, 1970.

Jensen, G., Liveright, A. A., and Hallenbeck, W. (eds.). *Adult Education: Outlines of an Emerging Field of University Study.* Washington, D.C.: American Association for Adult and Continuing Education, 1964.

Keller, E. F. "Feminism and Science." *Signs: Journal of Women in Culture and Society,* 1982, *7* (3), 589–602.

Kemmis, S. "Metatheory and Metapractice in Educational Theorising and Research." Unpublished manuscript, Deakin University, Geelong, Australia, 1989.

Klapp, O. *Overload and Boredom.* Westport, Conn.: Greenwood, 1986.

Knox, A. B. *Development of Adult Education Graduate Programs.* Washington, D.C.: American Association for Adult and Continuing Education, 1973.

Kokkonen, H. "Peace Education." In C. J. Titmus (ed.), *Lifelong Education for Adults: An International Handbook.* Oxford, England: Pergamon Press, 1989.

Lappe, F. M., Schurman, R., and Danaher, K. *Betraying the National Interest.* New York: Grove Press, 1987.

Law, M. "Adult Education, McCarthyism and the Cold War." In C. E. Warren (ed.), *Proceedings of the 29th Annual Adult Education Research Conference.* Calgary, Canada: University of Calgary, 1988.

Luttrell, W. "Different Women's Ways of Knowing: A Feminist Perspective on the Intersection of Gender, Race and Class in the Social Construction of Knowledge." In M. Zukas (ed.), *Papers from the Transatlantic Dialogue.* Leeds, England: School of Continuing Education, University of Leeds, 1988.

McHale, M. C., and Choong, P. (eds.). "Gender and Change." *Futures,* 1989, *21* (1), 1–110.

Marien, M. *Future Survey Annual 1988–1989.* Bethesda. Md.: World Future Society, 1989.

Merriam, S. B., and Cunningham, P. M. (eds.). *Handbook of Adult and Continuing Education.* San Francisco: Jossey-Bass, 1989.

Mosco, V., and Wasco, J. (eds.). *The Political Economy of Information.* Madison: University of Wisconsin Press, 1988.

Ohliger, J. "Is Lifelong Education a Guarantee of Permanent Inadequacy?" *Convergence,* 1974, *7* (2), 47–58, 74.

Ohliger, J. *Basic Choices in Adult Education.* Madison, Wis.: Basic Choices, 1985.

Owens, E. *The Future of Freedom in the Developing World: Economic Development as Political Reform.* Elmsford, N.Y.: Pergamon Press, 1987.

Phillips, L. E. "Is Mandatory Continuing Education Working?" *MOBIUS,* 1987, *7* (1), 57–63.

Poster, M. *Critical Theory and Poststructuralism: In Search of a Context.* Ithaca, N.Y.: Cornell University Press, 1989.

Prosterman, R. L. *Land Reform and Democratic Development.* Baltimore, Md.: Johns Hopkins University Press, 1987.

Purpel, D. E. *The Moral and Spiritual Crisis in Education: A Curriculum for Justice and Compassion in Education.* Granby, Mass.: Bergin & Garvey, 1989.

Rachal, J. R. "The Social Context of Adult and Continuing Education." In S. B. Merriam and P. M. Cunningham (eds.), *Handbook of Adult and Continuing Education.* San Francisco: Jossey-Bass, 1989.

Reardon, B. A. *Comprehensive Peace Education: Educating for Global Responsibility.* New York: Teachers College Press, 1988.

Ross, J. M. "Comparative Analysis of Recent North American Research on Women and Minorities." Paper presented at the

7th World Congress of Comparative Education, Montreal, June 1989.

Scott, N. A. *Returning Women Students: A Review of Research and Descriptive Studies.* Washington, D.C.: National Association of Women Deans, Administrators and Counselors, 1980.

Selener, D. "The Historical Development of the Training and Visit System of Agricultural Extension: Implications for Developing Countries." Unpublished master's thesis, Department of Education, Cornell University, 1989.

Slack, J. D., and Fejes, F. (eds.). *The Ideology of the Information Age.* Norwood, N.J.: Ablex, 1987.

Smil, V. *Energy, Food, Environment: Realities, Myths, Options.* New York: Oxford University Press, 1987.

Smith, D. *The Everyday World as Problematic: A Feminist Sociology.* Boston: Northeastern University Press, 1987.

Steidlmeier, P. *The Paradox of Poverty: A Reappraisal of Economic Development Policy.* Cambridge, Mass.: Ballinger, 1987.

Stubblefield, H. W., and Keane, P. "The History of Adult and Continuing Education." In S. B. Merriam and P. M. Cunningham (eds.), *Handbook of Adult and Continuing Education.* San Francisco: Jossey-Bass, 1989.

Titmus, C. J. "Adult Education as Concept and Structure: An Agenda for Research." Paper presented at the 7th World Congress of Comparative Education, Montreal, June 1989.

Titmus, C. J., Buttedahl, P., Ironside, D., and Lengrand, P. *Terminology of Adult Education.* Paris: UNESCO, 1979.

Touchette, C. "A Comparative Study of Andragogy (Adult Education) as a Field of Academic Study in the World." Paper presented at the 7th World Congress of Comparative Education, Montreal, June, 1989.

U.S. Department of Education, Center for Education Statistics. *Digest of Educational Statistics.* Washington, D.C.: U.S. Government Printing Office, 1987.

Veeman, F. C., and Singer, H. "Armed Forces." In S. B. Merriam and P. M. Cunningham (eds.), *Handbook of Adult and Continuing Education.* San Francisco: Jossey-Bass, 1989.

Vollmer, H. M., and Mills, D. L. *Professionalization.* Englewood Cliffs, N.J.: Prentice-Hall, 1966.

Wagner, D. (ed.). *The Future of Literacy in a Changing World.* Elmsford, N.Y.: Pergamon Press, 1987.

Watkins, K. "Business and Industry." In S. B. Merriam and P. M. Cunningham (eds.), *Handbook of Adult and Continuing Education.* San Francisco: Jossey-Bass, 1989.

Wilson, E. O. (ed.). *Biodiversity.* Washington, D.C.: National Academy Press, 1988.

The World Commission on Environment and Development. *Our Common Future.* New York: Oxford University Press, 1988.

Wright, J. W. "The Professionalization of Practitioners in the Institutionalized Occupation of Adult Education." Unpublished doctoral dissertation, Department of Education, Cornell University, 1970.

CHAPTER 16

Advancing the Study of Adult Education: A Summary Perspective

John M. Peters

The authors of this book have ably described the evolution of the field of study since the publication of the black book in 1964. They also speculated about the future of the field in terms of their particular chapter topics. In doing so, they identified the objects of discourse in the field, the tools that people in the field have used to forge their studies, the locations in which people work, and the aims and ideologies that have guided people's inquiries — all elements that Foucault (1972) suggests should be included in any analysis of a field of study. Important changes in these elements have occurred in the field of study over the past quarter century, changes that suggest themes that characterize the growth of the field and its potential for further development. My task in this chapter is to discuss these themes and to offer my own thoughts about how the field of study might be advanced from here.

Six themes can be discerned from an analysis of this book's contents. First, the field has significantly expanded its knowledge base and the composition of its several domains of

421

knowledge. Second, early dependency of the field of study on related disciplines has lessened. Third, the paradigms of thought concerning research methodologies appropriate to the study of adult education have changed. Fourth, scholars in the field have developed a better understanding of the relationship between the field of study and the broad area of adult education practice, and they have exhibited a more sensitive and sophisticated approach to integrating the two. Fifth, graduate programs have grown exponentially since 1964, and they appear to be developing a common core of course domains in adult education. And sixth, the field of study has taken on a stronger international focus. I will discuss each of these themes in terms of what has happened since 1964 and what might happen in the future.

The Knowledge Base

The predominant theme of this book relates to the epistemology of the field. It is not by accident that the authors and editors repeatedly refer to the *knowledge base* of adult education practice, as unwieldy as that term might be. Scholars and practitioners alike have added significantly to this knowledge base since 1964, building on but also departing from the outline drawn up by the authors of the black book. The knowledge base is constituted of the objects of scholar and practitioner discourse about the field and its many elements. It is represented by the theories, models, concepts, descriptions, and data that university faculty members and students usually are concerned with in their study of the field and by what they and practitioners in the field know from experience. This constitutes the body of knowledge of the field. Although university scholars do not have exclusive dominion over all knowledge in the field and practitioners of all sorts indeed share in the production of knowledge, the focus of this book is on university-based study of adult education, or what Long in Chapter Four calls "formal knowledge." I will focus here on the domains of the knowledge base that are generally associated with academic study but also address the problem of relating university study to the broader field of practice.

Several reviews of literature have chronicled noticeable

shifts in the topics and scope of our discourse about adult education since the era of the black book. (Dickinson and Rusnell, 1971; Long and Agyekum, 1974; Peters and Banks, 1982; Long, 1983c). Deshler and Hagan (1989) examined these reviews and identified "three somewhat overlapping phases of research history. . . . The first phase emphasized atheoretical program description. . . . The second phase emphasized improvement of research methods and designs patterned after the natural sciences. . . . The third phase, which is currently underway, emphasizes theory building and definition of research territory" (p. 148).

The first phase lasted into the 1960s, the second into the late 1970s, and as indicated, the third phase is taking place now. Reviews of the knowledge base have identified a variety of domains that have served as the focus of research and writing over the past quarter century. Long, who has published more such reviews than anyone else (Long and Agyekum, 1974; Long, 1977, 1983a, 1983b, 1983c, 1989), discussed in Chapter Four of this book six domains of knowledge that he believes illustrate our current discourse about adult education: andragogy, learning projects, participation in learning activities, perspective transformation, program planning, and self-directed learning.

Long's list suggests that the knowledge base is becoming more specialized and diversified. Except for the domain of program planning, the other five domains of Long's list could be considered as subsets of adult learning. Earlier lists of typical domains of research have referred only to the general area of adult learning (Deshler and Hagan, 1989), not to specific areas within that domain.

Long does not identify in Chapter Four an important trend toward further specialization in research on practice, a trend noted by Jarvis in Chapter One. This trend is very visible in the area of adult basic education, an area of practice that exploded with the infusion of federal funding in the United States in the mid sixties. Staff development programs in ABE required a knowledge base and university faculty members in adult education were called upon to serve this need. At least two journals have been developed especially for this area of the field, and the general literature in the area has grown significantly.

At the time of this writing, a new national research center for adult literacy is being funded by the federal government.

The knowledge base in other areas of specialization has also grown over the past quarter century. These areas include continuing professional education (Houle, 1980; Cervero, 1988), continuing higher education (Houle, 1973; Aslanian and Brickell, 1980), distance education (Garrison, 1989), and education in the workplace (Marsick, 1987). Major books on philosophy (Elias and Merriam, 1980), history (Knowles, 1983; Stubblefield, 1988), research (Long, Hiemstra, and Associates, 1980), comparative education (Charters, 1981), and learning to learn (Smith, 1990) are illustrative of the diversity and specialization that has characterized the knowledge base since 1964.

Other areas of growth include critical theory (Carr and Kemmis, 1986; Collins and Plumb, 1989; Merriam, Chapter Three of this book), and international adult education (Titmus, 1989; Cunningham, Chapter Fourteen). The literature on education for social change is also growing once again (Griffin, 1987; Thompson, 1980; Bell, Gaventa, and Peters, 1990). Cunningham points out in Chapter Fourteen how influences from the Third World have been felt in research circles in North America, although Rubenson (1982) criticized American scholars for their neglect of literature produced in other countries of the Western world. Most of the recent work in critical theory and education for social change has been presented in international forums, although it is appearing in greater regularity in North American forums (Cunningham, Chapter Fourteen).

Additional growth has occurred in related disciplines. One of the most significant areas of growth in the related disciplines is the area of adult development. In fact, many scholars in adult education view this domain as a domain of adult education research, even though the study of adult development is mainly the province of disciplines such as psychology, social psychology, and sociology. This area is so closely related to the interests of scholars in adult education that it frequently shows up as a topic of required courses in graduate programs (Peters and Kreitlow, Chapter Seven), and several important publications on the topic are written by adult educators, especially on its connection with adult learning (Knox, 1977). Cognitive psychology is also an area of growth within the related discipline of psychology. The advances made in knowledge about learning in this area have begun to transfer to adult education (Fellenz and Conti, 1989).

Knowledge in these areas is not additive, so the whole knowledge base is something more than the sum of these parts. In fact, the knowledge domains combine to produce a multifaceted knowledge base of adult education. The composition of the resulting knowledge base can be characterized as very general, very fragmented over several specialty interests, but showing promise of depth in some areas. The knowledge base continues to develop, but unevenly so. Concepts, typologies, constructs, empirical results, and descriptions tend to be set alongside one another rather than built on one another, thus spreading the knowledge base across ever-broadening territory. However, this is necessary (and expected) in a relatively young field of study so that people who study the field can have a menu of possible domains from which to choose the ones that offer the greatest promise of further development. The field of study needed to be put forward in this manner, however tentative and ambiguous it may initially be.

Scholars in the field have been particularly critical of the field's alleged atheoretical knowledge base (Boshier, 1978; Long, Chapter Four). However, Deshler and Hagan (1989) argue that "the call [for theory] has, for the most part, been heeded" (p. 154). They go on to suggest ways in which scholars have attempted to develop theory. They cite researchers' attempts to "generate theory unique to adult learning and development; build on critical theory; borrow and reformulate theory from different disciplines, test theory through international comparative research; and synthesize through meta-research" (pp. 154–155). Their review is one of the best indicators that a knowledge base in adult education is beginning to take on a distinctive form. However, the relationship of this evolving knowledge base to the disciplines and other fields of professional study remains an issue.

Relationship to Disciplines and Other Fields of Study

The initial relationship of the field of study to disciplines was described in the black book. The disciplines were a primary source of knowledge for adult education before the black book was published and for some years afterward. However, evidence suggests that the field is being weaned from its earlier dependency on the disciplines as a primary source of knowledge. The discourse of our field reflects this shift. Jarvis (Chapter One) points out that the knowledge base of related disciplines is omitted from adult educators' everyday thought and language and is regarded specifically as adult education knowledge. Jarvis further points out that this is a sign of growing maturity of the field of study.

Perhaps the strongest evidence of this changed relationship is contained in the present book. We set out to have selected authors describe particular disciplines and how they inform the study of adult education. However, we were probably not particularly reflective about this decision and assumed that the authors would summarize concepts, theories, models, and so forth found in disciplines that might "apply" to adult education. The chapters, for the most part, describe related disciplines *in terms of adult education*. For example, Tennant (Chapter Eight) examines potential contributions of psychology in terms of principles of adult teaching and learning, which he claims "have provided direction for the development of adult education practice and have set the agenda for the development of theory and research." Knox's review of administration in Chapter Nine, however, illustrates an important change in the way administration has been studied since 1964. Essert's review of administration in the black book was almost totally a review of concepts, theories, and models found in the related disciplines, but Knox's review is almost entirely in terms of adult education.

Griffin, in Chapter Ten, takes an even more divergent approach, questioning the wisdom of attempting to apply traditional sociological concepts to adult education. He expresses the concern that attempts to apply these concepts may result in a form of "reductionism" that occurs with overzealous attempts to apply psychological concepts to adult learning. He recommends instead that a critical sociology of adult education is a more appropriate way of conceptualizing the relationship between the two fields. Lawson (Chapter Eleven) also begins with a different perspective on what he calls the "interplay" between philosophy and adult education, which he says works in a variety of ways and at different levels. He argues that philosophy does not produce absolute foundations that are "immutable and incorrigible," and that adult education is not informed by a single area called philosophy but by many aspects of philosophy, including political philosophy, philosophy of language, and legal philosophy. In Chapter Twelve, Thomas claims that it is essential to understand that the relationship between adult education and political science is a two-way street, each field of inquiry having the capacity and the obligation to enrich the other. Collectively, these authors are saying that the days of defining adult education in terms of related disciplines may be ending.

The increasing independence of adult education from the related disciplines that is expressed by the authors in this book relates to assumptions made by Boyd and Apps (1980) in the development of their "conceptual model of adult education." They argue that adult educators should seek knowledge from disciplines based on a thorough conceptualization of the field of adult education and resist allowing knowledge from the disciplines to define the field for them. Plecas and Sork (1986) argue this point from a more extreme perspective, claiming that adult education researchers should avoid mimicking researchers in the other disciplines, and that they should stick to research that directly relates to a well-established definition of adult education. Boyd and Apps and Plecas and Sork also claim that concepts and research developed in situations not related to adult education cannot be directly "applied" to these situations since the research is usually done without regard to practical applications in the first place. However, examples of successful "borrowing" from the disciplines do exist (Cookson, 1983; Deshler and Hagan, 1989), and much of the research in related disciplines does assume an adult audience (Bright, 1988). Even Apps (1989) grants that much is to be gained from the related disciplines: "Adult education professors . . . need only to examine the research in sociology, psychology, nutrition, and geriatrics to see great interest in adults and adult learning today from a variety of perspectives and disciplines" (p. 24).

It seems that, even as the field of study has evolved from a position of being strongly dependent on the disciplines during its first forty years or so to a less dependent status over the past twenty years, leading scholars are still ambivalent about what ought to be the proper relationship between adult education and the related disciplines. Skepticism about the relevancy to adult education of research in the disciplines is clearly evident, yet Apps (1979) suggests that "Professors of adult education ought to develop cooperative research projects" (p. 29) with researchers in related disciplines. This has always been an admirable strategy, but what would scholars of adult education bring to the party? We need the disciplines, but do they need us? We must clearly identify what we do best, now that we have a knowledge base to build on. We need a focus, an organizing construct. More will be said about that focus in a later section of the chapter.

Research Paradigms

A critical dimension of a field of study that reveals its nature is the way in which it develops its knowledge base. Merriam, in Chapter Three, addresses the way in which research has contributed to the development of a knowledge base in adult education. Her emphasis is on how the worldview of researchers influences their method of research. She describes how the study of adult education at the time of the publication of the black book was dominated by the positivist view and how interpretive research and critical science methods have been adopted by an increasing number of researchers since that time — although the positivist paradigm remains the dominant view. A good illustration of the dominance of the positivist paradigm is found in Long's (Chapter Four) comments on the types of research used in building the knowledge base, in which he reveals his own bias toward this paradigm. He associates what he calls the field's phenomenological, subjective orientations and proclivity for atheoretical research, and he claims such an orientation hampers adult educators' efforts to agree on terms and content and ultimately defeats the development of knowledge. Such a view is widespread in the field, despite progress made toward the development of theory by such pioneering studies as Mezirow's work (1990) on perspective transformation and transformative learning.

The interpretive and critical paradigms are relatively new to the field of adult education but not to the social sciences. For the most part their introduction to our field roughly parallels the timing of their introduction to the broader field of education (Gage, 1989), but we are "behind" the social sciences in our experience with the two paradigms (Bredo and Feinberg, 1982). We can turn to literature in the broader field of education and the social sciences for guidance in the use of the interpretive and critical paradigms. However, the proclivity of adult educators to follow whatever trend is current may lead to our premature adoption of philosophical and moral perspectives on research that we do not understand well. Thus we should examine alternative models for doing research in the critical manner suggested by the critical paradigm itself.

The three paradigms discussed by Merriam will continue to coexist in the field of study, with the interpretive and critical paradigms gaining in influence with researchers in the future. The adoption of all three paradigms by researchers thus portends a richer production of knowledge for adult education. The success of our research, however, depends as much on an understanding of the relationship of the field of study to the broader field of practice as it does on an understanding of the similarities and differences in the types of research appropriate to the different paradigms of thought.

Theory and Practice

The relationship between theory and practice has been a topic of discourse in adult education for decades. Cervero (Chapter Two) claims that before formal study of the field began early in this century the relationship between theory and practice was practically a nonissue but since then at least three different perspectives on that relationship have evolved. There is a close parallel between the evolutionary phases of the perceived relationship between theory and practice and the evolutionary phases of changing research paradigms discussed by Merriam in Chapter Three.

Cervero points out that the relationship is not necessarily one of theory applied to practice but that it can take at least two other forms. One form involves locating theory in the practice and meaning schemes of adult educators and systematically interpreting theory in terms of improvement in practice. Another form of this relationship assumes that theory and practice are part of a single reality and that all theory and practice are mutually constitutive. In this latter view, both theory and practice are socially constructed, all practice expresses a theory, and the development of theory is in fact a form of social practice. In both of these forms of the relationship, theory is not something that is constructed separate from practice and applied to practice in the interest of its improvement, which is the more commonly held view of the relationship between theory and practice.

The three paradigms of thought reviewed by Merriam in Chapter Three can be mapped onto the three viewpoints regarding the relationship of theory and practice discussed by Cervero. The positivist paradigm of research locates the scientist-observer apart from the objective reality that is to be observed and explained. The scientific laws thus discovered can be used in building knowledge about the object of study (adult education). The observer and the laws are thus outside the world of adult education practice, but research findings can be applied to that practice, given appropriate qualifications in terms of context, situation, conditions, and so forth. However, the thrust of this attitude toward research is not in the direction of practice but rather in the direction of the knowledge base being built by formal study of the field. In the positivist paradigm, theory becomes the foundation of practice, the first of Cervero's theory-practice relationships.

The interpretative research paradigm assumes that there are multiple realities, not a single, objective world. In this view, beliefs, meaning, and actions are the focus of research. The emphasis on how people make sense of their lives brings researchers espousing this viewpoint closer to the worldview of the subjects of research (practitioners, learners); hence the assumption about the role of practical knowledge is somewhat analogous to the viewpoint that theory resides in practice.

The third paradigm, the critical paradigm, sees research as beginning in the world of the subject and as a possible vehicle for individual and social change. Thus it corresponds to the view that theory and practice are indivisible and are a part of a single reality; change in one involves the other. This view and the critical paradigm generally implicate practice as much as they do research.

The recognition of the philosophical and moral imperatives of the relationship between study and practice is a sign of maturity in the field of study. Merriam (Chapter Three) argues that to find a way to accommodate knowledge produced out of different worldviews and to assess whether knowledge from different views is equally valid we need to remind ourselves of some of the principles that underlie our practice. She goes on to say that research itself is an intervention, no matter how objective or distant from the phenomenon the researcher tries to be. Tennant (Chapter Eight) cites the tension between experimentation, which is concerned with control, and the reflexive nature of the relationship between adult educators and their clients. Tennant's view is supported by Usher and Bryant (1987, 1989), who question the so-called technical-rationality model, with its emphasis on application of theory to practice. They claim that this model is both "conceptually untenable and not in accord with the realities of practice. It isolates theory and trivializes practice" (1987, p. 211).

The growing concern about the appropriate relationship between study and practice strongly suggests that new conceptualizations are needed to forge an effective role for study in the improvement of practice. One way to form these new conceptualizations is to properly locate the field of study with respect to practice, other fields of study, and subject matter. Locating the field in this way would have profound implications for the definition of adult education in the academic community and for the professional development of practice.

I believe that there are at least four ways in which adult

education as a field of university study may more properly locate itself in the future. First, the field should locate itself in
the broader field of educational practice. Second, it should locate itself in the professional school of education. Third, it should
locate itself next to the social science disciplines, not in them.
Fourth, it should locate itself at the level of design of educational programs in terms of the subject matter to be emphasized. I will explore each of these points a bit further.

To locate academic study in the broader field of practice
is to admit that study is a form of practice (Usher and Bryant,
1989). Scholars engage in planning, organizing, operating, communicating, evaluating, and reflecting upon how their work relates to the needs of the field and its clientele just as surely as
practitioners do, except that their situation and the focus of their
work differ. Both scholars and practitioners pursue the various
aims of adult education, whatever those might be. Moreover,
practitioners engage in the study of adult education, formally
or informally, and scholars also teach, plan programs, and otherwise play the role of adult education practitioner. One of the
limitations of this book is that it may give readers the impression that study is restricted to the activities of university-based
researchers. Although the university-based community is focused
on in the book, it is not the only community engaged in the
study of practice. Thus, study is but a subset of adult education practice, a part of its territory, and hitherto sharp distinctions in the field of practice and the field of study need to be
ignored, except for purposes of analysis and accountability to
sponsoring systems.

It may seem puzzling for me to suggest that the field of
university study be located in professional schools of education,
since most graduate programs in North America are located in
them already. The exceptions and variations are not the issue.
Rather, my concern is how scholars of adult education identify
themselves, their students, and their subject matter. Ultimately,
this identification has to do with how adult education itself is
defined. Jarvis notes in the first chapter of this book that adult
education is first and foremost education, a point that is not
as widely accepted as one might think (Merriam, 1986). This

status is often made less clear by the tendency of some adult education scholars to identify more closely with supporting disciplines than with educational practice, not an uncommon occurrence among faculty members in professional schools (Schön, 1987).

Simon (1976, 1981) discussed the tendency of faculty members in professional schools to split into two rather distinct groups: those who are discipline oriented and those who are profession oriented. Knox's (1973) survey of graduate programs identified three dominant professorial roles, one of which was a discipline-oriented role and another a practice-oriented role. The lure of the more "respectable" disciplines can lead faculty members in professional schools to retreat from the world of practice. Simon (1976) puts it this way: "The discipline-oriented segment of the professional school faculty becomes dependent upon its disciplines of origin for goals, values, and approval. Sealed off from the practitioner's environment, that environment becomes inaccessible and irrelevant to them as a source of data, of research problems, or of development and application of innovations" (p. 350).

On the other hand, the so-called practical group of faculty members can become overly dependent on the world of practice as its sole source of knowledge. "Instead of an innovator, it becomes a slightly out-of-date purveyor of almost-current . . . practice" (Simon, 1976, p. 350).

A great deal of this split is rooted in what Schön (1987) calls the "rigor-or-relevance" dilemma. "The normative curriculum of the schools rests . . . on an underlying view of professional knowledge as the application of science to instrumental problems. There is no room for research *in* practice . . . [and] the schools' view of professional knowledge is a traditional view of knowledge as a privileged information or expertise" (p. 309). The reader will recognize this claim as one found in the view that theory should be applied to practice, described by Cervero in Chapter Two. Some faculty members simply prefer to associate with what both Simon and Schön refer to as the perceived "higher school" of the disciplines (versus the "lower school" of the professions). The rigor-or-relevance problem is not unfamiliar to adult education scholars, who practice in a broader field that has its own problems with respectability and identity. Moreover, a large number of adult education scholars received their advanced degres in the social sciences (and many more, their undergraduate degrees), and they are naturally inclined to seek research problems and methodologies from this disciplinary framework. Most of the adult education scholars in the era of the black book were trained in the social sciences, which may provide one explanation for their emphasis on social science disciplines as a primary source of knowledge (Griffith, Chapter Five).

The "territory" of adult education as a field of university study indeed includes related other fields of study; it is a multidisciplinary territory (Rubenson, 1982). It is reasonable to say that all professional schools and disciplines share the same territory of higher education, and that an implied hierarchy of system relationships among them does not exist (Clark, 1989), except, of course, in the minds of those who practice in universities. As Clark puts it, "Specialties and disciplines, and whole colleges and universities, may serve as mediating institutions that tie individuals and small groups into the whole of the system" (p. 8). This is the view that scholars in adult education should adopt, along with the position that they are first and foremost members of the education profession, not members of the disciplines. This position locates the field alongside the related disciplines, not in them. It should provide a focus for the profession, at least structurally.

My suggestion that the field be located at the level of design relates to the need to identify and focus subject matter, including the type of research appropriate to the field. Simon's (1981) ideas about the appropriate theoretical focus of professional schools are highly relevant to this concern in adult education. He argues that professional schools should do their own brand of research and theory building, related to but distinctive in focus from research and theory in the disciplines. He argues for a "science of the artificial," or, in other words, a science of professional practice on which to base research. Simon (1976) proposes the following solution to the problem of locating adult education in regard to practice and the related disciplines: "A full solution . . . hinges on the prospect of developing an explicit, abstract, intellectual theory of the processes of . . . design, a theory that can be analyzed and taught in the same way that the laws of chemistry, physiology, and economics can be analyzed and taught" (p. 354).

This theory of design is intended to bring together the two "subworlds oriented to university and practice" (Schön, 1987, p. 308). The idea of developing the study of professional practice around the concept of design should have particular appeal in adult education. Almost everything the field claims as its particular epistemology has to do with design. For example, program planning, an indispensable part of the field's knowledge domains, is essentially design (Rubenson, 1982). Houle (1972a) must have recognized this when he titled his planning book *The Design of Education*. The conceptual model for adult education proposed by Boyd and Apps (1980) is concerned with designing education to put into play the special interactions between what they label as transactional modes; client focus; and personal, social, and cultural systems. Even Cookson's (1983) criticism of the Boyd and Apps model rests on the assumption that adult education is centrally concerned with design. Cookson suggests that the second dimension of the model, client focus, is itself overly concerned with the motivations of the client rather than the program planner, who, of course, is a designer. The list of models concerned with design would include models that focus on facilitating learning (Knowles, 1980) as well as models that dictate a much more rigid form of designing instruction for adults (for example, Mager, 1962; Tyler, 1949).

Simon's (1976) idea of design is criticized by Schön (1987). Schön maintains that Simon embraces technical rationality as a viewpoint for his model, a viewpoint that assumes that knowledge is to be discovered by the scientist and applied to practical problems, even if the scientist is a faculty member in a professional school. Schön, on the other hand, believes that theory resides in practice and that practitioners have the ability and the right to develop that theory with the help of the professional school. Thus, while fundamentally agreeing with Simon, Schön proposes an alternative to the way in which Simon's idea would be put into play in the university. Schön describes a "reflective practicum" core to the professional school curriculum, one that focuses on the practitioner's own experience and ways in which theories of the disciplines and the professional school (design) may be integrated with the practitioner's theories. This model of the "reflective practitioner" has great appeal to adult educators (Cervero, 1988; Usher and Bryant, 1989; Mezirow, 1990), and various forms of it have been introduced into graduate programs in adult education (Ingham and Hanks, 1981). The important point is that such a model, based on the idea of design as the focus of study and research, should be even more seriously considered in the future as the central organizing construct for the university-based study of adult education.

Graduate Programs

Since the time of the publication of the black book, the number of graduate programs in adult education has increased dramatically. This growth has been accompanied by an eightfold increase in the number of doctoral graduates since 1964 and by the development of a near consensus on core course domains in graduate study in adult education. This consensus does not, however, extend to the areas of the related disciplines or various specializations in adult education that should be included in graduate curricula.

Houle (1972b) described four kinds of knowledge needed by practitioners in adult education. He later described this knowledge as being necessary for the professionalization of the field (Houle, 1980). This knowledge can be summarized as (1) what practitioners learn from work experience; (2) the body of knowledge that relates to specialties in the field, such as education for the aging or adult basic education, (3) the body of generalized knowledge that undergirds all specialties, such as the history of the field and knowledge about how adults learn; and (4) the findings of scholarly disciplines related to the field. Houle went on to say this about the importance of the third kind of knowledge: "The body of literature based on the practice of adult education lies at the heart of the graduate program and is the central purpose of its existence. Its mastery must therefore be the major concern of the student. If this knowledge is not made available . . . adult education has no right to a separate place in the university's program. If the body of literature in the field does not grow, the discipline of adult education cannot flourish and must eventually die" (p. 307).

Houle's statement reflects a very strong assumption held by most professors responsible for developing and maintaining graduate programs in adult education — that there is a foundation knowledge base that all adult education practitioners need to master, no matter their particular specialty. If one can further assume that the body of knowledge (and related literature) fundamental to graduate study is represented in course work required by most graduate programs, then the domains of knowledge are foundations (programs, agencies, history and philosophies, issues), program planning, adult learning, adult education methods, and administration. For doctoral students, the domain of research methodology is added (Peters and Kreitlow, Chapter Seven). These domains lie at the heart of most programs, but an increasing number of programs have added more and more specialty courses over the years in such areas as human resource development, adult basic education, and continuing professional education.

Achieving a proper balance in basic and specialized courses is a problem for program designers. This problem is confounded by a more fundamental problem discussed earlier in this chapter, that of relating theory and practice. Most practitioners involved in graduate programs find field-related specialty courses to be more relevant than foundational courses. It seems reasonable to conclude that different mixes of basic and specialty courses will have important but different relationships to practical concerns. Thus, should a program offer only basic courses on the assumption that "one size fits all," practitioners enrolled in the program may not feel that the content properly addresses their practical concerns. On the other hand, if a program emphasizes a particular specialization but not the full range and depth of basic coursework, practitioners in that specialization will not learn what many scholars consider essential knowledge for being professionals in the field.

Houle (1972b) argues "It is the recognition of [the similarities among all specialties] which turns individuals and institutions away from the parochialism of a narrow and restricted practice to a larger and freer kind of service. And it is upon such similarities that the field of adult education itself rests" (p. 306). A program that emphasizes only one specialty would exclude practitioners who practice other specialties. The generalized knowledge may be the commonality undergirding our discourse and the quest for professional status, but there is usually a considerable distance between this knowledge and its application to specific forms of practice, at least as perceived by practitioners. The question, therefore, becomes, How can we develop a general corpus of knowledge and also ensure its relevancy to a variety of specializations in adult education practice?

Some concepts that are endemic to generally accepted practice in the broader field of adult education may help us answer this question, and emerging models of graduate programs may illustrate how a balance in core studies and attention to specialized practice can be achieved. Brookfield (1988) outlines a rationale and a model for preparing adult educators at the graduate level, based on the orienting concept of the critically reflective practitioner espoused by Schön (1987).

The model is applied in the Adult Education Guided Independent Studies (AEGIS) doctoral program at Columbia University Teachers College. The program outlined by Brookfield incorporates widely accepted learning strategies such as peer learning, negotiated curricula and methods, and contract learning. Although these learning strategies are not new to most professors of adult education, they take on special and added importance when the focus is on the practitioner-student's own practice. This approach is not just a matter of relating theory to the experience of learners, it is instead a deliberate attempt to ground the development of theories in the ideas brought to the learning experience by the practitioners. However, not many practitioners are prepared to reflect critically on their practice in the way outlined by Brookfield (1988) and his colleague

Mezirow (1990), but fortunately the process of learning this type of reflection is an integral part of the program itself. This program presents a case in which adult education scholars have learned from the experiences and concepts of scholars outside of the immediate field of study (for example, Schön, 1987) and have combined these ideas with what they believe to be true about adult learning and program design in order to develop a truly practitioner-oriented program founded on a generalized knowledge base in adult education.

I would add the concept of design to the above model—a feature fully compatible with the orientation of the reflective practitioner—based on the rationale in my earlier discussion of the concept in this chapter. As Ingham and Hanks (1981) explained when they argued for the design focus, graduate program developers are strongly influenced by what Ingham and Hanks refer to as the arts and science model of graduate program development. In their view, this model stresses the creation of knowledge and its dissemination, "rather than the methods by which knowledge can be used systematically and humanely to design plans of action for changing existing conditions into preferred conditions" (p. 21). Although the current emphasis of our graduate curricula on the knowledge domains of adult learning, program planning, administration, methods, and surveys of the field would seem promising in terms of their applicability to design work by practitioners, these domains lack the central and integrating concept of design itself, and thus they lack a focus on the very core of adult education practice. This idea needs to be worked out by several professors and practitioner-students to determine the potential of design as an integrating concept for adult education graduate programs. Whether this not entirely new idea will capture the attention of a new audience remains to be seen, but readers are hereby challenged to react to this concept.

International Activity

The formal study of adult education in North America has taken on a much broader scope with the increase in international activity involving scholars and practitioners. The increase in activity has been especially evident in the past ten to twenty years, and the effects of this on the field of study in North America are now beginning to be felt. Even more important, increasing numbers of adult educators in North America seem ready to become much more involved in international activities.

Cunningham (Chapter Fourteen) discusses the scope and variety of international activities that have taken place in recent years, and she stresses the influence that people and institutions in the Third World have on the study of adult education by North Americans and vice versa. Major international conferences in the eighties provided arenas for much of the increased awareness of the needs and interests of other nations and cultures in adult education and the influence that research can have on those needs and interests. Even as the more visible of the activities of the eighties focused on the Third World, however, significant new links were being formed by North American scholars with their counterparts in more economically developed areas of the world. This increased level of activity promises to reverse what Rubenson (1982) criticized as a form of academic isolationism on the part of North Americans, especially U.S. scholars.

Rubenson has been especially concerned that an isolationist stance makes definition of the research territory all the more difficult, given the culture-specific nature of assumptions, traditions, and perceptions that govern the production and use of knowledge. He cites as evidence widely divergent approaches to conceptualizing, designing, and conducting studies among the scholars in countries most active in adult education research. Moreover, he claims that scholars from European and Scandinavian countries are more likely to read and cite North American literature than the reverse (Rubenson, 1982). Rubenson's views have been highly respected by scholars who know the international scene. However, several significant changes in the level of cooperative activity in the United States and other countries promise to correct the imbalances that Rubenson first wrote about a decade ago.

In the early eighties, the CPAE experienced an increase

in its membership from some countries whose interests were initially not well represented in the study of adult education as practiced by U.S. and Canadian scholars. The participation of these members has contributed to a heightened awareness of international interests by scholars in all countries involved. Concomitant with this change, but not necessarily because of it, U.S. scholars especially began to cite more often the publications of their colleagues in other parts of the world. A significant number of new books produced mainly in Great Britain and written by people from several countries have taken their place on American bookshelves alongside books produced on this continent and others. Moreover, two books that fall into this category received the Houle award for literature (Jarvis, 1987; Tennant, 1988). A new international scholarly journal, the *International Journal of Lifelong Education,* began publication in the eighties, and it has served as an important vehicle for the dissemination of scholarship around the world (see Brockett, Chapter Six). Many more examples of such changes could be cited. Cunningham's chapter provides more detail on these and other aspects of the trend toward internationalization of adult education.

The dramatic shifts in world power and ideologies that are occurring even as this book is being prepared for publication leave none of us a choice in the matter of international adult education. We will all participate in some manner at some level, simply because no nation's scholars talk only among themselves anymore and no nation's scholars have exclusive rights to knowledge, no matter its source. North American scholars are responding to the challenge.

Conclusion

Not long after the black book was published, Cyril Houle (1966) wrote, "In the Whiteheadian spirit, adult education came into the university curriculum more as a promise than as an accomplishment" (p. 145). Now it seems that a great deal has been accomplished, but does promise remain? It seems so, based on the trends that are developing in the field of study. Now that we have material to work with, it would seem prudent for us to take stock and see if we can exert some influence on the direction that knowledge in the field of study will take during the next quarter century. We do not have to ask who we are anymore, but we do need to ask who we might become.

References

Apps, J. W. "What Should the Future Focus Be for Adult and Continuing Education?" In B. A. Quigley (ed.), *Fulfilling the Promise of Adult and Continuing Education.* New Directions for Continuing Education, no. 44. San Francisco: Jossey-Bass, 1989.

Aslanian, C. B., and Brickell, H. M. *Americans in Transition: Life Changes as Reasons for Adult Learning.* New York: College Entrance Examination Board, 1980.

Bell, B., Gaventa, J., and Peters, J. *We Make the Road by Walking: Conversations on Education for Social Change.* Philadelphia: Temple University Press, 1990.

Boshier, R. "A Perspective on Theory and Model Development in Adult Education." Paper presented at the annual conference of the Commission of Professors of Adult Education, Portland, Ore., Oct. 1978.

Boyd, R. D., and Apps, J. W. "A Conceptual Model for Adult Education." *Redefining the Discipline of Adult Education.* San Francisco: Jossey-Bass, 1980.

Bredo, E., and Feinberg, W. (eds.). *Knowledge and Values in Social and Educational Research.* Philadelphia: Temple University Press, 1982.

Bright, B. P. "Epistemological Vandalism: Psychology in the Study of Adult Education." In M. Zukas (ed.), *Trans-Atlantic Dialogue: A Research Exchange.* Leeds, England: University of Leeds, 1988.

Brookfield, S. *Training Educators of Adults: The Theory and Practice of Graduate Adult Education.* London: Routledge, 1988.

Carr, W., and Kemmis, S. *Becoming Critical: Education Knowledge and Action Research.* London: Falmer Press, 1986.

Cervero, R. M. *Effective Continuing Education for Professionals.* San Francisco: Jossey-Bass, 1988.

Charters, A. N., and Associates. *Comparing Adult Education Worldwide.* San Francisco: Jossey-Bass, 1981.

Clark, B. R. "The Academic Life: Small Worlds, Different Worlds." *Educational Researcher,* 1989, *18* (5), 4-8.

Collins, M., and Plumb, D. "Some Critical Thinking About Critical Theory and Its Relevance for Adult Education Practice." In C. C. Collins (ed.), *Proceedings of the 30th Annual Adult Education Research Conference,* Madison: University of Wisconsin, 1989.

Cookson, P. S. "The Boyd and Apps Conceptual Model of Adult Education: A Critical Examination." *Adult Education Quarterly,* 1983, *34* (1), 48-53.

Deshler, D., and Hagan, N. "Adult Education Research: Issues and Directions." In S. B. Merriam and P. M. Cunningham (eds.), *Handbook of Adult and Continuing Education.* San Francisco: Jossey-Bass, 1989.

Dickinson, G., and Rusnell, D. "A Content Analysis of *Adult Education.*" *Adult Education,* 1971, *21* (3), 177-185.

Elias, J. L., and Merriam, S. B. *Philosophical Foundations of Adult Education.* Melbourne, Fla: Kreiger, 1980.

Fellenz, R. A., and Conti, G. J. *Learning and Reality: Reflections on Trends in Adult Education.* Information Series, no. 336. Columbus: ERIC Clearinghouse on Adult, Career, and Vocational Education, Ohio State University, 1989.

Foucault, M. *The Archaeology of Knowledge.* London: Tavistock, 1972.

Gage, N. L. "The Paradigm Wars and Their Aftermath." *Educational Researcher,* 1989, *18* (7), 4-10.

Garrison, D. R. "Distance Education." In S. B. Merriam and P. M. Cunningham (eds.), *Handbook of Adult and Continuing Education.* San Francisco: Jossey-Bass, 1989.

Griffin, C. *Adult Education as Social Policy.* London: Croom Helm, 1987.

Houle, C. O. *The Design of Education.* San Francisco: Jossey-Bass, 1972a.

Houle, C. O. "The Relevance of Research to the Preparation of Professional Adult Educators." *Adult Leadership,* 1972b *20* (8), 305-308.

Houle, C. O. *The External Degree.* San Francisco: Jossey-Bass, 1973.

Houle, C. O. *Continuing Learning in the Professions.* San Francisco: Jossey-Bass, 1980.

Ingham, R. J., and Hanks, G. "Graduate Degree Programs for Professional Adult Education." In S. N. Grabowski and Associates, *Preparing Educators of Adults.* San Francisco: Jossey-Bass, 1981.

Jarvis, P. *Adult Learning in the Social Context.* London: Croom Helm, 1987.

Knowles, M. S. *A History of the Adult Education Movement in the United States.* Melbourne, Fla.: Krieger, 1977.

Knowles, M. S. *The Modern Practice of Adult Education: From Pedagogy to Andragogy.* (Rev. ed.) Chicago: Association Press, 1980.

Knox, A. B. *Development of Adult Education Graduate Programs.* Washington, D.C.: American Association for Adult and Continuing Education, 1973.

Knox, A. B. *Adult Development and Learning: A Handbook on Individual Growth and Competence in the Adult Years.* San Francisco: Jossey-Bass, 1977.

Long, H. B. "Publication Activity of Selected Professors of Adult Education." *Adult Education,* 1977, *27* (3), 173–186.

Long, H. B. *Adult and Continuing Education: Responding to Change.* New York: Teachers College Press, 1983a.

Long, H. B. *Adult Learning: Research and Practice.* New York: Cambridge Books, 1983b.

Long, H. B. "Characteristics of Adult Education Research Reported at the Adult Education Research Conference 1971–1980." *Adult Education,* 1983c, *33* (2), 79–96.

Long, H. B. "Selected Abstracts of SDL Dissertations." Unpublished manuscript, 1989.

Long, H. B., and Agyekum, S. K. "*Adult Education* 1964–1973: Reflections of a Changing Discipline." *Adult Education,* 1974, *24* (2), 99–120.

Long, H. B., Hiemstra, R., and Associates. *Changing Approaches to Studying Adult Education.* San Francisco: Jossey-Bass, 1980.

Mager, R. F. *Preparing Instructional Objectives.* Belmont, Calif.: Fearon, 1962.

Marsick, V. J. (ed.). *Learning in the Workplace.* London: Croom Helm, 1987.

Merriam, S. B. "The Research-to-Practice Dilemma." *Lifelong Learning,* 1986, *10* (1), 4–6, 24.

Mezirow, J., and Associates. *Fostering Critical Reflection in Adulthood: A Guide to Transformative and Emancipatory Learning.* San Francisco: Jossey-Bass, 1990.

Peters, J. M., and Banks, B. B. "Adult Education." In H. E. Mitzel (ed.), *Encyclopedia of Education.* (5th ed.) New York: Free Press, 1982.

Plecas, D. B., and Sork, T. J. "Adult Education: Curing the Ills of an Undisciplined Discipline." *Adult Education,* 1986, *37* (1), 48–62.

Rubenson, K. "Adult Education Research: In Quest of a Map of the Territory." *Adult Education,* 1982, *32* (2), 57–74.

Schön, D. A. *Educating the Reflective Practitioner: Toward a New Design for Teaching and Learning in the Professions.* San Francisco: Jossey-Bass, 1987.

Simon, H. A. *Administrative Behavior.* New York: Free Press, 1976.

Simon, H. A. "The Science of Design: Creating the Artificial." In H. A. Simon, *The Sciences of the Artificial.* Cambridge, Mass.: MIT Press, 1981.

Smith, R. M., and Associates. *Learning to Learn Across the Life Span.* San Francisco: Jossey-Bass, 1990.

Stubblefield, H. W. *Towards a History of Adult Education in America.* London: Croom Helm, 1988.

Tennant, M. *Psychology and Adult Learning.* London: Routledge, 1988.

Thompson, J. L. (ed.). *Adult Education for a Change.* London: Hutchinson, 1980.

Titmus, C. J. *Lifelong Education for Adults: An International Handbook.* Oxford, England: Pergamon Press, 1989.

Tyler, R. W. *Basic Principles of Curriculum and Instruction.* Chicago: University of Chicago Press, 1949.

Usher, R. S., and Bryant, I. "Re-examining the Theory-Practice Relationship in Continuing Professional Education." *Studies in Higher Education,* 1987, *12* (2), 201–212.

Usher, R. S., and Bryant, I. *Adult Education as Theory, Practice and Research: The Captive Triangle.* London: Routledge, 1989.

Epilogue

Malcolm S. Knowles

Since John Peters has done such a thorough job of summarizing the main themes of this book in the last chapter, I feel free to take off in the epilogue and soar into fantasyland. I would like to take a fresh look at the future of adult education as a field of study and practice.

Which Hat to Wear?

Professional futurists have a choice of two kinds of hats to wear as they peer into the future. The one scholarly futurists usually choose is the academic mortarboard, since their commitment is to serious scholarship. The method they typically use is *forecasting* — a process of identifying current trends, carefully documenting the credibility of these trends through rigorous studies in the research literature, and then projecting the trends into the future on the basis of statistically derived tables of probability. Most of the authors of the preceding chapters have donned this hat as they glanced into the future at the end of their chapters.

A second kind of hat, the one most frequently worn by science fiction writers and nonacademic futurists, is the nightcap, because they are committed to unfettered dreaming. The method they typically use is *scenario writing* — a process of visualizing the world (or any part of it) as they would like it to be.

When the editors of this book asked me to write an epilogue and I chose to focus on the future, I debated with myself as to which kind of hat I should wear. After reading the manuscripts of most of the preceding chapters, it becomes clear to me that most of the authors were wearing mortarboards — their writing was so scholarly and well documented. So I decided to wear my nightcap and start dreaming. Here is what happened.

Scenario One: An Energy-Controlling Field

My first dream turned out to be sort of a nightmare. I saw a neat, tidy field in which all adult education is taking place within the framework of clearly stated goals, policies, rules, regulations, and procedures that are set and enforced by a national agency established by Congress. All activities are taking place in officially approved educational institutions, including public and private schools, colleges and universities, community colleges, and a variety of technical institutes. Curricula are prescribed, teachers and administrators are certified, and standards are monitored by the national agency. Teacher training and graduate study are responsibilities assigned to approved universities, which also carry on research under grants from the national agency. Only those research proposals that fit neatly within the boundaries of the national goals and meet criteria of scientific rigor are approved. It is clear that the dominant theme of our field is tight control by centralized authority. The people I saw moving around in this scenario had austere expressions on their faces; they did not seem to be enjoying what they were doing very much.

I woke up from this dream in a cold sweat.

Scenario Two: An Energy-Releasing System

A few days later I put my nightcap on again and began having a very different dream. A calendar on the wall indicates that the year is 2016—exactly twenty-five years from the date of publication of this book.

Nature of the Field. A panoramic vision of the entire field of adult learning (notice the dropping of the term *education* from the field's name), worldwide, appears in my dream. The vision is teeming with activity. Groups of adult learners are meeting in all sorts of places, but mostly in places of work, voluntary associations, and lifelong learning centers. By far the largest number of adult learners are in their homes, working alone or with two or three neighbors with multimedia packages, computers, television sets, videodiscs, and other equipment that is not familiar to me. (I fantasize the equipment to be thought transmitters and receivers—extrasensory perception enhancers). Similar activities are going on in other countries, and it appears that a good deal of communication is taking place between citizens of different nations via interactive television networks.

Schools and colleges are no longer operating as independent, often competing institutions but are amalgamated into lifelong learning systems, and learning resource centers are located within walking distance of every citizen in every community. The lifelong learning systems incorporate all of the learning resources in the community—including the established educational institutions, business and industry, governmental agencies, voluntary organizations, religious institutions, the mass media, professional associations, and informal networks of resourceful individuals—into a single collaborative enterprise. Each system serves learners of all ages and backgrounds.

The personnel operating these systems are very different from the persons we were familiar with in the educational institutions of the twentieth century. Each system has a governing board made up of representatives of the various types of learning resources in the system and the categories of clientele the system serves. In the place of teachers, counselors, and librarians, the systems have these personnel classifications:

1. Educational diagnosticians (with such subspecialties as early childhood, childhood, pre-adolescent, adolescent, young

adult, middle adult, and older adult), who administer di-
agnostic experiences (not tests) to individual learners alone
and in groups to help them identify competencies they need
to develop in order to progress successfully to their next
stage of development

2. Educational planning consultants (with subspecialties similar to those of the diagnosticians), who help the learners
design learning plans that specify their learning objectives
based on their diagnosed competency and development
needs, the resources they would use in accomplishing each
objective, a time frame for completing each objective, the
evidence to be collected to demonstrate the extent to which
they have accomplished each objective, and the means by
which the evidence will be validated (usually by some form
of performance assessment rather than information recall)

3. Subject-matter specialists, who are situated in various locations throughout the community and may be serving as
part-time or full-time resource persons to the system

4. Information (or media) specialists, who prepare and give
guidance in the use of multimedia learning packages, computer-based learning programs, videodiscs, and other learning materials

It is clear in this dream that lifelong learning has become
a top priority on the national agenda, and, indeed, on the global
agenda. But it is also clear that the removal of many of the obstacles to lifelong learning, such as poverty, inadequate housing, and urban congestion, have also become top priorities. I
can see vast housing developments across the landscape and people who look healthy and well fed. From the wide range of activities in which people are engaged, most of them involving
high levels of skill in communication, computation, and interpersonal relations, I take it that functional illiteracy has almost
been eliminated. The population is overwhelmingly adult, and
it looks as if almost everyone, of every age, has some sort of
learning project in the works. It has obviously become a learning society, dedicated to releasing a constantly growing supply
of human energy rather than controlling it.

Status of the Profession. Now, where are the adult educators in this picture? For one thing, the clear distinction between educators of children and young people and educators of adults has begun to blur, and even the term *educator* is seldom used. People seem to see themselves as facilitators and resource persons in a pluralistic, but holistic, lifelong learning system. There are national and international associations of lifelong learning to which all may belong, but there are also national and international associations for a variety of specialties, such as the national association for early childhood learning, the national association of adult learning, the national association of learning diagnosticians, and on and on. Most of these associations offer continuing professional development programs, many of which provide certificates of competence at various levels. A number of them offer advanced degree programs. A growing number of the "professionals" hold certificates of competence across several specialties and see themselves as generalists in lifelong learning. In fact, the distinction between "professionals" and "learners" (what we have known as "teachers" and "students") seems to be blurring as more and more "learners" take on resource roles in serving other learners. In a learning society, those who serve as learning resources are obviously accorded a high social status.

Status of Research. As my dream focuses in on the research that is going on in 2016, I am impressed with the fact that it seems to be going on almost everywhere. Every lifelong learning system has a research office, and each of the employees of the system seems to have some research project in the works as part of his or her daily activity. But I can also see a wide variety of specialized research institutes scattered across the globe, some of them funded by governments but many of them privately funded.

    I am impressed with the number of people who seem to be studying the physiology of learning; apparently this has become a major research concern in 2016. Some astounding breakthroughs seem to be occurring in regard to the chemical enhancement of the ability to learn. I see one group of experimental subjects demonstrating the power of some chemical to open their minds to new concepts and behaviors that previously they had been inhibited from exploring by preconceptions, biases, habits, and fears of failure. I see another group spraying a memory-enhancing substance up their nostrils and then exhibiting fantastic feats of memory. And, behold, in another laboratory, a group of subjects is being trained in "holistic" thinking — applying the ability of both the left hemisphere of the brain to solve problems logically and the right hemisphere to create totally intuitive solutions and amalgamating both kinds of solutions into plans for action that are both imaginative and feasible. Up the street a few blocks is what looks like a medical establishment (but not a hospital) in which people in white coats seem to be engaged in genetic engineering; at least the charts on their walls indicate that they have succeeded in raising the IQ scores of ten subjects by an average of what looks like 50 percent. Other charts indicate success in changing basic personality types. I do not dare to even speculate on where this line of investigation might lead our field in serving the needs of adult learners.

My vision scans across town and focuses on a laboratory in the Environmental Protection Agency in which a group of scientists is investigating the environmental factors that stimulate or inhibit learning. I take it from the bright colors with which their work space is decorated that they have determined that color is one factor. From the headings of charts on the walls I take it that they are investigating room shapes, chair characteristics, temperature, management philosophies, reward systems, and other factors the names of which I cannot read. From conversations I overhear, I learn that some of them have come up with models of ideal learning environments that are in the process of being field tested.

It is clear that the research tools of all the human sciences — historiography, psychology, biology, sociology, anthropology, economics, political science, philosophy, and even archeology — are being used. But it is also clear that most of the research undertakings are multidisciplinary or interdisciplinary and are concerned with both improving practice and building strong theoretical foundations. Obviously, the knowledge base about learning in general and about adult learning in particular is increasing explosively.

Role of the University. My vision scanned across a number of universities, and I awoke with a jolt and had to go to the bathroom. For one thing, I had a hard time finding the universities — they were so well integrated into the lifelong learning systems. A few professors were in their studies or laboratories, but most of them seemed to be wandering around among community agencies serving as content resources to learners of all ages, who were carrying out their self-directed learning projects. Some were conducting staff development activities with the "facilitators" employed by those agencies. But a number of them were in workstations preparing computer-based learning programs, multimedia packages, and other materials for use throughout the learning systems. Few students seemed to be living on campus; the dormitories were operated more like motels, with learners (obviously mostly adults) coming to campus for short workshops. I was impressed with the proportion of learners who were unquestionably senior citizens.

I was especially interested in trying to find out what was happening in graduate programs in adult education but had a hard time isolating them. The universities were not organized according to the traditional academic departments with which I was familiar. Universities had "foundational areas," such as human development, societal evolution, language arts, critical thinking, interpersonal relations, and the like. And there were also "professional practice areas," such as holistic health services, lifelong learning services, community betterment services, commercial operations services, and the like. Some people appeared to be specialists in adult learning, but they were working as members of teams with other types of specialists in the various foundational and professional practice areas. It seemed that people I had known as adult educators had moved from the edges of the educational establishment to its center. It seemed, too, that no prescribed curriculum for adult learning specialists or any other professionals in the systems existed. There were models of competencies for the various roles. Each learner developed a plan of learning, with the help of a mentor, for developing the relevant competencies for the role he or she wished to prepare for. When a learner completed a learning plan, he or she underwent a performance assessment demonstrating that all relevant competencies had been developed to the required level. The degree (or certificate of completion, as it seemed to be called) was then awarded. I concluded from this cursory exposure to the world of 2016 that a form of the external degree that was pioneered in the last quarter of the twentieth century had become the mode and not the exception.

How Reliable Are My Dreams?

Before sending the manuscript of this epilogue to the editors, I thought it would be wise to check out whether my earlier dreams about the future of adult education had panned out. The earliest dream that I had reported was described in the first edition of my *The Adult Education Movement in the U.S.* (1962). These were my predictions then:

1. The size of the student body will continue to expand.
2. The educational level of the student body of adult education will continue to rise.
3. The resources and facilities for the education of adults will gradually expand.
4. The curriculum and methodology of adult education will become increasingly differentiated from those designed for children and youth.
5. There will be a rapid expansion in the body of knowledge about the education of adults.
6. The role of adult educators will become increasingly differentiated from other roles, and training for this role will become increasingly specialized.

In the second edition of the book (1977) I document that these predictions were largely coming true.

I should report that I awakened from the dream described above with a glowing smile on my face. I felt proud to have been a part of such a dynamic and increasingly significant field of study and practice.

References

Knowles, M. S. *The Adult Education Movement in the U.S.* New York: Holt, Rinehart & Winston, 1962.

Knowles, M. S. *A History of the Adult Education Movement in the United States.* Melbourne, Fla.: Krieger, 1977.

RESOURCE

Standards for
Graduate Programs
in Adult Education

Since the Commission of Professors of Adult Education was established in 1955, the number of North American graduate programs in adult education has increased dramatically. A major reason has been the demand for qualified adult educators to assist adults who seek further learning in order to cope with the effects of technological changes, to advance in their careers, to make career shifts, to obtain a liberal education, to use leisure time wisely, and so forth. As a result, adult education has become a recognized field of graduate study with a distinctive body of knowledge that embraces theory, research, and practice relating to adult learners, adult educators, adult education processes, providers, and programs.

Rationale for Standards

A concern for quality must dominate the planning, conduct, and evaluation of graduate programs in adult education. This concern is reflected in such outcomes as the preparation of adult educators with needed competencies and with a commitment

Note: Reprinted with the permission of AAACE.

457

to lifelong learning, their placement in the field, and their contributions therein to leadership and scholarship. It is axiomatic that high quality outcomes result from a combination of high quality input and processes. Input embraces faculty, curriculum, resources, students' programs, and various services. It is especially important that faculty continue to teach effectively and to contribute to theory, research, and practice in adult education. Processes are those forces, such as communication patterns, that operate within an organization to give it its dynamic nature.

While there is no assurance that the setting of standards will guarantee the high quality sought in formal graduate programs in adult education, the standards presented here do offer some criteria on which to base graduate programs. As such, these standards provide established programs with guidelines for review and new programs with guidelines for establishing graduate study in adult education.

Standards for Graduate Programs

Standards for graduate programs in adult education must take into account standards, guidelines, and constraints that exist at the school or college in which a particular program is housed. These include faculty teaching loads and advisement. It is also recognized that, given the variety and scope of graduate study in adult education, the standards cannot apply uniformly to every program. Nevertheless, the standards presented here are deemed to be basic, and those responsible for graduate programs should strive to meet them.

Finally, it should not be assumed that the following discussion implies an endorsement of one-person programs, which have obvious limitations; it merely recognizes their existence. These standards might serve to enhance the development of such programs.

The standards are grouped under the following categories: Curriculum, Faculty, Organization of Graduate Study, Students' Programs, Resources and Facilities, and Scholarship.

Curriculum

The adult education curriculum clearly distinguishes between master's and doctoral levels in terms of beginning and advanced graduate study.

At the master's level, the core areas include the following:

- Introduction to the fundamental nature, function, and scope of adult education
- Adult learning and development
- Adult education program processes — planning, delivery, and evaluation
- Historical, philosophical, and sociological foundations
- Overview of educational research

These core areas are supplemented by additional study appropriate to students' needs and goals, which may emphasize specific leadership roles (e.g., administrator-manager, teacher, counselor). The area of specialty may relate to the study of a particular clientele (e.g., disadvantaged, career changers, aged) or of programs serving them (e.g., adult basic education, career education, gerontology). That specialty might involve study in other faculties. In general, because it is unlikely that any adult education program will contain all the courses that students require (e.g., business, educational psychology, philosophy, political science, sociology), students should be encouraged to supplement instruction by adult education faculty with other appropriate faculties.

At the doctoral level, the core areas include study that is at once more wide-ranging and more intensive than study at the master's level. The core areas include the following:

- Advanced study of adult learning (e.g., theory and research relating to specific issues)
- In-depth analysis of social, political, and economic forces that have shaped the historical and philosophical foundations of adult education

- Study of leadership, including theories of administration and management
- Study of issues that impinge on policy formation
- Advanced study of methods of inquiry, in order to conduct adult education research

Students who enter doctoral study with a master's degree in another field may be asked to take, as prerequisites, the adult education courses required at the master's level.

As at the master's level, the doctoral core areas are supplemented by additional study appropriate to students' needs and goals. This study might be pursued as a formal cognate area or simply as specialized study therein. At the doctoral level, the core curriculum may differ at institutions offering both the Ph.D. and the Ed.D. In general, the distinction between the two degrees is one of orientation. The Ph.D., which emphasizes theory and research, aims at producing a scholar-researcher who has, as his or her major goal, the advancement of knowledge. The Ed.D., which focuses on translating theory and research into practice, aims at producing a practitioner who will give leadership to the field. Institutions offering only the Ph.D. or the Ed.D. can provide for both orientations through individual programming.

Faculty

It is expected that institutions offering a graduate degree, major, or specialization in adult education (whether in small programs attached to or combined with other programs, in specific adult education programs of varying sizes, or in multidisciplinary programs) will have several faculty. At least one full-time faculty member will have an earned doctorate in adult education. (Other designations include "continuing education," "community education," and "cooperative extension education.") Other full-time faculty will have an earned doctorate in adult education or relevant fields (e.g., philosophy, psychology, sociology), with knowledge of and, preferably, experience in adult education. Other criteria are as follows:

- At the outset, at least one faculty member will possess a minimum of three years of graduate level full-time teaching experience in adult education; all faculty will possess graduate or undergraduate teaching experience
- Academic rank necessary for graduate status in a tenure track position
- A record of leadership, as evidenced by significant positions in the field, profession, and university
- A record of contributions to scholarship in adult education
- A continuing commitment to adult education theory, research, and knowledge of current practice

Part-time faculty consist of individuals whose adult education assignment is limited due to any of the following conditions:

- A full-time administrative role at the university (e.g., dean of extension, program planner, program coordinator, counselor)
- A major commitment in another faculty (e.g., educational psychology, instructional technology, philosophy)
- A joint appointment between adult education and another recognized unit within the university
- A research appointment relating to a grant or a graduate assistantship
- A full-time assignment outside of the university (business, government, voluntary agency, or as a private consultant)

Although selection of part-time faculty is based on their particular expertise and contributions, they will still need to meet the following criteria:

- An earned doctorate in the area of their competency, but suitable experience may be substituted when appointing a part-time faculty member from the field
- Evidence of interest in and concern for problems and issues in adult education
- A record of contributions to scholarship relating to courses

to be taught or to particular areas of theory, research, and practice (e.g., adult basic education, community development, continuing professional education, human resource development)

Organization of Graduate Study

A graduate program in adult education may be housed in a variety of colleges (e.g., education, agriculture) or form part of a multi-disciplinary group. At least one faculty member will be a full-time member of the graduate faculty and a member of the policy-making unit that administers the graduate program in adult education. The strength of a high quality graduate program lies in the caliber of its faculty, its students, and its graduates, their contributions to theory, research and practice. To ensure that faculty have sufficient freedom to continue making their contributions, the following organizing principles apply:

- The student admissions committee consists of at least one full-time or part-time faculty member with a doctorate in adult education
- The program committee for a master's student is chaired by an adult education faculty member. Whether a student selects the thesis or non-thesis option, the chair and student select committee members who will increase a student's competencies through advisement or mentoring.
- The load for master's advisement depends on certain variables (e.g., number of thesis students and number of non-thesis students, and number of doctoral advisees). For advisement and counseling, a distinction is made between full-time and part-time students.
- These variables suggest the following student-faculty ratios, which are maximum ratios for high quality programs:
  For students not writing a thesis or major paper—25 to 1
  For students writing a thesis or major paper—10 to 1
    (Where a faculty member has a large proportion of thesis students, the number of non-thesis students would be reduced.)

- The program committee for doctoral students is chaired by an adult education faculty member. The chair and student select committee members who will increase a student's competencies through advisement or mentoring.
- The doctoral dissertation committee is chaired by an adult education faculty member with an interest in a student's research. For special topics, co-chairs are selected from other faculties. Other committee members are selected on the basis of their contributions to the research problem or design.
- The load of doctoral advisement depends upon certain variables (e.g., number of master's advisees, number of doctoral students at program stage, number of doctoral students at dissertation stage). A distinction is made between full-time and part-time students as applied to advisement and counseling.
- These variables suggest the following student-faculty ratios, which are maximum ratios for quality programs:

    For students at the program stage prior to intensive dissertation advisement — 15 to 1

    For students assigned to a faculty member at the dissertation stage — 8 to 1, with no more than 4 students actually writing. (Where a faculty member has a large proportion of dissertation students, memberships on program committees or other dissertation committees will be reduced.) The ratios suggested above are based on the fact that students at the program stage require much less commitment of time and effort from faculty than do students at the dissertation stage. In particular, students actually writing dissertations typically require many hours of intensive help from faculty.
- The teaching load of faculty varies according to the number, level (master's or doctoral), and status (program, thesis, or dissertation). A graduate load for a faculty member with fewer than 3 master's thesis students, or fewer than 2 doctoral dissertation students, will not exceed 6 courses (3 semester hours each) during the year. Programs on quarter systems will have a higher number of hours, whereas programs on a year-long system will have fewer hours.

- The suggested teaching load for faculty having 3-6 master's thesis students is 5 courses per academic year; and, for those having 7-10 master's thesis students, 4 courses
- The suggested teaching load for faculty having 2-4 students at dissertation stage is 5 courses per academic year; and, for those having 5-7 students at dissertation stage, 4 courses

The above teaching loads will vary according to whether an institution is research-oriented or practice-oriented.

Other ways to enhance the process aimed at desirable outcomes are as follows:

- Formal and informal contacts with other faculties, in the interest of developing fruitful relationships that will benefit adult education faculty and students alike
- Systematic review of courses, programs, and procedures to provide evaluative data for improving the program; and peer review by external professors of adult education

Students' Programs

Since undergraduate programs in adult education are rare, students usually enter graduate study with little or no academic preparation, although they often have experience in working with adults. Hence, the orientation of many new students is narrowly directed to serving the field, and less concerned with acquiring knowledge related to theory, research, and practice. In order to gain competencies needed to function in particular roles (e.g., administrator, teacher, researcher), students will complete elements of the following program. Care should be taken to provide students with opportunities for flexibility and self-direction:

- The core curriculum discussed above
- A special area of study. On the master's level, this area takes the form of certain courses or a limited research study; whereas, on the doctoral level, it consists of courses in par-

ticular areas of adult education and/or a cognate area of study in another faculty.

- Research. On the master's level, it entails an understanding of basic statistics and research; whereas, on the doctoral level, research methodology entails methods of inquiry as preparation for writing the dissertation.
- Internship. To broaden the horizons of some master's students, an internship is incorporated into their programs. This experience equips students to function in a particular setting as administrators, teachers, evaluators, and so forth, and apply theory and research to practice. At the doctoral level, internships are more intensive and demanding; that is, a person assumes a certain role in an organization and even conducts evaluation or research.
- Independent study. On both master's and doctoral levels, students investigate specific topics in-depth. Such study draws upon the strengths of adult education faculty and/or the strengths of faculty in relevant disciplines.
- Thesis and dissertation. The master's thesis or project is much more limited in nature and scope than the doctoral dissertation. Typically, the dissertation requires investigation of a more complex problem, demands a broader theoretical base, employs a more sophisticated methodology, and utilizes the expertise of outside faculty.

Resources and Facilities

Graduate programs need funds to support full-time students in the interest of providing them with varied experiences through internships, which commonly offer administrative experience; assistantships, which commonly offer teaching experience; and research associateships, which offer experience in conducting research. Other resources are extension divisions, where students undertake assignments that give them experience and receive stipends that aid them in completing their dissertations. Finally, a comprehensive professional library, which includes periodicals is requisite, along with access to ERIC and other relevant data bases.

Scholarship

Outcomes of a high quality graduate program are as follows:

- Publications in refereed journals by faculty, students, and graduates
- Books and reports by faculty, students, and graduates
- Contributions of faculty, students, and graduates to conferences at local, regional, national, and international levels
- Exchanges, both formal and informal, of faculty and students, including international exchanges
- Service to the field and profession by faculty, students, and graduates
- Appropriate placement and performance of program graduates

Name Index

Subject Index

A

Academic issues, for adult education, 407–413

Administration: and adult education, 217–258; and attracting participants, 233–236, 248–249; background on, 217–221; and external influences, 226, 244–247, 249–250; functions of, 220–250; knowledge base for, 218–219; leadership in, 221–228, 248; and program coordination, 242–244, 249; and program development, 228–233, 248; research needed on, 247–250; and resources, 239–242, 249; roles and decision making in, 223–225; and staffing, 236–239, 249

Adult basic education (ABE): growth in, 148, 165; knowledge base for, 423–424; as specialization, 157

Adult Basic Education Act, 387

Adult development: and knowledge base, 87–88; and psychology, 195–196

Adult Education (book). *See* Black book

Adult Education (journal), 132, 133, 134, 329–330, 347

Adult education: academic issues for, 407–413; and adult learning, 273–275; advancing study of, 421–445; approaches to study of, 4; background on, 1–2; conceptualizing, in philosophy, 283–284, 290, 291, 294; conclusions on, 10–11, 441–442; and criticisms of society, 266–267; development of field of, 15–183; as energy-releasing system, 448–454; forces and trends shaping, 345–445; future of, 447–455; growth and challenges in study of, 1–13; institutionalization of, 351; international influences on, 347–383; issues in, 384–420; liberal philosophy of, 282–300; as movement, 21–22; multidisciplinary dimensions of, 185–343, 434; predictions about, 454; professional issues in, 24, 402–407; promise of, 441–442; public policy issues for, 413–414; and research paradigms, 58–61; scenarios for, 448–454; social issues

479